Redefining British Politics

Also by Lawrence Black

THE POLITICAL CULTURE OF THE LEFT IN AFFLUENT BRITAIN, 1951–64
Old Labour, New Britain?

AN AFFLUENT SOCIETY? (*edited with Hugh Pemberton*)

TAKING STOCK (*edited with Nicole Robertson*)
Consumerism and the Co-Operative Movement in Modern British History

CONSENSUS OR COERCION? (*co-edited*)

Redefining British Politics

Culture, Consumerism and Participation, 1954–70

Lawrence Black
Durham University, UK

palgrave
macmillan

First published 2010 by
PALGRAVE MACMILLAN

Palgrave Macmillan in the UK is an imprint of Macmillan Publishers Limited,
registered in England, company number 785998, of Houndmills, Basingstoke,
Hampshire RG21 6XS.

Palgrave Macmillan in the US is a division of St Martin's Press LLC,
175 Fifth Avenue, New York, NY 10010.

Palgrave Macmillan is the global academic imprint of the above companies
and has companies and representatives throughout the world.

Palgrave® and Macmillan® are registered trademarks in the United States,
the United Kingdom, Europe and other countries

ISBN-13: 978–0–230–55124–4 hardback

This book is printed on paper suitable for recycling and made from fully
managed and sustained forest sources. Logging, pulping and manufacturing
processes are expected to conform to the environmental regulations of the
country of origin.

A catalogue record for this book is available from the British Library.

A catalogue record for this book is available from the Library of Congress.

10   9   8   7   6   5   4   3   2   1
19   18   17   16   15   14   13   12   11   10

Printed and bound in Great Britain by
CPI Antony Rowe, Chippenham and Eastbourne

Contents

List of Figures

Acknowledgements

For tips, sources, interviews and ideas, I very much appreciate the help of: Kerry Barner, Angela Bartie, Laura Beers, Gidon Cohen, Denis Dworkin, Anne Etienne, Steve Fielding, Juliet Gardiner, Giles Gasper, Peter Gurney, Jim Haynes, Matthew Hilton, Kit Kowol, Peter Mandler, Lord Merlyn-Rees, David Moon, Peter Stansill, Pat Thane, Andrew Thorpe, Arnold Wesker, Dominic Wring and Philip Williamson. Thanks to the ex-Young Conservatives who responded to requests in the *Birmingham Post* and *Nottingham Evening News*, particularly Ann Franklin, John Wood, Richard Tomlinson and Peter Barwell. Thanks also to those who have commented on this research at conferences and seminars in Berlin, Berkeley, Birmingham, Bologna, Cambridge, Durham, London, Oxford, Sheffield, Warwick, at the UK Social History Society and Political Studies Association, North American Conference on British Studies, European Social Science History conference and German Historical Institute. For funding, I am grateful to the British Academy for a Small Research grant (SG-42672), the Arts and Humanities Research Council for a research leave grant (no.134782), the University of Texas, Austin's Harry Ransom Center and to departmental and faculty support from Durham University. Visiting Fellowships at Harvard University's Center for European Studies and St John's College, Oxford proved hugely useful. Michael Strang and Ruth Ireland at Palgrave and reader's comments were very helpful. I owe much to staff at various archives, particularly: Jeremy Mcilwaine at the Bodleian, the Conservative Party's Sheridan West-lake, Nigel Cochrane at Essex University, Louise North at the BBC and Gillian Longeran and Adam Shaw at the Co-op archives. I reserve the last smooch for LB.

Arts & Humanities
Research Council

List of Abbreviations

ACGB	Arts Council of Great Britain
AFL-CIO	American Federation of Labour-Congress of Industrial Organizations
ASA	Advertising Standards Authority
BAC	British Association of Consumers
BBC	British Broadcasting Corporation
BL	British Library
BSI	British Standards Institute
C42	Centre 42
CA	Consumers' Association
CBE	Commander of the British Empire
CC	Consumers' Council
CCCS	Centre for Contemporary Cultural Studies
CIC	Co-operative Independent Commission
CND	Campaign for Nuclear Disarmament
CoID	Council of Industrial Design
Co-op	Co-operative movement
CPC	Conservative Political Centre
CPGB	Communist Party of Great Britain
CPV	Colman, Prentis and Varley
CRD	Conservative Research Department
CRDS	Co-operative Retail Development Society
CTF	Catholic Teachers Federation
CU	Consumers Union (America)
CWS	Co-operative Wholesale Society
DIY	Do-it-yourself
FBI	Federation of British Industry
GLC	Greater London Council
GLYC	Greater London Young Conservatives
ICA	Institute of Contemporary Arts
IEA	Institute of Economic Affairs
IOCU	International Organization of Consumer Unions
IPA	Institute of Practitioners in Advertising
IPR	Institute of Public Relations
IT	*International Times*
ITA(N)	Independent Television Authority (News)
ITV	Independent Television
JWT	J Walter Thompson
LCC	London County Council

LPE	London Press Exchange
LSE	London School of Economics
MEP	Member of European Parliament
MRA	Moral Re-armament
MU	Mothers Union
NAA	Northern Arts Association
NOP	National Opinion Polls
NGO	Non-governmental organization
NLR	*New Left Review*
NUT	National Union of Teachers
NVALA	National Viewers' and Listeners' Association
PEP	Political and Economic Planning
PLP	Parliamentary Labour Party
PMG	Postmaster General
PPB	Party political broadcasts
PR	Public Relations
RAC	Royal Automobile Club
RICA	Research Institute for Consumer Affairs
RPM	Resale Price Maintenance
SET	Selective Employment Tax
SCWS	Scottish Co-operative Wholesale Society
SDP	Social Democratic Party
SNP	Scottish Nationalist Party
TRACK	Television and Radio Committee
TUC	Trade Union Congress
TVC	Television Viewers' Council
TW3	*That Was The Week That Was* (BBC)
UNO	United Nations Organization
WEA	Workers' Educational Association
YC	Young Conservatives

1
Introduction: Political Cultures

If the 2009 MPs expenses scandal was the acme of how remote Parliament seemed from the people, it also revealed more enduring popular frustrations with formal politics – that far from confined to Britain, were common to many liberal democracies. Musing on 'the contemporary condition... of political disaffection and disenchantment' in 2007 Colin Hay argued, '"Politics" has increasingly become a dirty word'.[1] And, as Lawrence's timely history of electoral conduct contends, both politicians and the modern media have effectively marginalized the public from political debate. Representative politics has been challenged not just by falling party membership and participation, but has been a victim of a secular decline in a range of other forms of associational activism. Given diminishing trust and interest in party, part of the alleged falling stock of social capital and health of the public sphere, and studies like *Why We Hate Politics*, a political version of Callum Brown's *The Death of Christian Britain* thesis might recommend itself to cultural historians aiming to capture the essence of politics' history since the 1950s.[2]

But the narrative in *Redefining British Politics* is of a shifting, mutating and broadening of the category of 'the political' – a redefinition both in this period and in historical writing about it. As Brown assesses not single denominations, but religiosity as whole through institutions, beliefs and practices, this study focuses on a cultural history of 'the Political' rather than a narrower, internal political history. Just as the Church was not the sum of religious history, nor was party or government the sum of politics. As Brown takes into account secularizing forces, so this study situates 'the political' as part of wider culture, in which its presence in everyday life could be (although not always) marginal and recognizing that the relative discreetness of formal politics was a facet of this culture. When 'politics' is said to be under attack or is invoked as a euphemism for self-serving or unnecessary, unconstructive dialogue, such discontent, cynicism, apathy or hate, have to be dealt with by historians as an integral part of political culture. This study's approach is that of cultural history, with politics as its

1

subject. So the cover image of a 'floating voter', nonplussed by some 1964 election posters, begs the question not only of who he will vote for, but whether he'll vote, how else he conceives of politics and what this discloses about the history of this period.

The definition of what was 'political' was itself loaded and contested. For the New Left, whose influence on historical writing has been extensive since the 1960s, politics was everyday life, apparent in the smallest minutiae or in what Frederic Jameson called 'the political unconscious'.[3] It (like power for Foucauldians) was everywhere, suffused in categories, practices, technologies and lifestyles that (self-) governed quite as much as the formal politics of voting or parliament. For many Conservatives, politics was ideally more discrete, less of a recipe for a fulfilled life or engaged public sphere – about governing (hard politics), but better kept out of the private sphere, civil society or cultural matters. This still implied a world view, even if not couched or defined in political terms. Such differences were muddied in this period as the political right was involved in demands for participation; in making the cultural and personal, political; and as a presence in civil society (a softer, but no less consequential mode of politics by other means). They demonstrate the difficulties in agreeing to a defined British political culture and constitute its analytical interest. They also related to historical debates. The shift from political bodies to the politics of the body and self, explored here in TV and consumerism (and elsewhere through sexuality, gender, imperial attitudes), politics reach was extended by being interlinked with the rest of society, but also rendered culturally relative, its distinctiveness made more common.[4] If politics included a wider agenda during the 1960s (in that sense that everything was political – homework, housework, holidays) and if the approach of this book is to register an array of pressure groups, social movements, activities and identities as part of political culture, there remains the paradox that in so doing historians encounter how parochial, ephemeral in popular culture, liminal or marginal to many Britons, politics was. Politics' apartness was part of political culture.

Redefining British Politics explores political culture in the period from the end of rationing in 1954 through the cultural shifts of the 1960s. Its method is to select core samples of ideas, movements, moments, identities, organizations and individuals that intersect social and political change.[5] Core samples are not simply case studies, but the sites and hosts of bigger debates. At best they inform general historical understanding from particular local knowledge – empirically testing theory, and using theory to offset potential narrowness. Identification and selection is then key. The core samples here have been selected because they traverse political and social terrains and formal and informal politics. Their claim to be representative or typical is partial. Nor however, are they arbitrarily selected. They explore new, old, successful and unsuccessful initiatives, since all illustrate the forces and landscape of political culture. They stretch from elite to grassroots politics and aspired to engage mass audiences. They bear then interpretive traction or significance beyond their immediate selves.

There is also purpose to this structure – aiming to capture the diversity of political culture, its awkwardness, unevenness and equivocalness. There are overlaps and sutures between the samples – assessed in the conclusion – but not an interlocking whole. This study is conscious that these are fragments of political culture, piecing together at best a partial picture – provisional, contingent, suggesting that politics is not as conclusive or neat as often imputed by contemporary political historians. In historicizing the category of 'the political', there are risks of normative judgement or that some dichotomies deployed here (popular-elite, formal-informal) prove insufficient.[6] But the approach here is to seek empirical detail to plot the ebbs and flows of politics' boundaries.

Besides contributing to the political history of the period, part of the exercise here is to expand the conception of politics into that of political culture. Familiar components of 'the political' – party, elections, government, policy – are vital, but should not be privileged. Shifting from the world of elite politics to integrate popular politics and considering parties not in isolation, but in competition, is essential. But these can still operate within received parameters – tacitly assumed forms or customary sources of 'the political' – overlooking how parties and activists often have more in common with each other than the rest of society. They insufficiently capture political *culture* – politics in its wider social setting, in which as a minority or occasional interest and identity, politics could bear a certain 'otherness', much as ethnicity or social class might. This suggests political culture might not be very political, measured in conventional terms. If that sounds an odd assertion for a political historian, the point is to exit the comfort zone of the politically 'given' and received terminologies or rehearsing the arguments of the day in the light of broader evidence than contemporaries. Political historians ought not to assume that their interest in politics was widely shared. Better to admit, as Lawrence does, to being 'sad enough still to find elections interesting'. When McKibbin, for instance, contends of inter-war political culture that 'never to talk about politics or religion is, after all, never to talk about two of the most interesting subjects in human history', we have to wonder (even if we sympathize) if that is an appropriate historical approach to political culture?[7]

Politics is treated as one cultural entity among many, embedding it in a wider sense of social history. By focusing on political *culture*, we can learn much about politics, but also about the broader social and cultural history in this period. Francis, for instance, uses elite political behaviour to explore gender and emotional history and here the Young Conservatives (YCs) are considered as a locus of middle-class youth culture. It also plots analogies with developments in society – how the professional and amateur and the private and public were played out in politics, how politics was consumed; how it faced competition from consumerism and TV, but also assimilated ideas and methods from them. It treats politics as an activity, not just discursively.[8]

Bernard Crick writing in 1962 saw politics, in that it was a debate about power relations throughout society, as an intrinsic human activity. He drew an analogy with sexuality. Politics was diverse, inventive, even fun, yet not always central to identity, an omnipresent, unavoidable, even if unconscious involvement. Crick also, germane to this book, stressed the volition involved, that politics was (in Britain) a free activity, not a reflex, an activity that was chosen if within a given context, but which was 'too often regarded as a poor relation, inherently dependent and subsidiary'.[9] Freeing politics up from being read as a corollary of other histories has been a hallmark of the 'new political history' outlined below. It also enables more cultural explorations of political identities, mentalities and organizations, treating politics not as independent, but co-dependent and interactive with society and that might interpret society not just reflect some prior reality. In this sense politics was just as interesting (for politicos at least) and indicative an activity and realm as more orthodox anthropological or cultural history fare of food, ceremony, coffee shops or cockfights.

And *pace* theorists of political and civic disaffection, recent studies have focused on a diverse history of political activity and civic engagement outside of party and this has brought empirical complexity to conceptions of 'the Political'.[10] The pluralism of modern British political life was not new – extra-parliamentary movements such as the Suffragettes or appeals to the citizen-consumer made by the Free Trade Union spring to mind. But some newer approaches can be charged with remaining quite party or election-centric – even on periods as late as the 1960s.[11] There are good reasons why parties and elections have been central to analyses of representative politics.[12] But party does seem less central to political culture and evidently much politics in this period happens outside elections and even against party. For this reason, Vernon and Lawrence's debate about when party came to dominate popular disorder in 19th and 20th century election meetings offer less access to debates about political conduct and popular participation in this period. Such debates were ongoing, but had moved outside party.

That is not to say elections are not important, just to recognize that they were exceptions, rare moments at which social barriers were broken down, power was exposed and unwritten political norms suspended. Or as Stacey's anthropological study noted, parliamentary elections provided a 'licence to say in public about a political opponent or his policies what it is otherwise taboo to say'.[13] Party and elections should not be then a privileged focus in studying political culture. But a discussion of political culture without party is like a party without fun – not uncommon but unfortunate. The search for alternative sources of political agency in minority identities can unduly marginalize conventional forms. Party remained potent as a formal nexus between politics and the people. And recent work on the cultural history of electioneering, posters, public meetings and the media has increasingly focused not only on the language and messages politics has constructed, but on its communication with people.[14]

Redefining British Politics also looks to assess politics' presence in civil society and in studying pressure groups and cultural politics stresses inter-actions with party – co-existence, appealing to and exchanging ideas, if also discontent with party's tendency to corral and speak for poly-vocal inter-ests. The concept of civil society – the sphere of voluntary activity and organizations outside the state, family, workplace – helps locate and under-stand party and other political entities. Harris points out ambiguities in defining civil society historically – its overlap with ideas of the public sphere and with pressure groups, social movements and non-governmental organiza-tions (NGOs). Whilst independent and resistant of state intrusion, it equally sought to influence it and was a resource on which the state drew. For some it was an alternative to the market, a public sphere based on non-commercial social relations, more akin to community. For others it was the essence of a free market in association by choice not circumstance – thus the pri-vate citizen *Bowling Alone* was less the decline of civil society than its quintessence.[15]

Like religion and the Church, party and political activity had ambiguous status in civil society. And part of the appeal of the latter (to contemporaries and to historians today) is that it seemed an alternative to the partisan polit-ical world – a sphere for a plural, participatory, democratic citizenship. But this can render it unduly anodyne, imagining politics out of it. Politics gene-rated debate and division, but also social capital, networks of trust and inter-actions that enabled democratic functioning and, particularly through parties and peak-level pressure groups, institutionally linked civil society to the state.

A subtext of this book, politics' apparent loss of power, has been echoed in historical writing about it. Since the 1970s and particularly the 1980s, political history, like national representative politics, has fallen out of favour and become one among many historical sub-genres – superseded by international relations and globalization and out-shone by histories sourcing identity in consumption, gender and sexuality. The approach here builds upon the 'new political history' that has thrived since the 1990s.[16] This moved away from an exclusive focus on political elites – those who Guttsman numbered in 1963 as between 2162 and 2212 MPs, Lords, paid party agents and pressure group lob-byists.[17] It also shifted away from 1960s' boom areas – social history's focus on activists 'from below' and from political sociology and Marxist approaches stressing the social forces underlying political change. Escaping the nar-rowness or determinism of such approaches, it embraced the cultural and linguistic turns in history.[18]

Stedman Jones' emphasis on *Languages of Class* in 1983 made it an ur-text of 'new political history'. But it has also shared with 'history from below' a commitment to a diverse source base, and shared with traditional approaches focused on state-level actors an interest in the potential of politics to manipulate and transform, not just reflect, popular opinion. As practiced in the 1990s, this asserted the creative power of party to influence popular political identities, rather than accommodating to pre-existing interests of supporters determined by their social position. This relative autonomy of politics recognized that politics was not a product of social forces, it *was* a social force – not unrelated to class or gender, but not reducible to them.[19]

If this brought politics back, asserting its ability to mobilize and impose, there has been a shift away from linguistic sources and explanations alone and my own previous work, whilst stressing political agency, showed how political rhetoric (in this case the left's condescension of prosperity) could distance voters.[20] If this emphasized how internal party culture and traditions influenced outputs and outcomes, focusing on political culture emphasizes how politics were delimited by the wider culture and the competition they faced from a range of other opinion formers for the public's attention. These included other parties, political groups and any number of influences from popular culture, the media or religion. There were social and cultural limits to the ability of parties to discursively or otherwise invent their own audiences or electoral success. Party could mobilize, but also alienate – as could other languages and forms of politics. Indifference and apathy were commonly encountered by all the initiatives studied here – amongst as well as beyond their own supporters. This is difficult to research. Eliasoph has analysed apathy not as innate or a by-product of ignorance or alienation, but as manufactured by the codes and exclusions of public debate and activity (in which 'politics' was seen as divisive or best avoided) – and crucially as part of political culture, not other to it.[21]

Akin to shifts in social history, 'new political history' has been as interested in the consumption as the production of politics – the reception besides construction of political rhetoric and practices, the popular traction and resonance of arguments besides their articulation. It questions the *ordering* of relations between political and social change, arguing that politics does not just reflect, but actively brings meaning to notions of class (and other categories). It also queries the *proximity* of these relations, qualifying the extent to which party can be seen to be either forging or reflecting identities. Parties relations with voters were rarely intimate enough to allow more than a contingent relationship between, say, electoral fortunes and political language to be deduced. Party utterances were rarely known to many voters in such detail as historians can excavate. Given this, party rhetoric can be more certainly read as evidence of the production of political discourse (and therein of party culture, perceptions of the electorate, mentalities of leaders, how activists understood change, rather than *actual* change). Participation through voting or membership was rarely rote, but need not involve wholehearted endorsement or knowledge of a political package. This is a model for assessing non-party politics too – recognizing vital, but mediated evidence in their popular reception.

So the case in *Redefining British Politics* is for spreading the focus beyond party, but not excluding it; for a focus on political *culture* rather than the more exclusive politics; and for the agency of politics, but one disciplined by popular reception and by a not always very *political* culture itself. The 'new political history', always more diffuse than even its anonymous title, seems to have culturally turned full circle in re-emphasizing constraints on political agency, although without returning to a social explanation. Its aim was only to offer new viewpoints, supplementing rather than supplanting existing work. An aim here is to bring perspectives that have enlivened studies of the 18th and 19th century – political space, the visual, performative and symbolic – to more recent periods. Its descriptive propensity, evoking the density of political infrastructures, in the quasi-anthropological mode of another of its 'founding texts', Samuel's *Lost World of British Communism*, brings out not only new evidence, but new meaning to existing questions.[22] Yet operating at a national level also often leaves it in need of some comparative dimension and if political history tended to assess divisions within politics, a more cultural approach can exaggerate similarities and continuities between political bodies or ideas. It brackets political life together, assessing its common features in wider society.

Contexts

A key context is relative affluence after rationing ended in Britain in July 1954. This afforded political salience for issues more concerned with the quality of life than the standard of living. Yet as Offer shows, wealth did not automatically translate into well-being – more was not better and generated a host of new disorders. The myriad economic and social consequences of affluence on attitudes, behaviour, choice, taste, knowledge, expectations and lifestyles lend it significant explanatory power. Offer does not detail the political ramifications of affluence, but it was clearly hot-wired into political besides social relations. 'The great transition' from social democracy and public welfare to more privatized values and market liberalism, *the* social and ideological shift of the last half century he contends, 'has been driven (in part at least) by the dynamic of affluence'.[23]

The 1960s saw the break-up of Britain's reputed political stability and civic deference. Leaving aside whether this was liberating or disturbing, it was more obviously a process whereby 'the political' was redefined. Discontent with existing political structures and demands for participation generated a more pluralist political culture, mostly located outside of party. Infused with the creative spirit and potential of 1968, Eley shows how 'the *boundaries* of politics – the very category of the political – had been extended'. Eley's account of this process whereby political space was opened up outside the traditional left, particularly the way feminism redrew political assumptions and the radical subcultures of sexuality, identity, counter-culture and new social movements, is compelling. But it was not confined or unique to radical, progressive politics, as is often assumed.[24] The do-it-yourself political spirit and flourishing of voluntary organizations was widespread and was latent before the sixties. This study notes the pressures for expanded participation within the YCs and Conservative party and the demands of the National Viewers' and Listeners' Association for viewer power and participation and frustration with Conservative politics and the religious establishment. The fragility of Conservative support was as recurrent as that on Labour's fringes. One Conservative agent told in 1957 of the sense of 'helplessness against the vast government machine' and the trade unions that many party supporters felt, but equally that 'they do not see the party political organizations as vehicles for making their presence felt'. There were specific causes for this – middle-class discontent over tax and prices – but it more generally signalled a de-centring of politics from party.[25]

One overarching concept of use to *Redefining British Politics* because it interrelates social change and political values and provides potential ways of analysing political culture, is 'post-materialism'. Ronald Inglehart argued that as core economic needs were met and new generations were socialized in conditions of relative abundance after the war, political values had accordingly become more focused on quality of life issues. Driven by underlying economic change rather than political clashes, a 'silent revolution' would result in generational and cultural conflict. First detailed in 1971, the very idea of post-materialism would seem to be a product of this context and to explain the rise of post-traditional, post-industrial and post-modern theories.[26]

The economic security and well-being fostered by affluence and the welfare state shifted values, which Inglehart plotted through extensive global survey data. Politics was increasingly about rights, tastes, culture, morality, environmental, post-industrial, even anti-materialist, desires and self-expression and less about needs. Inglehart supposed such values amongst younger generations, women's increased involvement, along with growing knowledge and ability to participate ('cognitive mobilization') would stimulate political activity. With resources of time, money and formal education, it was the middle classes that were primed to be the political storm-centre. Inglehart accepted that particular political conflicts would generate interest, but also that this narrative of a more politicized society seemed to falter after the 1960s. Stagnant or falling electoral turnout was the result of the decline of traditional mobilizing 'elite-directed' institutions (parties, unions, churches). This both stimulated and was a consequence of 'elite-directing' politics – single-issue campaigns, social movements, unconventional forms of activity and participation – more attuned to precise issues. Civic duty was not an inevitable victim of lack of trust in party or the state – the deficit was in the supply of formal politics not demand for political action. A more discerning, critical, irreverent, savvy (even cynical), less deferential electorate was harder for the main political parties to satisfy, manage or build alliances with. But by non-traditional measures, this was neither disengagement nor a retreat into domestic privacy, as some felt affluence promoted. In short, declining partisanship was not incommensurate with rising politicization.[27]

Inglehart's thesis has been much debated, critiqued and refined both for its method and results. But political historians have used it little. This is surprising for the 19th and 20th century where politics has been widely read as a proxy of socio-economic class and feverishly debated by Marxists, electoral sociologists and party activists seemingly possessed by materialism, if less surprising of historians of periods in which, say, religion was common political fare. Its mechanical understanding of cultural values as economically derived, revealed a lingering economic determinism, which further explains its limited appeal for historians, who since E.P. Thompson's 1971 work on 'moral economy' through to Vernon's recent work have understood scarcity as relative and mediated by custom and other cultural influences. Hunger did not determine political action and nor did relative affluence. Post-materialism was, paradoxically, a materialist theory. A residual determinism was also evident in its affinities to modernization theory. Inglehart has accepted that the USA showed prosperity could involve a quite conservative or non-secular set of cultural values, but as a 'deviant' case. Yet it is widely acknowledged amongst historians, that the likes of heritage and conservation are markers of the modern and as Chapters 5 and 6 of this study detail, cultural politics could play out in reactionary or traditional as well as progressive, liberal (modernizing) ways.[28]

For critics, greater cultural nuance was needed to understand not just the causes but the spread, extent and meaning of post-materialist politics. Even those who ratify Inglehart's findings that economic political motivations and agendas were being displaced by cultural ones, have here turned to Bourdieu's notion of 'cultural capital' that foregrounds culture as bearing centrally upon historical processes. Savage and Majima use Bourdieu to offer a more culturally complex (alert to national distinctions and specific social and group conflicts, rather than globally driven) and inter-subjective set of identity and value measures, which for Britain since the 1980s, they argue shows more stability than change. Nonetheless, post-materialism remains for Majima and Savage, 'the most empirically wide-ranging' and 'unusually sophisticated' and 'thorough attempt to explore value change from the perspective of global cultural politics'.[29]

Critics have also queried the efficacy of dichotomies of traditional/secular, libertarian/authoritarian, survival/self-expression and the one-dimensional materialist/post-materialist axis itself. They have questioned whether they were necessarily at odds with each other or if some mix of them might be held. It might then be that higher or rising value was being attached to post-materialist than materialist values, a trend towards post-materialism not that it was more prevalent, or that the two were not opposites or exclusive, or might be held simultaneously. The cultural agendas detailed in this book came with material implications as Britain's creative economy flourished in the 1960s, and the seeming materialism of consumer lifestyles could have self-expressive aims, aesthetic or symbolic appeals that were not necessarily at odds with post-materialism.[30]

Post-materialism need not then be anti-materialism, although Inglehart tended to counterpose them, suggesting for instance that in environmental concerns or unease with science, the 'anti-industrial outlook of some of the movement's ideologues could lead to neglect of the economic base on which post-materialism ultimately depends'. This exhibits again an under-lying economic determinism. Inglehart's defence was that in stressing not just escape from scarcity, but a generational socialization experience, he took into account tradition, religion, nation and other cultural differences. A degree of stability in the value systems of elder generations implied that affluence was not the only motor of value change and also pointed to how values were not just an economic reflex and thus that political 'action does not simply reflect external situations'.

There are other pointers within post-materialism to excising its latent materialism, its cultural 'blind spot' or 'marxism lite' as Houtman puts it, that neither escapes materialist explanations nor accords culture due power. As has been noted, this was hardly an uncommon framework – Offer and Eley, for instance, see politics driven by 'underlying' social and economic changes. Post-materialism offers a causal model of new cultural politics, but not a cultural, or post-materialist, approach for exploring them. This is despite Inglehart contending that 'being freed from the need to focus their energies primarily on the struggle for economic and physical security' meant mass publics could 'devote more attention to post-materialist concerns – such as politics'. Regarding politics itself as a post-materialist activity, offers a non-reductionist approach to political culture that corresponds with that outlined in the discussion of the 'new political history'.[31]

And this study also asks more about the supply of politics perceiving and articulating post-materialism. The Consumers' Association (CA)'s attention to dilemmas of choice and Whitehouse and Wesker's cultural agendas complicate the socio-economic drivers of Inglehart's post-materialism and suggest its politics played out more diversely and disputatiously. In their reception we can, tentatively, assess the extent of post-materialist political demand from the mass of citizens. Measuring popular values without taking into account the supply of political ideas, organizations, debate and mobilizing networks, risks substituting economic for cultural determinism – popular values do not translate into or correspond with fixed political positions any more than economic status does. Savage notes the importance of seeing values in relation to each other rather than derived from external forces, but says little about the production of politics, or how resonant politics was in popular values or how they became politically charged.

Post-materialism, like affluence, is used in this study then as a trend, rather than some definitive measure or quantitative threshold and as a qualitative shift (that ties in with a more cultural approach to politics). It is not as if *all* politics in this period were *only* about affluence or measurable along some materialist axis. The YCs, for example, were not post-materialist in cause or content, although their sense of belonging and associational motivations can best be grasped through such a cultural history. Nor, even more certainly, is it that culture, morality, consumption or the 'self' weren't political before this period. The case here is just that political culture both matters and illuminates.

Contents

Chapter 2 uses the Consumers' Association to explore consumer politics. Founded in 1957 and Britain's largest new post-war voluntary organization, CA initiated wide-ranging debate on consumerism and lends itself to comparison with the US consumer movement. A consumer testing organization, the CA not only invested washing machines with symbolic significance, but developed as a popular and effective pressure group, fashioning a consumer identity with social, political and citizenship implications. It was as much a prototype for alternative politics as the Campaign for Nuclear Disarmament and like them a mainly middle-class grouping. In the imagination of its founding figure, Michael Young, CA even aspired to challenge the main parties and redraw the political environment. Chapter 3 accesses related debates via the Co-op, whose comparative difficulties dealing with the consumer boom of the later 1950s were illuminating. The Co-op's part commercial, part political identity – the original modern social movement in many respects – straddles social and political change. The role of the leading Labour thinker Tony Crosland, also closely involved with CA, as chair of the Commission (1955–58) appointed to audit the Co-op's commercial and philosophical health, reveals the influence of consumer politics on his wider political outlook. Chapter 4 assesses party presence in civil society through the Young Conservatives. It traces their evolution from what was legitimately claimed to be the free world's largest political youth organization in the 1950s into one that was smaller, less social and more (in the formal, customary sense) politically-minded by the 1960s. The YCs vibrant social life enables historians to explore its internal culture in unusual depth and demands a social and cultural history to tease out its political meaning. The YCs debates about the strategic mix of social and political activities are used to glean insights into the broader political environment.

Cultural politics are surveyed in the National Viewers' and Listeners' Association (NVALA), founded by Mary Whitehouse in 1964 and which campaigned for 'traditional' moral values on television. As with the YCs, excavating the internal world of NVALA details how its characteristic strategies and language emerged, its frustrations with the political and Church *status quo* and how it experienced private TV viewing as a matter for public debate. The NVALA confounds assumptions about the generational and educational membership of emergent pressure groups, but also confirms their focus on post-materialist issues and the centrality of media and culture to such politics. Centre 42 (C42) (1960–70), Arnold Wesker's design for an arts centre in a restored Camden Roundhouse, the subject of Chapter 6, was a further instance of culture *as* politics. C42's urging of Labour and trade unions to take up this cultural agenda meshes with debates about the role of the state in the arts through to post-industrial use of buildings. Politically radical, in pressing what can best be described as an early New Left agenda, its own cultural repertoire was traditional, if 'progressive' and rapidly superseded by popular and counter-cultural tastes. It offers another test for the traction of arguments about the spread of post-materialist values and politics. The final chapter is concerned with the representation, conduct and reputation of politics. It discusses popular apathy and scepticism and politics' interaction with TV, marketing and polling. Besides new technologies, it uses evidence from satire to the presentation of party premises. In exploring the anxieties of party politicians at the impact of these media, their attempts to regulate them and how they shaped relations with the mass of Britons, it argues for continuity in terms of a sometimes boisterous, if distant relationship between political elites and the people, neither of which much pleased either. It notes the persistence of local and 'street' politics alongside the modernization and professionalization of party campaigning and signs of the neo-liberal consumer-voter and media politics more usually associated with the period since the 1980s. If everyday life seemed increasingly permeated by consumerism, this was no less true of political conduct.

Sources are diverse, using the detritus and minutiae of political activity, its material culture besides language and leading figures. They range from government papers to the politics of children's TV programme, *Pinky and Perky*; from washing machines to White Papers. To bring both formal and popular politics into the frame, it examines new or rarely used evidence and assesses traditional sources in new ways. Some sources have been neglected by political history's customary assumptions – notably the social life of the YCs, but without which their political import is inexplicable. It draws then on a range of state, organizational, individual and local papers. Whilst the book's focus generates some untypical sources for political history – say the BBC's Mary Adams who was involved with CA and in campaigning on the uses of TV and against Whitehouse – these are not read therefore as necessarily more typical political types.

A cultural history of politics does not just rest on new sources and can be read from the materials and assumptions in traditional approaches. Crick's study has been noted and for instance, Sir Ivor Jennings' three volume *Party Politics* (1960–62) was peppered with insights into politics' status in the wider society, much as it focused on constitutional, political history. For example, it recognized how parties competed not only with each other, but 'with the weather, television, sports and pastimes, and plain lethargy'. He noted how football was 'for most people, more important than the privy council' – a point alert to the gap between the people and politics and that explained the power held by elites. Party was marked apart for Jennings because 'keen local politicians' had 'the same interest in politics as so many of the people whom they claim to represent have in crime or football'. And this, for Jennings, implied 'that they are neither ordinary electors nor representative of them'. To reprise the dialogue with McKibbin, it was then 'false to assume that politics is the normal staple of conversation'.[32]

2

'Consumers of the world unite, you have nothing to lose but your illusions': The Politics of the Consumers' Association[1]

The consumer has become the lodestar of re-interpreting British politics from the 1940s and as a site on which historians can plot broader debates, something of an all-consuming subject. Zweiniger-Bargielowska has detailed the Conservatives' assembly of a popular alliance against rationing and control as key to its electoral recovery from 1945 and advantage over a left that struggled with affluence from the later 1950s.[2] 'The battle of the consumer', as Gurney has it, saw nothing less than the 'atomized figure of the individual consumer' became a 'hegemonic influence across both polity and civil society, shaping the epistemologies and languages through which the political and economic domains were... represented'. For Gurney, this 'helped undermine the Co-operative alternative to mass consumption', but Hilton sees the same process serve as the basis for new forms of citizenship and politics, in which the Consumers' Association (CA) was a prime mover. Mort similarly points to the increasingly common conception of political and consuming subjects, practices and discourses in this period, notably through the technologies of marketing and polling. Politics, no less than the rest of society, was consumerized or, critics felt, colonized by consumer values and practices.[3]

Founded in 1957, the CA assembles several themes that resonate throughout *Redefining British Politics*. It voiced the concern of consumers against producers, fused an amateur Do-It-Yourself (DIY) ethos with professional knowledge, research and expertise and operated outside orthodox party politics, as an attempt to influence, but also an expression of discontent with them. CA's magazine, *Which?*, made everyday, domestic issues into public and political matters. Like the cultural politics explored later through Whitehouse and Wesker, CA was contingent upon affluence, yet critical of it. It was preoccupied with how time and money were spent by Britons in conditions of relative well-being and where choice not need was a driver. It was motivated by issues of knowledge and participation as much as choice and by the perils of plenty as much as scarcity. CA highlighted new social issues that affluence produced and how affluence did not automatically translate into happiness and posed dilemmas of choice, taste and heightened the stakes of disappointment.[4] CA's politics were then post-materialist in content, but used more often as value for money guides by readers. CA's were not party politics, although they encountered many of the same difficulties as party (apathy amongst and beyond its own members and of claiming to speak for consumers other than its own members) and tried to influence and challenge formal politics and in Young's vision even supplant the party *status quo*. CA's were more a politics by other means and forms, a DIY 1960s-style pressure group whose campaigning rapidly assumed the form of a social movement with consumers at the centre of its worldview.

CA's importance lay not only in its scale, but the leading figures lured into its orbit, from Labour revisionist Tony Crosland to the BBC's Mary Adams. Its founding and driving force, Michael Young, and its chair from 1964, Peter Goldman, were key backroom research figures in the Labour and Conservative parties respectively – the key authors of the victorious 1945 and 1959 election manifestoes. That CA absorbed and attracted their energies hints at some displacement of party and how CA shifted the boundaries of politics and consumerism. CA was fond of claiming it had reinvented consumerism and other commentators did not think it so far fetched to suggest that 'Michael Young invented consumers', as a social subject and political category in post-war Britain.[5]

As the largest *new* voluntary association in post-war Britain, as much store can be put by the CA as signal evidence of a nation of shoppers as can be deduced about the potency of heritage in the national culture by Britain (and Europe's) largest voluntary organization, the National Trust. CA was as much of a prototype for the non-party politics that flourished in this period as the classic model of *Middle class radicalism*, the Campaign for Nuclear Disarmament (CND), founded in 1958. Even Whitehouse's National Viewers' and Listeners' Association aped CA's rhetoric of claiming to speak for the participatory rights of a key interest group – TV consumers. Pressure group politics like CA tended to be a more intimate monitor of specific social changes than parties, who were trying to assemble support across a range of members, electors and issues. CA articulated more than anything else the everyday concerns of middle-class suburbia. Yet literature on social movements has centred on radical demands, urban elites and more spectacular politics in the spirit of 1968. Yet CA experienced difficulties familiar to historians of political parties. For most members (subscribers to *Which?* had to take out CA membership) it was at most a single-issue pressure group; for its leaders and founders like Young, more a social movement that might address a range of issues – international, environmental and even national decline and in Young's imagination for forging a consumer politics to challenge the main parties.

CA was not simply a product of social change, it was a key articulator of the idea that Britain was now affluent and construed this in specific ways.

It made domestic, parochial commodities and practices – shopping, labelling, washing machines, as with TV discussed in Chapter 5 – into political and public matter. CA charged material culture with broader meanings and, unconsciously or not, made the personal, political. For Hilton its banality was at once its political weakness (lacking ideological cohesion) and appeal (populist and accessible).[6] CA lends itself to multiple readings: as a liberation of self-expression in the mode of the 1960s, an economic individualism that prefigured neo-liberalism and Thatcherism or, as its leaders preferred, a citizenship critically aware of the risks and possibilities of the market and with international and radical leanings. CA reveals tensions within post-materialism (in its self-conception as a movement of rational consumers un-interested in commodities' symbolic value and between CA and its less movement-minded audience) and in civil society, where CA served as both a critic of big business, but deployed a market-based language centred on empowering the consumer. Equally resonant in it were the legacies of Victorian social reform, echoes of Mass Observation's efforts to give voice to everyday life and the rise of the professional expert. It can also be read as a marker of Americanization (explored here through the influence of US consumer critics and comparatively with the US Consumers' Union, CU) and even of satire, as Chapter 7 discusses. Its success – in membership, lobbying and developing a BBC TV programme, *Choice* – contrasted with the consumer politics of the Co-op explored in the next chapter.

*Which?*craft: CA's internal culture

Launched in October 1957, *Which?* none too tentatively claimed by its second edition to have 'more readers than any other quarterly in the country, perhaps even in the world'. CA topped 100,000 members by the end of 1958. Local consumer groups, started-up in 1961 under CA's auspices as the National Federation of Consumer Groups numbered almost 100 by 1965.[7] The International Organization of Consumer Unions (IOCU) for which Michael Young campaigned, was founded in 1960. It had organizations in 27 counties by the end of the 1960s and several received start-up donations from CA.[8]

CA's own take-off was funded by the Elmhirst Trust, backers of Young's progressive *alma mater*, Dartington Hall. Dorothy Elmhirst made grants to the prototype consumer testing organization, the American CU, formed in 1936. By 1969 with 600,000 members, CA's expenditure and income exceeded £1 million and estimates of *Which?*'s readership were as high as four million. Five start-up staff had become more than 300 by 1970. Its first home in a decrepit Bethnal Green shed – a rags-to-riches narrative CA often related, reminiscent of the Co-Op's origins in a Rochdale back-street – became offices in Central London from 1960.[9]

Which? undertook what it described as 'honest fact-finding' – empirical, comparative research into the functional worth of consumer goods. 'CA's concern is with the design of goods from the point of view of their efficiency, their convenience and their safety, in relation to their price' *Which?* editor Eirlys Roberts explained in 1966.[10] Its strict focus on use-value meant campaigns like 'I'm Backing Britain', which fleetingly bloomed as Britain's economy withered in 1967, excited little CA support. CA was all for aiding the British economy, but by improving quality and value not through patriotic purchasing. The first edition of *Motoring Which?* in January 1962 criticized all six British cars it tested, finding a Volkswagen the 'best buy'. The *Daily Express* motoring correspondent felt such reports 'were gleefully seized upon by our foreign competitors' and accused CA members of 'paying to support a campaign against British exports, British industry and British employment'. CA director Casper Brook was keen to pursue a libel case against the *Express*. His more ameliorative successor, Peter Goldman, explained CA aided the national economy because its tests could 'show which foreign goods UK export products would have to compete with' and even touted testing for the government.[11]

Sensitive to this anti-British charge, CA was a quiet pro-European. It declared it had 'no view on the common market' during Britain's first application. But Young attended (as an observer) a meeting of consumer representatives from the six members in Brussels in 1961. Viewing Europe as a prospect for reversing the imperial, economic and sense of decline that had gripped post-war Britain, Young told the *Daily Mail* in 1962 that 'after contracting for so long, our immediate world may begin to enlarge'. His 1960 polemic, *The Chipped White Cups of Dover*, was firmly pro-European.[12]

Nor were style or fashion CA's métier. 'We can say that an electric iron is safe or a refrigerator efficient', a 1959 *Which?* editorial detailed, 'we cannot say that the iron looks good or that the refrigerator looks ugly'. It recognized taste was an element in consuming decisions, but not one on which it could designate a 'best buy'. A typically arch press release for a test of little black dresses in 1965 noted that whilst 'every woman knows that the right dress can do something for the wearer', most could not distinguish the couture model from others. Ergonomics apart, CA was 'not concerned with appearances', but endorsed the Design Centre set up in 1956 by the Council for Industrial Design for this purpose. Roberts often sat on its judging panels as 'a critic who would not be seduced by prettiness for prettiness' sake'.[13] This was a post-materialist agenda in so much as CA believed more goods alone were no guarantor of a better life, but it was not ethical issues that were uppermost in CA's mind. It admitted testing hair colour restorers on mice in 1960 and in 1967 the Manchester Consumer Group felt the only ethics of any worth to coat buyers was their right to know the actual fur content in their purchases.[14]

But by dint of its conviction that aesthetics were of secondary importance and the goods it was appraising, the CA could hardly avoid inferring value judgements on taste and lifestyle or expressing cultural or national preferences. Everyday commodities and activities were charged with qualities of national economic performance or consumers' skills and invested with partisan qualities, much as CA purported to be neutral. Its belief that enjoyment of affluence could only be realized through better goods and more discretionary consumers, not arrant materialism, could err towards the ascetic. An early *Which?* on 'drying the family wash' concluded the 'best method' was 'a country garden, a stiff breeze and a sunny day' – not terrifically useful advice to residents of high-rise housing, "Coronation Street" or rainy Britain. This inadvertently denoted *Which?*'s middle-class readership as much as critiquing the spurious claims made for spin-dryers.[15]

It is hard to envision the 'swinging sixties' from the pages of *Which?* dedicated to mundane matters, but this might refurbish our impression of the sizzling 1960s. Youth culture, for instance, despite being an expanding part of consumer spending, was largely absent from its pages. CA understood affluence to have given rise to greater expectations for an improved quality of life, but also to have generated new problems and social issues. More cars meant congestion, even more food – evinced in *Which?*'s tests on slimming – required expert managing to realize the prospect of affluence. CA retained an admiration for the self-control subsistence enforced and abundance threatened – 'don't eat between meals' potential dieters were told. This was a politics of rational recreation through consumption in the belief that too much was as morally dangerous as too little. But too puritan an image of the early CA would be mistaken. 'Pep' pills were tested and in 1963 contraceptives, even if this was only available as a special supplement and researched despite the unease of Catholic staff. The *Good Food Guide*, founded by socialist gourmet Raymond Postgate in 1951, was published in conjunction with CA from 1963.[16]

The CA's utilitarian tendencies contrasted with the Labour revisionist emphasis on the quality of life besides standard of living. For Tony Crosland (a CA council member from 1958), affluence afforded a post-materialist focus in which where the Webbs and Fabian emphasis on efficiency would yield to a more relaxed, pluralism of full enjoyment besides employment and aestheticism not asceticism. So too the free-market Institute for Economic Affairs (IEA) founded in 1955, which felt, 'with rising standards, leisure counts for more and the marginal utility of not bothering about marginal utility grows'.[17] Yet CA was invariably bothered about precisely the marginal utility of this or that washing machine. This lead consumer journalist Marghanita Laski to envisage a situation in 1958:

> when the shopper, thoroughly informed as to what is efficient, economical, labour-saving and useful, buys it and is sad, simply because the one thing she doesn't like about it is the way it looks. And we shall have got our values miserably wrong if we fail to weigh the pleasures of the senses against reason...[18]

Despite its revisionist influences, CA would not speak to this agenda and Laski, whose *Observer* columns were influential at the outset of the consumer rights and testing movement, was reluctant to join CA. CA's ethos was as much a product of austerity as affluence in its privileging of function over pleasure. In its own narrative and as Goldman explained CA 'got the timing... by judgment or by accident absolutely right', when rationing had ended, the shops filled up and 'people clustered for the information like hungry paupers round a soup kitchen'.[19] This self-conception related more to wartime and Cripps' Britain than the luxuries of choice and indecision afforded by affluence. In Young, revisionism's emphasis on the quality of life fused with traditional Fabianism. Profiled as the 'last of the Fabians', his dynamism as a social researcher was compared to the Webbs and there was more than a Fabian whiff in CA's dislike of the waste it saw in advertising and its anti-frivolous instincts. Roberts who very much 'set the tone for the magazine' had worked for the United Nations Organization (UNO) relief agency in post-war Albania and in Cripps' treasury as a public relations officer. If historians invest lifestyle with some symbolic store, *pace* CA, then Roberts' spoke volumes. She lived in a shabby Georgian house in London and drove a 10-year-old Morris Minor.[20]

In a related vein, *Which?* prided itself on no-nonsense language, illuminating the false claims and opaque rhetoric of advertising. Roberts believed 'legal language is often used to bilk the underprivileged'. But CA was apt to earnest and prolix vindications of its methodology. This was apparent to *Which?* readers, who in a 1971 survey complained it was 'too long-winded' and should 'come to the point'. Crosland remembered CA's governing council 'was not the most taciturn'.[21]

CA attracted and fashioned a similarly stern audience. Amongst criticisms of *Which?* in a 1962 reader's survey were: 'the use of English in *Which?* is becoming Americanised'; 'the use of colour... is a concession to glamour'; 'some reports are frivolous e.g. electric socks' and complaints at the occasional 'comic drawings'. Where popular pastimes were assessed, *Which?*'s sobriety was present. A test on beer admitted 'some of our members must be teetotalers by conviction' and that as fashion and habit shaped drinking preferences and 'tastes differ' abstained from naming a 'best buy'.[22]

In this respect, it is notable that Crosland was not CA's 'best buy' revisionist. That had been Denis Healey, who like Wilfred Fienburgh MP (revisionist, temporary CA office manager and key to winning it early press coverage), harked back to Young's Transport House days in Labour's research department. Healey was as forthright as Crosland, but less louche. Otherwise Crosland was an obvious choice, with knowledge of consumer issues acquired as secretary until 1958 of the Co-operative Independent Commission.[23]

Local and legislative campaigning evolved to supplement testing and consumer law also fell within CA's purview. It regularly submitted to government enquiries and claimed influence in the appointment of the Molony Committee on Consumer Protection (1959–62). Its close ties to the influential think-tank Political and Economic Planning (PEP) embedded it rapidly into peak-level policy networks and these assimilated leading CA figures. As a policy initiator and by 1980 the *Times* reckoned CA had 'filled more pages of the statute book than any other pressure group this century'. The first chair of the Consumers' Council, the regulatory authority and information service Molony created in 1963, was Baroness Katherine Elliot, an ex-CA vice president and honorary vice president of CA's Research Institute for Consumer Affairs (RICA). Jeremy Mitchell, *Which?*'s deputy research director between 1958 and 1962, joined the new National Economic Development Office in 1965 and succeeded Young as chief of the National Consumer Council from 1977.[24]

But CA took neither government money nor advertisements, fearing this would compromise the independence of its test verdicts. CA discouraged manufacturers citing *Which?* in adverts and referred 97 cases (a signal of the power of *Which?*'s 'best buy' trademark) to the Advertising Standards Authority in 1965. It was, like many critics of the affluent society, sceptical of advertising. In 1968 Roberts seethed that the £60 million Unilever and Proctor and Gamble spent advertising washing detergents could have built 20,000 new homes. Before rationing ended and as an adjunct to the symbolic washing machine, detergents were a key commercial battleground. Roberts highlighted a 1966 Monopolies Commission report requiring both companies to cut their advertising (and thereby prices) since total sales of washing detergent had not grown since 1956.[25]

Critics, like the IEA, charged CA was anti-advertising. Another business lobby, Aims of Industry, read Roberts' discussion of consumerism's 'egalitarian motive' and the potential for consumer action in her 1966 book *Consumers*, as 'practical anti-capitalism'. A favourite charge of such critics was of CA's hypocrisy since its own promotional spending was proportionally 'unmatched, so far as one can ascertain, in the world of commerce', compared to its professed *raison d'être* of testing and research.[26] CA found the nub of this charge irrefutable. In 1961–62 research expenditure increased by 52%, advertising by 230%, and expenditure on producing, distributing and promoting *Which?* exceeded that on testing. CA's defence was that *Which?* was not available at newsagents and that 'the great majority of new members only join as a result of our advertising'.[27]

CA was adept at self-marketing: even successful products like *Which?* needed promotion, as CA's example showed. Its launch received extensive press coverage and it rapidly established itself as a familiar reference point in the media and on TV. *Motoring Which?*'s launch in 1962 saw Roberts and (the aptly named car project officer) Maurice Healy on TV and radio news. The user-friendly accessibility of *Which?*'s 'best-buy', its clarity and media savvy, won it success by deploying very business-like methods, aping the sound-bite style of advertising and the language of free choice to critique big business. The same was true of Vance Packard, the influential US critic of affluence and consumerism whose squibs, published by Penguin in the

UK, left even sympathizers unsure whether they were reading a diagnosis or symptom of affluence's ills.[28]

Impressions mattered to CA, however wary it was of this in others. Professional designer (for Gala Toys and CND) Ken Garland was employed to re-design *Which?* in 1962.[29] It already used more photos than its main competitor, the part government-funded Consumer Advisory Council's *Shopper's Guide*. *Shopper's Guide* was revamped by Clive Labovitch and Michael Heseltine's Cornmarket Press in 1962. A song showed CA felt Cornmarket's other magazines, *Topic* and *Town*, would compromise test reports and some light-hearted anxiety: 'competition's stiff for *Which?* – with Heseltine and Labovitch – can't you see them arguing – when the first lab report comes in? – if brand "A" comes out too bad – *Topic* and *Town* might lose that ad'. With falling sales *Shopper's Guide* was folded by Cornmarket in 1963 and CA pursued its subscribers. Cornmarket got some revenge, issuing a *Which University?* (the first such guide) in 1966.[30]

In Sarah Franks' model, CA's skill was in expanding and dominating the consumer information market against the likes of *Shopper's Guide* and the Co-op. This booming market included romance publishers Mills and Boon. Elizabeth Gundrey, *Shopper's Guide* editor, was the most prolific presence. Besides *Which?*, 1957 also saw the start of a 'Value Judgement' column in the *New Statesman*, 'Information' in *The Listener* and what was to become Leslie Adrian's long-running (until October 1970) 'Consuming Interest' column in the Conservative weekly *The Spectator*.[31] Besides consumer rights, the column doubled up with recipe, wine, restaurant or travel tips, some authored by Elizabeth David. Adrian often drew on *Which?* reports and CA advertised in *The Spectator*.[32]

Further characteristic of CA's marketing-mindedness was its use of opinion polling: to target its members and to represent 'consumer opinion'. Polls revealed the products members wanted tested (TVs, washing machines, spin-driers and vacuums topped the first poll, with a quarter requesting washing detergents); their opinions of Resale Price Maintenance (RPM, whereby manufacturers determined retail prices, three-quarters were for abolition in 1961) and their socio-economic status.[33]

The CA was middle class in the main. Eighty-four per cent of *Which?* subscribers owned a car in 1967, compared with 48% of British households; 25% had a salary above the £3000 p.a. earned by 2% of Britons. It was middle-aged too. Only 11% were aged under 25 and 5% over 65.[34] Socially, CA was a consumer aristocracy, but its leaders thought this problematic. In September 1959 the Council agreed 'to broaden the CA into an organization for the purpose of representing the consumer at large'. Brook had urged the Council that as it was 'part of our terms of reference to spread consumer information as widely as possible', it 'ought to be favourably disposed towards the publishing of a popular *Which?*' He envisioned a *Which?* targeted not at 'the higher social/economic groups – presumably those who least need to be discriminating in their shopping', but at what was described as 'the less well-educated and much larger market'.[35] In short, *Which?*'s thrifty advice was being bought and used by those who could most afford it, but least needed it.

But limited progress was made towards informing working-class buying habits. Council member and Conservative MP Phillip Goodhart was 'horrified at the idea of a "popular" *Which?*'; Crosland felt CA was 'not professional enough yet' and should 'consolidate', but was more enthusiastic by 1962 that CA's TV collaboration with the BBC, *Choice*, might win it a broader audience. The best Roberts could conclude by 1966 was that membership had begun 'to spread, though slowly into the skilled working class'. Later in the 1960s, Goldman felt CA should go to working-class consumers if they would not come to *Which?* Besides reports in the *Daily Mirror*, Goldman's model was Austrian high street advice centres, cloned by CA in London from 1969. CA's limited progress here hints that class divisions were reinforced not blurred by affluence. Discriminating consumerism animated the middle class and even seemed a marker of its distinction from the working class. For Young it remained the state's role to breakthrough to working-class consumers.[36]

As a source *Which?* offers historians insights into middle-class life, with its guidance on tipping etiquette, airport customs, credit cards and au pairs. Many working-class shoppers in any case bought second-hand. By the later 1960s, *Which?* was a mainstay of middle-class life, tending to its niches, from a *Drugs and Therapeutics Bulletin* (another idea imported from CU) to, for those with alternatives to spending, *Money Which?* from 1968.[37]

In attitude too, CA was something of a consumers' aristocracy. It reveled in its member's reputation as 'some of the... most rational people in the country' who were 'more knowledgeable and articulate about consumer goods than the rest'. CA members were typically well educated – one-third had a terminal education age above 19, compared to 7% of all Britons.[38] In this sense they conformed strongly to Inglehart's typology of post-materialists. Psychologist Peter Cooper's research positing stages of consumer evolution, was seized by CA as evidence of its influence. The (first stage) traditional housewife wielding experienced management of the family budget had been replaced by (stage two) those with easy access to credit, but at the mercy of marketing. Stage three would see housewives draw 'on impartial information' of the sort offered by *Which?* to 'make informed choices and take control of their budget'. In short, *Which?* was helping 'combat the alleged deterioration in housewifery standards'. This placed it in a long tradition of well-intentioned middle-class attempts at educating working-class housewifery and to 'do good' to the working class more generally, a tradition revived and reoriented now that mass poverty had diminished.[39]

Whilst its members were the 'most consumer-conscious', CA simultaneously presented itself as a 'bewildered buyers club'. In imagining the consumer, CA supposed that expanded choice had also complicated choice via developments like self-service. For Goldman, mass production, distribution, credit and marketing, together with the technical goods 'which the Merlins of the laboratory have conjured into existence', meant 'the position of the consumer, though improving... in absolute terms, was actually worsening relative to that of the trader'. This then was a *Which?* to counter the hocus-pocus of the market, wizardry of technology and the spell this had cast over Britons. If still a 'David' compared to the 'Goliath' £360 million spent a year on advertising by industry, CA aimed to rebalance the market battlefield in consumers' favour.[40]

It was not only then that consumers were pressurized by advertising, bewitched by choice or mystified by technology, but that they lacked the prudence (and not only requisite information) to make informed choices. CA often took a dim view of consumers, particularly before or still un-affiliated to CA. As Roberts recalled:

> Remember (or imagine) your fellow-countrymen... in the early 1950s... The shops were full of goods, many... new and exciting... No-one, however intelligent, was much good at shopping... people felt puzzled, unconfident and even resentful. They were at the mercy of manufacturers and advertisers.[41]

Such thinking related to traditions critical of mass society and mass tastes since the dummy of the BBC's CA-derived *Choice* was dubbed 'scrutiny pro-gramme', echoing (like many on the unaligned political left) the serious tone less than the cultural conservatism of F.R. Leavis' *Scrutiny*. CA was hardly alone in so imagining consumers. Gundrey's book *Help* worried, 'half the time the bewildered citizen does not know... aids exist – or where to locate them' and 'flounders helplessly at the mercy of Government departments [and] big business'. The Molony Report reckoned, 'shopping has become more complicated', but 'doubted whether shopping expertness has kept pace with the advance in the standard of living', a consequence of new goods and selling methods and time pressure on shopping created by more women entering the labour market.[42]

Such perceptions of consumers – that they should be sovereign, but were unduly corralled by business – fed into the politics of consumer protection or education. CA believed consumers required enlightenment and were entitled to protection from the state but should not rely upon it. Too much protection might hamper the making of discerning shoppers. A quality label was only as useful as its reader or, as an initial draft of *Which?* put it, 'an ounce of self-help is worth a ton of spoon-feeding'.[43] On its tenth anniversary, CA declared a debt 'simultaneously to Adam Smith and Tom Paine'. It aimed to 'enlighten the ignorant' and 'wither the establishment by questioning the value of the goods and services it provided', all 'in the name of the rights of man' and in the belief that consumption was the essence of economic activity.[44]

Journalist Robert Millar's anatomy of consumers – commissioned by the CA as *The Discriminating Consumer*, but disowned when it emerged critical of them entitled *The Affluent Sheep* – reinforced CA's watchdog tendencies. Published in 1963, Millar concluded: 'because of their own apathy, careless-ness and irresponsibility, consumers are in danger of losing the war' over the benefits of affluence. He also found that some working-class shoppers thought *Which?* was 'in the pay of advertisers and manufacturers' and produced by 'do-gooders'.[45]

Even CA members complained it was prone to imagine that *Which?* knew better what was good for the consumer than consumers themselves. Almost half told the 1968 readers' survey that they found CA 'a bit smug about its own activities'. 1971's survey similarly unearthed a sense that 'reports are written with a self-righteous "know-all" air' or were 'too cocky, the con-sumer should be predominant, not the Consumers' Association'.[46] *Which?*'s repertoire and take on consumption patterns was evidence of CA's outlook above all else. More than reflecting consumption trends, CA's interest in new, household, domestic appliances freighted these with symbolic significance, largely by dint of the class and gender profile of its own consumers.[47]

As salient as any specific constituency was the breadth of appeal CA aspired to. Its 150 speaking engagements in the six months after October 1961 ranged from the British Disinfectant Manufacturers Association to the Institute of Contemporary Art, although Home Counties' Women's Insti-tutes, Townswomen's Guilds and homemaking evening classes were pre-ponderant. Politically, Young Conservatives in Hounslow, Epsom, Esher, Surbiton, Sevenoaks, Woodside Park, Lower Mitcham, Woodford, St. George's, Walton and Barkingside were addressed by CA, but just two Labour and one Liberal meeting.[48]

Women were central to CA's vision of consumers; particularly as house-wives, who CA's (chiefly male) experts would assist. 1957's Festival of Women was *Which?*'s planned launch pad, containing 'the precise section of the community to whom we wish to appeal'.[49] Other evidence queried such assumptions. A 1966 Marplan survey of CA joiners found it was more often husbands who sent in a subscription slip. *Which?* was alert to male consumption trends, the expanding market in male cosmetics for instance and, Hilton contends, the consumer was conceived in more gender-neutral terms by this period.[50] Gender certainly intrigued consumer writers. Poet Philip Larkin cast *Which?* (in TV form as the BBC's *Choice*) as mothering interference: 'Over to catch the drivel of some bitch – who's read nothing but *Which*'. The *Spectator*'s pseudonymous 'Leslie Adrian' was nurtured as an ambiguous, 'apparently hermaphroditic' figure by contributors like deputy editor Bernard Levin. A compendium of articles gave little away other than that Adrian was 'a fussy, voluble perfectionist who would like everyone else to be too'. Not least, anonymity guarded the writer against manufacturer's complaints or libel action.[51]

Choice

At its outset, CA sought legal assurance that criticism of goods and brands, based on testing, would not bring actions from manufacturers. Gerald Gardiner QC, a progressive who would be Penguin's defence lawyer in the *Lady Chatterley* trial in 1960 and Lord Chancellor 1964–70, advised Young in 1957 that 'the risk of an action being brought against consumer research was not such as ought to deter the founders from launching'. He predicted, in a signal of CA's populist appeal, that a jury was likely to be 'extremely sympathetic to a non-profit making body whose sole concern is to help the jury and their wives or husbands to spend their money to their best advantage'.[52]

Mary Adams, then the head of BBC television talks, was the motive force behind the BBC TV's *Choice* that started in 1962 and was based on the CA's research (with some *Shopper's Guide* input at the outset). Adams had been wartime Director of Home Intelligence at the Ministry of Information, was close to Mass Observation's Tom Harrisson and intimately involved with CA and its local consumer groups. As early as 1955 Adams noted Labour MP Elaine Burton's pamphlet *Value for Money* and touted a women's consumer programme, with participants such as Eirlys Cullen (*Which?* editor Eirlys Roberts, then on the Treasury's Women's Advisory Committee). But the proposed *Penny Wise* received contrary legal opinion about the naming of branded goods constituting advertising and infringing the BBC's charter. With opposition from Robert Fraser at the Independent Television Authority (ITA) too, it was abandoned in 1956. CA's emergence tipped the argument towards those who felt reporting tests results was 'a service to the public' and that this was a 'propitious moment' to offer this. *Woman's Hour* had reported CA's founding and early *Which?* reports, establishing a precedent that – as Gardiner advised and CA had discovered – malice or slander would be near impossible to prove against an independent body such as CA or the BBC rather than a rival trader.[53]

Adams was crucial since Young's relations with the BBC were fraught having broken a verbal agreement not to give out CA's address on BBC broadcasts. Adams had suggested a TV ad to boost publicity – 'it'll tell you what you need to know' was its plain-speaking tag line – and also approached the Independent Television (ITV) companies about a testing programme, although 'aware of the special difficulties this may present' given their dependence on advertisers. When ITV rejected the ad in 1959, Adams saw this as an 'opportunity to be able to make the fuss we had hoped'. Her approach to Hugh Carleton Greene (five months into the job) outlined how CA had not been prosecuted because of the 'accuracy and scientific impartiality' of its testing, claimed the Molony Committee had been 'the result of our progress' and how CA enjoyed the 'warm support of the political parties'. Adams was honest that the programme appealed to the CA as a means to access 'sections of the community at a lower income and educational levels than readers of our journal *Which?*'[54] Greene liked the notion of emphasizing that this was *Which?* research to negotiate the issue of naming brands. By the end of 1959 a pilot had been agreed. Legal caution meant slow progress was made and in the meantime CA pressed Molony for the BBC and ITV to report test results.[55]

CA was typically wary about the impact of the BBC entering its own market and determined to minimize any editorial divergence between *Choice* and *Which?* It was also determined to claim the credit 'that CA started the saga to get BBC publicity'. Although by the second series in 1964, presented by *Tonight*'s Derek Hart rather than Richard Dimbleby and which opened with an exposé of conman/entrepreneur John Bloom, 'the impression that everyone at the BBC is scared stiff of the subject-matter and its implications' had gone and it no longer emphasized it was simply reporting *Which?*'s efforts.[56]

Viewing figures for *Choice* were good. The Advertising Inquiry Council saw it as the 'most important development yet in consumer protection in this country'. But *Choice* aroused widespread business anxiety. Manufacturers' and retailers' associations queried the reliability of *Which?* research, the objectivity the BBC would lend it (since it was popularly known not to permit advertising) and the likelihood of impeding competition by recommending specific brands from a limited range. The Domestic Refrigeration Development Committee added its anxiety about the harm that negative reports might do to teething problems with its technology and efforts to eke out a new market, particularly if Britain entered the Common Market where *Which?* reports on British products were prone to 'misrepresentation by overseas manufacturers'. It believed *Which?* reports 'start from the standpoint that products are more likely to be bad than good'. The BBC was sensitive to these concerns and invited manufacturer's groups to discuss them. The use of hidden cameras, which had earlier been used in a piece on Bloom's salesmen, was reviewed, but the BBC also asserted the 'favourable public opinion' on the programme.[57]

The Federation of British Industry (FBI) gave *Choice* a tepid welcome. Amongst its President's 'grave misgivings' was that 'viewers are likely only to memorize the names of products which are either highly commended or severely criticized'. It complained that whilst readers of *Which?* were 'a reasonably sophisticated group' who would 'not therefore accept the conclusions of the reports uncritically', the mass TV audience was less discerning. Carrying 'the tremendous authority of the BBC' and 'the personal prestige of Mr. Richard Dimbleby' (the BBC's chief political and royal commentator), the FBI feared the programme's verdicts were too likely to be 'accepted uncritically'.[58]

Without doubt CA worried the business establishment. *Which?* sent 'cold shudders up and down the spine', of the retail journal, *The Grocer*. When questions about Unilever's artificial sweetener 'cyclamate' lead to a ban in 1969, industry leaders complained that 'unwarranted consumer action' that called 'their integrity and competency into doubt'.[59] Other criticisms were that: in its own market of testing goods, CA enjoyed the sort of monopoly it deplored elsewhere; that it tested the public sector less than the private; and that it inhibited entrepreneurial risk-taking. On the latter point, *Motoring Which?* prompted one motor trade journal to suggest readers 'might now be tempted to buy a bicycle'. The PR industry in particular, as journalist Michael Frayn detailed, argued testing was impeding rather than enhancing consumer choice, but this was really a cloak for its fears that a damning test report could damage a product's reputation.[60]

For Sir Harry Pilkington, chair of the St. Helens glassmakers: 'CA was a nuisance, didn't understand the problems of industry, was technically shaky'. CA admitted as much to the Molony Committee. There were amateurish, even dangerous errors in tests and advice. Rover received one of the frequent *Which?* apologies when it confessed it had used the wrong spark plugs and unjustly criticized the 110 model's performance.[61] Trade journals wondered whilst *Which?* 'has a strong sense of duty to the public... does it fully recognise its responsibility towards the trade?' Of four libel suits in this period one was lost and two unresolved. In the case of Imperial Domestic Appliances Ltd, a sometime Bloom ally, the owner shot himself after his action against *Which?* was dismissed.[62]

CA were litigious in defending their own corner. It encouraged the Board of Trade to investigate a rival-named British Consumers' Association in 1961.[63] Another legal case showed the CA's potency at making product tests into public matters. A 1966 test on car seatbelts in *Which?* had criticized Britax belts and was reported to Transport Minister Barbara Castle, who had made it compulsory to fit seatbelts to new cars from mid-1966. When this was reported by the *Sunday Times*, Britax sued on the grounds that CA had tested to European conventions more stringent than those in Britain, where Britax had won a British Standards Institute (BSI) kitemark. The case was envenomed by the Ministry using Britax belts in a road safety promotional campaign in 1968. With Leon Brittan as its legal counsel, the CA demanded the Ministry withdraw press and TV materials that tacitly endorsed Britax and prejudiced the case. This the Ministry did (including 40,000 posters), advised that it would lose a contempt case, but persuading CA from escalating the issue by appealing to its interest in public safety. The Ministry explained to Britax any other course of action would have dragged CA's criticisms through the courts again.[64]

More in tune with its founding mission to provide producers and retailers with useful feedback, as early as its second number *Which?* could claim to be improving standards: the Co-op Wholesale Society responded to criticisms of a kettle. In 1966 Roberts reported a number of safety measures taken post-*Which?* reports. CA was at pains to stress producers and retailers, whatever their instinctive unease, could use its research. In 1969 Lord Sainsbury, president of the supermarket chain, explained how: 'my own firm welcomed... the Consumers' Association... because we believe responsible retailers could benefit from a better informed consumer'. But Sainsbury, a noted supporter of Labour's social democrats, was an exception to judge by an early London School of Economics (LSE) study, that found *Which?*'s influence on business 'very slight'.[65]

To make it palatable to business was one reason CA constantly asserted the credibility besides independence of its testing. Its propensities were scientific, but it also improvised – in 1963, 100 people walked each day for six months over select carpets to test their durability.[66] When Goldman arrived as Director in 1964 he was minded, given his first council meeting heard about Imperial Domestic Appliances writ against *Which?* and an IEA poll of manufacturers, to water down CA's 'arrogant anti-manufacturer image'. He stressed CA's potential influence on design, citing a letter from a carpet manufacturer criticized in *Which?* who had responded positively and thanked the CA for 'not only serving the public but their suppliers as well'.[67]

Bloom

That the washing machine took on political dimensions was not solely down to *Which?* Like TV, it was a driver of domesticity, although launderettes also became widespread. Its political bearing was also abetted by self-made entrepreneur John Bloom – 'one of the most glittering of the success stories of Macmillan's England' and 'personification of the opportunities of affluence', a millionaire before he was 30. His bankruptcy and a Board of Trade enquiry from 1964 kept him in the headlines, as a figure of fun, featuring on the cover of *Private Eye* when his travel firm collapsed.[68] From 1958 Bloom sold washing machines at half the average market price as Electromatic (European imports) and from 1960 Rolls Razor Duomatics, Starmatics and Rolls 66's made at a North London factory. His (poorly produced) autobiography offers a risqué dash through his existence: as a fixture on the celebrity charity circuit mixing with Sean Connery, Jack Hylton and Stephen Ward (of Profumo fame) to the precarious production techniques and margins by which his companies kept pace with the demand generated by aggressive direct marketing. By 1964 with a fifth of washing machine sales, Bloom was second only to Hoover.

Marketed to housewives via celebrity football-singer couple Billy Wright and Joy Beverley, in 1964 Bloom signed the biggest single advertising deal with a national newspaper, the *News of the World*, and planned to advertise weekly in every national paper. The Advertising Standards Authority (ASA) attacked Bloom's adverts that masqueraded as news or editorial matter. His deals stretched the legal limits of hire purchase and direct mail order selling and were questioned by MPs like Philip Goodhart. From his company boat on the Thames he used a megaphone to heckle parliament: 'cut the purchase tax on washing machines... help the housewife'. Bloom marketed a bottled suntan, 'Man-Tan', had two television sets built-in to the end of his bed and was involved in pirate radio and a string of nightclubs (and associated scandals). His wedding cakes were replicas of the Starmatic and a forthcoming Rolls dishwasher and made the front cover of the *Daily Mirror*.

In aiming to get Rolls listed on the Stock Exchange, Bloom was introduced by the PR firm Westbourne Press to Conservative MPs Patricia McLaughlin, Reader Harris and Billy Rees-Davies – the latter two joining Bloom's board in 1961. Harris hosted Bloom's 30th birthday party in the Commons. Edward Du Cann, future Conservative Party Chairman and businessman, held 5% of the shares in Bloom's operations. By 1963 Bloom's financial wizardry was being courted by the Liberal party too.[69]

Sales were high, but competition (induced to slash prices by Rolls) was straining margins and Bloom's advertising budget. Ventures into TV rental, Bulgarian holidays, trading stamps (which featured his own face and on which he fielded a Levin interview on the BBC's popular TV satire show, *That was the week that was*), a gimmicky profile in the *Sunday Times* and factory closure did not help. But 'crucial' in ending public confidence was a damning report in April 1964's *Which?* on the new Rolls Concorde twin tub and its hire purchase terms, calculated to be more than double an average deal for an Electricity Board model (which could wash heavier loads). *Choice* followed up on this – on which Bloom 'made a poor case of defending himself' despite his inquisitor Derek Hart treating him 'warily', the *Spectator* felt. Sales fell by 55% in May 1964 and the share price plummeted to 1d by August. Desperate measures – a scheme whereby purchase of a washing machine enabled discounts on other Rolls goods was entitled Rolls Privileged Members to enable fun to be poked at another Bloom bugbear (RPM), and a hook up with Leon Seltzer's Imperial Domestic Appliances (another casualty of taking on *Which?*) only underlined Bloom's dubious reputation. Fascist Colin Jordan attacked Bloom (who was Jewish), whilst his defenders included the IEA, who contended he had made washing machines accessible and slashed costs and prices across the sector. Loaded with debts and share scandals in July 1964 Edward Heath ordered a Board of Trade inquiry.[70]

In the 1964 election, Harold Wilson span the national economic crisis in terms of Bloom's insolvency, charging Home with suffering from 'Bloom's delusion' – 'hiding from the nation the shock facts of the economic crisis facing Britain' and lacking firm economic grounding. The *Daily Express* depicted Home as Bloom. Wilson favoured bringing 'pressure on those who have made money by "immoral" if not "illegal"' means. Bloom was declared bankrupt in 1969, but by 1970, fearing implicating several luminaries, several charges were dropped and a £30,000 fine imposed.[71]

America

Studies like Vance Packard's *Hidden Persuaders* also imbued everyday, private commodities and consuming practices with broader social, political, even Cold War meaning. CA was part of a global movement, critically learning policy and adapting strategy from the CU. If US consumer models and business methods swept Europe, as De Grazia argues, then the same process was evident with US social criticism. American commentators were influential in the UK in the 1950s and 1960s – besides Packard, economist J.K. Galbraith, sociologist David Riesman, green hippy Charles Reich, H.H. Wilson (a member of CU's advisory committee, who wrote on the pressure groups behind ITV), environmentalist Rachel Carson, Michael Harrington on poverty and consumer rights activist Ralph Nader.[72] Trans-Atlantic comparisons were eagerly debated. On the BBC's Third Programme in 1958 Reuel Denney and Mark Abrams discussed, 'The American Consumer – slave or rebel?' Denney worked with sociologist David Riesman on *The Lonely Crowd* (1950). His latest book, *The Astonished Muse*, argued *The Lonely Crowd*'s conformity was being 'crumpled' by more creative demands and generational resistance to the idea that 'spending' your time was the US way. Western Europe and Britain were following US trends, but less revolt was apparent since elitism and unequal social structures were the norm. Abrams countered critics by arguing what many regarded as 'conformity – uniformity in consumption – is a pretty low price to pay for escaping from poverty'. Both agreed consumption had ideological implications. For Denney, the consumer 'becomes self-governing, not merely in the market place, but in the ideas that he relates himself to'; whilst Abrams stressed 'the itch for self government will seep over from consumption'.[73]

The parallels and linkages between CA and the American CU confirm some key characteristics of CA. Both were non-profit, voluntary organizations that hectored national governments to legislate, claiming to be the voice of consumers. Unlike many state-funded European organizations, CA and CU steered shy of state as well as business support. The *Harvard Business Review* felt this marked 'free enterprise at work, on the consumer side' and the 'decline of demand in recent years for greater government supervision'.[74] Both used commercial methods (for self-promotion) and grew in tandem with post-war affluence and self-service, advertising and the expansion of goods and brands that made its testing information priceless. Like CA, CU tended towards the earnest and austere, bred by its origins in the New Deal. It was wary that more did not necessarily mean a better quality of life. Buyers of *Consumer Reports* tended towards the upper echelons of the consumer market, like CA's. Of CU's 1954 members, 8.5% were in labour unions, but 43.5% were professionals. As one put it: 'it doesn't strike me that Joe Milkman reads *CR* and of course, he's the one who should'. Moreover, affluence saw consumer interests and duties more readily invoked and represented through spending not thrift and by business rather than consumer protection (by contrast with the 1930s); and this, combined with difficulties in acquiring a working class audience, meant CU was lured towards more middling tastes. In Elizabeth Cohen's estimation, as a 'buying guide' for an 'affluent, educated, professional middle-class' by the late 1950s, CU reconciled itself with the belief that consumers were as exploited by abundance as shortages. It also focused on influencing government. Longstanding demands were met via the Truth-in-Packaging and Lending Bills (1966, 1968) and like CA, it provided personnel for Federal schemes, notably Esther Peterson, who became President Johnson's Special Assistant for Consumer Affairs in 1964. President Kennedy's 1962 Consumer Message to Congress, feted CU with a 'significant role in expanding the horizons of an informed public'.[75]

Like CA, CU had a leftish reputation. This derived from its origins in a strike in 1935 to unionize staff at Consumer's Research, its interest in labour conditions (detailed in early *Consumer Reports* tests) and CU President Colston Warne's involvement with causes from the American Civil Liberties Union to Henry Wallace's Presidential candidacy. It was only cleared by the House Committee on Un-American Activities in 1954, but remained, like CA, subject to business suspicion and accused of impeding free-market dynamism. 'Clinical muckraking', 'laconic', 'contemptuous', 'anti-glitter' were *Sales Management*'s keywords for *Consumer Reports* in 1965, all qualities *Which?* emulated. Others detected only 'vestiges... of the sensationalism of their early years' from the mid-1950s.[76]

Ralph Nader, who crashed onto the US consumer scene with his pursuit of (and by) General Motors in 1965 and was elected to CU's board in 1967 restored some of this zeal, attending to Warne's warning for consumer activists to not 'unconsciously fall victim to love of ease and of approval'. Nader struck fame through an exposé approach that combined militancy with PR savvy. Barbara Castle, who as British Transport Minister introduced seat belts, breathalysers and speed limits, paid tribute to his influence.[77] Nader's confrontational approach differed in manner from Warne's vision in which 'consumer action groups could replace bowling teams and bridge clubs as a function of community recreation'. Consumer activity was envisaged as cohesive, not fragmentary or individualistic – as bowling *together* not *alone*![78]

CU deployed a language of consumer sovereignty and free choice to demonstrate their affinities to US values and to rile business by suggesting consumerists were the market's true believers. 'Uninformed choice is not free', Warne explained, 'you cannot boast of a vote of confidence [in a product] when the voter has been denied the knowledge essential to rational choice'. CU's technical director, saw it as 'a promoter of skepticism... opposed to the establishment which would have "freedom of choice" made simply on the basis of advertising claims'. Like CA, it believed commercial powers endangered the market's potential to deliver to consumers. Without 'the consumer as a rationally motivated, well-informed arbiter to the market-place', Dexter Masters, CU's director from 1958 explained, 'free competition becomes a kind of jungle warfare'.[79]

This allusion to Upton Sinclair's muckraking classic, *The Jungle* tallied with suspicions that consumers were prone to be herded by irrational forces, tastes and advertising. Schlink's early consumer studies depicted American consumers as *100,000,000 Guinea Pigs*, just as British studies saw them as *Affluent Sheep*. Nader saw market predators as evidence that 'we're still in the jungle'. US consumerists regarded consumers not as passive, but fallible and complicit in their own predicament. Thus as Nader's *Unsafe at any Speed* convulsed the auto industry, *Consumer Reports* stressed driver respon-sibility for auto deaths. What was needed, Warne estimated in 1961, was 'a degree of intelligence and skepticism on the part of the buyer – characteristics which [are] all too often absent'.[80]

In a signal of his sense of an international and historical movement, Young had copies of proposals that became Consumers' Research in 1929, in which the consumer was understood as 'an Alice in a wonderland of salesmanship', it being almost 'impossible for him (and more particularly her) to buy on a rational intelligent basis'. Dorothy Goodman, an American student in London, is credited with the first inkling of a British version of *Consumer Reports* (of which she would become an associate editor). Warne was at the 1956 House of Commons meeting that led to CA's formation and CU donated $6000 to it.[81]

Historians have rightly emphasized the American influence on the IOCU and CA, but in other ways the process was more one of adapting than adopting an American model.[82] Young reported of his 1958 trip to its Mount Vernon HQ that, 'CU has very few impressive people, except for Dexter Masters, but the set-up is very impressive'. CA thought it could better the Americans and achieved a proportionally higher membership as early as 1959.[83] There was then irony in CA's silver jubilee gift to CU in 1961: a map of IOCU affiliates, inscribed, 'greetings to the founding father from the pilgrims in London who would not have known *Which?* way to turn'.[84] The Atlantic was regularly tra-versed. Jim Northcott was the earliest Briton to visit CU in 1952. His 1953 pam-phlet, *Value for Money?*, argued stricter English libel laws made a private consumer advisory service unlikely. He was persuaded a public organization was more likely to succeed in reaching beyond 'the richer and better educated consumers, that is, those least in need of its help' attracted to CU and which he hazarded were likely to be drawn to a British equivalent.[85]

The differentiation of testing and lobbying roles the CA sought to combine was clearer in the USA partly by dint of tax regimes. There might be no British Nader (Young lacking the exclusive, persistent focus on consumerism of Warne or militancy of Nader), but, as Daniel Bell put it, likening Young's diverse research to social reformers from Chadwick to Booth, there was 'no American figure like Michael Young'. British political culture was more elitist, critiques of the market commoner and consumption less central to narratives of national identity. CA introduced into it a market-driven scepticism that made politics more like consumerism (and populist, Americanized) in style, besides *about* consumer issues.[86]

The politics of consumerism

Not that CA redefined politics as it wished. The Molony Report in 1962 criticized CA's governing council as 'oligarchic and self-perpetuating'. The number of 'ordinary members' who elected the council were expanded, in response, from 231 to 1343 in 1968. Until then, the council selected 'ordinary members'. 'Associate members' (without voting rights) could now apply, subject to council vetting. Vetting prevented a takeover by manufacturers or advertisers (or getting waylaid by periodic spats over water fluoridation).[87] Like council members, ordinary members were not to be engaged in the manufacture, distribution or sale of goods or services. But the seeming indifference of CA members was also a barrier to a more democratic, participatory CA. CA estimated its 'very active' members, who joined local groups on top of subscribing to *Which?*, at around 20,000 in 1962 – 6% of membership. As much as CA aspired to a constituency wider than its own members and to 'popularising the idea of discriminating consumption', it also faced activating its own members.[88]

A high turnover of members also sustained the council's control. Northcott, a founder member of CA's 1956 prototype, the British Association of Consumers (BAC), thought CA's 'democratization' prevailed against its wider aims, since the membership were less radically-minded than the council. 'The model *Which?* family', CA found in 1964, 'takes the *Daily Telegraph, Sunday Express* and *Reader's Digest'*. Gallup reported in 1962 that most *Which?* subscribers were 'intent on value for money', but there was 'no evidence that members joined for the purpose of achieving reform, reform being taken in the sense of manufacturing better goods for all, as a desirable end in itself'.[89]

In the post-Molony battles over CA's constitution, Crosland feared the membership might not be best placed to elect an appropriate CA leadership. Conservative James Douglas favoured integrating the CA's (unpaid) council and staff (like Roberts) further, to immunize CA's broader aims from any vagaries of its electorate. Apposite here was *New Society* editor Paul Barker's profile of Young in 1968 that his 'aims are classless, but his means usually bourgeois' and that 'there's not all that much democracy *within* a Young organization' however much it aspired to enable participation.[90]

CA's coterie were elite experts. Many had civil service backgrounds; were Oxbridge educated (10 of the 15 council members in 1967); and they were mostly male – there were calls for more women on council as early as 1958. 'Active members' of the BAC, besides Young, the Goodmans and Northcott (like Brook from *The Economist* Intelligence Unit), included staff from PEP; the British Productivity Council; the Government Social Survey and Board of Trade's Consumer Needs Division. Conservatives included the Bow Group's Michael Haynes and MPs John Vaughan-Morgan and Patricia Mclaughlin. From Labour were Sydney Irving and Bert Oram (both Labour-Co-op MPs), John Edwards (a leading common marketeer) and Elaine Burton.[91]

Whilst formally balanced in political terms, CA confessed to 'a pre-dominance of LSE people, Hampstead residents and... left-wing intellectuals'. This could inflect CA's approach and appeal. A 1965 survey found potential subscribers were put-off by perceptions of CA as 'anti-business, iconoclastic or left-wing'. *Which?* was distributed from Hertford, but CA staff were not a suburban breed. Attempts to move to Harlow in 1964 were thwarted. As Brook's assistant Alistair MacGeorge, remembered, 'the New Towns... and Harlow in particular, were not exactly... bastions of cultivated life, as far as CA's staff were concerned'.[92] As Hilton has shown in Birmingham, pro-vincial groups had a similar sociological composition. The likes of the *Bradford Buyword* or Durham's *Pick and Choose* outlined local initiatives. The Tyneside Group, with 222 members, reported in 1964 that it was 'regarded cautiously by our local chambers of trade although traders have on the whole (especially the better class of shop) been co-operative'. Janey Buchan, an actress and later Labour MEP, told the 1965 Labour women's conference of her involvement with the Glasgow group exposing Woolworth's price irregularities. Whilst backing government price information, she called on delegates to support local consumer groups as they 'needed a working class conscience'.[93]

The Labour revisionist presence in CA circles was discernible. Jackson argues Young himself has been 'underestimated' as a revisionist thinker. One of Young's pet projects borrowed from revisionism – though scuppered for fear of endangering test impartiality – was for CA to buy a share in Britain's top 50 companies. Young revived this in 1966 as a Community Interest Shareholding Association, independent of CA. Its representatives would attend shareholder meetings to encourage transparency in the public interest. Young in turn backed and funded revisionist projects like *Must Labour Lose?* that sought to modernize Labour's image.[94] Crosland, as the next chapter discusses, drew a series of broader points about political practice and thinking from his experiences in CA.

There seemed some correlation between revisionism, consumerism and quitting Labour. Bill Rodgers was a Good Food Club council member from 1965; Dick Taverne joined CA council in 1965 and Shirley Williams (Prices and Consumer Protection Minister, 1974–6) replaced Crosland on it in

1964. All later quit Labour and Williams and Rodgers were founders of the Social Democratic Party (SDP) in 1981, which Roberts and Young also joined. Elaine Burton, Coventry MP and consumer campaigner, a friendly critic of CA and irritated by Labour's non-committal approach to consumers, became SDP spokeswoman on consumer affairs. Michael Summerskill (later 1960s chair of the National Federation of Consumer Groups) was another notable CA leading revisionist and SDP member. Others were more Labour loyalists, notably Crosland and Gordon Borrie (a Birmingham Consumer Group founder, Director-General of the Office of Fair Trading 1976–92, Labour's Social Justice Commission chair 1992–4 and successor to Rodgers as Advertising Standards Authority chair in 2002).[95]

The Board of Trade Parliamentary Secretary, John Rodgers MP, told (the Liberal) Brook at a 1959 meeting that only one of CA's Vice Presidents and council members – Baroness Katherine Elliot (later Consumers' Council chair and an ex-chair of the National Union of Conservative Associations) – was on the political right. 'Too many', Rodgers continued, 'did ring a bell left of the political centre', for CA 'to claim complete political impartiality'.[96] These included the Liberal and Labour Party leader's wives; Jennifer Jenkins (wife of revisionist Labour MP and SDP founder, Roy Jenkins); Sir Julian Huxley (a CND founder); Francis Williams (ex-*Daily Herald* editor) and Gerald Gardiner, besides Young. Conservatives were tough to recruit – Lady Macmillan refused a Vice-Presidency and Young suggested Robert Appleby (Black and Decker managing director and FBI advisor) for 'ordinary membership' to redress the imbalance.[97]

The Conservative MP on CA council was Phillip Goodhart for most of this period. Dick Hornby had been the intended replacement for the first, Geoffrey Rippon, but was barred by his consultancy work for J Walter Thompson. CA Vice-president Jennifer Jenkins supplied her husband's appraisal of the candidates. Plumping for Goodhart, it described Ted Leather as a 'show-off', Julian Ridsdale as 'rather stupid' and Enoch Powell as 'clever, but unbalanced'. Crosland too was 'very much against' Powell.[98]

James Douglas, a CA founder and council member in 1958 and after 1962, had worked at the Conservative Party Research Department (CRD) since 1950 and was its Director from 1970. The Conservatives showed interest in the National Council of Women's consumer protection conference in 1956. The party's National Women's Advisory Committee liased with them; they were 'mostly conservative in outlook' and, it was predicted, were 'going to make a great point at this conference'. The centrality of the consumer as a subject was clear in Douglas' research for the Party's automation sub-committee which in 1956 concluded that automation ought to benefit consumers above all since 'only some of us will work with automation, but we are *all* consumers'.[99] Douglas remained convinced, he explained to Robert Millar, of the case in the pamphlet *Choice* he penned with John Wood (a free marketer who replaced Douglas on CA's council) and MPs Patricia Mclaughlin and Goodhart, 'that Conservatives see in the competitive system the principal safeguard for the consumer'.[100]

Yet Douglas closely monitored CA developments. Noting the 'rapid growth going on of local consumer groups' in 1962, he felt it 'a good idea if appropriate local organizations of the party kept in touch with this development which might turn out to be significant'. Douglas feared the left could 'capture the credit' for the CA. In this vein he encouraged McLaughlin and introduced her to Roberts and Brook. If Douglas did seek party advantage he was equally anxious to maintain the CA's balanced political constitution. His resignation in 1958 was because he anticipated active involvement in an imminent general election.[101] He recommended opinion research firms to the Party on the basis of work undertaken for CA; Young likewise quizzed Douglas about government discussions on the Consumer Council (CC) Molony created.[102]

CA's aspirant non-partisanship, intersected with that strand in Conservative political culture, which Chapter 4 discusses further, that preferred to practice politics incidentally, none-too-obviously, as a necessity rather than virtue in itself. When Mary Adams, who had been married to Conservative MP Vyvyan Adams, but who Douglas termed 'politically left-wing', replaced Young as CA Chair during his 1958 US trip, he explained to the Party Vice-Chair Mrs. Henry Brooke the ideal type of Conservative supporters CA needed. Since politics had little role in the CA, 'what is wanted is someone who is worth having for her own sake quite as much as worth having because she is a Conservative'. This was problematic since Douglas felt that 'when you are trying to find people who are unconnected with industry, trade or advertising who can spare... time for voluntary work, you are far more likely... to hit on a socialist than a conservative'. Douglas felt 'it would be a pity if the organization drifted to the left simply because Conservatives could not be bothered to take an interest'.[103] Conservatives and CA both grappled with the consequences as well as the difficulties of not appearing too political (as Chapter 4 discusses further).

Peter Goldman, CA's director 1964–87, was a firmly 'one nation' Tory and remained close to Heath. Director of the Conservative Political Centre (CPC) from 1955. Goldman came to CA having lost a by-election in the safely Tory, Kent suburban commuter seat of Orpington in 1962. This was variously ascribed to anti-semitism, the credit squeeze and in Liberal (the victors) and Conservative research, to 'the lack of provision of shopping facilities to serve rapid population growth' being blamed on the local Tory establishment. He was interviewed by five Labour party members for the post of CA director.[104]

Orpington corroborates Zweiniger-Bargielowska's case that Conservative support was more readily mobilized by consumer issues. The obverse was that Labour voters could seem relatively indifferent. Historians of Coventry in this period have noted how despite the city Labour Council's rebuilding of the shopping precinct, its citizens apparently found, 'connections between the availability of consumer goods in bright new shops and the ideals of municipal socialism... difficult to make'. Not that the Conservatives were automatic beneficiaries of consumerism or more able to voice or appeal to consumer issues – it could mean they were more sensitive to or likely to fall foul of consumers. What this attested to was how temporary, contingent and fragile Conservatives bonds with middle-class voters were. The Conservatives wrapped themselves in the trappings of affluence for electoral gain, but this cloaked profound uncertainties about its ethical values. They drew attention to the left's vocal puritans, but Conservatives hardly embraced what they saw as cavalier materialism. In debates on consumerism or advertising, Conservatives were, beneath their public façade, divided. They were sceptical about material advance representing progress – Goldman saw it in 1961 as 'an age darkened by materialism'.[105]

Labour struggled to reconcile workers and consumers, but the Tories were no less hamstrung between manufacturers, retailers and consumers. Debates around RPM demonstrated this. Many manufacturers, shopkeepers and Conservative-inclined groups like the Townswomen's Guilds opposed its abolition; whilst free marketers, large retailers and CA supported its ending. Adrian demonstrated Conservative tensions over RPM – having to resort to the Liberal journal *New Outlook* to criticize it.[106] Amidst what Mercer calls a 'cold war' between retailers and manufacturers, the political close call was whether Britain was more a nation of shoppers than of manufacturers and shopkeepers? Findley argues that abolition in 1964 cost the Tories the election, through the opposition of manufacturers, shopkeepers (whose support for the Tories fell by 30% compared to 1959) and backbenchers (amongst whom opponents of RPM's abolition, like Rugby MP Alfred Wise, increased their majorities).[107]

Rodgers' perception that CA leaned leftwards was one reason why it was not appointed to the Molony Committee in 1959. But Rodgers also told Brook he thought CA 'a very considerable force', lending credence to Young telling CA's council, 'we are obviously partly responsible for this report'. Hilton argues Molony's business-minded conception of the consumer matched CA's market-oriented notion.[108] But CA was 'fairly nervous' that Molony might fund a rival tester of goods. An emergency council in October 1961 stressed the expansion of CA's comparative testing, to raise the cost and decrease the likelihood of government funding a rival. Molony concurred that a testing body should be fully independent. *Which?* gave free pages to the CC to publicize its efforts, though this did not prevent it opposing the CC's proposed labelling scheme late in 1964 because of its lack of independence from manufacturers.[109]

CA's success was also used as a pretext for the CC's abolition after the 1970 election. The Conservative manifesto had praised it, but Anthony Barber's post-election 'mini-budget' ended its grant. The penultimate *Focus* warned consumers 'now you're on your own'. But Heath, who had been President of the Board of Trade when the CC was established, questioned its worth. Since there were 'other organizations' (a reference to CA) who covered its remit, Heath's policy was one of 'not using public money for objectives which can be achieved by private enterprise'. Crosland charged Heath with dogmatically pursuing a *laissez faire* policy, but one that was flawed since, 'competition will not work properly unless the consumer is well informed'. And Crosland deduced consumers were not well informed, since there was 'so little public protest' at the CC's dismantling. Many at CA suspected the appointment of Des Wilson as the CC's next director had sealed its fate. Wilson was the radical director of Shelter, the national campaign for the homeless and likened by some to Ralph Nader.[110]

CA's founding figures and thinking were *of* the left. Like Labour, it saw a 'world of bewildering variety, controlled to an increasing degree by large companies', in which 'the consumer stands almost alone'. The distinction was CA's embrace of the consumer – a category with which many on the left, being production-minded and attached to the category of workers, were uneasy. Equally, CA's market-based approach and preference for voluntary before state action put it at odds with the left.[111]

There was support in Labour circles for a consumer advisory service. Young first proposed a scheme in 1950 and it was periodically revived, such as in Northcott's Fabian pamphlet. Labour women discussed consumer protection, weights, measures, labels, overseas organizations and legislation through the 1950s. Young's proposal was cross-referenced, though they tended to opt for state schemes given their perception of gullible consumers. By the time CA was flourishing, Elaine Burton lamented that there ought to be a National Consumer Centre, one 'not based on subscriptions'. Burton was frustrated at Labour: 'I *do* mind that we have not done more' to address consumers, she exclaimed in 1958.[112] Labour Women's conferences regularly applauded CA, but still looked to state action. They scoffed at the costly advice of the free-market Conservative Peter Thorneycroft that disgruntled consumers had recourse to a solicitor, but also at CA membership at ten shillings per year.[113]

CA was born of frustration with Labour's indifference towards consumer matters. Burton wrote to Gaitskell early in 1956 warning, 'the time is ripe to deal further with this consumers' angle or it will be "lifted" from us entirely', a reference to CA's imminence besides direct political competition. Gaitskell had some CA leanings – he encouraged Northcott and attended CA's 1958 Christmas party, but these were never salient.[114] Labour's insouciance remained in some measure despite, if not because of, CA's successes. A Glasgow delegate at the 1970 Women's conference felt this had been fatal in the election and 'more should have been said about the Trade Description Act', passed in 1968 to boost impressions of 'what the Labour government had done for the consumer'. Symptomatic of the Labour movement's standoffishness was the

Co-op's rejection of the Gaitskell Commission's very revisionist proposals in 1958. The CA despaired at this, but exploited it to contest the Co-op's claims to represent consumers.[115]

Young

Young's background was as much influenced by PEP as Labour's Research Department, which he headed from 1945–50. In the 1930s PEP's *Planning* asked, 'can the consumer form some sort of "trade union"' or 'set... up voluntary research associations' and stressed consumer as well as producer responsibilities. And links remained – PEP entered the contemporary debate on consumer protection in 1960. Ray Goodman, who chaired PEP from 1946–53 and was then an executive at Marks and Spencer, was a CA founder before taking a post as a senior staff member at the World Bank.[116]

Young inserted into Labour's 1950 manifesto the promise that 'an independent Consumer Advice Centre will be set up to test and report on the various consumer goods... good manufacturers will be protected and unscrupulous advertising exposed'. The idea lingered. In 1983, under the same sub-heading as 1950 of 'Value for Money', Labour's manifesto vowed to 'establish a major public service facility... to test products and manufacturers' claims about them' and to 'set up consumer advice centres in all main shopping centres'. Young gleaned from the Treasury and Board of Trade that costs not the libel laws would discourage state involvement in 1950, but also the popularity of the idea, since it topped a Gallup Poll of manifesto proposals.[117]

Young also looked to a voluntary approach. The Attlee governments turned him against bureaucratic, statist approaches and seemed not to generate popular support. There was a DIY sense to CA at its outset, of an unpaid, volunteer corps of dedicated pioneers. Edward Shils described Young in 1960 as a 'bold amateur', incessantly inventive and realizing innovative organizations against the odds. Although through the 1960s this gave way to degrees of professionalization and specialization – competitively remunerated also, Roberts by 1964–65 had a salary of £3250.[118]

After Goldman's appointment in 1964 and as other projects consumed him, Young's involvement with CA became less intimate, although he remained one of its IOCU representatives and its public voice. And the CA remained axial to his conception of politics. In *The Chipped White Cups of Dover* in 1960 Young had contended 'class based on production is slowly giving way to status based on consumption as the centre of social gravity' in modern Britain. Since Labour and the Conservatives were producer-dominated by Unions and business respectively, he proposed a consumers' party. The Fabians (chaired by future CA supporter Shirley Williams) would not publish Young's freethinking. A Gallup poll found 25% of voters might support this new party – and more Conservative than Labour voters from the 1959 election, again suggesting Conservative audiences were more readily mobilized by consumer issues. Young envisioned a 'one nation' party to arrest Britain's decline – discerning consumers would improve the production quality and competitiveness of industry and could offset the inflationary wage-price spiral in a way the producerist parties could not.[119] For Young, the consumer movement was always less a single-issue pressure group than a new politics.

However, Young's idealistic consumer politics had to grapple with *Which?* research confounding the notion of 'one nation' of consumers, finding conflict rife at the point of sale. One assistant complained, 'we are treated by the majority of middle class customers as the domestics were treated 50 years ago'; another, endorsing the analogy, added, 'the newly affluent working classes are equally overbearing'. For their part, customers were 'fed-up with shop assistants who have no knowledge of the goods they are selling'. CA was a product of self-service shopping and demise of shop assistants. CA, and the labelling it put such store by, were substitute knowledge sources. In this role CA was perceived, so one assistant recounted, as accountable for customers who were 'after their "rights" which are being drummed into them, but do not know their "responsibilities"'.[120]

To judge from the way the main parties clamoured to associate themselves with CA, it was a potent political commodity. *Which?*'s 10th anniversary edition – a 'washing-machine edition' with 14 pages of tests of twin-tubs and automatics – carried congratulations from Wilson, Heath and Liberal leader, Jeremy Thorpe (Figure 2.1). Tribute to CA's success in raising consumerism's political stock and party attempts to assimilate this was further evident in the flurry of publications that accompanied the imminent Molony Report. CA was, equally, anxious to impress with the sort of political audience it could command.[121]

From the Rt Hon
Harold Wilson, OBE, MP

From the Rt Hon
Edward Heath, MBE, MP

From the Rt Hon
Jeremy Thorpe, MP

Figure 2.1   *Which?* (October 1967) genders and celebrates its political role
Source: Consumers' Association

And there was the danger, as Young told the 1967 Consumer Assembly, whose audience included cabinet ministers Crosland and Benn, of being assimilated by the existing system. Young warned that the plaudits CA won from the party leaders hinted it had become 'accepted and respectable'. 'The consumers movement is a movement with a small m' at present and Young's was a vision to 'enlarge its scope'. Young asserted that 'our strength is not that of a purely sectional interest group... without much concern for the welfare of the community'. 'Consumers are not a section of the nation; they are all of us' and 'if democracy is to be more than government by pressure group we need to assert this general consumer interest'. Young concluded in a 'spirit of militancy', arguing that the movement's other strength was 'the votes which consumers command'. 'Whether or not any new consumers party is formed... we are serving notice on the long-established political parties' should 'they fail to serve this newly asserted consumer interest'.

Young saw the broader context as one in which 'while the consumers movement has been expanding, the country of which it is part has been declining' and manifest in a national culture that worshipped heritage and ritual and was deemed too sick to be part of Europe. Such declinism made Young's understanding of British politics more familiar than his projected solutions. He explained that transcending pressure group activity meant consumerists 'shall be moving into the territory occupied by the traditional political parties'. This was territory 'lightly held' as Young mapped it, full of humbug, clinging 'to any symbol of past greatness like the sterling area' and because of their producer links, in effect 'the same party in two halves'. Young believed consumerists could 'activate a new kind of politics, the politics of prices to set against the politics of wages' and of the liberal, European, public participative not state-directed sort, as outlined in *Chipped White Cups*. To do so they also needed to 'build up local civic societies so that they effectively express the preferences of the consumers of planning' in schools, council houses and surgeries. The reception of Young's speech – and he was no orator – cautions against investing it with undue meaning. Some signed on to the vision – one delegate asked 'is not the quality of our environment more important than washing machines?' But other CA supporters were 'scared' a wider political role 'could endanger... the integrity and independence... of our Association'.[122]

Whatever else shifted in Young's vision, shaking up the main parties was a leitmotiv. And to judge by a speculative letter to Abrams in 1969 'about a possible new party', he continued to dream of the political realignment aired in *Chipped White Cups* even when his focus on pressure groups and social movements lead him to critique party *per se*. Unlike Crosland (as Chapter 3 details), Young's enthusiasm for pressure groups was less perturbed that a politicized civil society might impede democratic debate or governance. In encouraging new forms of participation to liven up what by 1969 had become a fashion for 'yawning about politics', Young cast party and the state as repressions to escape no less than poverty or inequality. Thus the 'Open Group' (as Young's liberal freethinkers denoted themselves) proposals were 'political, but not party'. Elections and party activity at Westminster were rituals and the media had cut politicians down to the size of a television screen, normalizing them. Power and authority were slipping centrifugally from Whitehall to voluntary organizations – unions, CA, Child Poverty Action Group, Shelter, even the Old Chiswick Protection Society. It was in these, admittedly 'few' in number, but vitally 'outside professional politics', that a new political agency lay. The 'multifarious pullulations' of these groups were a virtue of a pluralist system, but there were limits to the change they might effect, impeded by their multitude from concocting broader electoral alliances.[123]

Also cautionary, although of the challenges of post-materialism more than of the trajectory of the consumer movement or new forms of political activity, was Young's speech to the 1964 IOCU conference. It highlighted three dichotomies facing consumerists: between the needs of rich and poor consumers around the globe; between private goods and public services; and between the standard of living and quality of life. So far as the last was concerned, Young wondered, 'is there nothing to the good life except more and more refrigerators and TV-sets?... are consumers in fundamental agreement with industrialists... that all that is necessary to the good life is to produce more, better and cheaper goods?' He felt 'a fuller life... may for some people also be a simpler life'. By now sounding quite hippy-ish, Young felt people might 'make rational choices' and achieve 'individual fulfillment' through 'creative' or 'costless pleasures... the open air, the trees, the sky'. Consumerism, he urged, 'should be ready for them'.[124]

But Young's speech to the 1970 IOCU conference took on voguish '1968' critiques of affluence. He was not entirely unsympathetic to the New Left-hippy-West Coast critique, a fusion typified in Herbert Marcuse's work, of the spiritual paucity of the endless pursuit of material advance. But Young believed these were likely to remain the preserve of a relatively privileged minority, who were unlikely to 'take out more than one subscription to the journals of our organizations'. Young still asserted the *raison d'etre* of organizations like CA was to ensure 'consumers can benefit from... variety instead of being overwhelmed by it'. As such he was doubtful that once a level of basic demand had been met, this would undermine acquisitiveness or meant it could only be maintained by inventing demand. Rather, 'new wants have been generated as old ones have been met' and the 'need for self-assertion' in psychic, aesthetic and identity terms was met 'through making choices between alternative products'. Despite the seeming insatiability of human desires, Young also stressed the power of people to manage and mediate the assumed power of the state, party, business or advertisers. This co-existed uneasily with the CA's propensity to protect consumers. In a 1968 paper Young appeared more sceptical than the CA of the influence advertising wielded, something he saw both its critics and champions taking for granted. He was influenced by American sociologist Paul Lazarsfeld's work (*Personal Influence* and *The People's Choice and Voting*) assessing voters' and consumers' behaviour, which emphasized the importance of 'personal recommendation' by family and friends over potent commercial forces. This did allow him to conclude that as its persuasive powers had been unduly magnified, advertising ought to be more restrained.[125]

What Young advanced at the 1970 IOCU was a critique of the full, social costs of production and consumption of goods and services. Like other social movements at this time, notably CND, this amounted to an ecological turn. Young believed the costs on people, buildings, the environment, of deforestation, development, congestion, pollution and disposal (affluence's effluence), fell on 'the community and even posterity' and merited taking into account. He felt the consumer movement was culpable here for addressing consumers as individuals rather than 'members of a socio-ecological co-operative'. Attaching a 'social cost tag' might radically alter the price system and what looked 'good value for money from the point of view of the individual might turn out to be very bad value for money from the standpoint of the community as a whole'. Some work had been undertaken by European consumer groups on beach, exhaust, chemical and countryside pollution. Young was determined consumer tests ought to incorporate the social costs of production, advise consumers and governments on minimizing costs to others, reward manufacturers who cut pollution and that there should be IOCU collaboration on international issues like pollution. Young concluded in what was European Conservation Year, with a call for consumers and conservationists to unite.[126]

Young set about persuading Roberts and RICA to undertake 'ecological costing... of consumer products', with key questions for detergent production along the lines of 'which method of getting cleanliness produces the least dirt for others?'. Young anticipated that 'if CA doesn't do it, I don't suppose any other part of IOCU ever will'. Roberts was sympathetic, but doubted 'whether we could get the individual consumer to buy a more expensive product which cost the community less'. Roberts approached Manchester University's Pollution Research Unit with suggestions from river pollution to the working of the Civic Amenities Act on car disposal. If the 'costs of pollution of air, water, earth, silence and social costs more generally could be made a regular part of the testing of branded consumer products', Young believed this might be taken up by the IOCU and 'really be unique and (my guess) a world-wide sensation'.[127]

In fact, RICA had already looked at the social costs of the rising volume (it increased by half in the 1960s) of rubbish Britons threw out. The problem was not only rising consumption, but the expectation that private rubbish would be collected as a public service by local councils – a literal instance of private affluence and public squalor. John Green, deputy director of the

Local Government Operational Research Unit, proposed consumers be 're-educated' to dispose of more of their own rubbish and replace house-to-house collections.[128] Such concerns resonated with those of US critics (Packard's *The Waste Makers*, Carson, Reich), but were also reminiscent of CU's early reporting of the working conditions of production, thereby recognizing the wider impacts and meanings of specific commodities. Besides being a pointer to emergent environmental issues and green politics, this was another attempt to make a broader social movement out of practical material concerns, grafting them on to a post-materialist agenda.

Conclusions: the potential of consumer politics

Young showed the diverse potential of a consumer agenda and CA its wide appeal in this period, but also limits – encountering similar problems to the main parties, besides the parties ability to assimilate practices and even 'policy learn' from pressure groups. CA and Young also disclose the numerous dilemmas of non-party, pressure group politics and tensions in concepts like post-materialism and civil society. As a voluntary association that effectively bridged the private and public spheres, independent of yet influencing the state and policy-makers, CA generated an influential, critical voice. Yet it also held to an individualist, market-based model of citizenship – the rights of *shopping alone* by analogy with Putnam's *Bowling Alone*. This ratifies the ambiguities of the term civil society and its multiple trajectories. CA's leaders craved a movement to counter-balance producer power for purposes of consumer rights rather than their own material interests, but it was evident that was not their sole market appeal and that self-help could play out in other ways.

Whether CA represented a post-materialist trajectory in British political culture is hard to categorically answer. The content and vision of its politics was mostly concerned that more was not necessarily better and those who were active in CA conformed to Inglehart's sociological archetype: they valued knowledge more than wealth, were frustrated with and by existing (particularly party) political structures and deployed professional skills to remedy this. But most joined and used CA for more materialist ends. CA recognized this and it explained its reluctance to deal with questions other than those of use-value. Some commentators have suggested that the consumption of goods constituted a channelling of social and non-economic ideals, particularly in the private sphere, as identities blurred in public. One hardly need be a post-modernist to suggest that goods, commodities and shopping involved a (perhaps contradictory) bundle of sensations and had meaning other than in their use or exchange value. In short, post-materialism and consumption were compatible or not antithetical.[129] Yet this required goods to take on the symbolic qualities that CA was unwilling to judge or to address questions of lifestyle and taste. CA's consumerism was to assemble individual consumers acting out of what it saw as chiefly rational material interest into a collective movement, not always a comfortable exercise even before imparting any broader post-materialist agenda. Yet there was also a sense that CA was born out of scarcity into abundance, uncertain of its newer context. This all reflected tensions within post-materialism itself, a partially materialist concept by all accounts, as if it could not quite shake off materialist ties and culture.

Whilst this backs up those who doubt there was a post-material shift in British values, it might also suggest a more nuanced, politically variable notion of post-materialism is in order – one that allows for post-material politics to play out in more variable ways than the classic social movements.[130] After all, post-materialist agendas might be emergent without popular values becoming more post-materialist; political supply and demand need not correspond. Politics was an autonomous social force. CA's impact after all was no more determined by its audience or by some essential underlying socio-economic characteristics of consumerism, than it could invent or shape either to its own design. But before reaching decisive conclusions about themes in consumer politics and what they decode about the broader political culture, let's shed further light by visiting the Co-op.

3
Shopfloor Politics: Co-operative Culture and Affluence

If CA's successes offer historians valuable insights into key characteristics and trends in British political culture, then so do the Co-op's difficulties in this period. It too claimed to be the voice of consumers and thus provides a test of findings based on CA about the impact of consumerism. Like the CA it straddled politics and consumerism and had long combined them as a social movement – 'trying to sell a parcel of politics with a parcel of groceries', as it put it, charging shopping with meaning over and above its material functions.[1] The Co-op, like CA, can be used as an entrepot for a medley of debates about the politics of consumerism and other themes in *Redefining British Politics*, such as participation. Not least, organizations, practices and ideas that appear to struggle in this period, particularly in dealing with the emergent popular desires and tastes involved in affluence, as later in this book with NVALA and Wesker's Centre 42, are useful to historians. No less than those that flourish, they are illustrative of trends in and facets of political culture – its structures, resources, values and demands. The Co-op's purpose had long been to manage and escape material problems, yet it seemed to struggle in the very context in which post-materialism might flourish. Yet whatever the fact or causes of its decline, its principles of ethical, fair trade were also markers for the future.

If the Co-op's decline partly explains its marginal and diminished status for historians of this period, so do historiographical factors – political historians' predilection for party and a received 'formal' definition of politics; labour historians biases towards production and workplace conflicts; and cultural historians focus on the meaning of goods, wealth and poverty. This has meant less dramatic, eye-catching organizations like CA have, until recently, received little attention. But neglect of the Co-op has been greater, witnessed in its absence from Zweiniger-Bargielowska's otherwise comprehensive study. The same historiographical reasons explain why Tony Crosland's involvement with both CA and the Co-op has been overlooked by consumer and political historians alike. This chapter uses Crosland not only to remedy such (undue, it contends) biases, but to inter-

46

link CA and the Co-op and to show consumerism's influence on a key political thinker.[2]

More simply, that the Co-operative movement as a whole – the Co-operative Wholesale Society (CWS) and its Scottish counterpart, local retail societies and the Co-op Union which ran education and brought separate parts of the Co-op together – was such an everyday part of High Street Britain, goes some way to explain its by-passing. CA's novelty contrasted with the Co-op's enduring presence. This seeming durability was more fragile than it seemed and more an ideal, given Co-op local autonomy co-existed uneasily with national organizations and brands. But such was its size and omnipresence that 'the Co-operative movement', Elizabeth Gundrey, editor of *Shopper's Guide* wrote in one of her many handbooks for shoppers in 1962, 'scarcely needs to be described'.[3]

Yet the Co-op's quantitative claims to represent consumers were formidable. Its submission to the Molony Committee on Consumer Protection in 1960 reckoned two in three Britons had regular contact with the Co-op. One-quarter of Britons were members and half a million were Co-op employees. One-third of milk came from Co-op dairies and one in seven packets of cigarettes were bought from Co-op shops. The Board of Trade's 1961 Census of Distribution found just over 5% of *all* retail outlets in Britain were Co-operatives. One could live within a network of Co-op activities – besides factories and shops, there were the Women's Guilds, an Insurance Society, bank, building society (the Nationwide from 1970) college, youth movement, newspaper and political party – and even end life with it, since it was estimated around one-third of the UK funeral trade was undertaken by the Co-op.[4] But this bulk also served to seclude the Co-op, insulating its problems and culture from broader changes in consumerism. It was this paradox that the Co-operative Independent Commission (CIC, 1955–58) was charged with interrogating.

The Co-op's trading position was in fact quite parlous. Its share of the retail market fell by a third from 1957–70 to under 8%, losing out in the growth stakes to multiples like Marks & Spencer. Its strengths were in necessities like food and coal where spending was static rather than consumer durables (or 'dry goods' as they were rather dryly termed) such as cars and radio-electrical, where sales increased by 371 and 131% respectively from 1952–62 and where margins were greater. The motoring revolution overtook it, with less than a tenth of societies selling petrol and many fewer cars. As Sidney Pollard put it in 1964, the Co-op was 'tied to the geography of the tram rather than the bus or motor car'. It was poorly represented in the suburbs, new housing estates and the South, where population growth was stronger. More than half of its clothing shops were in areas that accounted for just 18% of national trade. Pollard admitted the Co-op's image was 'coloured by the drab and semi-derelict nature of their strongholds in the North', whereas 'there clings to the South... an aura of success and glamour which the chain stores… bring'. If there was a Northern chic to a post-industrializing Britain in the 1960s, then it was not acquired from the Co-op.[5]

In less tangible, qualitative ways too, the Co-op seemed at odds with the main trends of change. The Co-op's cherished, defining feature was the dividend. It was to the Co-op what Clause Four was to Labour. Accrued on Co-op purchases, dividends were based on earned, deferred pleasure and rewarded loyalty. But post-rationing consumerism was edging towards more immediate gratification, indulging desires rather than self-restraint in the realm of goods. Hire-purchase and credit detached spending from earning power and were often used to attain luxuries rather than to satisfy immediate needs. Co-op traditions of (if not preference for) cash-only trading were long gone and, in practice, as O'Connell has shown, informal credit networks had long existed amongst its consumers.[6] The Co-op offered generous credit terms in mutuality clubs, but remained wedded to the dividend rather than price cuts or trading stamps. That was until the symbolically seismic advent of a national stamp scheme in March 1968. Trading stamps encouraged a form of the shop or brand loyalty that the Co-op's 'divi' had long traded on. Bloom had a scheme and Green Shield stamps (modelled on a US scheme) were introduced in 1958 and adopted by Tesco in 1963. Co-op stamps were pushed by the CWS against opposition from tradition and from local retail societies. The Co-op's puritan moorings were still apparent in that the majority of societies did not sell alcohol. And such frugal, sober instincts were not absent from shoppers. As Walton points out the 'divi' had often been a form of saving and security, investing in the Co-op, but was less practiced by the 1960s' generation.[7]

The broader picture of this period is then more complex than a conservative Co-op, paralysed by modernity as Britons shopped in thrall to self-service supermarkets. The Co-op was less novel than can be supposed (it still made a surplus, even if that was democratically re-distributed) and in other respects an agent of change. Equally, the degree of change and contentment with modern shopping should not be overstated. Nor is the narrative here a dichotomy of private multiples good, Co-op bad, although Marks and Spencer were a self-selected point of reference for the Co-op. And equally, it was significant that commentators like journalist Robert Millar, believed the Co-op was past it and thus by-passed it in their tours of the emergent high street.[8]

There were structural reasons for the Co-op's malaise. As historians have shown, it was systematically marginalized from markets by trade associations and competition legislation, and excluded politically, from government committees like Molony. As the Co-op's stock was in decline amongst policy-makers, so its status as a consumer advocate was also challenged by comparative testing organizations, notably the CA. Where the CA flourished, the Co-op seemed afflicted by consumption patterns born of relative material well-being and, Hilton argues, 'lacked the imagination to step beyond an old politics of necessity'. [9] Yet the CIC reported that many of the Co-op's difficulties were self-inflicted rather than the result of social change. Without discounting structural factors, the evidence from the internal culture, inherited traditions and instincts of the Co-op's ethos, suggest these were as weighty. Culture, in short, matters.

The Commission (CIC)

Prescient warnings abounded before and after the CIC. In 1955 Jack Bailey, National Secretary of the Co-operative Party, anticipated 'intense competition' from the multiples, that the rate of amalgamation amongst local Co-op societies was 'too slow' and how 'modern methods of advertising and publicity' and their power to 'influence... public taste and consumer demand... threaten the accustomed levels of the dividend'. He welcomed the CIC as breaking down some of the Co-op's introspective fear of outsiders. William Richardson, of the late Co-op paper the *Sunday Citizen*, was moved by the 1970s to apply Dean Acheson's barb that Britain had lost an empire but not found a role in the post-war world, to a Co-op that likewise 'had lost its place on a road of progress... and was struggling to find its way back'.[10] The Co-op's problems were, as those of the nation were imagined, those of relative rather than absolute decline and of being an early innovator now facing a host of rivals. As early as 1951 a survey of the Co-op's 607 self-service shops found that it could reduce wage costs, satisfy customers and boost sales. It 'confidently predicted that self-service will extend', noting similar findings by competitors like Tesco, but recommended 'greater study' to refine the practice, since the Co-op 'cannot afford... to allow this new method of retailing to settle into a routine business operation' and there were 'signs that this may be happening'. Its authors, the Co-op Union's Research Officer (Hough) and manager of the CWS market research department (Lambert), felt 'it would be a pity if, having played the role of pioneers, the movement were to allow others to take more advantage of its work and pass it in the struggle for technical efficiency'.[11]

The CIC was chaired by Hugh Gaitskell and composed of: the author of the seminal 1954 study *Retail Trading in Great Britain, 1850–1950* and secretary of the International Association of Department Stores, J.B. Jefferys; J.T. Murray, an industrial consultant, member of the Scientific Advisory Council and manager of a textile firm; University of Durham economics Professor D.T. Jack; Alderman Pette, the general manager of the Middlesbrough Society and chair of the Peterlee New Town Development Corporation; the secretary of the Agricultural Co-operative Producers Federation and the Horace Plunkett Foundation (which furnished the CIC with London offices), Margaret Digby; and Colonel Hardie, a former chair of the Iron and Steel Board and member of the British Transport Commission, whose minority report argued for national co-operative societies for Scotland and for England and Wales. This composition was controversial. 'Is Gaitskell the right man?' wondered the *Co-operative Consumer*, which favoured a more traditional Labour figure, Alf Robens. Gaitskell's election as Labour leader late in 1955 placed the onus on Tony Crosland, as CIC secretary from 1956. Crosland's revisionist credentials were established the same year on publication of *the* revisionist text, *The Future of Socialism* and were informed by his CIC experience. Later in 1956 economist Lady Margaret Hall joined and the pro-revisionist Alan Sainsbury was touted as a member. The Co-op Union's general secretary expressed anxiety at the appointment of 'one of our competitors', borne out by Sainsbury missing a scheduled meeting because of opening the first New Town (Hemel Hempstead) self-service Sainsbury's.[12]

The revisionist tendency were regarded with suspicion. Walton shows how it chafed with the Co-op's inherited culture. Many Co-operators feared the CIC was a lever to modernize the Co-op, a rehearsal for what revisionists wanted to effect in amending the Labour Party's traditional working-

Figure 3.1 Members of the Co-operative Independent Commission, 1955: Left to right, Back row – Anthony Crosland, Robert Southern (General Secretary, Co-op Union) and, far right, J.T. Murray. Front row – Dr. J.B. Jefferys, Miss Margaret Digby, Professor D.T. Jack, Hugh Gaitskell, Colonel Hardie and Alderman Pette
Source: Co-operative College Archive

class appeal, and thus that its conclusions were pre-meditated. Crosland was up-front that 'our proposals to be of any use must be... so radical that the movement will not accept them in toto the year after we report'. He anticipated 'the minority of progressive leaders – the Jacques, Forsyths... should accept the rightness of our proposals straight away', but 'that the movement as a whole should adopt them in 10 years time'. The CIC tackled founding and core Co-operative principles. Some, like cash only trading, pure and unadulterated goods were deemed outdated or moribund. Others were updated and affirmed – democratic control, the distribution of surplus as dividend. Crosland figured the Co-op was not a non-profit organization so much as one that offered an alternative to the economic *status quo* in that it distributed its surplus (back to the community and customer-owners) in a way that offset and precluded private capital gains.[13]

Democratic control was the other lynchpin of the Co-op's claim to offer an alternative to the market and to represent its consumers. Yet for all the benefits of public service and social responsibility he acknowledged, Crosland felt market forces might be 'more efficacious' at making producers and managers more sensitive to consumers, particularly given the low level of participation in Co-op affairs. A 1954 Co-op College survey found 0.24% of those eligible attended meetings and 2.78% voted in local board elections. This could lead to 'faction-packing' at meetings, either political (Jefferys reported 'mutterings about the Catholic influence in the Beswick society disliking the Communist influence in the Manchester and Salford Society) or by Co-op employees, trumping the interests of consumers. But given the movement's growth (the average society was thirty times larger in the 1950s than the 1880s) lower participation was, Crosland deduced, neither surprising nor necessarily problematic. Where democracy could be 'an obstacle to efficiency' was if lay boards interfered in management decisions or local societies derailed national initiatives (as they did with amalgamations, CWS initiatives on marketing or the CIC's proposed retail development society).[14]

But such language and thinking trod on hallowed traditions of local autonomy and egalitarianism. This was also true of management, where the CIC wanted better-educated expert and specialist recruits from outside besides within the movement. Post-war educational changes meant its traditional recruitment from school leavers no longer guaranteed the Co-op the best working-class students and increasingly left it with what critics at the CA described as 'largely inbred' management, prone to reproduce its culture. Moreover, the CIC supposed, echoing Crosland's belief in the 'managerial revolution', management to 'have become more complex, more specialized' and to have assumed 'much greater importance' in determining the Co-op's fortunes. To this end and to negotiate low participation levels, the CIC argued the role of lay elected boards (inexpert, amateur, but democratically accountable) should be clearly differentiated from professional, specialist management. Yet for both local societies and national Co-op institutions, the CIC held there was no principled reason why skilled management and quality service could not operate in tandem with an egalitarian ethos and democratic control – indeed efficiency ought to be a byword for the Co-op.[15]

Another concern was mobilizing the movement's capital. The Co-op was 'supposed to be a dynamic trading organization, not a giant investment trust', the CIC complained, but exhibited an 'unhealthy preoccupation with the balance sheet at the expense of the premises'. The problem here was, in part, one of the traditional ethos – personified by the 'excessively prudent' general manager encountered at the Liverpool Society. Reserves certainly merited bolstering, but not at the expense of investment.[16]

Streamlining CWS production to better co-ordinate it with retail societies was laboriously discussed. There was no doubting the advantages of vertical integration of production and consumption (the retail societies owned the wholesale societies), but since Co-op factories didn't make everything the retail societies bought, it was felt the wholesale societies might wield their market power by buying for the retail societies. The latter lacked modern layouts or national marketing strategies for almost 200 CWS brands. In 1957 the CWS Market Research department found only 20% of window displays were dedicated to Co-op goods. The existing CWS retail society founded in 1934 was 'essentially a defensive mechanism', a last resort for societies, whose 'record is not very remarkable' the Market Research department confessed to Crosland. What was needed, the CIC's final report decided, was a professional, dynamic, federal Co-operative retail development society (CRDS), able to surmount local resistance, propagate best practice and develop national specialist dry goods chains. A point of reference here were the impressive central advisory services and Domus stores that Jeffreys, Jack and Crosland saw on a CIC visit to Sweden.[17]

By contrast the CIC's UK field visits made for a doleful audit of mid-century Co-operation, revealing an unpleasing decay and rarely escaped the ridiculous into the occasionally sublime. At the Royal Arsenal Society – Britain's largest – there was plenty of capital, but little imagination. Self-satisfaction emanated from the 'unimpressive' general manager and committee and union resistance to management trainee schemes meant university-trained recruits were sparse. At its Powis Street store Jeffreys found, 'lighting was dull, the fixtures were 30 years old... signing was ugly and careless'. There was a 'window display from 1930' and 'no real attempt had been made to develop the potential of the store to cater for the customers of 1956'. The CWS directors were only the most senior managers to impress the Commission with their amateurishness and complacency and an abiding impression (in this case from the Liverpool and Cheshire Farmers African Oil Mills) was that 'the buildings, the atmosphere and... the managers [were] rather dreary and uninspiring'.[18]

Huddersfield really agitated Crosland. Its 'fantastic number of huge shops of a positively Edwardian size and majesty' if 'often tarnished now', had seen off much private competition. But this 'grand jigsaw of palatial premises' caused 'vast waste', since they belonged to no less than 37 different Co-op societies in the city. The economist in Crosland saw it as 'a textbook example of the advantages of rationalization'. He compared Huddersfield's 'awesome grandeur' to 'a late Roman Emperor whose proud bearing and splendid robes conceal a fatal weakness'. Accounting for its management, Crosland turned to the Renaissance: '15th century Italy can offer nothing to compare with the ancient feuds... passed on from generation to generation, which rack relations at the Committee level'. Compared with this, Crawley, Britain's second new town, provided modernist relief. Its expansive plans were funded via a low liquidity ratio and its Epstein sculpture and 'remarkable' lunch with wine and Irish coffee, left Crosland contemplating 'what a dreamworld it would be if all Co-operative societies were like this'.[19]

Image was the subject of the most memorable parts of the final report. The '"image" of a Co-operative shop in the public mind', it declared, was a 'ponderous, unrestored and unimaginative grocery-cum-butchery-cum-drapery, built in the early 1900s, still operating counter-service, the window display old-fashioned, the exterior clumsy and badly in need of paint, the interior frowsy and unattractive'. There were 'too many such Co-operative premises, especially in parts of Scotland and the North' that leant the 'whole movement a name for backwardness and drabness'. Its retail outlets lacked the quality that the consumer, who was 'more exacting than her predecessor of even two decades ago' and would 'no longer endure blowzy buildings and dowdy display', expected. Its clothing lines had 'a certain dowdiness' and were 'not always "smart" enough to appeal to the younger generation'. Individual correspondents compounded this impression. A Wrexham correspondent complained Co-Op products were expensive and sold with a 'take it or leave it attitude'. The commission was told by Elizabeth Wilson how 'women in Southampton don't buy their clothes [at the Co-op] because they are made of cheap, shoddy material and not modern in style and at a dear price' and of the grocery department's reputation 'for very bad service'.[20]

This was a common impression of the post-war Co-op. In 1947 that London shoppers' felt private shops offered more luxury than the 'drab' Co-op was noted by Mass Observers, as was how at a Women's Co-operative Guild meeting, 'there was no attempt at smartness in the "Hollywood" sense'. Infamously, Herbert Morrison's boast of shopping at the Co-op was derisively greeted by one heckler – 'and my god, you look like it'. If partly a hangover from rationing, this also stemmed from the Co-op's instinctive focus on subsistence needs and its egalitarian propensity to regard con-sumers and staff as equals. But this ill-fitted the relative affluence of the later 1950s. On the CIC, J.T. Murray welcomed the 'creative minority of experts' made up of designers and advertisers. There was, he argued, 'no more pernicious idea in socialist thought about industry than the belief that modern creative merchandising techniques, which are in effect an attempt to create new satisfactions for the consumer of which he would unaided probably never have dreamed, is amoral'. Murray warned the Co-op management who subscribed to such a fallacy that they were failing to 'recognize their creative responsibilities'. Crosland concurred, rejecting distinctions between innate needs and invented wants and insisting the Co-op 'must give the consumer what he thinks he wants as well as what it thinks he wants'.[21]

The CIC aspired both to highlight how democracy had the potential to make the Co-op responsive to customer demands, but also to the high standards it saw at Macy's or Printemps. The final CIC report declared:

> the slogan should be that 'nothing is too good for the co-operator'; and the ambition should be that the word 'co-operative' comes to be a synonym for both leadership and dependability in respect of price, quality and service... In many areas the word 'co-operative' is, we fear, associated with a drab, colourless, old-fashioned mediocrity; and too many societies are... complacently and unimaginatively, quite content so long as dividend is being paid. It must be said dogmatically that this is not good enough for the consumer in 1958; indeed it betrays a somewhat patronising and insulting attitude to the wants and expectations of the ordinary co-operative member.[22]

As the CIC saw it, the Co-op was 'no longer appealing to a working class which is barely above the subsistence line, but to consumers whose tastes are changing and rising rapidly' and thus was allowing social change to bankrupt it. To rectify this it insisted 'the greater proportion of co-operative capital expenditure in the next few years should take place, not in the production, but in the retail field' and that the wholesale societies should become 'more retail-minded'. National assistance was needed to help those societies 'not yet awake to the higher and more varied expectations... of today's shoppers'. Otherwise its recommendations dealt with the four areas of management, amalgamation, the Retail Development society and wholesale societies. What would likely impress an anthropological reader of the weight of evidence in the Report were the Byzantine qualities of the Co-op as a whole – qualities that were to entangle, assimilate and, arguably, overcome the CIC.[23]

Reception

Historians have differed over the report's reception. Birchall writing in the 1990s, considered the CIC report was met, if not implemented, with enthusiasm. Sidney Pollard, writing in 1964, felt it went 'largely unheeded'. Battle was joined well before it was published in May 1958. Newcastle Society's General Manager, J.T. Fair, admitted the Co-op faced difficulties in the Dry Goods trade, but was 'not interested in the Independent Commission... we have the brains... let us get down to the job'. Others, like Jacques, who Crosland identified as a progressive, defended ideas of more potent management structures. But most were instinctively resistant. Leonard Cohen, Managing Director of a Manchester store and member of the Retail Distributors' Association council, depicted a depressingly complacent organization that saw fit to leave the report for six months before formally debating it. Just weeks before the report was formally debated, the London Co-op, according to *The Times*, had no time to discuss the report.[24]

Within Co-op circles the sense was that the CIC proposals modified 'the traditional conception of Co-operative democratic control in the pursuit of business efficiency' – sacrificing democratic control to the managerial revolution. Critics, like the *Sunday Times*, provocatively agreed it amounted to 'bouquets for capitalism'. Foes and friends agreed it attended to the lack of integration between producers, wholesalers and retailers. Both the revisionist *Socialist Commentary* and Communist David Ainley, doubted the loss of lay democratic control was worth the gains in efficiency.[25] The *Economist* and *Tribune* agreed that this was 'a radical report aimed at a stuffy, conservative organization' for whom 'apathy is often a greater enemy than capitalist competition'.[26]

Once the report was delivered Gaitskell urged 'don't defer and defer and defer!' Alive to the resistance it had already met, a group (including Co-op MPs Bert Oram and George Darling) held a conference in Nottingham in July 1958. Its pamphlet, *Four Things First*, urged establishing the CRDS, a national chain of specialist stores, amalgamations and wholesale reorganization. The debate at November's Special National Congress in Blackpool, vindicated Robert Millar (the socialist, not consumer journalist) wondering whether 'history and tradition can be overthrown so ruthlessly?', especially once the Co-op Union's Central Executive rejected parts of the Report. Gaitskell expressed his 'disappointment' and Crosland, unsurprised like his party leader, saw the attempt to downgrade the CRDS to CWS control as evidence that producers dominated consumers in the Co-op.[27]

Blackpool saw controversy rage – even the timing of the debate on amalgamation (after lunch, when it was reckoned the executive might find delegates more pliable) was controversial. The case for amalgamation – 44 North East societies with under 1000 members were described by the Barnsley British delegate as a 'colossal waste' – was thought by a minority best not entrusted to the Central Executive. But when a delegate suggested that 'parochial instincts... in the average board' might work against the wider movement, the Executive and societies like Rushden and the Rochdale

Pioneers invoked the spectre of compulsory mergers to defend their independence.

Debate on the proposed CRDS exposed further divisions. St. Albans, Pontycymmer and Stockton's Resolution K to have the Central Executive initiate the CIC's proposal for a CRDS narrowly passed. This was despite opposition from the Executive, Scottish CWS (SCWS), Norwich and Birmingham who argued too much work was being placed on the CRDS and the Enfield Highway society, who argued it was not a pressing need. The Executive assured congress it was 'not running away from the problem', but reminded local societies that an independent CRDS might overrule them. Despite its defeat, the Executive promised to action the resolution, prompting Letchworth and Hitchin's delegate to complain that the 'approach of the central executive to this matter is completely inadequate'. To complicate matters, a Resolution M to develop the existing retail services, was passed by a majority of 6790 votes, compared to K's 91.

As fractious was the debate on recruiting more skilled personnel. A delegate from Redding welcomed the executive's efforts not to *implement* but *encourage* societies to examine recruitment, insisting 'do not let us allow too many of these educated men into this movement', otherwise rather than '"These Things shall be" we shall be singing "Land of Hope and Glory"'. University types would 'bankrupt us in no time' and 'think it below their dignity to enter a co-operative shop'. Although denounced by speakers from Kilmarnock and Barrow (who noted whilst preferable to have employees whose 'heart is in the movement... it is not their heart that pays the grocery bills' and the likely press ridicule should such an amendment be passed), the sum effect was to deflect the question of implementing reform.

The Executive wanted to *refer* the CIC report to the wholesale societies, but modernizers wanted *acceptance* recommended. Edinburgh's G. Gay argued 'that the central executive appear to be as bold as lions when making proposals to concerning the future of retail societies but as mild as lambs when making proposals – or failing to make proposals! – with regard to the future of the wholesales'. A Royal Arsenal delegate held the CWS directors had been too quiet on the CIC report. But the Executive argued they could not pre-judge the CWS response and they were abetted by a Doncaster delegate arguing that discussion was best deferred since problems ought not be aired in the presence of those he ritualistically denounced as 'our enemies' in the press. But Watford argued that the CIC had not gone far enough in proposing a SCWS-CWS merger and that the Wholesale Societies were acting for themselves not the movement *en masse* and still others that too many decisions were being deferred. In short, as Pontcymmer's H.C. Greening argued, the 'report cannot be treated in bits and pieces', only as 'an integrated whole'. But central indifference, inertia and local autonomy triumphed.[28]

By 1959 the Executive admitted it did 'not see eye to eye with the Commission on... the amalgamation problem'; would neither rein in local societies to enforce amalgamation nor specify whether it would prioritize Resolution K or M in developing retail services. Reports in *Co-operative News* through 1959 corroborated CIC findings. Forty societies were accused of having 'fallen hook, line and sinker' for a deal from a combine of Westons, Ranks and Spillers that was 'crippling the co-operative baking trade' and showed the lack of co-ordination between retail and wholesale. Mark Abrams, a revisionist who was supplying polling data for the CRDS Negotiating Committee, showed multiples' market lead in areas like clothing and electricals and tied this to the CIC's argument that they were more adroitly winning clientele from the newly prosperous working class.[29]

By 1960 the CRDS was the issue between pro-CIC modernizers and their critics. At Blackpool again for spring congress, the modernizers on the CRDS committee – Gay, Greening, Cyril Forsyth from Nottingham, with Oram as secretary – issued a minority report. They accused the Central Executive of stalling negotiations, trying to 'frighten the movement about its capital position in relation to CRDS' and of exploiting the majority Resolution M had over K to relegate the CRDS to CWS control. The executive countered that neither the minority (arguing for an autonomous division of the Co-op Union) nor majority reports argued for an independent CRDS, as the Commission had (and as Watford and Stockton societies still wanted). They argued that the CWS had commenced a national chain (Shoefayre), that they had conceded retail society representation (from where most modernizers originated, but not proposed by the CIC) and accused the modernizers of 'guerilla tactics' since their Nottingham conference. As think-tank Political and Economic Planning (PEP) concluded, 'the rebels, even if successful, will go only part of the way to implement the independent commission's report'.[30] This was a measure of the extent to which the CIC report's was at odds with established Co-op culture, but also assimilated by it.

Culture blocks modernization

Evidence of resistance to change was abundant beyond the national debate around the CIC report. The Co-op's submission to Molony harked back to the 1940s Utility scheme as 'a guarantee of good quality and a fair deal'. Its preference for state regulation (a ministry of Consumer Affairs indeed) rather than the voluntary efforts of the British Standards Institute and quality kitemarks that replaced Utility after 1952, did not seem to be tempered by any awareness of consumer pleasure or empowerment at the ending of such regulation. Communists like Ainley held the Co-op should not and could not compete with the 'glittering supermarkets, neon lights' to 'please and dazzle the customers'.[31]

Critics kept the CIC's agenda to the fore. For Roy Hattersley writing in 1966 – and his context as Crosland's protégé was as pertinent as the flowering of sixties culture to his style guide – the Co-op remained 'the home of drab uniformity... and shapeless clothes'. Leslie Adrian, consumer correspondent of *The Spectator*, thought the Co-op had been forgotten in the attention lavished on the newer CA. Its goods were 'not by any means as bad as the Co-op's opponents like to claim', but its public image was such that its 'virtues tend to be overlooked and vices exaggerated'. Despite efforts and achievements at retail modernization, it retained an old-fashioned image and its shrinking social and retail base 'made it parochial' and revealed 'traces of in-breeding:' Adrian concluded that in Co-op culture 'the past has too much influence on the present and may undermine the future'.[32]

The editor of *Stores and Shops* also thought 'parochialism' was the Co-op's 'besetting sin'. It stuck to 'selling cloth caps to people who want trilbies' and had 'an inbred, subconscious reluctance to make too much money or to join too vigorously in the skirmishes and battles which rage up and down our High Streets in the 1960s'. Management consultant Nancy Hewitt highlighted this 'inward looking attitude' and the Co-op's inattention to Public Relations. Combined these tended 'to keep Mrs. Jones out of the Co-op' and gave the movement an 'inferiority complex' which meant that rather than seeking her trade it preferred 'to concentrate on its existing members'. Trading failures that could 'more properly be ascribed to bad public relations', were instead put down by the Co-op to shopper's 'political prejudice and lack of loyalty and idealism'. Hewitt felt the Co-op underestimated both 'the potential attraction of their unique ethical background' and shoppers. Most people 'could not care less what party ticket the directors of a business wear', but the Co-op's unique brand as 'a living symbol of its belief that people do not exist to make a profit out of each other' could yield ethical dividends from exploiting aspects of shopping other than its material ends, particularly amongst new youth markets.[33]

Less partial and more sympathetic sources also chimed with the CIC. The Co-op 'boasted... too quietly' of its 40 goods approved by the Council of Industrial Design (CoID)'s Design Index, Bonner felt. A Croydon co-operator complained in 1960 that her local store did not push CWS brands in tandem with TV ads and that staff were 'very lax about assisting', PEP, in an allusion to the CA's activities and a reprise of the theme that it wasn't the Co-op's goods but its techniques that were remiss, lamented that the Co-op did 'not sell its worthwhile consumer educational publications as energetically as a private enterprise publisher would'.[34]

Modern publicity seemed to adulterate Co-op values, emphasizing image (for Bonner, a realm in which the 'biggest and most persistent lie' prevailed) over ideals. This was despite a long history of innovation and of ranking in the UK top 20 advertisers for expenditure, as Schwarzkopf has shown. This unease was apparent towards commercial television after 1955. Despite busting the BBC's monopoly, the advent of ITV correlated with the Co-op's declining use of film and was feared by the Co-op as evidence of Americanization, of private commercial power and for being beyond the finances of individual societies. Burton shows the Co-op's attitude towards ITV was also pragmatic. After all, many societies sold TV sets, if the Co-op's own were branded as 'Defiant'. The CWS applied for a commercial licence in 1952, Burton suggests as a ruse to force the government to address the danger of control of programmes by manufacturers. CWS took out adverts from ITV's outset and overriding the anxieties of local societies, developed national strategies for its brands and for the Co-op itself in 1968's 'Operation Facelift', with a uniform logo.[35]

Most often then, it seemed that modernization was half-hearted or flawed as much as resisted. Assessing the Co-op's relationship with the CoID, Whitworth contends the Co-op is too easily dismissed as out of touch, unfashionable and disengaged from consumers. Design historian Woodham has related the difficulties the CoID experienced in bringing modern furniture design and marketing to Co-op production and retail practices in the late 1940s and 1950s. The CA likewise painted a mixed picture. Positive reports in *Which?* suggested 'co-operative products may be among the best available', whatever 'shoppers' casual gossip' insinuated. But gossip counted and was not helped by un-enticing 'dowdy window-displays in their local co-op store'. CIC supporters, like Forsyth, Managing Director of the Nottingham Society, saw potential in the progress made by his own society, but could not demur from more generic criticisms.[36]

The Co-op's relationship to self-service was paradigmatic of this flawed modernization. It was a pioneer and innovator – 90% of self-service stores in Britain in 1950 were Co-ops, but by 1960 less than half and just one-quarter by 1968. Its fondness for this retail development was fading too, suggesting this was not simply the competition catching up: in 1954 66.5% of Co-op stores were self-service – by 1957, 58%. A similar pattern occurred with supermarkets – the Co-op ran two-thirds of these in 1953, but scarcely a third by 1960. The geography of self-service shops revealed a familiar pattern – in 1957 three-quarters of Northern Co-ops were self-service, but in the South less than one-third, well behind the multiples. Shaw, Curth and Alexander have stressed the multiple forces at play in the 'Americanization' of food retailing and how self-service and supermarket development was constrained until 1954 by rationing, building restrictions, shortages and RPM. Once these passed, so did the Co-op's advantage, which was in conversions rather than building new, larger outlets.[37]

Mobile shops were an alternative, in which the Co-op was also a leading innovator. Serving housing estates and rural areas, they boomed between 1946 and 1959, commanding 3% of national trade. The Co-op ran around half these by 1959, mostly in Scotland and Northern England. And bar

50 self-service mobiles, their success drew upon the expertise of their salespeople.[38]

The Self-Service Development Association reckoned Co-ops lagged behind competitors in having a higher ratio of storage to sales area. A Board of Trade survey of self-service had the Co-op behind the pace in sales per checkout or shopfloor area, although competitive per assistant. Research into self-service and management suggested firm institutional resistance to the sorts of change the CIC envisaged. In 1960 the (ever-progressive) Nottingham society compared the performance of 45 product groups in an experimental self-service store (Farnborough Road) against a yardstick store (Dungannon Road). Techniques such as grouping related products, attention to customer flows and space allocation, making delivery and credit available and the active marketing of Co-op brands (not just by price incentives) saw the experimental store increase sales significantly. The authors from the Co-operative College concluded: 'the counters of stores have been removed, but the attitude of many managers is still a counter service attitude... apparent in the lack of an adventurous merchandising and in the unprofitable control and utilization of floor and shelf space'. Hough and Lambert's fear in 1951 that the Co-op had embraced such changes expediently not wholeheartedly and would be outpaced by competitors, had been realized.[39]

Self-service was a useful, but not definitive register of modernizing trends, since it met an uneven reception. For all the time it gave shoppers, they complained of checkout queues (complicated in the Co-op by the dividend issue), lack of a personal sales touch and knowledge and the anonymity of supermarkets. The CA's rapid growth, after all, had much to do with the dilemmas of choice posed by self-service. Nor was the adoption of self-service unproblematic by the Co-op's commercial competitors: the process of learning from US models and practice was, as for the CA, not uncritical. It was not then simply a lack of innovation or that private enterprise was innately more adroit at modernizing or that self-service was necessarily the way to proceed, but that Co-op uncertainties were compounded by its potent culture and by a range of other restraints.[40]

Uncertainties in modernization also stemmed from a sense that political and democratic attachments to the Co-op, as well as corporate, economic loyalty amongst it shoppers, were slipping. The *Sunday Citizen*, as *Reynolds News* had been re-badged in tabloid form in 1962, was symptomatic of this. It struggled on until June 1967, but like the TUC-owned *Daily Herald*, which had been taken over in 1961, its almost exclusively working-class readership weakened its advertising profile. This caused strife between the Wilson government and Co-operators like Alf Morris MP, Lord Peddie and William Richardson who felt some Arts Council-style arms length subsidy was warranted in line with the concern of the 1962 Royal Commission on the Press to sustain smaller papers. Co-operators were aggrieved the government did not send more public information advertising the *Citizen*'s way. The government remained persuaded by the need to reach the largest audience and to avoid, as Kaufman told the Prime Minister, being seen to favour a paper 'with its own special party political complexion'. But both the *Herald* and *Citizen* also suffered because, Stuart Holland noted, Co-operators, like Labour members and trade unionists, 'preferred to buy other papers than those backed by the movement'.[41]

The New Left's Raymond Williams argued the Co-op was part of working-class culture's collective institutional alternative to capitalism, but few it seemed saw this as an appealing vision.[42] Halsey and Ostergaard's study found the Rochdale Pioneers meant nothing to 89% of members. Most saw the Co-op instrumentally, as a shop not social movement, permitting them to conclude that 'active public participation is characteristic only of a small minority' and that a 'secular drift towards apathy' was pronounced in the Co-op, if not unique to it. Participation in the Co-op beyond shopping, they described in 1965, as 'a *diminuendo* on small numbers'. Less than 0.5% of members attended society meetings and 1.41% voted in the 1960 board elections – by all comparisons this was the 'lowest extremity of member-ship apathy'. PEP estimated that of the 12 million eligible to claim divi-dends, the number who took a 'lively interest' in their societies was 'probably well under 100,000'. Not that participation had always been as high as such concern implied – Ostergaard's 1954 survey plotted a decline since 1933, but from the far from ideal level of 1.53% attending meeting and 4.22% voting. Crucially, all this was diagnosed as amounting to not only a democratic loss, but a trading deficit too. A 1960 survey found that besides being more male, middle class and likely to be a Co-op employee than the average Co-op member, active participants in the local Co-op (Ten Acres and Stirchley in Birmingham) also shopped there more.[43]

The issue of dividends could be, the Central Executive explained in 1958 – arguing for less publicity for a 'dividend day' and for societies to encour-age members to save them in share accounts – as beneficial to other traders as an advert for the advantages of Co-op shopping. 'What are we to do', a Coventry Co-operator asked MP Richard Crossman in 1955, 'when our members draw the "divi" to spend at M&S'? Even such loyalty as could be detected in the Co-op's insularity, had the effect, PEP reckoned, of robbing Co-op consumers 'of their sense of discrimination'. They were poorer because 'the devoted co-operator will prefer to buy at his own shop even though a manifestly better buy is on offer in a free enterprise shop'.[44]

Economic attachment to the Co-op also seemed to be slipping. Average annual sales per member fell by one-sixth between 1940–60 and 10% of the average working-class wage packet was spent at the Co-op, where this had been one-third in 1881. The 'divi' it seemed, was not enough to induce loyalty – it too was in decline with more than half of societies cutting their dividend rates in 1962–63. Average capital holding per member fell by two-thirds in 1938–59, leaving many with merely nominal shareholdings. This problem grew through the 1960s as a younger generation withdrew family holdings. Rotherham suspended repayment in 1967 and even large societies like Barnsley British were impacted. Meeting with the Friendly Societies Registrar in 1971, Senior CWS officials 'fully accepted' that this 'arose from poor management' and the 'failure to adopt up-to-date ideas'. The CIC suggested withdrawable schemes be supplemented with longer-term investment opportunities. This was realized in a CWS ten-year escalator bond scheme, but only by 1971. Critics feared it would supplant local schemes with central control.[45]

The Co-op's political and social aspect generated limited interest. Politics and groceries were not irreconcilable, but evidence suggests they were not easily combined given what was being sold, how and to whom. Membership of the Women's Co-operative Guild and of Co-op youth groups was in decline. Even socialists, according to John Gorman, 'shopped at the Co-op for the "divi" rather than from socialist conviction'. Formal politics were not part of the CIC's remit, due to ongoing discussions between the Co-op Party and Labour. These concerned the rising number of Co-op MPs (peaking in 1955), but that Co-op MPs did not always adhere to Parliamentary Labour Party (PLP) standing orders, demanded their own election broadcasts in 1955 and paid scarce affiliation fees to local Labour parties (contrary to popular myth and unlike Trade Union-sponsored candidates), indeed often duplicated constituency party resources. Labour's proposals for a capped number of Co-op Union (rather than locally) selected MPs and for a formal affiliation to Labour, seemed to the Co-op to threaten its political independence.[46] At Royal Arsenal, the only society to affiliate direct to Labour, the CIC found this put off as few members as it attracted. Only one of 204 respondents to a 1958 survey of new Manchester members joined for political reasons: a third joined for the 'divi', 17% had no particular reason; 41% were introduced by family, 14% by Co-op Roundsmen; 70% joined at grocery stores, only 4% at furnishing stores.[47]

Most commentators assigned sluggish modernization – typified by amalgamations which reached the upper level of 300 societies proposed in the 1958 Report only by 1972 and were made more out of financial necessity than conviction or choice – to a failure of will rather than knowledge. This kept the Co-op hamstrung in a state of anxious self-examination on the one hand, alongside complacent conservatism and inability or unwillingness to address its well-established problems on the other.[48] Through the 1960s a steady stream of surveys and commentators, from within the Co-op as much as competitors and critics, probed this affliction.

A 1963 Co-op College and Union survey underscored the case the CIC had made about the quality of management, recruitment, training and salaries. It found woeful contact between societies and career's offices at Grammar schools or Universities meant few managers had a degree (1% at assistant department head level or above). Of 885 senior vacancies between

1956–61, only 10% were filled from outside the movement. College diploma recipients (of which only three were women since the 1930s) reportedly felt that lay boards favoured length of service over talent in promotion and that the multiples offered not only better salaries (the Co-op feared alienating managers from the shopfloor), but more clearly defined career paths.[49]

The managing secretary of Nottingham Co-op and a Vice chair of the Manchester Fabians, restated the case for accelerating amalgamations to 30–40 regional societies and referenced Swedish national and specialist Co-op chains.[50] Bernard Rhodes, formerly the Co-op Union's development officer and the head of the London College of Distributive Trades' management department, highlighted its difficulties in 'trades where fashion... style and design are of great importance' like clothing, hairdressing and record sales and how no Co-op outlets were featured in the *Good Food Guide*, it ran no wimpy bars and few espresso bars. A 1960 Alfred Bird & Sons survey found 40% of Co-op shoppers were aged 55 or over and only 17% under 35. Teenage spending was, a Coutauld survey found, notably lower at the Co-op. The 'typical co-op shopper was a working-class woman, aged 45 or more and living in the North of England', it concluded. This resistance to change, Rhodes saw as both cause and effect of local Co-operative local boards being elected by and from 'a restricted circle of Guildswomen, employees, staff of other co-operative organizations and interested socialists'; an ethos, Rhodes believed, that encouraged 'an unwillingness to experiment and a narrow conception of a specifically "co-operative type" of consumer'. Twinned with the lack of 'one undisputed source of national authority' to press for amalgamations and to rid it of the intangible impression that whilst many working-class shoppers had traded up in their aspirations, it hadn't, the Co-op was 'behind the times'. This all made for familiar reading to those versed in the CIC Report.[51]

Co-op and CA: speaking for consumers?

Another commentator, socialist historian Sidney Pollard reconciled his initial criticisms with the CIC by 1964. In a Fabian pamphlet he argued for modernizing the Co-op by refashioning its ethical vision. The CWS, SCWS and Co-op Union should merge, a move that retail societies and the SCWS scotched at the 1964 congress. Only such a body would have the power to effect reform and sustain the 'divi' in the anticipated onslaught from multiple retailers after the abolition of RPM. Pollard drew on Hewitt's assessment of Co-op management that it needed to be drawn from a broader social base. But his advocacy, like Hewitt's, was not simply business-minded. Retail societies should 'remain proselytizing agencies for their own form of trading as a superior form'. To reject the new affluence was aimless, because whilst he shared the Co-op's 'healthy suspicion' of advertising (indeed he found it 'difficult to think of any licit economic activity... more harmful to social health'), it was equally the case that the 'dull and unglamorous routine of the Victorian working class home were not ideal for the development of the human spirit'. To counter commercial advertisers, Pollard looked to the Co-op Union Education Department's 1964 collaboration with the CoID, *Eating, Sleeping and Living*. The CIC slogan 'only the best was good enough for their members' was apt, marrying the Co-op's hope of making capital servant not master of people's lives with modern post-materialist agendas of the quality of life. Pollard attempted to persuade the Co-op that 'these new social tasks are different in kind, but they are not inferior in importance to those with which it began its career as the consumers' organization'.

Pollard also noted the rise of competitors (if sometime collaborators) in the CoID and its design centre and most notably the CA. Such developments had 'largely by-passed the co-operative movement', but seemed to Pollard to have a more contemporary appeal and garnered more media attention, although he was uncertain whether this was because of their vocal criticisms of goods or by virtue of being more compatible with a liberal market economy. Pollard believed this new consumer movement was at present too middle class and structurally limited. Their initiatives were 'static and passive... they cannot by themselves initiate production or use the purchasing power of a large membership or of a large chain of shops'. In this lay the potential for the Co-op to 'recapture the initiative in this field' and realize the consumer movement's 'countervailing power'.[52]

For its part, the CA saw the Co-op as 'the neglected opportunity of the contemporary consumer revolution' and its Director, Casper Brook, suggested 'what the Co-ops need is a Dr. Beeching' to enforce the CIC's Report and prune its inefficient proliferation of societies. Its failure to actively involve shopper-members in decisions negated its democratic potential and claims to represent consumers. It was a 'producer-oriented organization' where the CA maintained independence from producers. This was the essence of CA's typically robust defence of its claim to represent consumers. Ex-PEP researcher Leonard Tivey of the Birmingham Consumers Group, argued the Co-op, despite its size, did not represent consumers in general, but only Co-operative consumers. Much Co-op activity was concerned with production, thus like Labour and the TUC – whose consumer interest claims Tivey dismissed as 'amiable nonesense' – it was insufficiently consumer-centred. The CA was, Tivey reckoned, presently 'the main focus of independent consumer knowledge and thinking'.[53]

The International Co-Operative Alliance's head of economics research retorted that 'to inform a consumer about the relative merits of different products enables him to become a *discriminating* consumer rather than an *active* consumer'. 'Only when consumers are organized and their consumption becomes creative' did they 'become active consumers'. 'By feeding back to producers and distributors, whose activities they control by ownership' it was possible for consumers 'in Co-operative societies to do something that the new consumer movement cannot'. More generally, the Co-op echoed sceptics like Raymond Williams and J.B. Priestley, who felt the very category 'consumer' as CA applied it, was complicit with market-oriented individualism, private acquisitiveness and a restricted view of citizens. Its submission to Molony bemoaned collaboration with the CA was limited (by CA's strict independence from producers) to work on consumers' legal rights, but also suggested CA's testing was of more interest to traders than consumers.[54]

That *Which?* aided manufacturers was a common charge, one CA claimed as testimony to its facilitation of consumer-producer dialogue (except where it was perceived as in the pay of business). Like Young, Crosland repeatedly asked, 'what influence is CA having on manufacturers?' Other Co-op critiques of the CA's approach disclosed its own resistance to change. Bonner thought 'scepticism of advertising by the more intelligent consumer' was 'not enough' to compensate the consumer 'deprived of the assistance of knowledgeable retailers' in the self-service era.[55]

At stake here was the form of modern consumer politics – in short, consumerism versus consumption – CA's consumers asserting their individual power and right to choose in the marketplace, vying with the Co-op's collective attempt to provide an alternative to the market. But there were also resemblances. Crosland was a link between the two organizations and his Co-op associations did raise questions about the impartiality of the CA towards the Co-op. Although Conservative council member James Douglas rebutted this – maintaining the CA's non-partisanship – and reckoned test reports showed the CA was 'not unduly prejudiced in favour of the Co-ops and their products'. Crosland was after all critical of the Co-op. He could certainly be partisan, opposing the appointment of Conservative Peter Goldman, as CA director in 1964.[56]

And the CA's claim to speak for consumers had evident limitations. One in four Britons might see *Which?*, but CA's membership, like the Co-op's, saw it foremost as a value-for-money guide before any broader aspirations. For this reason, just as the CIC criticized the role of lay boards and local autonomy waylaying a national Co-op strategy, Crosland's proposed CA constitution in 1964 persisted in distancing policy-making from direct membership control, despite the criticisms of the accountability of the CA leadership made by Molony. Crosland argued, 'people join CA (as it now is)... to purchase a service, namely, reports of consumer tests' and this made it more 'like the Automobile Association or RAC... than a political party or trade union' and majority rule less pressing. Democracy would escalate 'the risk of capture by an unscrupulous minority pressure group' since (in a phrase revealing CA leaders disparaging attitude to its members) most CA members 'would be incapable of an intelligent selection amongst competing candidates'. Like other CA leaders, he was anxious to develop an audience beyond the middle class and by 1962 argued CA should have access to ITV to help it 'reach a mass' besides the 'mainly middle-class audience', attracted by its BBC programme, *Choice*. CA's membership, impressively rapid as its growth was, remained too small to claim broader representation or to be a peak-level interest group in its own right. Tivey conceded that, so far as the majority of members were concerned, any claim by CA leaders to speak for them was as invalid as a newspaper claiming to be the voice of its readers.[57]

Crosland

Historians and biographers have overlooked Crosland's relationship with the consumer movement. Jefferys' summary of the CIC notes this was Crosland's first foray into policy after writing *The Future of Socialism* and was a 'bitterly disappointing' failure that amounted to a period of 'marking time' for Crosland. Fred Inglis likewise adjudges it a 'brief interval', despite highlighting Crosland's grasping of a vital popular distinction between public welfare and the private realm of consumer culture. Crosland had a populist, consumer eye that recurred in his language and conception of politics and the public sphere, that was indebted to his CIC and CA experiences. Not least the £2000 he was paid as CIC secretary was welcome since he had lost his parliamentary seat in 1955.[58] The CIC earned Crosland's 'rapt attention', attested to by a hectic schedule of meetings and visits in his diary. His wife's biography notes little more than how despite Crosland's 'bad temper' at the report's rejection, his association with the Co-op's progressives helped him secure the Labour nomination in Grimsby, whose MP he became in 1959. As Harold Wilson's 1955 organizational tour of local Labour parties gave him a sense of the broader movement and a base in the Labour Party outside his parliamentary reputation, so did Crosland's three years as CIC secretary, somewhat offsetting his louche, revisionist, Oxford-educated reputation. Crosland's intellectual and personal closeness to Michael Young is widely acknowledged. And Susan Crosland even notes how her husband was 'irritated by consumers voicing complaint to one another rather than doing something about it' – but none mention his formal association with the CA.[59]

Crosland's interest in the Co-op and consumer politics persisted after the CIC report in 1958 and pre-dated it to. In 1954 he reviewed the free market economist Basil Yamey's case against RPM in the International Co-operative Alliance's journal *Cartel* and (incorrectly) predicted there was little prospect of the Conservative Party attacking what amounted to a manufacturers' prerogative. Ellis covers the evolution from the 1940s of Crosland's thinking on the psychology of consumerism and its relationship to democratic socialism, but like Reisman's, Jackson's and Nuttall's studies, does not factor in the context of Crosland's associational links with either the Co-op or CA.[60]

Hilton has detailed Young and Crosland's proximity and their centrality to rethinking social democracy along more consumerist lines. Both exaggerated Labour's historic hostility to the market and the extent of its production-mindedness, but as Jackson notes what particularly unified and defined Young and Crosland was the notion that 'there was nothing necessarily unsocialist about equalizing access to high levels of personal consumption'.[61] If Crosland left his mark on the Co-op rather more than the CA (where his day-to-day involvement was minimal), both helped shape his thinking. He drew analogies with the broader Labour movement from the Co-op and the CA was a model for his understanding of pressure-group politics. The CIC and CA influenced his understanding and characteristic thinking on: participation in the public sphere; modernization of Labour and Britain; professionalism as the antidote to both national decline and Labour's egalitarian belief in amateurism; Scandinavia as a reference point for social democrats; the 'managerial revolution' (the thesis that in complex businesses, power over operating decisions was held by managers more than the owners of the means of production); besides consumer politics.

If Crosland seemed more at one with CA's consumer politics, then this wasn't only because of a shared belief in the individual consumer-citizen and that the market could be made to deliver for consumers and that educated, rational consumers were preferable to a more paternalist approach. It was also acquired and learnt from the CIC's critique of the Co-op and the Co-op's response to it. This preference in terms of consumer politics – and it was a preference rather than a definitive choice – was also cultural. CA seemed more modern compared with the Co-op – apparent in its use of polling, which, like his near neighbour Mark Abrams, Crosland advocated to further Labour's ends. He regarded its 'often rude comparative comments on goods and services' as one of *Which?*'s qualities. This appealed to Crosland's tendency, as Benn described it, to use 'informality' as 'a sort of substitute for radicalism', contrasted to the Co-op's traditionalism.[62] To those embedded in Co-op ways of thinking, he seemed to treat its traditions irreverently, exploiting its language for purposes that marginalized or even mocked it. In 1973, as Labour's policy swung leftwards towards public ownership, he asked a Shadow Cabinet meeting: 'Why don't we nationalize Marks & Spencer to make it as efficient as the Co-op?' At 1972's Festival of International Co-operation, he argued for a voluntary prices-incomes policy, against Co-op and especially trade union instincts, by invoking 'a return to the old cooperative Rochdale spirit – a sense of obligation to the wider good, thought for others as well as ourselves, and a more Puritan self-government of our own desires and lives'. Yet the Co-op remained a reference point for him, if often negatively. Crosland was, after all, equally aware of the limitations of CA's audience and it could be subject to his irreverence. He remembered the proceedings of CA's council often 'bored him' when discussing the more banal details of product testing and would read the *Evening Standard* in such moments.[63]

Like Young, Crosland was sceptical of those who supposed the pervasive influence of advertising. Here he locked horns with American critics like Galbraith, with whom he differed over the extent to which the 'managerial revolution' meant big business could manipulate the market as well as the power of advertisers over consumers. Crosland highlighted failed campaigns and recent tastes and trends that had arisen without advertising, from Marks & Spencer clothes to pep pills and the Liberal Party. Lazarsfeld's work was, as for Young, a clear influence, but it was more that Crosland was wary of an authoritarian, paternalism about others lives that could patronize or needlessly distinguish needs and wants in popular tastes. This pertained to the Co-op's weakness in reaching beyond working-class material needs, but also to the state's role. State intervention was on Crosland's radar and he vigorously defended the Consumer Council, but chiefly to offset biases in the market. His preference was for the CA and Co-op to play a 'dynamic pro-consumer role', to 'fight against undue producer-domination' and combat misleading advertising. His point echoed CA's belief that the market could be made to work for consumers, provided their voice had equal power to producers, retailers and advertisers. Moreover, 'if the consumer is given a fair deal against the producer', then 'he can be left to express his choices freely through the price-mechanism'. This had 'the overwhelming merit of reflecting the libertarian judgments that... individuals should have what they want, and that they themselves are the best judges of what they want'.[64]

For all that Crosland and Young's concerns were co-terminus around the classless, lifestyle politics afforded by higher income elasticity of personal liberty, education and consumer choice that Young outlined in *Chipped White Cups*, there were differences. Crosland certainly concurred that 'a left-wing party should always be in the van of consumer radicalism' and agreed that Labour wasn't at present, but was uneasy about Young's tendency to develop a consumer politics outside Labour through the 1960s and thought his touted consumer party 'amusing'. And whilst, like Young, his attention was turned towards newer forms of pressure group participatory politics, Crosland was warier and remained more party-centred. Crosland championed voluntary movements in the early 1960s, as a counterpoint to those in awe of the power of commerce and advertising. In the 'sensational growth' of the CA, Civic Trust, Advertising Inquiry Council, Viewers' and Listeners' Association, *Good Food Guide*, Noise Abatement Society – he detected the potential that 'sustained voluntary effort (though it is sometimes a slogging uphill task) *can* overcome producer or bureaucratic interests, and often public indifference as well'. He suspected this was 'a major breakthrough' and that 'voluntary civic activity' in 1960s Britain would 'transform for the better our whole physical and cultural environment – towns, countryside, housing, schools, television programmes, shops and restaurants, as well as material consumer goods'.[65]

'Participation' – an issue for immigrants, workers, students, women, nationalists, viewers, consumers in the 1960s – was a concern for Labour. As a prospect it receded for Crosland, because of the radicalism of '1968', though also because he was a senior government minister and saw operations from the inside from 1964. By the 1970s he feared 'the stability of democratic society and the possibility of peaceful reform seem more and more threatened by angry workers, students, squatters and even middle-class amenity groups'. After Labour's 1970 election defeat, Crosland pondered whether Labour ought to 'argue trendily for some fashionable version of the "new politics"?' of the sort Young was touting, but affirmed he believed 'profoundly in a non-violent parliamentary system, even an imperfect one like ours'. Here, he was airing some of the liberal unease that would become widespread, that pressure groups or identity politics might corrode democratic through voluble rather than critical debate.[66]

The Co-op itself was largely excluded from *The Future of Socialism* by reason of Crosland's ongoing authorship of the CIC report, bar a few allusions such as to how the Swedish Co-ops were more 'venturesome' than the British movement.[67] But historians have paid little attention to the overlap between the projects. Notably, the CIC helped forge and clarify recurring themes in of Crosland's thinking, not least that democratic society need not have notably high levels of political participation, measured by conventional public sphere-service type registers. For the CIC this was a means to marry the traditions of internal democracy but low levels of voting and participation by Co-operators with their emphasis on more professional management and efficient selling techniques. But it became a leitmotiv of Crosland's broader political outlook. Such thinking marked Crosland apart from mainstream labour movement thinking, that sought to tackle not accommodate what it tended to regard as apathy. It also sprang from Crosland's desire to liven socialism up against its more moralist practitioners and strictures and to relax its insistence on public sphere service, by recognizing that it was 'nonsense to say people can't be perfectly happy on sex, gin and Bogart – and if that is what they want under soc[ialism], well and good'.[68]

The CIC's discussion of 'first principles' coincided with Crosland's concluding work on *The Future of Socialism*. In a discussion from February 1956 Crosland noted that 'we do not want the entire population to "participate" or feel responsible for all the world's ills or fuss around in an interfering manner constantly attending meetings. An evening, for the ordinary citizen, is something which should be spent at home or with friends, private and quietly drinking. An active minority of 3% is quite sufficient. Let the rest of us cultivate our gardens'. In the CIC report this was deployed as an explanation for why Co-op activism was so low (3% was approximately the proportion voting in Co-op board elections) – that only 'a small minority of the community... will ever wish to devote their evenings to voluntary public work', since 'most people wish to attend to their families and cultivate their gardens'.[69]

It was a principle Crosland developed in general political discussion. In *The Future of Socialism* he contended, 'we surely do not want a world in which everyone is fussing around in an interfering and responsible manner and no one peacefully cultivating his garden... If one believes in socialism not on paternalistic grounds, but as a means of increasing personal freedom and the range of choice, one does not necessarily want a busy, bustling society in which everyone is politically active and spends his evening in group discussions and feels responsible for all the burdens of the world'. The point was shared by revisionists who valued less public community-citizenship activities or state-sanctioned redistribution as the route to liberty than individual freedom, private choice and autonomy. Gaitskell remarked in 1956 how he was 'impatient with those who think that everybody must continually be taking an active part in politics or community affairs! The vast majority find their happiness in their family or personal relations, and why on earth shouldn't they?' In this respect revisionists were at odds with the Co-op's proximity to 'traditional' working-class culture, but also with Young's (in his Institute of Community Studies persona) foregrounding of family and kinship in public policy.[70]

Crosland's understanding of participation was informed by his experience with the Co-op and CA, which had similar levels of 'really active' involvement, and as models of consumer and pressure politics. In a talk delivered immediately after the Heath government had done away with the Consumer Council in 1970, Crosland revived and developed his point. He cautioned the left against uncritical celebration of a flourishing 1968-style advocacy of popular participation. Warily and wearily reflecting a more politicized civil society in the later 1960s, he suggested the prospect of 'a busy, bustling society in which everyone is politically active' was doing Labour few favours since 'the majority prefer to lead a full family life and cultivate their gardens. And a good thing too...' Feminists, Marxists and student activists were his target here, but not political or civic participation *per se*. His point was rather that the private sphere and individual action (here he cited Bertrand Russell) ought 'not to be regarded as ethically inferior to that of social duty'. Moreover, it was idealistic to hope to supplant indirect participation through elected representatives with some Athenian ideal of mass participation in decision-making via local forums or mass meetings. It was unrealistic 'in a society as large and complex as ours' and because the left had both Conservatives and 'public attitudes to contend with'. Crosland's evidence of the latter was not gardening, but that there had been 'so little public protest' over the dismantling of the Consumer Council. Nonetheless, appropriate voluntary pressure groups – he referenced CA, Shelter, the Child Poverty Action Group, Campaign for the Protection of Rural England, Civic Trust and World Wildlife Fund – still impressed

Crosland. These existed 'to exert pressure from the outside, rather than to participate from the inside' and were, Crosland held, a 'countervailing power' on the state and business. He held that Ralph Nader's activities in the US consumer movement were 'less trivial' than the feminists who attacked the Miss World pageant in London in 1970. Some, like conservation groups, were elitist in aim and middle class in composition. So without suggesting such movements transcended class differences or negated a role for the state or indiscriminate support for them, Crosland argued 'on balance' the left should seek to 'extend and strengthen their activities'. He added the proviso that it 'must seek ways of involving the majority in what is so far largely a minority movement' – for which Crosland looked to (Young's latest brain-wave) the Association of Neighbourhood Councils.[71] In short (by analogy with the CA's take on prosperity), whilst more participation could be good, this did not mean less was necessarily bad or dangerous to democracy.

Crosland returned to the fate of the Co-op in 1971, addressing the Co-op Party's annual conference. Explaining that whatever his American wife's tastes, he retained an 'emotional commitment' to the Co-op, he welcomed the integration of the retail side and CWS, which had seen the latter buying *for* societies (as the CIC advocated) and 1968's 'Operation Facelift' which had introduced a national advertising strategy and new blue and white insignia. He applauded the Co-op Union regional plan for amal-gamations, (now Lord) Jacques' idea of a national society and the perfor-mance of the Nottingham Society, the Insurance Society and Bank. But all this was tempered by the continuing downward trends in market share and capital position. Yet Crosland was confident the Co-op had more to it than simply competing with Marks & Spencer and with a characteristic nod to Sweden and reprising a nostrum of the CIC report, asserted, 'there is no contradiction between a socially-involved, campaigning consumer move-ment and a high level of efficiency'. To this end he outlined expanded roles for the Co-op College and for housing and development partnerships with Trade Unions and the private sector. Above all, consumer representation agitated him. The CA was too middle class, but equally he held 'the agencies which claim to represent the working class have not yet found the right formula to mobilize and express working class needs and opinions'. And with the 'mean and petty murder' of the Consumer Council in 1970, Crosland sensed an opportunity, since 'the Tories have deserted the field; we must occupy it' Crosland explained he was 'a firm believer in competition', but reprising his criticisms of Heath's axing of the Consumer Council, felt this further stacked the market against the consumer and lead him to share US consumer campaigner Nader's anxieties that the economy was too dominated by 'semi-monopolistic giants which are often immune from the full rigours of competition'. So, opposition to monopoly, prices and incomes policies, CA-style advice centres, legal protection and educating consumers were grounds for the Co-op to tend.

In this role as a critical and consumerist friend, Crosland wound up by arguing the Co-op had the right to expect help from Labour, but had to demonstrate its viability 'and this it has not shown unambiguously in the last ten years'.[72] Co-operators might have felt this was rich, given how fraught relations were with the Wilson government. Some affinities were apparent. Government support, via a MinTech innovation grant, had helped create a computerized CWS warehouse in Durham, that bought for retail societies. Though by 1971 many in the CWS scheme felt this was driving costs up, not down and wanted to regain their autonomy.[73] But divisions were more apparent – over Labour-Co-op Party relations and the *Sunday Citizen* and most fractiously the Selective Employment Tax (SET), introduced in the 1966 budget. An attempt to shift the tax burden from manufacturing (to stimulate exports) to distribution and retailing, the tax might be read as simultaneously a tribute to the growth of the consumer sector and evidence of the continuing priority afforded to production in Labour thinking. Its burden fell heavily on the Co-op by a series of anomalies, for instance that there was relief if coffins were made separately from a funeral business, but not if done by the same company – and because the Co-op was not subject to exemptions like Universities, the Post Office and nationalized industries as a service provider (a role it claimed to play, particularly in remote, rural communities). Doubled in 1968, by 1969 SET payments absorbed half the net profit of consumer co-ops, further straining its capital reserves and, so it told the government, being passed on in price rises such that 'its impact is unfair on poorer consumers'.[74]

Other Co-op criticisms were that it failed to distinguish between luxury and necessity goods and that it showed a disregard for a retail sector that was more efficient than strike-prone manufacturers. The Co-op campaigned for the tax to be applied equally to the self-employed and exemptions extended to disabled, part-time and elderly workers (which the Co-op employed more than the private sector) and for it to be truly selective and ring-fenced to benefit only export manufacturers. On its introduction Sittingbourne Co-op described SET as 'a vicious stab in the back'. By 1969 the Co-op Party felt that what it described as 'political spite' and 'cynical abandonment' (the assumption that Co-operators would support Labour come what may), but also the ineffectualness of Co-op MPs in negotiations with the government, had the effect of 'questioning the whole basis of our being in politics and in particular the value of our relationship with Labour'.[75]

In meetings of Co-op Union officials and MPs with the Prime Minister and Chancellor in 1966 and 1969, the government held that SET was the fairest way of raising revenue for other social reforms. And evidence of the Co-op's faltering modernization was adduced in these meetings and weighed against it. The Prime Minister's briefing for the 1969 meeting noted the Co-op's social as well as commercial aims, but also its 'stuffy and old-fashioned image' and 'reluctance... to adapt itself to modern conditions'. This came just a year after 'Operation Facelift' had sought to reno-vate the Co-op with a new logo and stamp scheme. In 1966 the CWS man-agement and directors were replaced by professional executives and a part-time board elected by retail societies – bifurcating management and democratic control as the CIC proposed. But by 1971 several senior figures had resigned, including Keith Willoughby who introduced the new logo (and joined Woolworth's) as the trading position continued to decline.[76]

Conclusions: the limits of consumer politics?

The Co-op's resilient culture discloses much to historians about its fortunes. In 2000 another report critiqued the trading performance, directors and 'old fashioned image of grocery stores' of the Co-op. Chaired by TUC gen-eral secretary Alan Monks and with Alan Donnelly, former Labour leader in the European Parliament as secretary, the Commission's evidence and con-clusions were distinctly reminiscent.[77] Equally, its enduring ethical appeal as an alternative to capitalism, has revived its commercial and political fortunes since the 1990s in green, fair trade and anti-capitalist agendas. The Co-op still operates more shops than any other UK retailer.

That, as this suggests, the cultural resistance to the CIC was enduring and embedded does not necessarily confound Gurney's case that this period 'witnessed the effective marginalization of the one significant consumer movement Britain ever had' so much as offer alternative explanations for it.[78] That consumer politics were dynamic and influential was apparent in Young and Crosland. And CA's footprints were multifarious – in opinion research and satire, to the idea that all could be ranked or commodified, at once subversive of established hierarchies and enabling of consumer rights, popular choice and bolstering market philosophies. Much as a model for pressure group politics, CA were archetypal post-materialists: they valued knowledge more than wealth, were frustrated with and by existing (parti-cularly party) political structures and deployed professional skills to remedy this. The Co-op undoubtedly no longer set the agenda of consumer pol-itics, as certainly as the CA was more centrally involved in *Redefining British Politics* via the private, public and political meanings and boundaries of consumerism and indeed of politics itself.

But CA did not do so entirely to its own design or irrespective of its audience. The limited participation and differing agendas of its own mem-bers, not to mention those beyond its reach did not determine, but con-strained its influence. The rapid assimilation of its discourse by the main parties and in legislation was a tribute to its success, if also to the ability of party to refurbish themselves and of Hilton's case that its politics posed scarce alternatives to dominant market models. Turner Morris's conclusions about CU were as apt for CA: 'the social reformers... hoped for a mass move-ment; they got a class movement'.[79] The Co-op too remained class-bound

– and so, it is hard to avoid concluding, was consumerism. Yet this was as likely the limits of consumer politics as articulated by the CA and Co-op as limited popular demand. Just as CA could not invent its audience or shape consumers in its own image, nor did it simply reflect or translate some essential socio-economic characteristics underpinning consumerism. It read and conveyed affluence in critical, even austere terms, prioritizing use over pleasure and this limited its purchase on it. A post-materialist context did not mean a post-material politics would emerge or capture mass popular support. And in the Co-op too we can also see that the ways an organization construed change – mediated strongly in its case by inherited culture, customary assumptions and a resistance to change – *did* to a large extent fashion its fortunes. Consumer politics emerged rather as a mixed bag of organizational culture and popular interests and thwarted potential.

4
'The largest voluntary political youth movement in the world': The Lifestyle and Identity of Young Conservatism

As a social institution organized under party auspices, the Young Conservatives (YC) intersect political and social change, like other core samples in *Redefining British Politics*. Making a virtue of its apolitical reputation to recruit a mass, if mainly middle-class membership, the YCs deployed a rhetoric of service and citizenship to embed themselves in local civil society through the 1950s. Its low key, light-hearted and associational appeal attests to the persistence of strands identified by historians of inter-war Conservative political culture – deftly avoiding the appearance of being political or partisan in much other than name. If this amounted to evidence of a relatively unpolitical culture, it was also testimony to party's ability to negotiate this. After *The Macleod Report* (1965) into the YC's falling membership, debate ensued about the impact of social change on YC fortunes, whether the ratio of social to political activities needed adjusting and whether a smaller membership of greater political quality was preferable. The 'politicization' of YC activity initiated by *Macleod* was not uncontested, but provides a means of tracing shifts in the texture and parameters of not only YC and Conservative, but the wider political culture.

Despite the legitimacy of its sonorous claim to be 'the largest voluntary political youth movement in the world' (sometimes adding for good Cold War measure, 'the free world'), the YCs were the subject of much ridicule through the 1960s.[1] Whilst popularly disregarded as a 'middle-class marriage bureau', BBC TV's *That was the week that was* satirized the YCs as puppets of the party leaders. Most (in)famous was the YCs role in Tony Hancock's *The Blood Donor,* broadcast on BBC TV in 1961. Hancock craved: 'To do one unselfish act, with no thought of profit or gain... something for the benefit of the country as a whole. What should it be...? Become a blood donor or join the Young Conservatives. But as I'm not looking for a wife and I cannot play table tennis, here I am'. *Impact*, the YC national journal (1964–69) felt this 'was all very funny', but 'the tragedy remains that this is the way in which most people think of the Young Conservatives'. It vowed to 'give the lie to this dancing puppet image and get around... to representing the vigorous and progressive youth of our generation', but by 1967 found the 'unhappy truth is that we can still be effectively satirized as an effete social club catering only for political lightweights'.[2]

Historians have been as dismissive. The YC's chiefly social dimension placed it outside the métier of political historians and orthodox definitions of 'the political'. Its social character has not been as alluring to policy- and election-minded historians as it was to aspiring politicians and partner-seeking middle classes at the time. Equally, studies of youth culture have focused on cutting-edge sub-cultures or youth 'problems', rather than the less remarkable lifestyle of YCs. That the YCs have fallen between the pre-occupations of both social and political history explains their absence from recent synoptic studies of this period.[3] This has rendered it something of a sub-culture (notwithstanding its conformism) and the YCs, this chapter seeks to show, can redraw the history of youth as much as the norms of political history. Tempting as it is to ascribe the YC's neglect in historical accounts to it being simply *social*, this would be to ignore the varied opinion behind its pliant public face that Catherine Ellis has identified in its 1960s policy groups.[4] Equally, to dismiss the YCs as *simply* social is to ignore the purpose and effect of this dimension. YC's values, social life and practices disclose as much to historians as formal political pronouncements and are just as imperative to deducing the public perception and internal culture of the YCs. The YCs thus both enable and demand a cultural history of politics, one that includes but moves beyond conventional 'political' categories alone and locates it in a broader set of meanings, activities and contexts.

Despite the neglect of the YCs, the question of youth was rarely absent from politicians' minds, since around 7% of the electorate at each general election was made up of new young voters. And interest was accentuated in this period by anxieties over 'youth culture' and the voting age reduction to 18 in 1969. Peaking in 1949 at 160,000 members, although with unofficial estimates as high as 600,000, the YCs were very much part of Conservatism's public image.[5] The YCs hint that in the 1950s, when their social presence was most salient, that this image was more youthful than the Edwardian stereotype attached to Macmillan. The YCs demise from their 1950s heyday contributed to the ageing of the Conservative Party. By the 1990s it had a reputation 'as essentially a retired person's club' – dubbed by one historian a 'gerontocratic rump'.[6]

If sometimes joked about in the 1960s, the YCs were a dynamic presence in the 1950s. In 1955 opponents estimated that 'more young men and women under 30 voted Tory and worked actively for the Tories this time than in any election since the war'. The YCs were launched late in 1944 and were a key part of the organizational review after the 1945 defeat. They were not only a revival of successful inter-war predecessors like the Junior Imperial League, but in a long Conservative tradition of social organizations that built electoral support. Pugh describes the Victorian Primrose League, as a 'genuinely popular organization', whose role in the 'political socialization' of voters came by 'embedding the Conservative cause into the routine social life of many communities' via a 'vast array of social activities', lending it a 'degree of immunity from the vagaries of political issues and policies'.[7] The same might be said – although Pugh does not – of the YCs. Their associational culture and social reputation was its key as a political resource. It recruited effectively by offering a mode of political affiliation for the un-political, in what such success hints was a relatively apolitical culture. The YCs not only forged party political identities, but also the partly political identity of young, middle-class voters.

Despite decline from their membership peak in the late 1940s, the YCs retained a significant competitive advantage. By 1965, one-third smaller than at its peak, it had double the number of Labour Party Young Socialist (YS) branches and each branch (averaging 80 members) had double the members. Nevertheless the YCs' influence cannot be read just from the quantity of its members. The world of YCs explored here was succeeded by a smaller, ideologically-motivated youth cadre in the 1970s and during the 1980s they were matched in size by the more transparently 'political' Conservative students. The two generations of Young Conservatism are encapsulated in the style of two internal histories: Holyroyd-Doveton's antiquarian, rose-tinted, anecdotal amble through his time in the 1950s' and 1960s' YCs and Evans' more schematic analysis of the 1970s and after, befitting of a libertarian sectary.[8] The Federation of Conservative Students that prevailed in this image of abrasive, Campaign for Nuclear Disarmament (CND)-pillorying, Greater London Council-baiting Conservatism (the YCs, which survived until 1998, remained more 'wet', and although more sectarian than in the 1950s and 1960s, still hard partying) was disbanded in 1986. In Jo-Anne Nadler's witty recall, the comparatively few women in it were 'more likely to pay homage to Hayek than dance around their handbags'. Nadler's Wimbledon YCs were more sedate: a 'throwback to the social clubs of the 1950s... hardly political at all and definitely not ideological – rather what the Tory party itself had been before the advent of Thatcherism'.[9]

Ewen Green has challenged this notion that Conservatism was not best understood ideologically before Thatcherism, anxious that historians should not uncritically replicate the assumed rupture – and rather reading this as a characteristic Conservative conception of politics. Green accepted that, as Michael Oakeshott argued, Conservatives thought they had 'not a creed or a doctrine, but a disposition', but argued this was nonetheless 'indicative of a particular view of the world, in which being "non-ideological", "atheoretical", or even "apolitical" were intrinsic parts of adhering to Conservatism'. Mckibbin holds that 'a "non-political" discourse to which people could retreat' pervaded inter-war society, but was chiefly of Conservative benefit. As Leon Epstein suggested in 1954, that Tories were 'said to reject rationalistic and *a priori* doctrine', were 'tireless in disclaiming the type of ideological prepossession considered the curse of socialism' and prized those 'values regarded as "given"' in British politics, constituted a set of political positions worth investigating. This de-politicizing urge – Daniel Bell's 'the end of ideology' would have been an apt slogan for YCs – was political. Conservative historians have, likewise, tended to obscure or neglect ideology and explain Conservative appeal by its lack of apparent ideology, whereas (symptomatically) Labour historians have often craved it and explained the shortcomings of 'labourism' by the same absence of ideology. The YCs hardly confound this sense that Conservatives were less ostensibly or conventionally political. They were more able to 'informally capitalize', Harrison judges, on routines of national, local and family life or were more at one with civil society, which they aimed to preserve as a sphere independent of what they regarded as undue politicization. This suggests that whilst civil society was not politically neutral, its persuasion was not pre-determined.[10]

Since YCs were apt to regard their politics as an instinctive mode of living and thinking, tilling their social terrain is essential to understand the political, as much as social meaning of the YCs. Such an approach avoids a propensity in political history to privilege certain sources and a received set of parameters defining 'the political'. As suggested elsewhere, one model for this is Raphael Samuel's evocation of the 'Lost World of British Communism'. This articulated a sense of political belonging and consciousness that, whilst not unrelated to social being (class, gender), was far from determined by it.[11] Samuel's approach might seem to have little application, since by contrast with British Communists the notoriously sociable YCs revelled in an apolitical style. But Samuel offered a method of examining the politically-affiliated, from ideology to the rituals of branch meetings and how such identities inflected their everyday behaviour and private and public outlooks that is eminently useable for historians investigating the world the YCs inhabited. Samuel's approach drew on deliberately diverse sources: novels, family life and the detritus of political life, besides political historians' regular fare. And it used traditional sources – policy, leaders and elections – in novel ways to explore the cultural history and symbolic meanings of politics and the mentalities of participants. Collapsing boundaries between political and cultural history enables the very category of 'the political' to be interrogated. Moreover, this approach attends to criticisms of Conservative historiography that maintain it has focused too readily on national leadership, institutions, on 'high' politics – in short, an orthodox, 'given' conception of 'politics'.[12] Even more innovative recent works centre on party elites[13] and histories of popular Conservatism have scarcely mentioned the YCs.[14]

Socializing politics

The YCs offered 'organized gregariousness for the children of the middle class', as sociologists Philip Abrams and Alan Little saw it. They tapped into 'the culture of the suburbs' and their politics were as semi-detached. Their motivations confound more than conform to some materialist/post-materialist axis, but err towards the latter in that they were chiefly associational. Angela Povey, a receptionist, regular council candidate, and Birmingham YC Vice-Chair by 1969 explained: 'a number of young people join tennis clubs – I joined the Young Conservatives'.[15] The style in local YC publications was light and carefree, affecting an everyday sociability. Jennifer Titchmarsh, a secretary, was profiled in Birmingham YCs' *Looking Right* as 'Ginny Jen' whose likes were 'chips with everything (including boys)' and 'boys with everything'. Branch reports related canvassing escapades, excess at social events and occasional 'all night drinking, smoking and telling dirty stories with those nasty YC boys'. This style was further cultivated in light-hearted titles for when discussion did turn to politics proper (with a certain politics secreted in the wit). Templedown YCs debated whether 'Peking is the chink in the iron curtain' in 1961; the Filey holiday weekend 1958 promised YCs not 'immature political theorists' but 'politics with a smile' and debated the motion that 'a greater contribution has been made by Marks and Spencer than by Marx and Spencer'?[16] The philosophy espoused by *Buff Orpington*, 'life is a funny proposition, but why worry? Join the YCs and be assured of a happy evening', neatly echoed Oakeshott's view that to be Conservative was to prefer 'present laughter to utopian bliss'.[17]

On rare occasions when YCs did outline a worldview, they professed 'a duty to God, the queen, my country', but that beyond this, 'the philosophy underlying a political party often is hidden'. YC style – casual, self-confident, banal even – set them apart from a left that was, whatever else, rarely indulgent of matters it perceived as trivial. For the more policy-minded, there was the Bow Group, but Conservatives were more apt to think of themselves, as Viscount Hailsham (Quintin Hogg) paraphrased Oakeshott in 1959, as practicing 'not so much a philosophy... as an attitude'. This was, Crick observed in 1962, a longstanding Conservative disposition – the type who could be rather cynical about ideas and experts, preferring appeals to experience and loyalty and 'who claims to be above politics'.[18] Peter Walker, YC National Chairman 1958–60 and President of the YC National Advisory Committee in 1968, personified this. According to a fellow MP in 1967, Walker was 'the archetypal YC... successful, energetic, confident' and 'aggressively non-intellectual'. In the 1980s as a prominent 'wet' in Thatcher's government, he readily brandished Macmillan's phrase 'let sleeping dogmas lie'.[19]

'Young Conservatism is built on themes of leadership, responsibility and service', Abrams and Little reckoned 'and not on issues of policy' – 'most members remain almost a-political', but embodied and identified with a 'compact of feeling for the nation... the established order... not the politics of party conflict'. *Looking Right* outlined in 1959 how the YCs provided 'entertainment and friends', the 'chance of becoming knowledgeable in the nation's problems' and to 'play a useful part in the life of the city'. Jennings noted how in YC quizzes on matters ranging from the Empire to litter bins in local parks, any 'obvious propaganda of the games is dropped'. But their importance was to associate the Conservative Party with 'loyal, patriotic, nationalist and imperialist sentiment' and, as crucially, 'with fun and games'. In both the (junior) Young Britons and YCs, Jennings found, there was 'no emphasis on party policies'. If there was more to life than politics, there was also more to politics than party. YCs contrived to wear their politics lightly, exaggerated by their lack of formal political responsibility and a deferential sense that they should be seen but not heard.[20]

In this vein, YC language avoided the conflictual terminologies of opponents. Courses at the party's Swinton College encouraged YC leaders to recruit 'all types, age groups, occupations – for want of a better word – classes'. As a commentator in the YCs national paper (1954–58) *Rightway* saw it: 'this word, short and bitter, never mentioned in front of the children and whispered only among close friends, has become a secret disease... the offender? Class'. Politics was ideally a rather discrete sphere and discreet business – on this YCs and later Thatcherite Conservatives, who urged student politics resist broader political agendas, were at one – much as Geoffrey Beaman, a Conservative trade unionist and YC advisory committee member explained in 1955, that the state should leave trade unions to bargain collectively and trade unions should stay out of politics.[21] Swinton principal, Reginald Northam, told students that 'conservatism is not a dogma but a way of life. Conservatives should show how hard they are prepared to fight for their values by the way they demonstrate them in private life. Politics should be a personal challenge and a crusade', although Eldon Griffiths MP, clarified in 1966 that 'this does not mean parading like some latterday CND'. CND were YC's chief competitor in youth politics in the late 1950s (as in the 1980s) with a social and political appeal and large middle-class membership, if the antithesis of the YC's demure style.[22]

Rather, YCs stressed a service ethic and how 'youth and dignity are not incompatible', exemplified by (future MP and Europhile) Geoffrey Rippon, who became Mayor of Surbiton at the age of 26. The most obvious way in which YCs socialized and converted private into public practice was through family values. Nadler recalls her YC mother was 'a typical Conservative' since she 'did not consider herself especially political'. Nadler took her parents 'seldom stated politics as a way of life', and amongst 'the political messages implicit in her upbringing' was that Labour meant 'Politics with a capital P'. The YCs were family and home-centred: two-thirds of Birmingham YCs lived with their parents in 1969. Amongst these was Stella Knight, who was 'a YC as much by heredity as by conviction', since her parents had met in the Junior Imperial league.[23]

In the YC family, schisms were to be avoided, especially if antagonized by personal ambition. In David Walder's fictional account of Conservative branch life, when one prospective candidate, Inglis questioned a rival, 'the YCs turned and looked at Inglis as one who had asked a hostile question', frowning disapproval. YC leaders were 'encouraged to cultivate authority', and in turn to display loyalty to party leaders. This disposition towards figures at the top nurtured the YC's docility. This was manifest in YCs' reverence for elders and tendency to act as if 'embryonic elder statesman' by 'affecting mannerisms such as the cleaning of... glasses, the deliberate cough, and the "umming" and "ahing" that he imagines are part of politics'. It entailed the prospect, so one YC modernizer in the 1960s depicted, of encountering a 'succession of little Quintin Hoggs, little Mr. Marples, and even little Sir Edward Boyles' at YC rallies, and was 'useless as far as any original thinking is concerned'.[24]

Ellis found that when YCs thought in the Policy Groups set up by Rab Butler in 1960, they thought much like their elders. Some post-material interest in leisure issues was detectable. On welfare and the individual in society, they accepted state involvement if the agencies of civil society were ineffective. This hints that on social matters and in their conception of civil society many YCs were less wary of the state than in favour of the market (as Chapter 5 further suggests of Conservatism). It was also significant as Green argues this preference for an organic civil society, rather than one politicized by state involvement, linked libertarian and paternalist Conservatisms (as much as Thatcherism's market penchants strained civil society to breaking-point). It was most significant in that civil society was the focus for the YCs' practical activities both before and after its 1965 'politicization', and paradoxically suggesting it recognized and fed the 'politicization' of this realm.[25]

YC's diaries were crammed with dances, fêtes, factory visits, tennis, yard of ale contests or beach parties, as much as any more ostensibly political occasions. The Ball was the highlight, invariably graced by an MP, dignitary or aristocratic sponsor and providing the prized opportunity in 'middle-class circles of mingling with the upper crust of local society'. Sub-committees attended to the tiniest detail, like East Midlands YCs' insistence that the raffle should be drawn 'out of the ballroom in order not to interrupt the dancing'. Its 1963 summer fête, held at Swithland Hall by courtesy of the Earl of Lanesborough, had 50 special constables, the St. John's Ambulance in attendance, and signposting by the Royal Automobile Club (RAC). Advertising was taken in the *Sunday Express* and *Sun* for South Buckinghamshire's 1966 Ball at London Airport. Large attendances were needed to break even: in 1967, Preston needed 850 attendees to cover the hire of the Top Rank Ballroom (who loaned its 'bunny girls' to run the Tombola), and succeeded in attracting 1300.[26] Elaborate planning was lavished on table tennis tournaments as much as Balls, all integral to the YCs' appeal. As Holyroyd-Doveton recalls, the YCs 'provided a complete social life'. A 1956 South Kensington survey found 83% of members joined for social reasons. The glamour and scale of these events made them fixtures in the local season, just as it led opponents to feel 'the YCs are a bally-hoo social group bent upon enjoying themselves at parties'.[27]

If not in the Conservative Club, YCs assembled in local hotels or pubs, being less inhibited by drink than the Left. At its outset in the 1940s, it offered social opportunities that were, so Abrams and Little have it, 'difficult to find elsewhere' in the suburbs. Its pitch was different to rougher urban working-class clubs or dowdy church halls, although there was some overlap with the latter. For instance, the Honorary Treasurer of the Central Council of Birmingham YCs in the 1960s, Kenneth Johnson, had also been chair of the Methodist Association of Youth Clubs. Nor were all events glamorous. Beetle drives were a YC staple: nothing to do with pop music or cars, but a dice game in which competitors drew sections of the insect. Others recalled that the YC's appeal was that compared with church groups, scouts and Round Table, it was gender-mixed and had no uniform. What the YCs practiced and offered was a togetherness and sense of social belonging. 'I was on my own', 'most of the people I liked seemed to belong', 'I joined for the tennis' were among reasons given to Abrams and Little in 1965. If the YCs ingratiated themselves with local civil society and received unofficial support from local business, hotels, Rotary Clubs, the Women's Institute or Young Farmers in rural areas, they were also a vehicle for assimilation into the national culture. Nadler tells how her father, a Jewish-Polish émigré, found at the Kensington YCs Christmas dance in 1949 that 'standing there amid the music and the chatter he did not feel like an alien'.[28]

One could 'live' within the YCs, although not in the same sense as the Co-op's network of organizations and this was a more outgoing, less self-referential world than many political groups. By 1965, Colchester YCs ran their own club, three hockey, two table tennis and football, tennis and bridge teams, organized its own holidays to Majorca and – confounding the usual merger of business and pleasure – a 'purely political' Blue Group. There was indeed no uniform, but as Elizabeth Wilson recalled, by the late 1960s dress was a means of distinguishing YCs – particularly the male garb of 'cavalry twills and paisley cravats', by turns modern and traditional – from other activists. And a corporate style could be acquired in the form of YC scarves, blazer badges, ties (with regional variations), car badges, key fobs and windscreen slips.[29]

YCs were also avid motorists, forever participating in rallies and treasure hunts. Publications were peppered with details of how to soup-up a pre-war

Austin; reports on the Monte Carlo rally, by 1953 runner-up, Ian Apple-
yard; and celebrations of queues at the British Motor Show, contrasted to
those during rationing.[30] In the car, Conservatives saw a rising standard of
living and sense of freedom and were more likely than Labour activists
to own one. No campaign was easier to rally the more politicized post-
Macleod YCs than Peter Walker's 'Kill the Transport Bill' in 1968. The
National Advisory Committee discussed offering preferential motor insurance terms to YCs. Cars were also a resource for mobilizing the electorate.
In Bristol in 1964, for example, the cars owned by YCs were identified as a
factor in holding the city's North West seat.[31]

Birmingham YCs boasted the only RAC-affiliated political motor club in
Britain, formed in 1954 and based at an Edgbaston hotel. By all accounts
the Club was purely social. Although it was also an effective vehicle for YC
membership since, as car buff and later Lord Mayor of Birmingham (and
son of a prominent local Conservative), Peter Barwell, found, one had to be
a YC to join. Fun was the watchword, but the Club also served as a 'flying
squad' at elections, ferrying voters and candidates around. Rallies were
organized with typical precision: with marshals, RAC listings and its own
magazine, *The Innovator*. The RAC affiliation was necessary to use and sign-
post public roads and another instance of how social activity embedded the
YCs with organizations in civil society.[32]

Birmingham was notable in this regard. *Looking Right* carried up to
80 adverts in its 58 pages, which was witness to its affinities with local
businesses, like the senior party. A glossy, professional production, it
had impressed Harold Macmillan. Other components of Birmingham's YC
culture included a drama group, the Chamberlain Players, a Guy Fawkes
bonfire party, the first of its kind in post-war Birmingham, and a YC investment club. Aided by the Wider Share Ownership Council and a local stockbroker, this aimed to invest for YCs, their friends and parents.[33]

As *Impact* irreverently observed in 1965, there were many 'constituencies
where the executive and branch committees read like an imperial general
staff's veterans parade'. Demobbed officers helped the YCs advance at its
outset. As with other areas of YC life, recruiting was undertaken with a military precision that belied the YCs easy-going manner. Courses at Swinton,
which were attended by as many as 3000 YCs annually, detailed how, since
'the personal touch is the only effective way' to recruit it was advisable to
meet potential recruits before meetings 'as many young people are shy'.
Emphasis was placed on recruiting a 'cross-section' of the local community
and to this end, besides attending Church on Sundays, a strategy of 'raid-
ing other organisations' – tennis clubs, youth groups, amateur dramatic
societies – was recommended. The process – as a 1956 cartoon, 'Sally joins
the YCs', in *Rightway* imagined – was one of low-key political education
and socialization, reminiscent of Conservative approaches to new women
voters in the 1920s. Shy Sally's reluctance to talk politics was overcome by

convivial male YC officers over table tennis, until she became an effective debater and canvasser.[34] Thereafter, as the National Vice-Chair, Marcus Fox, told a 1958 leadership course, the perennial problem was how to make politics interesting and role-plays at Swinton included devising methods to raise the political quota in socially-minded branches.[35]

The social side of YC life was integral to a well-drilled political machine. The rigmarole of planning a dance or jumble sale provided vital training in skills of lasting political use. As Layton-Henry noted, the 'sacrifice of leisure time' for YC activities was 'part of a recognized apprenticeship' on the political ladder. And the YCs were the training ground for 11 members of the Macmillan and Home governments, upwards of 600 local councillors by 1968 and some 90 MPs (all male) by 1970.[36]

Gender and class

In 1967 David Walder MP saw YCs as the 'essence of the middle middle class', in both 'mini-skirted giggly branches and more senior waist-coated branches with over-age chairman'. YCs were resolutely middle class – in Birmingham, for example, two-thirds lived in owner-occupied properties.[37] But gradations within the middle class were acutely observed by YCs: ranked by parents' jobs, property and education. In Birmingham Edgbaston YCs 'thought of themselves as the cream'. They were educated privately and living in the detached homes of directors, solicitors and medical consultants. By comparison Hall Green Primrose Young Unionists, who were the progeny of teachers, local government officers and shopkeepers, lived in semi-detached houses and were direct-grant schooled. Whatever deference there was to wealth or breeding, the YCs offered the politically-ambitious minority access to and apprenticeships with local councillors and MPs. The YCs were a tool and emblem of social mobility, a place to be seen and mix. 'For the ambitious young clerk or salesman, an entrée to his community's Conservative clubhouse', was judged by Epstein to mark a sizeable 'step on the road to well-being'. Walker found Gloucester YCs a means of establishing business and social contacts. By contrast, Abrams and Little found YS members comparatively unbothered by being 'well off', 'getting on' or even 'personal relationships'.[38]

A proto-typical YC was to be found in Colin Grant, chair of South-East Essex YCs in the mid-1960s. Grant was a retail furnishing director (and furniture was, as Alan Clark revealed, a class and status marker in Conservative mores – new money bought furniture, old money did not have to). Interviewed 'in a Rayleigh local', he confided his middling tastes: his favourite drink, a dry martini; his favourite music, Andy Williams; his favourite authors, Nevil Shute and Ian Fleming. He disliked jazz, traffic jams and Beatniks' scruffiness. With a dash of snobbery he related how having attended Rayleigh primary school his 'mother heard the new language I had learnt' and he was sent to boarding school. 'Most people believe I am only interested in making money', but he assured his interviewer that he also liked cars and found 'women very interesting'.[39]

Gender was salient in YC life, although since membership was equal – 52% were male in Birmingham's 1969 survey – few contemporaries commented on it. But this was also because the YCs both cultivated and appealed to a sexist culture – one in which they would not have been too bothered if they had recognized it as such. They inhabited a world in which a gendered division of labour was taken for granted. Sampled from 1960s' branch programmes, men comprised 88% of branch chairs and 85% of treasurers, although more than 90% of social secretaries (a vital YC role) were women.[40] A masculinist appeal was integral to 19th century Toryism and if it sat unremarkably in Conservative and YC mores, it was hardly absent elsewhere in political life. As Geoff Eley and Jonathan Green highlight and the case of Centre 42 in Chapter 6 shows, trade unionism, the radical and New Left, counter-culture and underground press in the later 1960s were notably male-dominated – indeed this was a well-spring of feminism.[41]

Impact's board discussed that they were all male in 1964 and to redress the balance opted for journalist Juliet Gardiner, who was not even a YC. Lynda Chalker chaired the Greater London YCs (GLYCs) in 1969, but all other National Chairs were men. At the 'Action '67' rally in the Festival Hall one regional organizer, Elizabeth Steele, a solicitor and later a judge, was female. The rest – an insurance broker, three chartered accountants, a management trainee, teacher, stockbroker, surveyor, engineer and cooper – were male.[42]

Misogyny was commonplace. In *Roundabout Rushcliffe* a contributor held forth on 'birdwatching', explaining his 'own particular favourite' was 'the YC bird, conservative by name if not by nature' and the uses of a car for such ornithology. In Lowestoft a typical YCs diary apparently ran, 'Monday-choosy-Wendy-Thursday-Heidi-Saturday-Cindy'. *Rightway* reckoned 'a prerequisite for the success of any revue is a supply of attractive young ladies', and reviewed Ilford YCs as 'well off in this particular form of talent'. Jarvis' case that the 'numerical predominance of women in the YCs was regularly exploited' is less sure-footed than his assertion that a certain 'glamour' was a large part of the YC's appeal.[43]

The YC world was attentive to women, but via a male gaze. As Campbell argues, women's presence in the party was organized around patriarchal norms of 'the acceptable face of femininity' in society. Conservative policy addressed women voters in a range of identities, but in internal party culture they were, by-and-large, powerless. Their local contributions received gallant thanks, but were taken for granted. This was a state of responsibility without power – a status shared with the YCs, who nevertheless reproduced their parent party's gendered culture. For Birmingham YC Vice Chair

Angela Povey, political education was 'all very well for the male members of the branch, the ladies need time to absorb and digest', but that YC women internalized these attitudes grated with Gardiner. 'The little woman in the sweet pea hat' who tittered 'oh me, I'm just not political' was dealing a 'death blow' to 'our equality' she argued. Citing 'considerable discrimination against women at candidate selection meetings', Gardiner believed women could be their 'own worst enemies'.[44]

Yet, a *Times* profile in 1964 argued that the YCs had a definite, enduring appeal to women. Future MP Julian Critchley's mother considered the YCs 'to contain much the nicest class of girl' compared with other political parties in Hampstead. Critchley recalls 'much titillation, little consummation', tennis, a little canvassing and 'gentle political indoctrination'. Paralleling the experience of many Conservative women, he recalled 'we were not encouraged to think... it was not our pens that were wanted but our feet'. The prospect of meeting partners was part of the YC's appeal. A West Midlands YC was also a member of Labour, Co-op and Church groups, but the YCs had cars and girls and 'girls were the attraction rather than politics at that time'. He duly met his wife at the YCs. This was a world 'couched in the language of rugby club bars', in which the 'fair hair and blue eyes' of girls at YC dances were noted and 'women drivers' bemoaned.[45]

More morally conservative parts of the party cannot but have noticed the sexual subtext to YC life, which by the 1960s purported to be quite hedonistic. Rushcliffe YC parties were 'like sex, they cannot be described, only experienced'. Helen Seaman, a North Ealing delegate wondered in 1965, 'why is YC Conference synonymous with orgy in the eyes of all but the delegates?' The ratio of five boys to each girl at Butlins had prompted the question 'who did you get off with?' 'Gossips had to get going so that the YCs did not lose their Tony Hancock image. Everyone knows that the YCs don't play ping-pong!' Indeed – one YC infamously strip-teased in 1965. She resigned as Chesham YCs chair, but was re-elected. As controversially (if depicting what many thought), the cover of *Crossbow* that discussed the YCs in 1967 pictured a semi-clad woman with a glass of wine.[46]

Miss YC beauty contests demonstrated YC values. Adjudicators, including MPs like Keith Joseph, assessed: poise and deportment, dress-sense, beauty, charm and intelligence. Miss YC 1968, Gosforth's Karen Murphy, embraced summer-of-love themes like 'make love not war', but only, she added, explaining her support for the US in Vietnam, 'if everyone agrees'. Her case that 'fifty years of electoral equality have not put women level with men in politics' was no feminism. Rather it was 'because women find it difficult to be rational amongst administrative complexity – anyway she would much rather be ruled by a strong man than a stubborn and misguided woman!' *Looking Right*'s pin-ups of Miss Birmingham YC competitors became racier as the 1960s proceeded. Cars and women were conflated in Birmingham's

1966 contest – a 'concours d'elegance' in which the bodywork, paintwork and chassis of the competitors was whittled down to the final 'high performance models'. The car analogy was given regular outings, with car buff Barwell described as 'going into production' for his first baby, with his wife, the 1960 Miss Birmingham YC.[47]

No political party had beauty contests on the YCs scale. They could boast a Miss Great Britain, Leila Williams, originally of Wolverhampton but by 1959 of South Kensington YCs, and one of the original presenters of BBC TV's *Blue Peter* from 1958 to 1962. Williams appeared at the Royal Festival Hall YC National Rally addressed by Macmillan in 1959 alongside the reigning Miss YC to illustrate the YCs 'brains with beauty'. This was for some a career. Autumn 1957's *Rightway* front cover featured Barbara Hellaby of Asbourne YCs who was also Miss Derbyshire Young Farmer 1955–6. When the Empire games were held in Cardiff in 1958, Miss Empire Games was a YC, of whom *Rightway* saw fit to remark: 'she is not only a member, but takes an active interest in politics'.[48]

Miss YC was not uncontroversial. Some areas resisted selecting entrants for the national contest, although there were as many as 47 for Miss GLYC in 1963. Nor was Miss YC always pliable. Miss YC 1963, Margaret Fundell from Cardiff, rejected insistences that she should speak at the party conference. Although the YC's National Advisory Committee abandoned the national competition in 1967, this was reversed a month later, but by 1972 the competition was ended.[49] YC gender traditionalism limited recruitment through the 1960s of professional women, although occasional profiles of YC women with careers in the press and ITV were to be found. And the YCs were, as a rule, rarely immune to cultural trends, especially amongst the young. *Trend* told readers in 1966 that for 'the single girl who chooses not to marry, a good time can now be had' and reviews of women's and men's fashions were frequent.[50]

Image, modernity, tradition

But cultural change and modernity were mixed blessings for the YCs. Pop music, of the Beatles variety in particular, vexed the YCs. Government Minister Bill Deedes told in 1964 how the Beatles 'herald a cultural movement among the young' that was 'part of the history of our time' and were evidence that 'the young are rejecting some of the sloppy cultural standards of their elders' and of the 'the human instinct to excel... and the human faculty of discrimination'. But his audience of London YCs listened only 'in respectful silence'. The *New Statesman* ridiculed the whole episode as 'whimsy' and a crude recognition that the Beatles were 'electorally valuable', so much so that Prime Minister Douglas-Home and the (admittedly liberal) Bishop of Woolwich were doing their best to fit into the pop scene. But the political left (as Wesker's C42 shows in Chapter 6) had no greater affinities with pop culture. The author of this piece (Paul Johnson) was as damning of Beatles music and fans as of Conservative cleaving to it, expressing his preference for the commanding heights of the 'mainstream of European culture' and Beethoven's 9th.[51]

Tony Bowers, elected Birmingham YC chair in 1969, sported a goatee beard, but was always pictured in a tie. Smart attire was preferred – if less formal than Conservative grandees in Brigade or school ties, then less causal than those on the left.[52] A 1965 report on 'Birmingham's new citizens' recognized problems of housing and education and how immigrants posed a challenge to the YCs' ambitions to represent a cross-section of society. Many YCs were sympathetic Common Marketeers, as a well-off group of young people who holidayed in Europe, which for some involved an experience of a 'camaraderie [that]... knows no international or racial barriers'. Close ties were maintained with the pro-Common Market Conservative and Christian Democratic Youth Community and exchanges undertaken with the German Christian Democrats.[53] But imperial visions were as likely to be encountered. In Rushcliffe, Roger Neal, sustained a tirade against crime and sexually transmitted disease amongst 'coloured people' and on how the Commonwealth in 1966, unlike the Common Market, was yet to achieve its peak. The 'political honesty' of Peter Griffiths, the racist victor in the 1964 Smethwick election, was applauded and, by the later 1960s, Enoch Powell was YCs' pin-up MP.[54]

YC's sense of tradition demanded deference to elders, but they were not unduly haunted by the party's past. Amongst its characteristic dispositions, in Oakeshott's taxonomy of conservatism, was a preference for 'the familiar to the unknown... the near to the distant'. Not that the past was hard to find. In Birmingham, the YCs were 'still in thrall to Joe Chamberlain', and known as Young Unionists, as they also were in Scotland to 1965. YC attempts to make politics 'fun', and their belief that it was not such a rational business, if at odds with its decorousness, were manifest in nostalgia for heckling. Area speakers' competitions in the early 1950s appointed an 'official heckler' and YCs were 'strategically placed' at opponents' election meetings. Heckling and unsettling opponents through mockery or by crunching walnut shells under their heels, as Edward Heath recalled of the YCs during the 'packed' but 'good-humoured' meetings of the 1950 campaign, were traits admired by candidates besides YCs. A 1965 Birmingham recruiting campaign, culminated in a motorcade and speeches in Chamberlain Square, where one speaker, YC organizer Tony Shaw enthused, dealt with heckling for over an hour.[55]

In the public imagination and for mocking critics, the YCs were a 'middle-class marriage bureau', a phrase in common currency by the 1950s. As Iris Harvey put it, the YCs were a 'breeding ground' of conservatism. But this was double-edged since, as the *Macleod Report* found, 'young marrieds' were most prone to cease YC activity. In Walder's *The Short List*, Rupert Inglis of the 'Stepney Group' fights Netherford East with the support of the YCs and an aristocratic backer and against suspicions of his lack of a wife and donnish philosophizing. The novel features a canvassing encounter with a newly married ex-YC who confesses she had been 'quite active until I had my first baby'.[56]

As Geoffrey Johnson-Smith, the party Vice-Chair saw it, that 'the YCs have so many attractive people that they want to marry one another says a great deal for the quality of the membership'. Almond and Verba's measurement of partisanship though parent's attitudes to children's marital choices found Conservatives more concerned about party affiliation than Labour, if indifferent by European standards. Marriage was celebrated and whilst there was no official discouragement of 'marrying out', the notion of 'partners' was frowned upon. When the Athertons became the youngest married YCs in the Nottingham area in September 1965, they were rewarded with a clock from Lord Belton. Barely a branch report went by without some nuptial notice. It was quite an occasion when *Looking Right* announced in July 1967 that, 'strangely… there are no marriages or engagements to report'.[57] Such marriage culture also helps explain why Edward Heath's unmarried status was such a preoccupation.

YCs hardly had a monopoly on social allure, but its cachet was more enduring and as even opponents attested was located in greater social acumen, not just larger budgets. As Samuel recalled, the Conservatives were 'the party of people… who had cars… who dressed up… carried themselves with poise'. In 1955 the Young Communist League's *Challenge* warned the left 'should not scorn to learn from the… colourful and attractive methods of the Young Conservatives', and by 1968 was copying *Crossbow*'s semi-clad YC image in the hope of aiding recruitment. As Waite notes, *Challenge* had long used cover images of female Communists, their healthy appeal arguably a distraction from 'politics' in 1956, but again illustrating the male-centredness of 'politics'.[58]

Other studies noted the left's comparatively limited social skills and resources. But more common was to dismiss the YCs, as the New Left's Edward Thompson did, as 'providing a slap up "social" life', which he equated with political apathy, or to dismiss them as Hugh Gaitskell did, as 'nothing more than a glorified dancing club'. Labour's difficulties were not only that its youth movements tended to be more political. Jennings noted how in 1960 that whilst it was 'slightly humorous to find the Conservative Central office running boys and girls clubs, it would be downright hilarious to ask Transport House to do it'.[59] There were YC activities that were more acceptable in the unofficial culture of party life, but it seemed more *laissez-faire* than the left. In 1961 one YS member reported to Gosling that 'she would have to join the Young Conservatives if she was to continue her sailing without being victimised'. Sailing was no longer such an elite pastime; and one that under Heath was tacked to the Tory image. The YC's success, so Gosling saw it, was that it was 'run by the young people for the young people'.[60]

As *The Times* saw it in 1959, the YCs combined 'politics with fun and zest' and a faith that young people were 'willing to serve'. The key point, as John Vaizey argued in the *Observer* just after the 1959 election, was that the left had no conduit to bring 'decent non-political people and party zealots' together in a climate other than formal political meetings. However:

> the Conservatives have created such a bridge for themselves. It is usual on the left to sneer at the Young Conservatives. They hold dances and tennis parties and rarely pass resolutions. But in a few years they have created among young people in the suburbs a genuine sense of shared values and assumptions, which has led to really effective political action.[61]

YCs were very image consciousness. There were constant exhortations that 'our sales talk must be big and effective' in cyclostyled local YC magazines as well as Birmingham's benchmark, *Looking Right*. Titles such as *Trend, Blue Horizon, Progress* or the popular *Enterprise* (of both Spalding and Southend YCs) denoted YC's endeavour to be modern and forward-looking. *Impact* launched itself as YC national magazine in 1964, tempting advertisers with the 'opportunity of reaching thousands of today's most important spenders – the affluent 16–24 age group'. It was glossier than the samizdat style in vogue on the left and which appealed to a sense of underground radical élan of 1960s, but could not prevent Labour journals like *New Advance* or *Focus* folding in 1967.[62]

Efforts were made to win subscriptions from schools, libraries and newsagents. Marketing executives told *Impact* of the parity of consumers and voters, the commodity-like qualities of candidates and how the traditional fête might be 'out of touch'. Business-like efficiency was rewarded from 1955 by the Finsberg 'National Efficiency' trophy, named after YC chairman, Geoffrey Finsberg. In Birmingham, minute books were kept in good order by the prospect that in an efficiency contest tie, they were a deciding factor.[63]

According to Abrams and Little, the YCs were modelled 'on an advertiser's image of modern business leadership... bland and professional', encouraging the diplomatic language that distinguished the YCs from the 1980s' sectaries. This was the 'politics of [the] managerial revolution' since YC leaders advanced through business rather than politics where 'the pay is so bad', but imported such values to the party. The YCs were the subject of national Conservative TV and radio broadcasts early in 1961. Others feared that modern, national PR communications would diminish the value of a mass membership and that enthusiastic use of them derived from, but exacerbated the YCs' passivity and could denude their role as foot soldiers or 'unhidden persuaders'.[64]

Between 1956 and 1958, the YCs won endorsements from high-profile celebrities and sports stars. The former included actress Shirley Eaton (see Figure 4.1), later famed for her role in the Bond film, *Goldfinger*, but who also starred in three *Carry On* films. Amongst sport stars, cricketers were numerous: Robin Marler, captain of Sussex and Arundel YC chair; Yorkshire's Jimmy Binks; Hampshire's Colin Ingleby-Mackenzie of Portsmouth YCs, Colin Cowdrey, captain of England and Kent (Petts Wood YCs) and test batsmen Tom Graveney, described as 'amongst Bristol's keenest and most hard-working conservatives' (and with Cowdrey, Ingleby-Mackenzie and Marlar, later a chairman of the Marylebone Cricket Club, Cricket's world governing body until the 1990s).

F.J. Parker, the British high hurdle record holder was a Sheen YC. Boxing YCs included: Terry Spinks (a gold medallist at the 1956 Olympics) a West Ham YC. Other sporty YCs included Angela Buxton, the first post-war English Wimbledon finalist; show-jumper Dawn Palethorpe of Kidderminster YCs and Douglas Baker, England rugby union player of Hampstead YCs. Most exposure was given to racing driver Stirling Moss signing up in 1956 to the Victoria Lunch Hour YCs, since 'he doesn't have much time for political work'. Moss's input was minimal and in an epitaph to the YC's incidental footprint, confessed, 'I do not have any memories of the Young Conservatives, even though

SHIRLEY EATON, *outstanding young T.V. and screen star, adds real talent to her obvious glamour. She's chosen a hard profession; long may she be right at the top !*

SOME MEMBERS OF A GROWING COMPANY

THE Young Conservative movement is out to attract people who mean to win life's prizes. Here are a few outstanding winners, all genuine Y.C.s.

They have special talents which you may not possess, but YOU can copy their determination to reach the top. And YOU, like them, will find it worth while to become a Y.C.

Figure 4.1   Shirley Eaton in *Rightway* (October 1956)
Source: Conservative Party, Bodleian Library

it is true I was a YC'. But such endorsements served to project a youthful image and affiliate the Tories with sporting success in the 1950s, if sometimes coming uncharacteristically close to a formal politicization of civil society.[65] A Southern skew and absence of more working-class sports such as football or rugby league was noteable here. The YCs self-confidence survived the traumas of Suez and sales of its regalia, blazer badges and so forth, peaked in 1959. But such endorsements – with occasional exceptions like England cricket captain and Conservative candidate in the 1964 election Ted Dexter's contribution to *Impact* – faded in the early 1960s in tandem with the fortunes of the government.[66]

Sometimes the social aspect of YC life trumped the political. Hornsey YC cricketers disaffiliated and in Walder's Netherford the routine of YC activity, sausage suppers, bingo and the annual fête was disturbed when 'along comes this bloody by-election and spoils it all'. In 1955 the South East Area passed a resolution 'deploring the cancellation' of the annual holiday and tenth anniversary weekend in Scarborough (no longer needed it was decided, so shortly after the general election victory) and turned up nonetheless.[67] And the social aspect could get out of hand. After a weekend school at Butlin's Ocean Hotel in Saltdean in 1954 'the bad behaviour of YCs' was 'the subject of comment and complaint, at the hotel and by local residents', and adjudged 'inimical to the prestige of the Conservative Party'. At Buxton in 1966 for a YC holiday weekend many felt the 'food and accommodation at the Spa Hotel were deplorable'. A certain 'togetherness was… strengthened by prevailing circumstances', but the 'ravishing' women and a party that only stopped at 4am were no compensation for the fact that the 'place was littered up with some local scruffs', that the bar ran out of gin and Roger Neal had his car spotlights stolen. For all their inclusive claims, some elements attracted to YC events were unwelcome. At Hayes and Keston's 1958 'February Fandango', the presence of two teddy boys was irritably noted. By the 'March Hare Hop' at Keston Village Hall, three teds were present, although it was unclear whether this was 'regrettable' because they 'glowered' at the YCs, were admitted for free or bagged seats by the radiator.[68]

Politicizing the YCs

The social-political balance in YC life was a source of constant debate. In 1960 Butler instituted policy groups to link the YCs to the main party and boost their political content. In 1965, Iain Macleod's Report addressed the decline in YC membership. Precise figures and even trends in membership were elusive, but in 1963 it stood at half the 1949 level and fell by 30% to 58,344 by the end of 1964. It could nonetheless still outrank the Young Republican or Democrat organizations in the USA. The *Macleod Report* aimed to enlarge the YC's political activities and restore its social prominence. It noted the impact of affluence, popular culture, education and housing since the YCs launch in the 1940s on those aged under 30. Targeting a membership of half a million, it envisaged 'a more flexible, informal and yet more politically-conscious youth movement' in the belief that 'youth will not be attracted to a movement that provides only social entertainment'. Simultaneously with *Macleod*, the Young Britons, for those of pre-YC age, were closed down.[69] Crucially, *Macleod* differentiated between political and social activity, countering the YCs original conception and coming up against its abiding culture. Conservative preference for a tractable, discreet political style was strained in the later 1960s, not only by social and cultural change, or from without by the likes of Whitehouse (see Chapter 5), but by the choice to 'politicize' the YCs.

Most discussion of *Macleod* concurred the YC's thinning membership was the result of social change, but some political factors were registered. East Midlands YCs felt the political spurs for joining at the YCs inception in the second half of the 1940s had diminished during the long period of Conservative government and it was felt YCs should 'concentrate on making our views heard rather than defending the Conservative party'. This 'did not mean we should be completely political', but 'should stop apologising for being a political movement'.[70]

But mostly it was agreed social factors were working against the YCs. Demographic change perturbed Conservatives. It was not only that their appeal appeared to be receding as the post-war baby boom came of YC age in the mid-1960s and that the birth rate dropped sharply from 1964, but also trends like earlier marriage – paradoxically given the YC's 'marriage bureau' reputation.[71] Marriage was seen as good in itself, but there remained the problem of keeping married YCs active. In Birmingham 77% of YCs were single, its 1969 survey found, and there was often a vacuum between novices and more careerist, party hack elder YCs. Addressing the Conservative psephology group in 1960, Mark Abrams thought 'neither party seemed to have appreciated the trend towards earlier marriage', and they thought in terms of teenagers rather than those with family or career responsibilities. YC policy groups did consider issues like mortgage rates, and in Colchester a baby-sitting service run by women in the senior Association freed time for young marrieds to canvass. To this end *Macleod* proposed 'supper clubs' meeting monthly 'in people's homes, in restaurants, hotels or clubs' and at which 'informality should be the key note'. In short, the dinner party might rival the ball in YC life.[72]

YCs also asked if 'in an affluent age people can find enough social entertainment without joining the Young Conservatives', and most reasoned that they 'simply cannot compete... with the professional pastime makers'. Although Essex's *Trend* reckoned popular culture was a recruiting sergeant: 'many of the go ahead young people of today are clamouring for something more to occupy their leisure than just television, the cinema and other "canned" entertainments'. Either way, *Impact* concluded that 'the political work of the Young Conservatives [was] being hidden from... potential members'. A new member from a comprehensive school was wielded by *Impact* as evidence of the need for a more political appeal. Interested in jazz, drama and banning arms sales to South Africa, he reported being told on joining the YCs: 'don't worry we talk about everything here except politics'. He thought YC 'girls... never had a political thought in their life' and YCs on the whole were 'young in age, but old and stolid in their ideas'.[73]

Much was at stake in *Macleod*'s reception. It offers historians a vantage from which to dissect Young Conservatism as it voluntarily ditched its traditional codes. It signalled the end of the YC's preference for displacing formal politics to maintain a social presence in civil society and of the conditions in which it could achieve this. The distinction it introduced between social and political activities, that had been studiously avoided previously, left YC culture in a liminal state. It is noteworthy that not only did established YC culture resist and persist after *Macleod*, but that there were continuities in the proposed content of YC life after 1965. It was not entirely unpolitical before and sustained a focus on service in civil society after – more repackaged than reinvented. This suggests it was not only social change, but how YCs read it and what they chose to do about it that determined their fortunes.

This uneven application of *Macleod* was testimony to the vibrancy of inherited local YC culture and uncertainties over membership targets and an age limit of 35, despite office holders being capped to 30. Some remained convinced that a period of Labour government would revive interest. Others believed the expansion of higher education (something Conservatives were wary of in any case) had provided competition amongst the YC's social and generational base. According to *Macleod* however, 'the tendency for YC branches to demonstrate a very unintellectual approach towards politics' accounted 'for their inability to attract university graduates'.[74]

Macleod, after all, tackled a well-entrenched YC culture. That 'in the public imagination "Young Conservative" means a half-baked, if not half-naked socialite who organizes successful dances and the occasional not so successful merry whoop down the council estate at election times', 'Geordie' told 'Basil' in 1967, in a mock North-South debate, was a product of the YCs' dominance by safe, Southern constituencies. Their complacency meant the 'Conservatism gets forgotten' and so did the Northern Area YCs who had no Cabinet-level speaker between 1952 and 1965. For Walder the YCs were a misnomer by 1967, a category requiring 'inverted commas': neither notably young nor Conservative, identity was 'social for the non-political' and 'insignificant for the political' and correspondingly hard work to politicize.[75]

Opinion surveys for Central Office in 1966 revealed – besides how seriously the Party took them – continuity in perceptions of the YCs, necessitating the 'Action '67' campaign to progress *Macleod*'s proposed change. Opponents saw the YCs as an opportunity to 'enjoy yourself... no word of politics is ever mentioned'. Conservative voters agreed: YCs were not as 'earnest or dedicated as socialists', if 'steadier... not always shooting their mouths off'. Even the respondent who felt they were 'snobbish' admitted it was 'a good association to find a girlfriend'. One respondent explained that he 'would join if I found my social life depleting'. This tallied with a larger survey that found one-quarter believed 'people joined the YCs only if they are rather lonely'; the same proportion as thought it 'primarily a political organization'. Many more believed people joined 'because their parents want them to' or 'to meet important people and make business contacts'. The 'potential' for YC growth, it was optimistically reckoned, lay in the large majority of working-class respondents that thought the YCs 'with it' not 'square'.[76]

The heavy leisure quotient of traditional YC programmes rendered them sensitive to changes in this sphere. Backing *Macleod*, Edward Lear, Birmingham YC Chair, complained that premises used by YCs were often 'the same drab, uncomfortable schoolroom they used 20 years ago'. John Selwyn Gummer, who worked in publishing and edited *Impact*, agreed: 'young people are richer, more sophisticated... yet the YCs still provide them with a fare which we first served up in the days of austerity'. Alan Haslehust, who had been an ICI commercial assistant before becoming YC National Chairman in 1966, argued the YCs needed to match modern youth's tastes for skiing or more lavish balls.[77]

So the idea that social activities were eroding the political point of the YCs and that renewal rested on the quality, rather than quantity, of recruits was not unchallenged after 1965. The popularity of a local disco in Lowestoft in 1969 prompted some YCs to propose they 'take advantage... of entertainment which could provide an immense source of revenue'. Even the more striving 'political' London YCs could party – Lynda Chalker's Chelsea YCs hosted the Bonzo Dog (Doo Dah) Band after a Quentin Hogg talk in 1967. Branches with social reputations remained convinced YCs ought to offer a primarily social menu. In Birmingham, Povey countered talk of politics proper: 'Politics – nothing was further from my mind when I joined the Young Conservatives... I was going to meet a group of friends and even if I found the meeting itself rather a bore, there was always the drink and chat afterwards'. In distinguishing between social and political activities, then after Macleod, the less social, like Tony Shaw (*Looking Right*'s editor and a notoriously poor dancer, contemporaries attest) were supposed to be in the ascendant. But both *Looking Right* and Birmingham's Motor Club struggled as participants moved out of the city.[78] It was not that YC-style social activities died out – marriage rates after all peaked in 1971 – but that competition in provision marginalized the YCs.

Macleod also *renewed* the traditional YC ethos of service before party, bolstering voluntary activity in churches or local authorities. In 1962, Macleod had called YCs 'to service – not because you are Tories but because you are citizens'.[79] In 'Action '67' a focus on community service as a demonstration of the YC's use emerged. YCs should 'exist to stir such people into a more active contribution to society', to convert 'good friends and neighbours' into 'excellent citizens'. Activities could range from the Voluntary Services Organization (set up under Macmillan) to campaigning on the local environment. The qualities of likely recruits did figure in Conservative calculations here:

> ...was an appeal stressing a social and general interest approach losing out?... This would be a ludicrous situation: trying to shield that we were political when it was the thought of our not being sufficiently political which was keeping people away from us... These people... revolt against the idea of being mere spectators in society. They want to be doers.

YCs marched for Oxfam (Gosforth), tidied local gardens (Middlesbrough) or recycled silver paper (Birmingham's Harborne YCs, copying *Blue Peter's* 1964 guide dog appeal). Here the YCs were repackaging their civic-service ethic and citizenship activities in a more political language. The YCs became socially useful rather than party animals, then, in the belief that 'political organisations will only ever interest a small percentage of the community'. Crosland had reached similar conclusions, but for YCs the logic was also that, as South Buckinghamshire reported, 'the reliable members, the best organizers, are those who are politically interested', not the 'more volatile social branch'.[80]

The East Midlands area Chairman, Peter Le Bosquet, endorsed this aim 'to provide a medium through which younger people can play a full part in the affairs of their local community and the country by involvement in public life and by service to their fellow citizens'. YC's associations with 'hunt balls and Bar-B-Qs' contrasted with CND and Oxfam who had 'gained the support of young people because underlying them is the idealism which many people desire'. 'One could hardly associate the YCs with this kind of idealism', and this explained 'why we have failed the serious-minded youth of this country and we are facing a situation where many branches are nothing more than glorified youth clubs'. A Birmingham YC invoked the Salvation Army's slogan, 'For God's sake care', to critique the carefree YCs. 'We Young Conservatives sitting in our dream world of dances, cheese and wine parties and jumble sales', Fowkes despaired, 'have the cheek to sneer at long-haired university students who protest about everything'. 'At least they are doing something', whilst YCs 'have debates on nearly every subject except politics', then 'recoil into our own social world' where everything is 'jolly good'. To Fowkes it seemed imperative to 'make our own policy independent of the senior members... let's not conform'.[81]

Yet despite the official preference for a more political focus, the YCs were grudging about the reduction in voting age to 18 in 1969. Objections ranged from questioning teenagers' maturity to discontent that the age for candidates was not similarly lowered. A real fear was that new voters were 'more uncommitted than ever before and less likely to accept guidance from their parents or propaganda from any political party'. The age reduction also seemed to make a case for the pre-*Macleod* YC emphasis on volume, rather than quality, of members – just 1% of newly eligible voters in Birmingham in 1969 were YCs. London rebels argued that falling membership was a consequence of YCs' lack of status within the Conservative Party. YC leaders countered it was smaller, but more influential. In Birmingham, a contemporary political language was deployed, but the view remained that size was a prerequisite of effectiveness: 'for any pressure group and I feel sure that this is what we would like to be classified as, to be effective, it must have strength in numbers in order to have its voice heard'.[82]

Efforts at a more serious image could nevertheless falter. In 1969, '50 well-fed, well-housed Young Conservatives spent a weekend in a stately home', and it did not seem to strike Hugh Holland of the National Advisory Committee as in any way odd that they were discussing homelessness, watched *Cathy Come Home* and were addressed by the director of Shelter, Des Wilson. The difficulty for the YCs was to disturb its traditional, lingering disposition against excess political thought – or as another YC urged, that 'politics, unlike charity, requires people to think before caring'.[83]

Politics also generated and exposed division. Brought to the fore, it was not as if YCs exhibited a state of political unanimity. And they were increasingly susceptible to the ebbs and flows of political debate. YC national chair, Terence Wray, joined Labour over the issue of Rhodesian independence in 1967. Juliet Gardiner felt too many YCs had the 'prejudices of middle age', being unable to differentiate 'between drug-taking – a very serious problem – and the permissive society, which is a blanket name for a lot of things that have recently made our lives fuller, more colourful', especially for those simply escaping the 'grey monotony of their jobs'. Her career as a YC journalist ended when she reached conclusions about Charles Reich's *The Greening of America* that were too favourable for Conservatism's tentative environmentalism. *Impact* generally took a liberal line, but more authoritarian voices were apparent. At the 1967 YC conference, for example, Gummer blamed the permissive society for social problems and those of a more clement mind on the drugs issue were out-voted in 1968. The danger here, Lynda Chalker surmised, was that 'we are considered old-fashioned'. But in other ways, the YCs seemed in tune. Pirate radio animated YCs, allowing them to support the free market and youth culture and critique as state killjoys the Labour government's attempts to ban them.[84]

Not that YC life was bereft of formal politics before *Macleod*, however much those who saw the earlier generation as practicing 'pale pink' policies under Macmillan came to the fore in the later 1960s. For those anxious to root them out, paternalist, authoritarian and libertarian strains were all present. Below their quiescent surface politics, the YCs were no more homogenous than their elders on issues like Europe. When it was decided to join the Common Market in 1961, Central Office warned the '61 Group' of Northern Home Counties YCs that there were appropriate channels for opposing entry. Some YC leaders were involved in the Anti-Common Market League, but at party leaders' behest, the YC rank-and-file heckled anti-Europe speakers at the 1961 party conference.[85] The most consistent YC politics was anti-socialism, in which scaremongering (Labour would abolish cricket) and mockery (an identikit socialist based on *New Statesman* personal ads) was rife. But opposition to what YCs saw as the 'claim of one set of men to dictate how the rest shall fashion their lives' united pre- and post-*Macleod* YCs and later generations.[86]

YCs also often echoed their opponents, sharing in the fortunes of party politics as a whole, bemoaning apathy amongst YCs and non-YCs alike. The 'coffee bar generation' and playwrights of John Osborne's ilk were denounced – 'these people are not the don't knows, they are the don't cares' – but the YCs opened their own coffee house as early as 1956 in Croydon.[87] By the late 1960s 'teach-ins' proved popular, although in YC-style East Midlands held theirs in 1968 at the Grand Hotel, Leicester. In 1968 the three main parties' youth wings united to 'fight world poverty' and the liberal *Impact* even seemed to contract some 1968-style campus alienation from 'the comfortable materialism and intellectual limitations of suburbia'.[88]

An unintended consequence of a more 'political' YC movement was less readiness to exhibit loyalty to party authorities and instead for more involvement and power in party decisions – very much in tune with 1960s' demands for participation. Eric Chalker's campaign in London to boost YC influence was the first time YC elections had slates of candidates and 'open political campaigning'. London GLYC rebels grouped around *Democratory*, which cast itself as the 'voice of protest representing 12000 YCs in London alone' and 'the million or so young people in London who are so frustrated by the lying incompetence of one major party and the inertia of the other that emigration seems the only way out'. This outspoken stance, critical of Party bureaucracy and its stage-managed conferences, coincided with Enoch Powell's Presidency of the YCs from 1966. GLYCs opposition to the Miss YC contests was a desire for 'proper' politics, not a feminist gesture.[89] *Set the Party Free*, produced for the 1969 party conference, combined Powell's critique of the leadership, with Chalker's proposals for inner-party democracy (presently comparable to the Freemasons, it argued), a desire for the YCs to assert themselves as policy-makers and a foreword from Macleod. Powell and Macleod's presence in the shifting tenor of the YCs after 1965 was significant: both were figures whose technical intellect, Green explains, could put them at odds with Conservatism's preference for a more unflappable, sceptical style.[90]

The London revolt was decisive, but YCs dissent surfaced in moderate quarters and was further legitimized by the unexpected number of YCs who became councillors in 1968 after extensive Tory gains in local elections. The Party Chairman warned Heath in 1967 that 'the YC leadership is often more interested in cutting a political or public dash than in developing the movement'. Besides Chalker's rebellion, Heath was criticized by Alan Haslehurst. When he stepped down as YC Chairman in 1969, Haslehurst told Heath that the YCs were under extremist control. A 'Bolshie' YC that 'could prove politically embarrassing' saw Heath welcome an election moratorium, facilitate a parliamentary-YC liaison committee and the Chelmer Committee to review party democracy in 1970.[91]

Conclusions: YCs and political culture

What, then, do the YCs disclose about the wider political culture? They suggest that facets of inter-war political culture persisted after 1945 and this in itself redefines the later period. McKibbin argues that 'apolitical sociability' came to characterize social networks and personal relations, particularly amongst the middle classes in England in the 1930s. Differences of politics, sex or religion were negotiated by humour or deferred, as associational life aimed to cultivate an environment that was 'notionally unpolitical'. Rotary and Lions clubs burgeoned, as in Southern England did Ratepayers Associations, under whose non-partisan banner Conservatives regularly campaigned locally. By enmeshing themselves in such institutions in civil society, a 'definition of Conservatism as "non-political"' emerged and enabled it to seem 'common sense', whereas Labour, 'dragged "politics" into everything', 'took everything so seriously' and emphasized 'conflict instead of good humour'. Conservative appeal and crafting of an everyday culture 'in which people did not talk about politics much' lent it a comparative advantage over Labour. For McKibbin these 'apolitical set of silent assumptions', could entail 'a taboo on talking politics at home' or only 'according to well understood conventions' in public, but 'were, in practice, deeply political'. McKibbin rather agrees with contemporaries who 'found these codes trivializing or enervating, or simply dishonest', but equally acknowledges this (a)political climate fostered a 'civility' in public, private and political life that obstructed the 'politicization of all relationships which did so much damage to European society as a whole in the interwar years'. Conservatives neither naturally exuded nor benefited from this style. They had to adapt their imperial edge into a more inclusive, parochial style to ensure liberal non-conformist networks and new associational organizations were 'ineluctably drawn into the wider network of the Conservative Party'.[92]

Light's account of relations between (lower case) conservatism and the Conservative Party in the inter-war period tallies with McKibbin's. That it was 'the least articulate level of conservatism' gave it an intangible 'taken-for-granted' quality that explained both its influence and the difficulties and dearth of analysis of it. It was *passim*, rather as Raymond Williams' *Keywords* contained no entry for 'conservative'. Its reticence at articulating itself ideologically and propensity to be 'indifferent to Politics at large' demanded both a political and cultural history. Regarding it as an 'emotional economy rather than, though it might accompany, specific views on the economy of the state', Light avers 'conservatism likes to see itself... as a politics which eschews politicking; a system of beliefs and values without systemization; an organic and inevitable way to be: socialists and radicals are those who "interfere"... with people and their lives'. Such apparent insouciance or 'throttled emotion' in either government or comportment did 'not come easily', although Conservatives liked to imagine it did. There is evidence of the persistence of this Conservative political culture. Crick noted in 1962 the type of 'non-political Conservative' who likes 'to settle public matters privately'; whose point of political entry was anti-doctrinaire, manifest as a general mistrust of politicians; who took up Gibbon's regard for 'the usefulness of Christianity to civil polity' and, all in all, 'likes to be thought above politics'.[93] Not least, this was apparent in the YCs. Their virtually un-political, sociable, service ethos seemed a Cold War re-working of the Rotarian civic-business practices that De Grazia has highlighted. McCarthy is doubtless correct that there was much more of a democratic and participatory impulse to such civic associationalism than the anti-socialism stressed by McKibbin, but it was also evident that the YCs operated in ways that fit with McKibbin's account.[94] YC strategy incorporated the limits to party support as a means to gently counter such indifference, but also sustained it as a political style.

Political scientists like Blondel noted Conservative Associations were 'rightly called "associations" and not "parties"', since they were 'primarily social organizations'. That Conservative clubs were chiefly social venues, Tether holds, immunized them from shifts in politics and relatively resilient to the suburbanization of Tory support and the politics of the inner city (where most were, dating from Victorian or inter-war period). They barely declined (by just 10% to 1987) in number from the 1500 in the Association formed as a limited company in 1948. 'The atmosphere' in Clubs was 'tangibly apolitical', although 'overt political disloyalty can be taken seriously'. Jennings likewise noted in 1960 that whilst 'political activity outside the London Clubs is small... membership of a club must lead to increased political interest' and retained allure for an 'ambitious young man' seeking 'to promote his career'. For Blondel, the skill of Conservative Associations was to enlist 'lukewarm supporters or, at any rate, people who are not very interested in politics'. This meant that many middle-class 'businessmen and professional men... still consider that membership of... the local Conservative association is as natural as membership of the local golf club'. 'Most Conservatives... consider politics as a hobby', Blondel deduced, whereas for 'Labour politicians... their real life, is the political life'.[95]

Frankenburg thought Labour the 'most political' of the main parties. It seemed a more incidental activity for Conservatives, whose agents, as the Blackpool incumbent explained in 1957, were 'expected to... join all the Oddfellows, Foresters, Buffaloes and Homing Societies and assist all his local horticultural, Chrysanthemum and charity shows'. Though there was obvious electoral reasoning to such inveigling of support. Edward Heath described how he 'joined most of the sporting, cultural, business and purely social organisations' – from dental to angling – and the 'interminable dinner-dances' of his 1950 election campaign in Bexley. Such affiliations and community ties did not fall into Conservative's laps, they had to be earned.[96]

Anthropological accounts like Frankenberg's, or Stacey's study of Banbury, showed the associational networks entwining Conservatives in local civil society. This seemingly un-political presence was something Conservatism had to make, not an innate quality of a politically neutral civil society. Its nexus with the Churches, Bowling Clubs, Chamber of Commerce, even the Sweet Pea Society, made Conservatism an unofficial part of everyday life. Labour were regarded as 'always bringing class into it' by the middle classes, who would 'avoid social relations' with Labour supporters from their own ranks. Stacey found 'politics are little discussed' or 'got round by a good deal of joking and backslapping'. As one Banbury club motto, put it, 'No religion, no politics, good comrades all'. This 'taboo on discussing political questions outside the political arena' enabled 'opposed groups to live and work together'. For 'beneath the taboos, the issues remain profound', when periodically unleashed by the 'safety valve' of parliamentary elections. Local Conservatives also worked hard – there were seven YC branches canvassing in Banbury in 1955. By 1968, except for the 'rise of local pressure groups', little had altered and the 'joking relationships' between parties continued 'to cover, and also reveal, their awareness of political differences'.[97]

As a political practice, this style was well illustrated by *The Birmingham Diary and Year Book*, a publication which Birmingham Conservative Association's advertising director explained in 1964 'will be on the desks of all worthwhile companies'. He was equally at pains to 'make it clear that despite the fact that it is being published by the Conservative Association', it 'will not be at all political in nature and content and will not in fact carry the name of the Party'. The types and strategies which McKibbin noted meshing Conservative and civic bodies were then still evident. In 1954 Southampton Conservatives formally amalgamated their longstanding (since 1933) electoral alliance with the Ratepayers' Association. In the age of mass party membership, Conservatism cut a low profile; as an acquaintance of Samuel's noted, it 'was something you took for granted... like God, it was there'.[98]

The senior party reproduced, then, many of the YC's qualities in this period, just as it passed these down to the YCs. In terms of such informal, socializing, assimilative propaganda, despite Trade Union support, Labour had 'many disadvantages' compared to the Conservatives. For example, in Keith Joseph's Leeds constituency, a 'predominantly Jewish golf club' with a membership of over a thousand were, with minimal party prompting, 'Tories to a man'. Property resources and 'snob appeal' for fêtes, garden parties and dances impressed Jennings. Echoing McKibbin, Light and Green's reading of Conservatism, Jennings reckoned in 1960 that 'for the average Conservative his ideas are sensible and non-political; it is the other fellow who insists on being "party political"'. This was a signal of the low key political culture that Conservatives, and not least YCs, had assiduously cultivated or attempted to fashion as an (un)political norm. But it also generated the sorts of problems the YCs encountered in the 1960s. For instance, discussing how to rejuvenate the Party's research department in 1959, James Douglas explained that whilst they could reach out to lawyers, universities, managers and directors, the basic disadvantage the Party suffered was 'because left-wing types are more inclined to think in political terms'. The façade of seeming relatively un-political was neither easily achieved nor unproblematic.[99]

Traces of this political culture persisted, eroded as it was through the 1960s. Nadler's Wimbledon YCs in the 1980s were a 'hangover from the 1950s', a 'cosy dating club' meeting in a Conservative club and mainly charged with lowering the average age at cheese and wine parties. Hoggart's mid-1990s portrait of Farnham in Surrey conveyed a casual, ingrained conservatism. Church, authority, tradition and Conservatives were inseparable. 'To be a socialist is almost unthinkable' amongst the middle class who 'assume active Labour members are loud-mouthed demagogues'. The *Farnham Herald* was 'more right than left', but did 'not push its politics much' and was less bothered with party than 'local voluntary political action'. Commuters and their families were 'habitually' conservative, with weekends dominated by gardening (a 'civilizing occupation') and golf.[100]

The YCs were the Tory party at play. Its provenance was middle class, Home Counties, suburban, provincial small-town, aspirational types. It was no Primrose League-like bridge to the working class (more alienating judged by their minimal participation), but the YCs helped secure middle-class support for the Conservatives, mobilizing existing support and building it amongst the next generation. It was always conscious of the electorate's fragile support. As a Birmingham YC saw it, 'when one remembers how short the memory of the public is', they could not be relied upon to punish Labour, however apparent its shortcomings. Their social aspect concealed, and made them relatively immune to, political issues – the YCs did not much register that mid-1950s wavering of middle-class support Green has plotted or evident in this study in consumer politics and Whitehouse's campaign – but sensitive to changes in lifestyle. The ghost that haunted the YC's demise as a mass organization was a fragmenting of the middle class and of its support for Conservatism. No less than Labour feared transformations in the working class, so Conservatives saw a more diverse, larger middle class, much now employees of the state and unionized, as less politically reliable. YCs perceived themselves to be grappling with competition from a pullulating popular and commercial youth culture, but also demographic and educational trends. As 1960s cultural change seemed to loosen traditional class and political affiliations, the YCs were aware, as the East Midlands Chairman put it in 1966, that 'the days are past when any ordinarily intelligent young man or woman could be assumed to be ready to join the YCs'.[101] The YC's composed, convivial façade crumbled then, but not only because of social change.

The YCs cultivation of a low key political presence was both a product of and contributor to a relatively unpolitical culture. And it was a practice that enabled them to operate in conditions where, as Jennings saw it in 1960, 'the best propaganda is the private conversation in the pub or club, the bus or the railway carriage, the canteen or the luncheon room', rather than that which was more blatant, organized or delivered by political fanatics.[102] The YCs were adept at seeming incidental, everyday and not political, at informal propaganda and socializing activities. If this demonstrated the limits of party appeal even in the so-called 'golden age' of turnout and membership, so it demonstrated the skill and resilience of party in negotiating this. The expansion in the parameters of 'the political' during the 1960s – a politicization of civil society and everyday life, popular culture and new, non-party modes of political activity, a process evident in the recesses of popular conservatism as Whitehouse's example in the next chapter shows – made the traditional YC approach of decreasing relevance. This was also a process that the YCs abetted. The YCs were sensitive to social change, more so than to political issues before 1965, but their fortunes were not determined by these alone. Its membership was in decline before *Macleod*, but the decision to undertake more formally 'political' activities and to define existing activities with a more political rubric marked not only a shift in the political culture, but undermined as much as any external social changes the conditions in which earlier practices and language succeeded.

The more self-expressive, febrile political culture of the 1960s ill-suited the YCs culture of restraint[103] – that which it inherited and sustained from the senior party and inter-war period, indeed was a prime expression of in the two decades after 1946. But if the YCs were victims of political irreverence in the 1960s it could not be said they had not contributed a certain scepticism towards politics. If suburbia seemed a less benign environment for the Conservatives by the later 1960s this was, at least in part, connected to the YCs' diminished presence as a fixture of middle-class life as much as the competition (from pressure groups above all) party politics faced in connecting with civil society. The decision to politicize their activity changed the YC's character and impetus and made it an agent of this more emotive political culture – not least in stoking debate about party democracy, but also in that the erosion of the YCs benign social presence took a brake off these social changes. Its falling membership through the 1960s was not just a symptom of social change, but of its choice to cultivate a membership of greater political quality, which it assumed to be necessarily of smaller quantity.

5
Whitehouse on Television: The National Viewers' and Listeners' Association and Moral and Cultural Politics

If seeking an alter-ego to Howard Kirk, Malcolm Bradbury's 'history man', as a portal on the sixties, it would be a struggle to invent anything better than Mary Whitehouse's career as a moral campaigner. Their mutual penchant for politicizing the personal apart, if Kirk was the quintessence of sixties radicalism, Whitehouse was its antithesis – quite as stereotyped and exaggerated, but no work of fiction. This chapter uses Whitehouse's campaign to 'clean-up TV' and the National Viewers' and Listeners' Association (NVALA) as a register of shifts in the form, content, style, motivations and strategies of politics, and more specifically of how culture and morality became politically charged, a process most readily associated in histories of this period with the New Left and feminism. Like the Consumers' Association (CA), NVALA's politics were not of the party or parliamentary kind; they were middle class in its core participants but national, even international in its aspirations, concerned with consumers rather than producers and with the politics of everyday life. It offers historians not only insights into the politics of culture, as further discussed in Chapter 6, but into the texture of political culture. Television increasingly figured in the communication and representation of politics as Chapter 7 discusses, but this chapter is concerned with the politics *of* television itself as a cultural form and activity and contends this was as much a key way in which British political culture was redefined.[1]

Launched in 1964 by Whitehouse and Norah Buckland, the 'Clean-up TV' campaign entered the public spotlight at a large, rowdy meeting at Birmingham Town Hall that May. The campaign's manifesto, with 366,355 signatures, was delivered to Parliament in June 1965, the year in which the campaign became the NVALA, purporting to be the voice of viewer opinion, feeding this back to influence broadcasters. It combined its case for a viewers' council with a torrent of invective directed at political leaders, programmes (the 'disbelief, doubt and dirt that the BBC projects into millions of homes through the television screen', as its manifesto put it, see Figure 5.1) and Whitehouse's real life nemesis, BBC Director-General

CARVED ON THE WALLS OF BROADCASTING HOUSE—

"This Temple of the Arts and Muses is dedicated to Almighty God by the first Governors of Broadcasting. It is their prayer that all things hostile to peace and purity be banished from this house, and that the people inclining their ear to whatsoever things are beautiful and honest and of good report may tread the paths of wisdom and righteousness".

THE MANIFESTO

1. We men and women of Britain believe in a Christian way of life.

2. We want it for our children and our country.

3. We deplore present day attempts to belittle or destroy it, and in particular we object to the propaganda of disbelief, doubt and dirt that the B.B.C. pours into millions of homes through the television screen.

4. Crime, violence, illegitimacy and venereal disease are steadily increasing, yet the B.B.C. employs people whose ideas and advice pander to the lowest in human nature, and accompany this with a stream of suggestive and erotic plays which present promiscuity, infidelity and drinking as normal and inevitable.

5. We call upon the B.B.C. for a radical change of policy and demand programmes which build character instead of destroying it, which encourage and sustain faith in God and bring Him back to the heart of our family and national life.

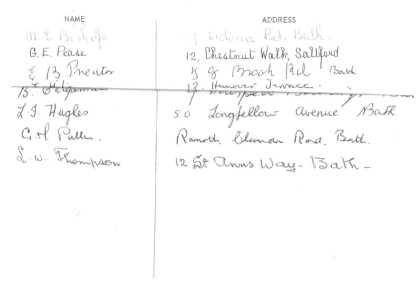

Return to—

Mrs. E. R. WHITEHOUSE, Postman's Piece, The Wold, Claverley, Nr. Wolverhampton.
Both Sides of this may be used for signatures preferably with addresses.

Figure 5.1   The 'clean-up TV' petition and manifesto
Source: Mediawatch UK, Essex University Library

Hugh Carleton Greene.[2] The BBC, as a publicly funded and accountable corporation, was its target much more than commercial ITV. With broadcasting pivotal to its worldview, it shot off diatribes on issues from abortion to satire and pornography, the whole gamut of liberal permissiveness *or*, as it experienced it, profanity. What started as a single-issue campaign, rapidly developed aspirations to be a broadcasting pressure group or NGO, voicing viewer opinion and held forth on a host of broader issues to take on the façade of a social movement.

The NVALA can then be understood in terms of the history of non-governmental organizations (NGOs) and social movements. Quite contrary to its portrayal in narratives of the period, it seems emblematic of the 1960s. A non-party, extra-parliamentary, anti-establishment, grassroots campaign utilizing the media, led by a woman and employing a parti-cipatory rhetoric of viewers' rights, seemed modern in form, if not content. But NVALA rarely features in surveys of social movements, which have taken peace, environmental and feminist movements as their model; echoing New Left assumptions about their liberal-radical politics. The NVALA offers the opportunity to review the dominant assumptions in this literature.[3] NVALA was avowedly traditionalist and critical of progress and modernity, more readily comparable to Powellism, the New Right and later the Country-side Alliance and the US evangelical Christian right, although not achieving anything like the latter's influence or media access.[4] Being systematically excluded from policy networks both frustrated and mobilized NVALA. Nonetheless, historians can learn much from about the wider political culture from NVALA's difficulties and marginalization.

NVALA's campaign was not, as with many campaigns, to repeal or for new legislation, but for enforcement of the BBC's professed values (the manifesto quoted the dedication to 'almighty God' and 'peace and purity' at BBC Broadcasting House) and the 1964 Television Act that prohibited broadcasting material that 'offends against good taste or decency or is likely to encourage or incite... crime... disorder or to be offensive to public feelings'. It claimed to influence the 1982 Indecent Displays Act and the Broadcasting Standards Commission established in 1988 (OfCom from 2003). Affinities between Thatcher and Whitehouse (made a CBE in 1980) were grounded in authoritarian and moral notions of 'Victorian values' (or 'back to basics' for John Major), if often strained by free market economics. Whitehouse became one of the 'populist heroines of the right' – reactionary, but also a portent of the future.[5]

NVALA was critical of yet contingent upon popular affluence. Like the Co-op it struggled with the value shift away from self-restraint and deferred pleasure. It was preoccupied with how Britons spent their time and improv-ing this, like CA and Wesker's Centre 42. Like these, debates about TV turned on matters of choice, taste, impacts on social attitudes and, most distinctively for NVALA, morality. If affluence diminished concern with instrumental economic interests, it seemed to afford a more expressive pol-itics, particularly middle-class concerns with moral and cultural issues. Parkin's contemporary study *Middle Class Radicalism* focused on CND and shifts away from mass, party politics and in which moral issues were increasingly salient. Since it was preoccupied with values, NVALA makes demands of concepts such as Inglehart's post-materialism and its proposition that such quality of life issues were political drivers for a relatively well-off, well-educated generation in a modernizing society.[6]

Suggestive parallels can be drawn with the New Left, which like NVALA defined culture and the power of the media as politically paramount. Richard Hoggart and Stuart Hall, key New Left figures and originators of 'cultural studies' in this period, were occupied by similar debates to NVALA. As the New Left and CND were products of discontent with the conventional politics of the left, so NVALA grew from what it perceived as a loss of values in the Church and amongst Conservatives. Like CND, its Christian core of activists hinted religion was more of a factor than modern British political historians (who, other than when addressing multiculturalism, have tended to assume processes of secularization) have allowed.[7] Whitehouse was a sort of moral entrepreneur; an initiator of 'moral panic' not just *through* the media, but from below and *about* the media.[8]

In other ways, NVALA resonates with established themes in the history of this period. It deployed (exploited, critics argued) the rhetoric of participation that was rife in 1960s Britain – opening up the BBC to viewer power, as women, workers, students, consumers and nationalists tackled other institutions and hierarchies.[9] For Nash, Whitehouse personified not only moral retrenchment against permissiveness, but the post-colonial fears and isolationism that coincided with European integration.[10] NVALA's vision of Britain was firmly declinist – the essence of its narrative was the demise of authoritative cultural values and moral standards. But Mary's perversity and contrariness was also apparent. Whilst most commentators targeted amateurism, NVALA criticized professional control of broadcasting with a case for balancing this with non-experts, a case it advanced in emotive terms at odds with the increasing professionalism and rationalism of formal politics.

NVALA made the personal viewing experience political; albeit as an unfortunate necessity out of which it made a strategic virtue, born of TV's domestic invasiveness, rather than any more self-conscious identity politics. 'TV was an intruder into private homes', one speaker exclaimed at the 1965 Grosvenor House meeting that formed the Viewers' and Listeners' Council. 'Our living rooms are the stage', the TV can 'talk *at* us!', supporters complained in *The Viewer* in 1968, 'we can never talk back!'. As Whitehouse saw it 'atheist liberals' were ignoring 'the basic reality and responsibility of television – that it comes into the home'. If TV had to invade the home, she asked at Birmingham Town Hall, 'why concentrate on the kitchen sink when there are so many pleasant living rooms?'[11]

From protest to participation: pressure group to social movement

NVALA's working assumption was that TV was 'responsible for forming public opinion and taste – and not only reflecting it'. This was something 'any manufacturer or advertising expert can vouch for'. The causal link was unquestioned – battles between Mods and Rockers were stimulated by TV, NVALA believed. In fact, advertisers were conscious and anxious that attention and recall of what was viewed on TV was very partial.[12] Such was the power of television that Whitehouse imagined 'drug-taking through the television screen' as a consequence of TV-watching itself as much as in coverage of Jerry Rubin or Allen Ginsberg (in the UK for the Dialectics of Liberation conference). The key question for NVALA was then 'how are we to ensure that we are master and not servant of this great medium?'[13] Here, the diffuse, diverse social power and reach of TV was turned to NVALA's advantage. Whitehouse told the Grosvenor House meeting that the fact that the medium had grown 'so vast and powerful that it can, and indeed does, control the thinking and actions of millions' also meant it could ' play a very real part to bringing the solution' to such problems. Instead of 'close-ups of the technique of love-making' or programmes 'weighted against the church', it 'would be wonderful if the BBC put on plays that showed how people can stay together in the home happily without drinking and smoking and flying out of the door in bad tempers'. Instead of a 'law unto itself' as at present, the power of the BBC, properly directed and regulated by a viewers' council was conceived of, quite as CA conceived of its critical consumerism, as a potential remedy to national issues. As Whitehouse explained to Postmaster General (PMG) Ted Short in 1966, the campaign had 'begun to articulate something of the contribution we feel television could make in solving the many personal, industrial and social problems which confront us as a nation'.[14]

But the toxic language and apocalyptic tenor of the Clean-Up manifesto was rarely far from NVALA's surface. Nor was Whitehouse the only one to vent such invective. Clean-up TV's Major James Dance, Conservative MP for Bromsgrove 1955–71, described a BBC *Wednesday Play* from summer 1964, *Diary of a Young Man*, as 'sheer sordid worthlessness' in which it was a scandal that 'the squalid, amoral, idle, dirty and completely charmless couple of deadbeats should be presented as objects of interest, instead of as they are: ugly cancers'.[15] But Clean-Up TV's morphing into NVALA aimed to forge a more constructive role. This built upon its initial impact, but distanced itself from such language by emphasizing the responsibility of broadcasters not just the censure of viewers. The expansion of its remit was also prompted by the opportunity to exploit the 1964 general election and invite candidates 'to express themselves, not only on the issue of clean television', but about the legalization of homosexuality and whether 'public funds continue to be used by the Arts Council and local authorities for subsidizing the "theatre of dirt and cruelty"?'[16]

The idea of a viewers' council sustained NVALA, almost irrespective of other setbacks. When Lord Normanbrook died in June 1967, NVALA saw an opportunity in the appointment of a new BBC Chairman to renew its demands. PMG Short resisted, but Whitehouse won from him an admission that 'a consensus of opinion' decides what is broadcast. 'We submit', she replied, 'it is only through... an independent representative council that this consensus can be obtained'. The new Chairman was Lord Hill, an ex-Conservative Minister, whose appointment by Harold Wilson was part of his skirmishes with the BBC and who at the Independent Television Authority (ITA, who regulated commercial TV) until 1967 had treated Whitehouse more diplomatically than the BBC. Hill raised hopes sufficiently for NVALA chair, James Dance to convene a meeting of prospective council members at the Commons in 1968. Present besides NVALA members and associates from Whitehouse's links with Moral Re-Armament (MRA) like GP David Sturdy, were Conservative broadcasting spokesman Paul Bryan MP, banker Jonathan Guiness and bodies with NVALA affinities – the Headmistresses Association (represented by Mrs. Manners), Baptist Union, Women's Institute, Young Wives groups and Rotary Clubs. Dance commended NVALA's programme monitoring and the meeting heard how a viewers' council would be able to respond to those MPs who 'indicated how very valuable reports on programmes of the kind produced by *Which?* on consumer goods, would be'.[17]

Such a model, with viewers as critical watchdogs, used the participatory rhetoric that was rife in 1960s Britain. Whitehouse increasingly conceived of NVALA as 'a consumer movement' and one that might 'draw in more supporters' by cultivating 'a role as a middle-class value-for-money, help-for-the consumer organization'. After all, the NVALA claimed to campaign about broadcasting 'not simply as a moral issue but because we pay for the licences'. Whitehouse wound the Commons meeting up by making NVALA's case for broadcasters exercising 'responsible control' via viewer opinion and defending this seemingly more pluralist approach, not as a timid shift from stricter controls, but in the belief that 'a truly healthy society will be producing many viewers' and listeners' associations'. But ultimately, such a consumer model was vitiated by NVALA's astringent values that made it more prone to police culture than feedback a range of views. To take the Consumers' Association as an example, NVALA was suspicious of its assessments of the use-value of goods alone. When a report on impotence alluded to aphrodisiac literature and contraceptive advice and was featured on BBC radio's *World at one*, Whitehouse's ire was aroused.[18]

This approach aimed to exploit Hill's arrival and Greene's departure in 1969, but induced little elasticity from the BBC. After a rare visit to Broadcasting House in June 1969, Dance and Whitehouse emerged critical of the lack of public transparency and mandate the existing BBC-appointed advisory councils enjoyed. In response to domestic setbacks, international efforts increased in the later 1960s. Viewer and Listener Associations were promoted in Germany, Australia and Denmark (the focus for much debate about the pornography industry); Whitehouse met the Pope in 1971 and addressed the Congress of the Union Internationale d'action morale et sociale. There were dealings with the National Audience Board and Nixon's Commission on Obscenity and Pornography in America; and NVALA's concerns were appended to a European agenda via groups opposed to liberal social regimes, like the European Union of Women (whose leader Gabrielle Strecker, a founder of the West German Christian Democratic Union and leading anti-communist, was close to NVALA). In the 1970s NVALA helped spawn the Nationwide Festival of Light, as the UK branch of a global evangelical Christian revivalist initiative against various manifestations of moral pollution.[19]

NVALA broadened its aims as a defence against its limited progress with broadcasters, but a viewers' council remained central to its thinking. This was a secular proposal, but premised upon NVALA's faith that Britons' 'believe in a Christian way of life'. Thus, such a council would revive a Christian ethos and even a Reithian purpose at the BBC, if one less broadcaster-dominated and more interactive with viewers. For Lord Reith, the BBC's formative Director-General, this had meant a civilizing mission. Reith judged, as early as 1963, Greene's regime to have indulged 'the disgusting manifestations of the age... he gives the public what it wants... the dignity of the BBC has utterly departed'.[20]

Viewer-producer interactivity was, allegedly, the point to a Council. Announcing his conversion to NVALA in 1970, future Conservative MP Neil Hamilton argued, 'viewers and producers should not be seen as two opposing sides', but that a council would increase broadcaster's 'responsiveness to our views' and fight the 'silent censorship... wherein opposing viewpoints are suppressed by editors or... rendered unacceptable... by a subtle ridicule'. There were attempts to attach the council to other initiatives. Home Office research into violence in 1969 (sparked by evidence in the Mary Bell trial) was greeted by Whitehouse as potentially opening a dialogue 'between those who make and those who receive programmes'. It reiterated its case to the Annan Committee on Broadcasting (1977) and even critics of its reactionary views recognized its aspiration to be a third sector force of viewer opinion by inviting it to the 1981 National Consumer Congress.[21]

Another reason for shifting to the viewer representation model was to negotiate the other charge, besides its MRA links, that regularly dogged the campaign – that NVALA were censors. NVALA's case was that the real censors were the liberal elite who used 'any weapons to silence any opposition to their "progressive" ideas' and that the BBC had imposed 'blanket censorship' on covering the NVALA under Greene. But it was easy to see where these charges originated when Whitehouse wrote in her 1967 book *Cleaning-up TV* that: 'if it were the only way of preventing the gradual erosion of our Christian values... we would not hesitate to call for control over certain influences which confuse liberty with licence'. And when seemingly innocuous children's programmes like *Pinky and Perky* were censured for fostering juvenile delinquency by disrespecting parents, this seemed signally sinister.[22]

Censorship was regularly discussed, with NVALA arguing for the rights of the viewing public to dictate content rather than have it decided by producers or the market. 'We believe in self-control... exercised by responsible citizens', a 1967 discussion concluded, but accepted this was 'an ideal'. Control by viewing figures would not suffice since it would mean programming that appealed to 'those most easily satisfied'. Artists themselves were more likely to indulge in 'mutual back-scratching' and government regulation would be draconian. What *was* needed, was public control via 'a body chosen on the widest possible basis, with the permanent, constant duty of relating the output of both BBC and ITA to the accepted standards of public taste and morality'. Such a body, rather than prohibiting creativity could encourage writers towards more appropriate standards than their 'present pre-occupation with sex and violence'. Failure to achieve some public-BBC dialogue might, it was predicted, result in some crude form of censorship injurious to programme producers and consumers alike.[23]

The government matched the BBC's resistance. In 1968 PMG John Stonehouse outlined, in Whitehouse's presence, why there was no need for a broadcasting equivalent to the Press Council. If at 'arms length' from direct political control (as well as from the broadcasters they regulated), the BBC governors and ITA were ultimately accountable to parliament. To 'superimpose another statutory body' would 'lead to bureaucracy and dilution of responsibility' and 'curb the creative genius which we want from broadcasters'. NVALA queried this accountability and its 1966 letter to MPs highlighted what it considered the PMG's and parliament's impotence *vis-à-vis* the BBC. NVALA asserted its 'campaign is a grassroots, spontaneous movement in which differences of religious and political conviction are merged in a common determination to halt the destruction of moral values within our national life, particularly in relation to television, and to establish the right of those who pay £67 million a year in licence fees to have their views taken into account'. To NVALA the licence fee presently amounted to 'taxation without representation'.[24]

Strategy

NVALA's tactical flexibility belied its doctrinal rigidity, but denoted its strategic setbacks in the culture wars. It was litigious – Whitehouse personally and for prosecutions under obscene publications and blasphemy laws. Besides monitoring programme content, it instituted a TV award and 'teach-ins' in the later 1960s. Its basic repertoire (like most campaigning NGOs) was of recruiting members, public meetings, media coverage and lobbying authority by phone, letter and heckling. Petitioning parliament

(and delivering the petition to parliament was an experience Whitehouse l
ovingly recounted in its arcane detail as the 'moment of a lifetime') evinced
its critique was less of systemic failure than of liberal conspiracy. The structures of governance were basically sound (a viewers' council apart), but the
personnel and culture at the BBC and in government were wrongly manned.[25]

The BBC's response was to minimize NVALA's impact by starving it of
publicity and not rising to its baiting. This strategy worked (in that Whitehouse was marginalized), but bolstered NVALA's case that the BBC was
immune to criticism. Privately the BBC was more nervous. Observers were
sent to NVALA conventions. The BBC's Information officer in Birmingham,
Kenneth Bird's report of the Birmingham Town Hall meeting typified this
uncertainty. Bird noted the farcical (the Methodist speaker who could not
recall the message God gave her that morning) through to the sinister,
ruthless way that non-Christian opinion was suppressed by what otherwise resembled a Women's Institute meeting. And Whitehouse's presence
disclosed anxieties about their audience. *Woman's Hour*, on which Whitehouse had first appeared in 1953, feared having her on when *Cleaning-up
TV* was published in 1967, because editor Monica Sims felt 'if Mrs. Whitehouse did give her views, I'm afraid a majority of our listeners might write
to support her'.[26]

David Attenborough, Controller of BBC2 urged producers to respond
rapidly to correspondence from 'of all people Mrs. Whitehouse'. To fail to
do so was to 'show considerable tactlessness and lack of political sense'.
Welcoming letters could be as dangerous and when the head of drama,
Sydney Newman, noted a 'sincere note' in a Whitehouse missive, the
Director of BBC television Kenneth Adam feared he was being 'naïve' and
'Mrs. W might exploit Sydney'. From 1965 it was decided that 'all letters
from avowed members' of NVALA 'should be referred unanswered to the
secretariat'. When, later, Whitehouse began phoning departmental heads
direct, they were advised to be 'careful not to be drawn into an argument'.[27] Peter Black in the *Daily Mail* scorned both the BBC's refusal to give
Whitehouse's new book screen time and at its author, by proposing 'there
are more ways of killing a dragon than by holding its head under water'.
The power to marginalize – as Whitehouse's absence from Goldie's study of
televised politics shows – was wielded by the BBC.[28]

Macmurraugh-Kavanagh's account of one of Whitehouse's main targets,
The Wednesday Play tallies with such evidence. This tempers a picture of
either a liberal-radical regime under Carleton Greene and an unflappable
1960s BBC (an image propagated variously by Whitehouse and historians
like Marwick). She argues it 'survived the 1960s in spite of the BBC, not
because of it', persistently undermined by critics from without and anxious
programme controllers within like Adam. Whitehouse was a factor in this,
in producer's minds, as much as Carleton Greene and Wilson skirmished
about criticisms of the government and the licence fee.[29]

The NVALA's legal shenanigans unnerved the BBC, but more through threat than real prospects. An episode of *Omnibus* shown in November 1968, which used a Jimi Hendrix soundtrack and performance to discuss tensions in US society, had Whitehouse beside herself. She told Carleton Greene this had been the 'most obscene' programme, showing a Vietcong prisoner being shot (a scene Whitehouse felt 'took us straight back to the days of the public executions'), besides Hendrix's masturbatory guitar technique. She pressed her supporter, Chief Constable of Lincolnshire, John Barnett to prosecute, but he was rebuffed by the Director of Public Prosecutions, Norman Skelhorn, on the ground that intention to deprave would be hard to prove and that these were isolated incidents in the programme. The BBC's Audience research did record the lowest reaction index for this episode and when a repeat was scheduled for May 1969, Whitehouse told the new Director-General Hill that the NVALA was pressing for prosecution under the obscenity laws. In Lincolnshire officers assembled reports on the 'grotesque and extremely crude' images in the programme. Hill's defence was that the music reflected a violent society, although personally, he found 'gyrating noisy performances like his [Hendrix's] repulsive'.[30]

In litigation early in 1967 over an unscripted aside on *World at One* by writer Johnny Speight (most famous for the BBC TV sitcom-satire, another bugbear of Whitehouse, *Til Death Us Do Part*), that Whitehouse was worse than a fascist since she cloaked her beliefs, the BBC's counsel grasped their resistance to any 'capitulation so far as this lady is concerned'. But he advised the BBC 'to nip this one in the bud', in preference to 'giving Mrs. Whitehouse the opportunity to appear in the role of a martyr' and bringing up the entirety of her 'voluminous correspondence'. 'To stifle the complaint now' counsel even suggested offering Whitehouse airtime to discuss her new book or to debate with her critics as a sop, or at least to prevent her exploiting her previous lack of airtime as an issue. A similar approach was adopted to the NVALA's awards. BBC management opted to be 'cool and non-committal'. For *Dixon of Dock Green* (which won the first award for its portrayal of the police, although criticized for showing how crime was undertaken) to accept might give NVALA valuable publicity, but to refuse since 'Mrs. Whitehouse had consistently attacked fellow actors and used violent language about the BBC' was likely to generate even more. It was decided not to boycott the awards, but to avoid comment on them, a minor concession to avoid a major one.[31]

NVALA and Whitehouse tailored arguments to suit multiple scenarios – evidence of TV's multifaceted reach she claimed, but of bandwagon politics, critics held. In 1967 she argued that football hooliganism no less than industrial conflict or 'the satirizing of public men and national institutions' were evidence of the 'moral vandalism fostered by the "hippy society" with its cult of softness', in which '"culture" is mass produced but beastliness increases'. She wrote to Wilson when he became Prime Minister in 1964 arguing economic growth depended 'upon the character of the British people'. This, she argued in an elision of morality with morale, was being 'devitalised by the constant portrayal of sex, violence and destructive satire, from stage [and] TV screen'. She regularly reminded Wilson of Labour's origins in a militant Christian faith and invoked a wartime spirit. She conjoined her anxieties over sexually transmitted disease rates with the PMG's 'self-imposed impotence' over intervening in programme content. The latter discouraged viewers from complaining and proved the need for new procedures.[32] When the licence fee was raised from £5 to £6 (colour from £10 to £11) in 1968, the NVALA campaigned for a pensioner's (one of its core constituencies) exemption. It suggested the increase be referred to the Prices and Incomes Board since at 20% it exceeded government policy.[33]

In 1968 Whitehouse, part of the cocktail of Birmingham race politics, made a case for including broadcasting in the Race Relations Act. Targets included *Til Death Us Do Part* and airtime with Tariq Ali, Ruth First and Stokely Carmichael. For Whitehouse such broadcasts were inflammatory and demonstrated the 'lack of understanding amongst television professionals of the power of television to accentuate problems'. But broadcasters countered that they were reporting attitudes not inciting them.[34]

Direct action was mooted. Echoing the symbolism of CND and the US civil rights movement a women's march on London was contemplated in 1964 by the Reverend Harold Goodwin. Another leading supporter of NVALA from its outset Chief Constable John Barnett, proposed civil disobedience against a licence fee increase in 1965. Barnett argued NVALA should 'make a political issue of our cause' and, drawing parallels with a dock strike, rise against 'conditions unsatisfactory'. Such militancy 'disturbed' the Archbishop of Westminster's representative, who preferred to 'proceed with great prudence'.[35] But NVALA rejected turning off or switching channels – this it thought to be 'the philosophy of "I'm alright jack" taken to the ultimate'. 'Silence means assent', 'Don't moan, Phone!' were its slogans. It encouraged (short, polite) letter writing, an activity that reinforced the middle-class biases in the membership, besides legitimizing and empowering housewives and giving them the 'gumph' (as one put it of her newly acquired protesting 'know-how') to express themselves.[36]

Suggestive both of Whitehouse's media savvy and awareness of the limitations to other strategies or weight the movement could wield through membership alone, was correspondence with high profile BBC or political figures. If this revealed a certain faith in existing power structures, it more often aimed to convert private discussions into the public domain via open letters. If this suggested a readiness to by-pass a mass movement strategy, it also recognized the resistance that NVALA had encountered to meeting deputations or public debate and its limited access to the media. Petition support was brought to the signature of such missives – '366,000 supporters' was the sign-off on

Whitehouse's June 1965 letter to the PM. Missives themselves became an issue. The etiquette of whether replies could be cited in NVALA literature was raised. A reply from Wilson that got lost in the mail in 1965 generated questions in the Commons. No.10 concluded: 'Mrs. Whitehouse is clearly a most tiresome woman, out for all the publicity she can get'.[37]

However often NVALA were informed 'as you know from previous correspondence the government does not intervene in matters of programme content', they proved tireless. A public telegram after the 1967 New Years' Day *Til Death Us Do Part* informed Wilson that this 'dirty blasphemous' programme could only have intended to 'insult the viewing public' and implored the PM 'to take responsibility', asserting the government's 'obligation is moral rather than legal'. Seeking to clarify once and for all the limits to the government's ability to intervene, this lead to a letter being drafted that it was hoped 'with the authority of No.10 behind it, will make a lasting impact on... her organization'. Whitehouse had even less chance of twisting the arm's length policy in the hands of Short's successor as PMG, Roy Mason, who simply asked her to stop sending NVALA material. Nor did the new Tory government of 1970 increase the prospect, with the Minister of Posts and Telecommunications (as the PMG was renamed), Chris Chataway, adopting the same line of not confusing the existing BBC and ITA machinery.[38]

Yet NVALA interest in a programme could agitate the government over and above their perseverance. Peter Watkins' nuclear drama *The War Game* – about the impact of a nuclear detonation over Southern England, banned in 1965 and not broadcast by the BBC until 1985 – allowed Whitehouse to fuse her case about the moral effects of TV and the balance of power between the government and BBC governors. Whitehouse told Wilson that a Civil Defence Officer in Kent predicted *The War Game* would 'have a terrible effect on the public morale' and if this were so, wondered whether it ought to be the Home Office and not the BBC who decided whether it should be aired? Both No.10 (for exposing the inadequacies of civil defence) and Lord Normanbrook (for antagonizing the government during licence fee negotiations) were apprehensive that Whitehouse had got wind of the contents and equally that any government intervention should not be seen to be creating a precedent for other interventions.[39]

Part of NVALA strategy was, unavoidably, Whitehouse herself. She was certainly image conscious. The *Daily Mail* reckoned by 1970 'the sophistication of the television personalities and other public people she now meets' had 'rubbed off on this former schoolteacher' and she 'looks more up-to-date'. Her (MRA) colleague Mrs. Sturdy reported she 'picks her clothes with television and the public platform in mind'. She visited the hairdresser every ten days. Her method was to exploit the same media she was criticizing. The Birmingham Town Hall meeting, in all its dramatic asides – playwright David Turner defending his work, stewards blocking cameras and nuns stamping to drown out protesters chanting 'we want sex' – was covered by the BBC. She was in Bernard Levin's opinion, 'skilled in the art of lobbying behind the scenes while fussing in front of them' and at obtaining 'widespread coverage in the newspapers' via sound-bites (and a spell as *Daily Sketch* TV critic in 1967) as much as controversial views. However excluded NVALA were, they made good copy *because* they transgressed the prevailing norms of public discourse.[40]

Whitehouse's charisma was a resource for the movement – if her singular personality rendered NVALA a virtual mass movement. What also lent NVALA everyday force and made it newsworthy was rooting arguments in specific programmes – Britons' common cultural diet. NVALA had opinions on all and sundry programming – from violence and horror in *Dr Who* to the pilot of Frankie Howard's classical camp, *Up Pompeii*, which was 'an insult to the average viewer' and 'sordid' (a fear that its star also entertained).[41] Like New Left reviewers who could see 'in almost every programme... *some* view of life, some implicit or explicit social or moral attitude' and 'worried about the sheer volume of television material dealing with violence or with the implied virtues of materialism', NVALA could detected meaning in all programming. This rendered its outbursts a predictable part of the entertainment of the TV landscape. Whitehouse herself rapidly acquired an iconic infamy in popular culture that dogged her career to the 1990s – mocked by comedians and impudent pornographers. As early as 1964 David Turner (resident playwright at Coventry's Belgrade theatre, who Whitehouse criticized but refused to let speak at Birmingham Town Hall) broadcast a BBC radio skit *Sizzlewick*, in which a 'Mrs. Smallgood' from the Midlands started a 'freedom from sex campaign'.[42]

This could verge on the post-modern when she launched tirades against TV characters, dismissing her nemesis *Til Death Us Do Part*'s Alf Garnett as a 'silly and vulgar old man' in 1967. Whitehouse was endorsed (to her chagrin) by Garnett in an episode of *Til Death* in February 1967 (just after Speight's outburst). A gastroentiritus afflicted Alf was reading Whitehouse's newly published book, *Cleaning-up TV* and suggested 'she ought to go out and clean up all the country, get rid of all the dirty foreigners and their dirty disorders'. Blaming his disease on 'those coons your 'arold Wilson keeps letting inta the country' whereas 'that woman is concerned for the moral welfare of the country... better than all that filthy muck the BBC put on'. Rather as liberals had created Garnett, they 'subconsciously welcomed' Whitehouse as a godsend, affirming their progressive credentials. *Humanist News*, for example, could not help but compliment Whitehouse's 'moral seriousness' and that she was 'not rich... not educated... single-minded and energetic'.[43]

Before NVALA there were 'clean-up' branches in South Wales, Birmingham, Mansfield, Nottingham, Manchester and London. But the extent to which this was a sham behind the accoutrements of a mass movement was revealed by Dance agreeing the council and executive roles could simply be swapped in 1967 between the London and Birmingham committees. By most accounts despite the annual convention the executive was self-perpetuating and criticism of Whitehouse was sacrilege – all credence to critics who thought it an MRA front.[44]

Its claim to represent the viewing public was hard pressed. Membership was 7000 by 1968 and peaked in the mid-1970s. But Whitehouse told the 1968 Convention that with Church support, plus manifesto signatories, some 'one million people have, in some practical way, expressed their support of our work'.[45] In correspondence to the BBC Whitehouse claimed to speak for ³/4 million viewers and was amazed it considered them a 'fringe movement' rather than 'representative' like peak-level bodies such as the British Medical Association. But BBC Secretary, Kenneth Lamb, disputed NVALA's claims, since it was reluctant to say which organizations affiliated *en bloc*. Normanbrook exploited the lack of any provably close link between the 'clean-up TV' petition's signatories and the outpourings of the NVALA leaders, to refuse to meet with them.[46]

NVALA was a movement of the elder generation and the provinces, with a palpably non-metropolitan appeal. It occasionally targeted the young (Cliff Richard won its 1970 TV award). Whitehouse was 53 when the campaign started and many activists were retired or housewives and with time for activism, as much as TV enabled domestic forms of activism. There was a curmudgeonly element in NVALA. NVALA members the Priests of Norwich felt the 'ghastly long haired young men with strange musical instruments' on a 1965 *Radio Times* cover, 'cannot be a good influence on the style of impressionable young people'. Many took a dim view of TV *per se* not just programming. Malcolm Muggeridge, a Christian and NVALA convert in the 1960s, a noted critic of the Beatles, drugs and contraception and himself a media personality, confided to Whitehouse in 1967 that TV, whether 'vicious or wholesome', was 'a tenth rate medium at best and always will be'.[47]

And NVALA's manner as much as anything distinguished it from its liberal quarry. Conservative MP Michael Clark-Hutchison felt the BBC was propagating 'low schoolboy humour' and wondered 'how can men like David Frost', the presenter of the satirical *That Was The Week That Was* (TW3), 'be allowed to earn up to £600 a week and decry our way of life?'. A Warwickshire councillor's wife complained at Birmingham Town Hall that the BBC was 'behaving like an adolescent' rather than 'maturely'. And yet, as the meeting's chair Councillor Pepper put it, the BBC dismissed complaints in a 'smooth, urbane' way and this irked NVALA. Pepper warned of danger 'if we allow ourselves to become over-emotional', yet concluded, 'if we stand by and say nothing while the decline is going on we can't complain when the ultimate fall takes place'.[48]

Wilson was informed NVALA represented the 'repugnance which exists in the provinces for much of what has come to be known as "swinging

London" and for which the BBC appears to have a predisposition, thus moulding the climate of opinion rather than reflecting it'. Inducing political support, Whitehouse estimated it would 'be a wise politician, and wise party, who realizes that the future lies with whoever has the courage to grasp this nettle'. This appeal to the interests of a less vociferous majority of citizens was one that British politicians had been conscious of and keen to make since the 1920s. It also offers an interesting contrast to the assumed effect on politics of changes in values proposed in 1971 in Inglehart's 'silent revolution', focusing on an elder generation and moral retrenchment not modernization.[49] Laying claim to be a moral majority (or 'silent majority' as Nixon put it in 1969) in advance of the term achieving popular currency in 1970s America, NVALA bears comparison with the US pro-life, anti-liberal Christian right. Both exploited fear of change, appealed to an anti-establishment populism, seemed more mobilized by moral than material agendas and had a developed sense of grievance and sacrifice for the movement. Perlstein's account of Goldwater's divisive unsuccessful 1964 Presidential campaign details the liberal context (Betty Friedan, Michael Harrington and Rachel Carson published liberal landmark works in 1963) and a range of campaigning techniques and organized extra-party conservative networks that emerged. NVALA can be seen similarly as part of the kindling for the New Right.[50]

By 1970 NVALA imagined itself 'the voice of the silent millions', not 'a noisy pressure group representing a tiny minority, but a manifestation of an awakening democracy conscious of its power and responsibility'. Whilst open to all, 'as our national institutions are founded on... Christian concepts, so VALA reflects... the values inherent in our national heritage'. In its mind's eye, NVALA saw itself not as a single-issue 'man-made movement concerned simply with raising the standard of broadcasting', but as a 'movement of the spirit' uniting those with 'a passionate desire to enrich the quality of life'. With 'groups all over the country' it envisioned reaching out to 'every sphere of the nation's life – education, politics, social and moral issues'. Its hope was that if broadcasting 'was the launching pad of the permissive society', then 'in the 1970s it could become the pacemaker of the responsible society'. To achieve this depended 'on the courage and vision of creative people who care more for society than for their own need for self-expression'. It also depended on – a familiar activist injunction – nothing less than the 'willingness of each one of us'. There was no lack of certainty in its sense of a national and historic mission: 'as in the last century it was inevitable that Trade Unions should become an essential part of industrial life, so today it is natural that a viewers and listeners association should arise in order to protect the interests of a viewing public and to raise the standards of radio and TV programmes generally'.[51]

Building support

Prominent NVALA patrons came from military and religious elites: Air Chief Marshall Sir Theodore McEvoy; the English secretary of the World Methodist Council, Benson Perkins; the Lord Bishops of Hereford, Blackburn, Argyle and the Isles, plus personalities like Muggeridge. Dowager Lady Birdwood, who dabbled in far right groups in the 1970s and had like Whitehouse (an obituary attests) 'weird taste in spectacles', lead NVALA's London branch through the late 1960s.[52]

In attempting to assemble support with cognate groups in civil society, NVALA, like many NGOs, faced difficulties once speaking beyond its immediate campaign and membership. Other groups were resistant to the idea of appearing 'political'. There were successes – the Scottish Housewives Association, whose Secretary Mrs. E. Pattulo was a Whitehouse supporter, shifted its support from Cyril Black's Public Morality Council in 1964, something he regretted, whilst supporting Clean-up TV. Black was Tory MP for Wimbledon, a temperance campaigner and President of the London Baptist Association.[53]

Churches were NVALA's best recruiting ground and it advertised in papers like the *Baptist Times*. Of the mass of letters in its archives, most were from non-conformists – Presbyterians, Evangelical Free Churches, Baptist Chapels – and from outside of England, where Protestantism remained stronger. The Clean-up manifesto and petition was collected for by the Ulster Women's Christian Temperance Union, National British Women's Total Abstinence Union and Royal Society of St. George (whose particular objection was to TV attacks on the Royal family). The Catholic Church's opposition to permissiveness was, in general, more resolute, so disgruntled Anglicans were more apparent amongst the grassroots. Amongst non-religious groups, typical was Rotary International that explained its 'strictly non-party approach to political matters' precluded institutional support for NVALA's licence fee campaign in 1968, although individuals might help. Replies in this vein were also received from the National anti-Vivisection Society, St. John's Ambulance, Girl Guides and British Legion Scotland.[54]

The Catholic Teachers' Federation (CTF) backed NVALA, requesting parents, staff and pupils sign the manifesto in 1965. This was countered by Charles Curran (to be Carleton Greene's successor and like him, a Catholic) and adult educationalist and future Arts Council Secretary-General Roy Shaw. Tony Higgins (the Nottingham CTF President and also involved in the Society for Education in Film and Television) worked to reverse the decision internally rather than making it a public issue, in which case it would be harder for the Federation to recant. Higgins had his work cut out in Nottingham, where Kenneth Adam was heckled at a CTF meeting shortly after *Up the Junction* aired as *The Wednesday Play*. Higgins and Curran questioned the propriety of NVALA's campaigning and research methods, highlighted other Catholic media initiatives (notably the Catholic Radio and Television Centre, of which Curran was an ex-Chair) and a Papal encyclical ('Miranda Prorusus') that emphasized parental and educators' besides broadcasters' responsibilities. Curran stressed to Alderman Shiell, the CTF's secretary, that the Clean-up campaign was 'too sweeping and there is a lack of discrimination'. By 1966 the CTF was inched away from supporting Whitehouse. Higgins concluded of campaigning against NVALA that 'their attitude is based on emotion not reason, they are not open to argument'.[55]

The Mothers Union (MU) briefly embraced the campaign at its inception. MU's President explained that its own TV groups shared the campaign's interests. But the manifesto only won the support of two of the 13 area dioceses it was dispatched to. 'Though sharing a common concern for declining moral standards', most felt that 'to indict the BBC alone for propaganda which undermines standards and morals' or 'to suggest that the BBC is contributing any more than any other field of the mass media to the many signs of ill-health in our society', was 'neither fair nor realistic'. They felt 'the writers of the manifesto had invalidated it as a responsible or constructive document by their use of intemperate language'. The 'sweeping accusations made by the manifesto against the BBC' were 'grossly exaggerated'. The Norfolk Group wanted 'a less aggressive tone' and to persuade broadcasters 'in the normal way by discussion, preferably not of the heated, over-emotional type reflected in the manifesto'. To this end it favoured clearer categorization of programmes 'so that the use of the switch could be brought in before the damage is done', a 'practical' measure it thought 'could be pressed for immediately'. After just five months, in July 1964 the MU's President told the *Church Times* it would not be collecting signatures as an organization although individual members might. Such conclusions were relished by Doreen Stephens, head of BBC TV family programmes. She nursed the MU as a barrier against 'this other "monstrous regiment of women" ... the Birmingham Women "Vigilante" group'.[56]

Another characteristic was NVALA's suspicion of professional experts – be they in TV, research or playwrights. Its great fear was 'being dominated by the broadcasting professional unless viewer's representatives of all kinds... make sure that their voice is heard'. It saw as 'one of the most ominous developments' that 'playwrights are demanding that... they alone shall say what is fit for the public to see' and that the BBC appeared 'more concerned with the rights of young playwrights than with the community'. Though this was more a revolt of TV consumers against producers than against professionals *per se* Whitehouse's case was that related experts – police, doctors and also parents – had as legitimate a claim to control output. The amateur-professional dichotomy was recurrent in debates about TV. The government-appointed Pilkington Report (1962) regarded professionalism as the BBC's advantage over ITV, where good broadcasters operated against the grain of a culture dominated by advertising and head count judgements of a programme's worth. It also bore on NVALA's model for participation. David Frost, speaking at NVALA's 1970 Convention, argued pre-broadcast vetting by a Viewers' Council would kill new besides bad ideas, since 'an amateur cannot be expected to make a judgment'. His belief that viewers were too intelligent to be brainwashed was, revealingly, met with cries of 'no'.[57]

NVALA reveled in its oppositional status, its non-professional everyday DIY activism, appealing for funds for Whitehouse's 'spartan' office from where she tackled the mighty BBC. In this vein Whitehouse celebrated the 'I'm Backing Britain' movement of Surbiton typists – who after devaluation in 1967 promised to work through their tea breaks – in a letter to Wilson penned, in a sure sign of commitment, on New Years Day.[58] Its case for morally re-arming Britons was delivered with frank force. It seemed rather naïve by contrast with the educated, younger, satirist ethos – if this lent it a disarming appeal, it alienated many more. NVALA tactics were also a reaction to the professionalization of politics discussed in Chapter 7 – that party now seemed managerial, utilized the machinery of public relations and was delivered by TV. NVALA's repertoire – public meetings, leaflets, petitions, heckling, not to mention more underhand tactics – was more traditional and less contingent upon professional expertise or funding. If political parties struggled to address a plurality of issues that pressure groups more readily tackled, then it was also the way such groups went about politics that unsettled the main parties.

Like CND, NVALA's politics were symbolic and expressive more than instrumentally aimed at specific material ends. There were not the badges or dress sense that for Parkin characterized CND, but it was no coincidence that the movements title, National VALA was pronounced 'national valour'.[59] It also defiantly expressed the values of housewifery and parenting. These were lodestars of Whitehouse's worldview, evident from her early newspaper writing and radio broadcasts in the 1950s that emphasized 'the part that ordinary housewives can play in spheres far beyond her home', from the Cold War to homosexuality. Appearing on *Woman's Hour* on the eve of the coronation suggested Whitehouse was hardly ordinary, but as evident was how the domestic and personal were here rendered political. Although her intention was to preserve the demarcation between the two spheres in so much as the public ought not invade the private, but should embody its best qualities. She eagerly submitted evidence to a Home Office Committee on Privacy set up in 1970, even though broadcasting was outside its remit.[60]

The femininity deployed by the group, first formed as 'Women of Britain', was conservative. Whitehouse was formally listed as Mrs. E.R. (Ernest) Whitehouse, her husband's moniker. As Buckland told NVALA's founding audience only a minority of programmes were 'corrupting', but the lack of a resolute Church response meant 'many women feel that the training they are trying to give their children is being undermined by the television'.

And this was the reason Whitehouse gave for resigning her teaching job in 1964 to devote herself to campaigning – because 'influences outside education are undercutting the character training we are trying to give' as parents and teachers. This linked NVALA with more liberal-minded groups (and in its focus on children, with CND). The 1959 Standing Conference on Television heard from leading TV researcher Joseph Treneman that prospects for educational television were limited by the (mostly commercial) champions of the right to choose and enjoy. The place of education in the cultural hierarchy, as with other traditional sources of authority, was slipping.[61]

Contexts: Christianity, conservatism, TV

A key context for the NVALA was the waning of Christianity as relative economic and social security undermined the security sought in religion or rigid cultural norms. This was all the more apparent following a period of church growth immediately after 1945. For Callum Brown, the 1960s saw 'discursive christianity' abruptly diminish in constructions of the self, sending 'organised Christianity... to the margins of social significance'. Besides declining church numbers, it was secular personal morality – the self-liberation, shift away from restraint, questioning of authority and institutions like the church, marriage, family, Sunday and the state fostered by affluence and permissiveness – that provoked the NVALA. These seemed notable in 1963: Profumo, the pill, *TW3*, relaxing of BBC codes. Brown argues these secularizing trends were particularly borne by women – and three quarters of NVALA members were women. If affluence relaxed traditional codes, it simultaneously agitated post-materialist cravings to fill this spiritual, ethical void and, more simply, some defence of them. As Peter Fryer presciently declared in his 1963 study of prudery, 'Mrs. Grundy is with us still'.[62]

Whitehouse was one free radical amongst much broader theological and philosophical disputes in the 1960s. Secularization was not sociologically determined, but involved intellectual shifts too. As Roodhouse shows, debate between reformers and conservatives within the Anglican Church (not to mention other varieties of Christianity and religion), were longstanding and had been public since the 1960 *Lady Chatterley's Lover* trial. The Church contained multiple views on social change in the 1960s, but through the decade these were reduced to whether the Church could continue to speak for the nation and how Christian it should be; those unwilling to countenance either sect-like purity or adapt to a more civic-style religion were squeezed out. This was easily polarized in the media as Whitehouse versus the radical, liberal Bishop of Woolwich, John Robinson. McLeod also stresses a more variegated religious and social process than Brown and how Whitehouse was at the 'conservative end of the spectrum of Christian opinion' and 'far from being representative'. But he concurs that the role of TV and the BBC's shift to a plainer-speaking ethos were vectors in secularization and 'in that respect, Whitehouse had correctly identified the enemy'. However unrepresentative, Whitehouse became Britain's most recognizable Christian, more so than any formal church figure.[63]

Muggeridge, accepting Whitehouse's invitation to deliver the 1967 Convention keynote, saw NVALA as 'awakening' a 'Christian resistance movement' to the 'Pagan society' that would 'make people see that materialism, with its black mysticism of violence and obsessive eroticism is... a poor way of living'. In no uncertain terms, NVALA equated moral rectitude with Christianity, as vital to social cohesion. Whitehouse's view was that Britons faced 'as grave a danger in the field of morals and faith as we faced on the battlefields twenty years ago'. The 'manoeuverings' of humanists, communists and media were daily and made this 'enemy... more subtle'. NVALA offered, in short, a campaign on television and a wider philosophical package. Tracey and Morrison concluded this amounted to a desire to 'recolonise social life for God' and create a 'theocratic state', but adjudged this an unlikely prospect. This faith that Britons were at heart Christians, sustained the NVALA and gave its activists a characteristic optimism, whatever setbacks were experienced.[64]

The NVALA blamed the Church response as much as secularization – itself questioning established authority. Like politics, the Church was 'so fearful of appearing authoritarian – that dirtiest of all dirty words – that they have forfeited their moral authority'. The Church, McLeod holds, struggled in a more plural society to speak with a common or authoritative voice. John Robinson's *Honest to God* (1963) seemed to swim with permissive tides. Robinson situated god in man's earthly actions, not in heaven and as one chapter was titled 'prescribed nothing – except love', including easier divorce and contraception. For those of NVALA's ilk, this was heresy – as with the BBC's 'new morality', a shorthand for the precise opposite. Michael Ramsey, Archbishop of Canterbury was criticized, but Robinson was the liberal enemy – a defence witness for Penguin in the *Lady Chatterley* trial, opposed to nuclear weapons and the death penalty and a Labour member until he quit over 1968's Commonwealth Immigrants Act. Whitehouse felt the church was too timid, too liberal in its attempts to be relevant and Robinson's 'situational ethics', insufficiently prescriptive or doctrinal. NVALA supporter Arnold Lunn's *Cult of Softness* (softness was a NVALA keyword, denoting, like Thatcherism's 'wet', a fatal irresolution) wanted less indulgence of individual weakness and more moral guidance.[65]

Whitehouse's involvement with MRA since the 1930s also discouraged church and political support. MRA preached love, honesty, purity and unselfishness and encouraged members to engage with social and political matters, combating issues from alcoholism through to communism. MRA's tactics of organized letter writing and clandestine air infused NVALA. NVALA's willingness to by-pass ecclesiastical teaching and structures for a personal connection to God and to emote righteousness and the private self as public politics also echoed MRA. Its sect-like style, as much as specific beliefs, fed into the charismatic-New Age revivalism that contested church authority and made for a more plural, diverse Christianity through the 1960s. In 1963 MRA's leader Peter Howard wrote *Britain and the Beast*, lambasting the 'dirt' peddled by the BBC, the excesses of the Edinburgh festival and endorsed Whitehouse's campaign shortly after its Birmingham Town Hall meeting.[66] MRA's Blanford Press published Whitehouse's first book and NVALA newsletters advertised the MRA's Westminster Theatre, which hosted plays by Peter Howard and in 1965 Alan Thornhill's popular *Mr Wilberforce MP*, which drew parallels with Churchill's wartime and Clean-up's efforts – 'under God causes which start off being hopeless to all appearances end up in a mighty triumph'. Much discussed in Labour MP Tom Driberg's 1964 expose, NVALA's MRA links were not denied but its controlling hand and finances (the charge of critics like Roy Shaw) were.[67]

NVALA asserted its authenticity as a 'spontaneous' (suspiciously recurrent in its lexicon) 'expression of the determination of ordinary people... to preserve their homes and families from the seeping immorality... portrayed on television'. And Buckland found just 5% of members were MRA active. But there was a conspiratorial, furtive, extremist aspect to NVALA. It associated the BBC with communism and was itself compared with fascism (by a BBC staff bulletin and by James Halloran, a leading TV researcher and member of the BBC Midlands Advisory council). TV writer and Labour Peer Ted Willis accused NVALAers of scare tactics and threatening letters and by the 1970s it frequented right-wing para-politics. Willis was wary of those forwarding an explicit cultural agenda, be it Wesker or Whitehouse, and believed her advocacy of censorship made her 'a very dangerous woman'.[68] TV was a focus for Cold War paranoia and conspiracy theories, as ex-controller of BBC TV Stuart Hood regularly pointed out when he became *Spectator* media columnist. ITV had been 'a villainous plot hatched by financiers, advertising agencies and unscrupulous politicians', whilst the BBC politically vetted job candidates and held to received truths about state broadcasting. Hood regarded 'the governors of the BBC, members of the ITA, Mrs. Mary Whitehouse and her grass-root puritans' at one in 'the great conspiracy to protect the British public'.[69]

Also unable to offer much support to NVALA was the Conservative Party, hamstrung by a modernity it had facilitated in legislation on divorce, gambling, obscene publications and TV. Anxieties about the break-up of traditional values and youth crime were regularly voiced by women's sections and MPs like Dance. Dance had strongly opposed the Wolfenden Report on homosexuality and prostitution that had differentiated between crime and sin and declared sin no concern of the law since it was a private not public matter. Party leaders concurred that material well-being had bred rather than assuaged social and moral problems and whilst sensitive to church opinion, were keener to advocate family and individual responsibility than more rigorous state action. Besides an ideological aversion to imposing a moral agenda on a more pluralist society, Conservatives were politically wary of tampering with popular tastes they had introduced via ITV in 1955. Jarvis argues that debates about crime, youth and TV, initiated by Butler at the Home Office, more than laid the ground for modernizing, permissive legislation of the later 1960s and, as Brown terms it, the de-Christianizing of much of the British state and law. The notion of the Anglican Church as 'the Tory party at prayer', was fragmenting – just as the Church of England was no longer so Tory in inclination (to judge by Robinson), nor was the Tory party so keen to be seen to pray.[70]

The chances of the Conservative Party (which had some sympathy for MRA in the late 1930s) acting on Whitehouse's strictures were then limited. Just as the chances were limited of Labour taking up the moral battle against ITV and commercial triviality that Pilkington had urged – for the same reason of not being seen to interfere with people's private leisure. What Hugh Gaitskell wrote to Richard Hoggart, Pilkington's main author, that 'had the report been less naïve and more based on solid research' then Labour might have acted, held true for Conservative dialogue with NVALA. The Conservative leader from 1965, Edward Heath, 'evacuated the arena of popular politics', Campbell argues, in favour of a 'cool corporatism'. This 'distanced him... from the keepers of the party's moral conscience – women' meaning Whitehouse's appeal could still resonate there. Lukewarm as he was, Heath claimed to Whitehouse to stress individual, moral and family responsibility 'more than our opponents' and was most effusive in congratulating NVALA on its fifth year.[71]

TV was a delicate issue for Conservatives. Having battled to break the BBC's monopoly, ITV had been mauled by the Pilkington committee and the response of the BBC to ITV competition had prompted Whitehouse's moral-Christian backlash. Belief in the efficacy of the market seemed to be undermining conservative morality. Whether Conservatives felt a responsibility that overrode their resistance to state intervention, largely turned on whether TV was believed to influence society and behaviour. They were divided on this, although Butler, Deedes and Eccles accepted that it was a matter worth researching.

But there was grassroots Conservative support for the campaign as local activists, programme monitors and in local motions, especially by women in the party. Their voices were regularly heard at party conference from the later 1950s arguing for a more authoritarian moral stance and indicting TV as a cause of crime, delinquent behaviour, cultural debasement and family breakdowns. This was very much the social world that Whitehouse inhabited – an elder generation on fixed incomes, uneasy with the effects of working-class prosperity and downwardly mobile in differential terms by dint of inflation. NVALA articulated and liberated visceral elements in popular conservatism. In this respect, its reliance on moral instinct and common sense over more ideological, dispassionate or academic stances (a facet of YC culture as the previous chapter noted) resonated with conservative hearts (more than heads).[72]

Like CND for Labour, NVALA pricked Conservatism's moral instincts. It showed, as with consumerism, the brittleness of Conservatives' middle-class support. NVALA signalled the discontent with party and willingness to engage in extra-parliamentary protest that Marsh detailed and the party's difficulties in dealing with moral politics. Whilst part of the boom in pressure groups, Whitehouse was herself wary of them. Vocal minorities on abortion and homosexuality, she felt, had prompted permissive legislation passed under the Wilson government, to which she might have added the evidence in HH Wilson's seminal *Pressure Group*, on the commercial lobby behind ITV.[73]

'The campaign', Jasper More, Whitehouse's own MP, warned Prime Minister Douglas-Home in June 1964, 'is assuming the dimensions of a mass movement'. Since its 'leaders are conservative supporters', More worried this might damage party support. A month later, Bill Deedes proposed a 'consumers council' for broadcasting. The Cabinet rejected this, arguing that it would interfere with the jurisdiction of the ITA and BBC governors; that responsibility lay with parents not the state and that it was wisest to await the results of research initiated by Rab Butler as Home secretary. Deedes stressed TV was not the sole influence on 'manners, morals and a standard of values', but his 1966 speech to the NVALA's first convention admitted that influences like school were struggling to compete with television and the movies.[74]

Six Conservative MPs were present at the February 1965 meeting that set up NVALA: five from the party's broadcasting committee, Dance, Harold Gurden, Greville-Howard, Michael Clark-Hutchison, R.G. Grant-Ferris, plus the vehement opponent of immigration, Cyril Osborne. Whitehouse addressed the party's Broadcasting Committee, but there was little discussion of NVALA's agenda other than Dance suggesting competition from ITV had been bad for the BBC, until Julian Critchley (a speaker at NVALA's 1972 convention) revived some notion of a Broadcasting Council in 1970.[75]

For the radical left, NVALA's broader agenda was a deterrent, even if nodes of agreement (for example with some feminists, on pornography) occurred. Some commentators felt the left were too inhibited in debates about emotional or moral well-being and gave up this terrain too easily.[76] Labour had little truck with NVALA – suspicious of MRA and, with odd exceptions, more liberal-mannered and minded. Tony Benn, a nonconformist, interested in more participatory democracy and critic of the BBC establishment, whilst disagreeing with NVALA views on programmes, acknowledged their right to voice them. As PMG, Benn forwarded NVALA motions to the BBC, believing they ought to 'consider expressions of public opinion about their service' and agreeing the power balance between government and BBC governors was a key question. In 1971 Benn described the BBC's response to Whitehouse as 'grossly offensive'.[77]

NVALA could transgress partisan politics. Labour MP Jeremy Bray agreed, 'politics should say more about morality and personal conduct' and 'abandon the prudishness that will not speak of god'. Bob Edwards, Labour MP for Bilston (Wolverhampton), was an early NVALA supporter, but would not attend its 1966 convention because it had 'become too involved in political aspects'. Conservatives also rejected the politicization; Richard Nugent MP told a NVALA-supporting constituent in Godalming, whereby 'moral issues got blurred and tangled in those of freedom of speech'. Jim Prior pointed out in encouragement of a NVALA constituent that the BBC received more complaints from the left (such as Harold Wilson, who believed the BBC 'a nest of Tories') about its bias than from Conservatives.[78] As divergently as such politics could play out, there were clear limits to the purchase NVALA's case acquired popularly and no decisive political cleavage could be forged (as in the USA) between an anti-metropolitan, politicized Christianity and liberal elites. When it came even Thatcherism's repudiation of sixties values was rather muted, Harrison notes, with Conservatives believing Britain was now a more secular society.[79] If this suggests the culture shift effected by and during the 1960s was well entrenched by the 1980s, it also suggests 'culture' had its limits as a political force and issue or as NVALA applied it.

Equally, the way the NVALA raised the issue hampered its popularity and traction amongst Conservatives. Much as NVALA's campaign was intolerant of the shift to a more self-expressive, less deferential culture, its own lack of restraint put it at odds with those strains of Conservatism that eschewed dogmatism and abrasiveness and preferred to appear low-key, demur, almost un-partisan (if for partisan reasons), verging on the unpolitical. The politicization of the YCs in the later 1960s chafed with these same instincts. NVALA valued deference, but was decidedly un-deferential in going about restoring it. This was its un-doing, since in other ways it articulated widespread Conservative concerns about TV. Leading Conservatives were key to marginalizing Whitehouse – locating her as beyond the pale of acceptable politics. Most Conservative support was tacit. The National Women's Advisory Committee chair suggested meeting, but only once she had appraised levels of local support. Paul Bryan MP, who was close to Whitehouse, turned down an offer to speak at the 1969 Convention, assuring Whitehouse of his support, but that they best not appear to be in league. Jasper More's professed support was likewise curtailed by his role as a government whip. In 1971 MP John Selwyn Gummer, the son of an Anglican minister and who later sat on the Church of England's General Synod, took a foray into *The Permissive Society*. But he mentioned Whitehouse only once, despite dealing with her precise canon – professional liberals, drugs, sex, abortion, theatre, literature, legalized pornography in Denmark, the 'lilac establishment', Church and TV. And the sorts of MP that did openly associate with Whitehouse – Dance, Gerald Nabarro and Neil Hamilton (NVALA chair in 1972 and editor of the *Feudal Times and Reactionary Herald* in Aberystwyth) – were outsiders.[80]

Besides secularization and Conservatism, TV mobilized NVALA. Britons' most common culture in this period was as much a storm centre of public debate as consumerism. Politicians quickly put their finger on how TV not only hosted debate on other issues, but excited it itself. As John Stonehouse explained in a 1968 speech, TV 'has long ousted the weather as the most frequent talking point'. Even CND, reviewing the debate over TV stimulated by the 1962 Pilkington report, considered this 'indicative much more of the state of the country than ever the failure to maintain an independent deterrent was'.[81]

By 1970 more than 90% of Britons had a TV and they were Europe's most avid viewers, living what one commentator termed 'a withdrawn and inarticulate life'. Such elitism has been rife. Critics across the political spectrum have freighted TV as the cause of a range of social ills. Despite this, the prosaic nature of TV has discouraged media historians from paying it the attention film has attracted and lead them to focus on institutions, elites and programme production rather than its everyday, domestic setting and popular consumption. The same prosaicness steered historians away from consumer institutions dealing primarily with everyday consumption. Yet historians might benefit from watching TV more closely. If a church habit declined, some of its power switched over to TV. Offer sees the activity of TV-viewing involving a misanthropic, acquisitive, materialist outlook on life, which might account for NVALA's subconscious unease towards it irrespective of content it found offensive. TV has been central to debates about social capital and political participation in modern democracies. Most have concluded it was corrosive and disengaging – 'the villain of the piece' in a survey of British citizenship. Even those, like Norris, that have argued TV might inform or mobilize citizens have tended to regard TV as one-step removed from politics, rather than having a history as a political issue in its own right.[82]

TV politics

TV had long been a cause for political debate. Rival pressure groups contested the advent of ITV in 1955 and the (in)activity of televiewing and content of programming were widely debated. The NVALA was countered from 1965 by COSMO (founded in Bloomsbury's Cosmo Place) and TRACK (Television and Radio Committee). TRACK was chaired by Roy Shaw, with Richard Hoggart (like Shaw a member of the BBC advisory council) and TV writers like David Mercer amongst members. COSMO started out as the

Harlow Housewives League, rebutting Whitehouse's claim to speak for women and campaigning for artistic freedom. Its leading light was Avril Fox, very much Whitehouse's antithesis. A Communist until 1956 and now Labour councillor whose children had left home, her beliefs meshed Sufi, feminism and science fiction and assessed the 'holiness of sex' and 'arch paternalists'. The NVALA dismissed COSMO as liberals of the worst sort, supporting the likes of Lenny Bruce and supported by the *Daily Worker*. It saw the two as BBC collusions – and the two did coincide, with Hoggart wanting Fox to step aside to let the professionals run the counter-Whitehouse operation. But COSMO could boast a membership of 500 and it survived to campaign for the abolition of the Obscene Publications Act at the end of the decade. A measure both of the unease NVALA created in the BBC, for all Greene's public unflappability, but also of COSMO's impact came in the instruction to all BBC departments in 1965 to 'lay off inviting Mrs. Whitehouse or Mrs. Fox on to our screens <u>for the time being</u>'. Whatever else, TRACK and COSMO were tribute to how NVALA redefined the debate about TV.[83]

The Standing Conference on Television (Television Viewers' Council (TVC) from 1963), pre-dated NVALA's interest in viewer-programmer dialogue. Formed in 1957, it was backed by the BBC, ITA, Gulbenkian Foundation and National Council of Social Service. It assembled parties interested in broadcasting: the Consumers' Association, teaching unions, Advertising Inquiry Council, Council for Children's Welfare, the Society for Education in Film and Television and the first Viewers' and Listeners' Association (historian Peter Laslett's educational TV experiment, a fore-runner of the Open University). TVC participants included Tony Higgins, Hoggart and researchers like Halloran, Joseph Trenaman and Hilde Himmel-weit (who sat on its Central Committee). The 1962 conference, debating Pilkington, heard Hoggart argue that because programme producers had to estimate what their audience wanted, there was a 'need for much closer liaison between producer and consumer'.[84]

TVC's chair and moving force was Mary Adams, who was also closely involved in the Consumers' Association. TVC's purpose, she explained, was 'to express viewers' viewpoints... to communicate with the providers'. Adams drew explicit parallels with the consumer movement. 'Television viewers' she argued in *Consumer News* 'are consumers of a kind ... the viewer, like the ubiq-uitous consumer of goods and services, needs information and advice... and protection [and] an organization to represent him'. Besides Pilkington made moral and social questions central to TV debates and the TVC felt 'the role of the viewer' was changing because television was 'ceasing merely to reflect social behaviour and current affairs', but rather 'beginning to change them'. The key point for TVC was that 'the professionalism of the providers calls for reciprocal expertise and receptivity by viewers'. 'The methods by which such scrutiny could become creative' required: 'information generously and frankly exchanged between providers and viewers, and... participation by viewers in the notion of public service broadcasting'. The latter had tended to apply to providers, but it was 'time the recipients played a more virile part'. On-screen quizzing of producers was proposed and a more accessible alternative to the BBC's advisory councils – all 'to strengthen the consumers' contribution and influence'.

But there were differences with what NVALA envisaged later in the 1960s. TVC had no ambition to be 'an unofficial television ombudsmen' and aimed to creatively engage broadcasting professionals by dialogue with viewers. Its tone was lighter-hearted, recognizing 'that much screen time is for entertainment pure and simple, relaxation after a boring day'. The TVC was determined to remember that 'pleasure is part of the serious business of television' much more than the NVALA ever managed. Still parallels with Whitehouse's intent impress, for Adams outlined how TV had moral, artistic and political roles and how 'in this duty the viewer must jolly well play his part'. But by this Adams meant much more than 'a thousand letters or telephone calls to programme providers', which would 'mean little in an audience of millions'.[85]

Whitehouse suspected the TVC to be a BBC front since Adams (assistant BBC TV controller 1954–58) was from the BBC elite and in 1965 appointed to the ITA by Benn. By then the TVC was moribund other than sponsoring research and local community TV projects. But its influence lingered. Brian Groombridge, an adult educationalist, also involved like Adams with CA, later wrote a Penguin Special about the potential for greater popular involvement in television as part of a more general programme for democratic participation in public life.[86]

Cultural politics

The TVC co-sponsored (with Gulbenkian) research at Birmingham University's Centre for Contemporary Cultural Studies (CCCS). Hoggart chaired CCCS from 1963, with former *New Left Review* editor Stuart Hall as research fellow and funding from Penguin. Rachel Powell, who had been involved with Hall in early New Left campaigns in Notting Hill, researched and explored the relationship between television and society and the history of bodies concerned with this. She favoured the TVC model, criticizing NVALA for disregarding academic evidence and suggesting its criticisms were evidence of the BBC's populism. She also critiqued the state of audience research – too one-way, 'audience reaction to something given', to do justice to the complexity and plurality of producer-consumer relations or enable dialogue.[87]

The NVALA and CCCS helped draw the parameters of the culture wars. For Whitehouse, Hoggart was the *'eminence grise'* behind Carleton Greene. But despite helping liberate *Lady Chatterley's Lover* as a defence witness in 1960, Hoggart, like Whitehouse, was more often represented as a puritan, moralist 'enemy of the people's joy'. This was especially the case after the Pilkington report criticized the trivial content and vulgar commercialism of ITV and of which Hoggart was reckoned to be the chief author. Roy Shaw regarded the moral tone of Pilkington as a 'reproach to faint-hearted or corrupted Christian' and evidence that Hoggart was 'doing a Christian job without the support of Christianity'. The New Left too, in the vanguard of the culture wars was cast by its opponents as of rather puritan tastes.[88] Hoggart's review of *Cleaning-up TV* thought it posed legitimate questions about TV's role in society, if invariably coming up with the wrong answers, ignoring academic research and the dangers of censorship and misreading wider society.[89]

The two could sound similar. Hoggart's *The Uses of Literacy* conceived materialism as corroding the ability to discern quality through an uncritical acquisitiveness. In a radio talk Hoggart explained, courtesy of de Tocquville, 'that some commonly accepted ideas in democratic society unbend springs, not corrupting but slackening, make people soft and materialistic'.[90] Like Whitehouse, Hoggart was accused by critics of moralizing in interpreting evidence about TV (particularly the influence of advertising) and Hoggart exhibited a touch of her frustration with academe. He felt that 'social scientists talked as though, if you scientifically studied the evidence – of audiences, responses and so on – then value-judgments would simply emerge from it'. For Hoggart (as for Whitehouse) these were less of a science and more a matter of values. He asserted Pilkington's right to work on assumptions about TV's impact and deduce policy decisions and cultural judgements, since 'you can't *scientifically* demonstrate imaginative debility' in its output. Debates about TV were for Hoggart (as for Whitehouse), nothing less than 'a microcosm of warring views about the nature of a free society'.[91]

Another parallel between conservative and radical cultural critics Hoggart's review of *Cleaning-up TV* highlighted was the 'firesiding' effect of TV drama. As Pilkington was occupied by the triviality of ITV output, so NVALA saw TV 'trivialize and cheapen human relationships and undermine marriage and family'. Sex and violence desensitized viewers by reducing social issues to spectacle. Here Whitehouse sounded like Marcuse, whose analysis of popular culture was that in exposing such issues it served to contain them rather than pose radical solutions (although the contribution of another *Wednesday Play*, *Cathy Come Home*, to the homeless organization, Shelter, confounded this). Whitehouse's critics occasionally let slip these parallels. Ned Sherrin, producer of *TW3* in a *Daily Mail* piece (for whose other content Whitehouse successfully sued), started out by arguing that TV 'dulled people's capacity for shock'.[92]

Early in 1966 Hoggart invited Whitehouse to talk to the illustrious CCCS seminar and to 'meet privately and talk'. Either option Hoggart felt would be better than the sort of public confrontation Whitehouse had recently had with Hall. But Whitehouse's refusal led Hoggart to drop the conciliatory tone and accuse her of refusing to read CCCS research and of falling for inaccurate press reports of Powell's research. Whitehouse was indeed selective with the press – and academics. CCCS was not to her taste, but others were, such as David Holbrook, an opponent of pornography and obscenity.[93]

Where the figureheads of the TV wars differed was on the merits or pit-falls of professional control. For Hoggart this was the BBC's saving grace, but Whitehouse's scruples were that television's potential was unchecked by moral self-control on the part of programme makers and audiences. But aside from this, the power and agency of the media impressed both the NVALA and the New Left, for all that both officially declared viewers to be possessed of critical faculties. They believed, as Raymond Williams put it, that culture *teaches*. Both rejected viewing figures as a useful measure of a programme's worth or impact and detected manipulations or emotional blackmail, be it by the liberal elite or advertisers. After editing *New Left Review* until 1961, and particularly as a secondary modern teacher and writing *The Popular Arts* with Paddy Whannel, Hall's concerns overlapped with Whitehouse's. These were driven by widespread debate in the Trade Unions about culture (as Centre 42 in the next chapter shows) and parti-cularly debates in the National Union of Teachers (NUT) about TV's impact and 'debasement of standards'. For Hall the NUT too readily blamed cul-tural producers, was too dismissive of the cultural value of popular activ-ities and 'too eager to think in terms of censorship and control'.[94] In 1960 Hall wrote of how:

> The figures of sexual sensation take their place in the general montage of 'success', seducing our consciousness, undermining and corrupting moral standards, encouraging a weak, flaccid, self-indulgence at odds with the adult critical standards demanded by life. Sex has become the universal salesman of prosperity, on the hoarding, the television screen... Capitalism which emerged with the Methodist Sunday School and the gospel of work, now offers a week in Monte Carlo and the gospel of promiscuity.[95]

This is a telling extract. Whitehouse would hardly have demurred from it, indeed might have intoned it. And it was suggestive that so far as cultural politics were post-materialist, they shared certain qualities and terms of debate, vehemently opposed as their politics were.

Culture – which like femininity and domesticity, NVALA conceived of traditionally – was another battle front. Birdwood tried to bring a private prosecution against Kenneth Tynan's nude Roundhouse spectacular *Oh Calcutta!* in 1970.[96] Whitehouse took on the Arts Council's Working Party on the Obscenity Laws in 1969. This argued for a suspension on the now familiar post-Wolfenden grounds that obscenity 'was a matter of private taste or distaste and not the concern of the law' and Arts Council of Great Britain (ACGB) participation was excused on the equally familiar grounds of it operating at arms length from government. At a public meeting she won support from a NUT spokesperson, but locked horns with ACGB chairman Lord Goodman and the head of BBC radio drama, Martin Esslin. The fall out from this public fracas was typically fractious. On BBC TV's *Quiz of the Week*, Whitehouse's local MP and NVALA member Gerald Nabarro was presented with a photo of a disgruntled looking Goodman being confronted by Whitehouse and asked to imagine words into his mouth. His response – 'you hypocritical old bitch' – was widely reported as Nabarro's opinion of Whitehouse. Nabarro made good by speaking in the Commons, along with Dance, against the Working Party's report and deploring the 'decline in moral standards in recent years' associated with the permissive society and its 'depredations of drugs, obscenity and pornography'.[97]

Research into the social impact of television was ineluctably drawn into this conflict. LSE social psychologist Hilde Himmelweit's study into the effects on children ascribed limited causal effect to TV – programmes 'aroused aggression as often as they discharged it'. Whitehouse noted the study accepted that television was 'gradually, almost imperceptibly' fashioning youth values. Himmelweit privately admitted anxiety that violence in BBC westerns like *Tenderfoot* and *Bonanza* was being copied and that, 'it is not the public, but the producers image of what the public is like which determines the level of the programme'.[98] The NVALA preferred William Belson's work, who Himmelweit steered the TVC away from. Belson's work posited a more direct link between exposure to TV and social behaviour and was publicized (in less circumspect terms than Belson himself used) by NVALA related groups like the Festival of Light. But even his 1959 study, commenced as chief psychologist in the BBC Audience Research Department as an adult companion to Himmelweit's study, distinguished effects '*caused* by, from those... *correlated* with, the possession of a television set'. Whilst posing a strong relationship between television and behaviour, Belson proposed this could also have effects likely to please NVALA-types – drawing the family together or, for example, boosting attendances at arts galleries.[99] Like Himmelweit's study then, conclusions were mixed and lent credence to either side in this partisan debate.

The Television Research Committee at Leicester University, appointed in 1963 by the Government and which funded researchers like Himmelweit and CCCS, took much of Whitehouse's flak. This was targeted at both its duration (its first report took six years) and the interim conclusions of its secretary, sociologist, James Halloran. Halloran was a recurring Whitehouse foe, who also helped the ACGB's efforts to suspend the obscenity laws. Committee working papers stressed the complexities and contingencies of relationships between the viewer and medium and of forging suitable research methods. Halloran agreed the NVALA's simplification of the issues and the 'efficiency of that Association's public relations' fed a popular sense that TV ought to be considered a factor in violence, delinquency and attitude formation. But definitive conclusions and thus policy implications were harder to reach – 'the picture is not clear' and 'an unequivocal answer cannot be given'.[100] BBC audience research picked up on the multiple causes of delinquent and aggressive behaviour and TV's role as both trigger and release. Nor were equivocal results unwelcome for politicians keen to defer debates about commercial TV or having to declare on moral questions in a pluralist society. But by neither proving nor disproving TV's impact, nor assuaging the concerns of the Conservative rank-and-file, it meant debate ensued on Whitehouse's terms.[101]

But NVALA, mistrusting professional experts, pilloried 'the rather "precious" sociological research into the effects of TV violence... at Leicester'. 'They have declared that violence on TV has little or no effect. But research of this kind asks the wrong questions and inevitably comes up with the wrong answers – if any answers at all!' It was a 'basic fact of human psychology – that people, and especially children are deeply affected by their environment, of which TV is an all-pervading part'. An exasperated Barnett complained that it was 'years before their results become public knowledge' and as the NVALA-supporting Stoke Rotary Club president put it, on such issues all that 'was needed was good sense'. Whitehouse too craved more certain and quicker answers. Nor were NVALA the only group to express anxiety about the Television Research Committee. The liberal-left *New Society* welcomed the Committee's medical, legal, educational and psychological experts as an advance on the 'endless ignorant pontification which goes on at present', but was surprised there were no members with 'expert knowledge of television or indeed of the mass media' and one member who confessed to not owning a TV. It feared that as the Kefauver Committee in the USA had 'failed to obtain conclusive evidence either way' on the relationships between television, crime and juvenile delinquency', its work would 'not be easy'.[102]

NVALA's own research sought representations of womanhood, family life, relationships, authority, violence, sex, crime and Christianity and disclosed predictable insights into the NVALA mindset. A reviewer of a programme about World War One Soldier songs concluded: 'War is a terrible thing, but if the mood of these scriptwriters were followed, they themselves would not now be free to subvert our children. Perhaps it would not have been a bad thing! There can be too much freedom'. Its report on schools broadcasts in 1970 (duly dispatched to Education Secretary Thatcher) found social history programming emphasized injustice and discipline to an extent likely to encourage revolt. Results did not always corroborate NVALA's public stance. A 1966 Mansfield survey found, for instance, that ITV sinned more than the BBC in advocating greed, showing crime and family life as divided, although the BBC lead in terms of ridiculing authority and misrepresenting Christianity.[103]

Halloran's own work could resonate with Whitehouse's, notably in the case study of ITN coverage of the October 1968 anti-Vietnam war demo in London (which generated much concern amongst politicians like Crossman and Benn that TV might stoke violence). Halloran argued that the content of print and TV news media was monolithic and despite multiple outlets worked within key shared assumptions. They were prone to unconsciously edit out (censor, for Whitehouse) alternative opinions in a way deleterious to democracy.[104] The point here, as with the parallels with Hoggart and the New Left, is not to assimilate or legitimize Whitehouse, but to foreground correspondence in the terms of debate.

Conclusions

Opponents struggled to define NVALA – drawing analogies with Poujadism (for its populism, petit-bourgeois opposition to taxes and crypto-fascism) and McCarthyism (for its conspiracies of communists ensconced in the BBC hierarchy). Sociologists in the 1970s were much concerned with moral panics and middle-class protest and pressure group influence on government. They considered NVALA an 'excluded promotional' pressure group – neither defending a material interest nor with ready access to the major means of communication. Parallels with NVALA were located in work on the US temperance movement that likewise used coercive rather than assimilative methods.[105]

Wallis analysed the NVALA as a less-educated fraction of the middle class at odds with a younger upwardly-mobile generation of more secular values. If there were structural causes for the NVALA, there were also cultural ones – voluntary choices not unconscious reflexes induced by class. If NVALA had a class basis, it was not *about* class – materialist conceptions of class alone were explanatorily insufficient and concepts of status and cultural defence emerged. If sections of the middle class suffered a differential erosion of their material position and security, so their traditional values of self-discipline (the protestant work ethic, in short) were threatened by the pleasures affluence promised. The impact on traditional domesticity was born out in NVALA's majority female membership. Wallis termed the NVALA's ideology 'cultural fundamentalism' drawing out its religious inspiration, but also its opposition to pluralism, to a society reluctant to make value judgements about what to NVALA, seemed uncontrolled and rapid social change. NVALA craved stability, respect for the order of things in its vividly imagined recent past. The trajectory of cultural values seemed – more so to NVALA than any other section of 1960s' society – to be towards hedonism over asceticism and against self-discipline in arenas like sex and consumption and even violence seemed to it manifestations of a deficit of self-restraint. The post-Reith BBC seemed as much victims as perpetrators of these values shifts to the NVALA.[106]

These studies hint at conceiving the NVALA as a social movement. But studies of these have remained centred on feminist, environmental and peace movements – progressive in their politics and echoing the assumptions and influence of the New Left and *soixante-huitards*. The NVALA scarcely features (if at all, as the enemy, as if social movements are defined by their progressive content). NVALA's exclusion from such literature would not have surprised Whitehouse, whose critique of liberalism as in practice intolerant, even coercive, was a central plank of conservative moralist and emergent New Right thinking.[107] NVALA merits consideration as an 'other', a rejoinder to assumptions about the social and political nature of recognized social movements. By accepted definitions – 'a collective, organized, sustained and noninstitutional challenge to authorities, powerholders or cultural beliefs and practices' – NVALA qualifies in form. It exhibited key concepts in the taxonomy of social movements: affective ties; charisma; (a paradoxical) media savvy; tactical innovation and, however rhetorically, participatory democracy.[108]

NVALA's values were less anti-materialist – business and ITV were spared its harshest criticism – than post-materialist, trying to prioritize morality. As for Conservatives, the market and morality could find themselves at odds in the NVALA's vision. NVALA criticism of capitalism and advertising's impact on values was less prevalent than of liberal state-sponsored permissiveness. Although as Cliff noted credit card culture ('keep the waiting out of wanting', as Barclaycard ads ran) corroded traditional values. On the other hand, NVALA did lose such support as there was amongst Conservatives by querying the values of pirate radio. And it was notable that two-thirds of NVALA members in a 1969 survey favoured funding the BBC through an increased licence fee rather than advertising.[109]

The NVALA can be read as post-materialist both in that it saw the materialist philosophy of communism as a global threat, and because it tried to set the agenda, in terms of culture and the quality of life. As most NVALA members saw it material wealth far from preventing 'human failings' seemed to be fuelling them: 'what we've got is a non-materialistic problem' for which the answer lay in Christian values. Or, as Muggeridge told NVALA's 1967 national Convention, the 'greatest lie' the mass media perpetrated was that 'it is possible for human beings to live happily, usefully, serenely, seeking only sensual and material ends'. Whitehouse told Heath that her 'experience... speaking around the country' and the lesson of his 1970 election victory was 'that concern over the libertarianism of the "permissive" society ran even deeper than anxiety over the economic state'. Essex VALA, in a letter to election candidates in 1970, argued 'however much politicians may focus attention on economic matters... we shall continue to be in trouble until the moral issues are sorted out' and proposed 'to give maximum publicity to these matters'. Parkin saw CND as evidence that 'groups and individuals may be as deeply concerned about the defence or propagation of secular moral values which are unrelated to material and economic interests'. Secular apart, this holds for NVALA.[110]

Like CND, NVALA offered opposition to 'the establishment' couched as a choice between good (and God, for the religious element in both) and evil and rather sceptical of the merits of the modern and technology. And unlike CND, in Parkin's depiction, NVALA mobilized 'house-bound wives'.[111] More generally, sixties Britain saw debate about the efficacy of representative institutions sparked by a wealthier, better-educated electorate, by the concentration of power in Whitehall, the welfare state and industry and by a sense of powerlessness and national 'decline'. And pressure groups saw participation and accountability as watchwords. NVALA seemed at one with this, but its social profile complicates Inglehart's generational and educational patterning of post-materialism (and Parkin's portrait of the on-average young, well-educated, CND members). If anything, NVALAers were downwardly mobile in class terms and from an elder generation socialized in less affluent times.

Perhaps the NVALA were the exception that proved Inglehart's rules. But the NVALA might also be read less as an upshot of an emergent post-materialist polity, than an agent of it. Inglehart after all posited that 'the transition to postindustrial society will entail a renewed emphasis on spiritual values', particularly amongst post-materialists afforded time for ethical matters. And these values were not necessarily, NVALA shows, bound to be progressive or modernizing (as Inglehart normatively proposes) or effect a particularly 'silent' revolution (as Inglehart's early work posited) in values, since the NVALA was nothing if not noisy. NVALA's post-materialism at the very least suggests a more contested, uneven process.

NVALA does provide supporting evidence of Inglehart's projected fading of the gender gap in political participation and of the drift away from elite-directed (state, party, unions, church) to elite-directing participation. In NVALA's case this was not due to the rising levels of education, so much as the decline in trust for conventional politics and its difficulties convening constituencies across the breadth of issue, like television, that made the personal political. The NVALA was both a product and cause of that doubt in existing institutions and collective belief systems, religious and political. The NVALA questions not post-materialism *per se*, but nuances it, suggesting a less economically determinist, more culturally manifold process and more varieties of politics than Inglehart's. The NVALA might be exceptions that proved Inglehart's model, or suggest that it needed and could incorporate more diverse constructions of post-materialism, that operated through contestation and difference in the political and cultural spheres. NVALA were post-materialists, but not as Inglehart knew them; indeed they countered the values, cultural tastes and political trajectory of the younger generation he focused on.[112] Cultural and moral politics seemed then to be post-materialist in form, but neither necessarily radical or progressive in content nor the preserve of the young or better-educated.

6
Cultural Turns: Wesker's Centre 42, the Roundhouse and the Politics of Culture

A 'cultural turn' in post-rationing British politics was evidenced by increasing interest in culture and leisure from political practitioners, as much as in politics by sixties cultural practitioners. Contingent upon relative popular prosperity, the cultural turn was akin to Inglehart's emphasis on the shift from the standard of living to the quality of life or post-materialist values. Thus a range of issues became more politically salient and such politics could play out in multiple ways as the case of the NVALA suggests. As with consumerism and TV, political debates about how to spend time and money on 'culture' involved the professional and amateur, the state, issues of taste and choice and the private made public.[1] This chapter explores the multifaceted, fluid politics of culture in the 1960s and what these disclose about political culture. It uses playwright Arnold Wesker's Centre 42 (C42) project as a site on which politics and culture encountered each other. A Jewish socialist, Wesker had found fame with a trilogy of 'political-kitchen sink' plays – *Roots*, *Chicken soup with Barley* and *I'm talking about Jerusalem* (1958–60). Urging greater attention to culture in a 1960 Trades Union Congress (TUC) motion (no.42, hence the moniker), Wesker's movement ran local festivals in 1962, then inherited an old railway turning house, the Roundhouse in North London, which became its spatial and imaginary home and for which it attempted to raise the finance to create a cultural hub.

Distilled in the Roundhouse and C42 were a series of debates about the meaning of 'culture' in which the dramas of the transition to a post-industrial society were enacted – debates about popular, elite and counter-cultural content; economics; the state; London and the regions and the post-industrial use of buildings. By 1970 C42 came to the end of the line – struggling to put down popular roots in cultural life, derailed by the failure to secure funding from the trade unions and Arts Council of Great Britain (ACGB) and superseded by popular and counter-cultural activities at the Roundhouse. In its own terms it had failed. But in the longer-term it can be argued to have been a model for post-industrial arts centres and in forging 'culture' as a political terrain. In any case, the terms of its failure tell historians much about the pattern and extent of the 'cultural revolution' of the 1960s and suggest the limits of cultural politics and post-materialism. For Coppieters, the idea of a Centre controlled by artists was radical enough to generate political unease, threaten commercial dictates and question artistic hierarchies. Its potential was 'betrayed' by elite opposition and union antipathy. Marwick, by contrast, notes that Wesker's efforts to transform the Roundhouse into a political theatre 'inevitably flopped'.[2] This chapter seeks to move beyond the failure-betrayal dichotomy, to use C42 to explore the intersections of politics and culture and bring nuance to a narrative in which the New Left is usually (and uncritically) authoritative.

Cultural politics were not intrinsically post-materialist. The 'arts' (like, for instance, sport) had long had a commercial aspect. But the 1960s saw culture commercialized in a way that is quite recognizable to post-1990s rhetoric of the creative economy and cultural industries. Moreover, post-materialist values could make good political and commercial sense. This was apparent in Harold Wilson's government under Britain's first Arts Minister Jennie Lee, who until her appointment in 1964 was actively involved and sat on C42's council of management.[3] C42 is also then a test-bed for how post-materialist British political culture was. The argument here isn't that 'culture' suddenly became political. John Arden, a contemporary radical playwright of Wesker's, held that 'the theatre, being a place of public assembly is obviously part of... political life'. But however much the debate about the ending of the Lord Chamberlain's powers of theatre censorship in 1968 brought this to the public fore, this was in no way unique to the 1960s.[4] There was an enduring tradition of what Davies calls alternative, experimental theatre in which Wesker's efforts can be located and for Itzin and Shellard, the heyday of radical theatre (from agit-prop and avant-garde to black and gay), was the 1970s.[5]

Over and above Wesker and C42's own significance, it was that they were emblematic and encapsulated wider cultural issues. C42 generated as well as hosted cultural debate. Noel Coward, a critic of the 'dustbin school of drama', disparaged Wesker's efforts in 'all those dreary English towns organizing dreary festivals for those dreary people'.[6] Other cultural warriors saw C42 as more sinister. In 1968 Whitehouse drew attention to 'the headquarters of the left wing organization Centre 42... the Roundhouse is used for activities of the "anti-university" and had hosted a conference on the "dialectics of liberation"... whose neo-Marxist ideas have kindled much of the present unrest in Europe'.[7]

Wesker's sixties celebrity was notable. He was close to Lee and Wilson and, albeit infrequently, a member of the government's Youth Service Development Council from 1960–66, alongside Hoggart, Tony Crosland and the Conservative and ACGB executive member, Edward Boyle. *Tatler* profiled him and by 1967 *Roots* was an A-Level text. He commanded 10%

of the box office, such that a week run of *Roots* could earn him some £1000. *Roots'* off-Broadway run in 1961 had critics comparing Wesker to Clifford Odets. *Chips with Everything* was a Broadway hit in 1963, starring Corin Redgrave – 'as rollicking as Sgt. Bilko', the *New York Daily Post* reckoned, casting Wesker as part of 'the British invasion'.[8] The buzz was such that the film rights became valuable, sold by Wesker for £10,000 in 1964 to kick-start the Roundhouse appeal. Wesker's notoriety was greater abroad than at home. He was feted in Japan by a 'Project Wesker 68'. He told ACGB chairman Lord Goodman in 1965 of the 'attention the fortytwo project has excited abroad'. He was shortly to be 'an "honoured guest" of the Swedish social democratic society of cultural workers', but without the ACGB support (he was trying to prize from Goodman), 'what am I to tell them?'.[9]

His part in the sixties radical odyssey added to Wesker's exoticism. Active in CND and a founder of the Committee of 100 in 1960 along with Doris Lessing, Lindsay Anderson, Shelagh Delaney and John Osborne, Wesker marched to Aldermaston, was arrested on a sit-down protest and served a month in Brixton Prison in 1961. He also argued sit-downs were insufficient without industrial action. By 1962 C42 limited his participation, but the Roundhouse was used by the Committee of 100.[10] Despite Communist Party (CPGB) members like David Mercer amongst C42's helpers, relations with the CPGB and Soviet Union were distant. Cuba, which Wesker visited at length in 1964 and 1968, was his preference – an antidote to 'England, an enfeebled country... with grey political leaders'. He criticized Castro's persecution of homosexuality, but the British-Cuba Association HQ was at the Roundhouse. For critics like Bernard Levin all this meant that 'on political matters' Wesker 'has a brain made of apfelstrudel'. And much as C42 was part of the late 1960s warren of networks operating outside official party channels, Wesker did ricochet around the left – a signatory of the original *1967 New Left May Day Manifesto*, criticizing the Wilson governments, whilst at the same time requesting state support for C42.[11]

By the end of the 1960s, like C42, Wesker's political and artistic light had dimmed. His creative output slowed and in the case of plays like *The Friends* and *The Four Seasons*, won less critical adulation. In 1969 *The Times* theatre critic proposed that 'Wesker seems to have abandoned the stage for good works'. His dramatic output imitated C42; its betrayal, in Wesker's eyes, or as Patterson has it, Wesker's disillusionment. *Their Very Own and Golden City*, first performed in 1966, was an allegory of C42, about an architect's ambitions for making the city beautiful, thwarted by business and trade union curmudgeons. It had also predicted the dilemmas C42 would pose. The closing line of *I'm Talking about Jerusalem* insisted: 'visions do work and even if they don't work then for god's sake let's behave as though they do – or else nothing will work'.[12]

Politics' cultural turn

The uses of leisure preoccupied commercial and consumer commentators, journalists, academics and politicians. As a *Sunday Times* series put it in 1962: 'we have more money and more time to spend on leisure, the subject has aroused the anxieties of sociologists and the anger of the self-appointed guardians of people's pleasure'. America was a point of reference – notably the 28 volume 1962 congressional report, *Outdoor Recreation for America*. On TV, ATV's *The Warning Voice, Leisure* in 1962 had Mark Abrams grilling Bill Carron on whether campaigns for shorter hours required trade unions to attend to what their members did with this time; Himmelweit on the pitfalls of TV; and Wesker on the responsibility of the artist, how the arts were as valuable as football and plugging C42's festivals. A 1963 *Guardian* series asked 'if money in their pockets hasn't made men virtuous, why should time on their hands?', but noted neither political party wanted 'to risk seeming to be telling people the way they ought to be spending their spare time'.[13]

But government and political parties were increasingly interested in this realm. Wilson's keynote 'white heat of technology' speech at the 1963 Labour conference had outlined the possibility of 'leisure on an unbelievable scale'. The short-lived Department of Economic Affairs had a long-term group on leisure from that assessed sports and regional arts associations. The nostrums of Lee's 1965 White Paper, *A Policy for the Arts*, made for good business and infiltrated government thinking. The Society for Industrial Artists and Designers quoted the President of the Board of Trade, Douglas Jay, at 1965's 'Profit by Design' exhibition: 'There is more and more evidence that good design pays. It is a vital weapon in the armoury we must use if we are to sell British goods... all over the world' and as such required the 'standing and qualifications of a professional'. As Henry has it, the 1960s' Wilson governments operated thinly but across a broader area than predecessors via the new Arts Minister, Sports Council and legislation on preservation and countryside access.[14]

Much discussion of cultural politics in 1960s Britain has centred on the New Left. And C42 saw itself as something of a New Left cultural wing, notably influenced by Raymond Williams' work. Culture was the New Left's keyword and for C42 it was second nature that culture, in both content and practice, was political. Yet in most accounts of the New Left there was a waning of its own vibrant London cultural life and interests as its 'second' generation, from 1962, patronized theory rather than its Soho Partisan café, Left Clubs, new wave cinema via Karel Reisz and Lindsay Anderson or Wesker plays at the Royal Court.[15]

Relations between the New Left and counter-culture, Jonathan Green recalls, were estranged. Even the *May Day Manifesto* movement (1967–68), a revival of the first generation, edited by Williams, said little about 'culture'.

However much 'culture' was a keyword in theory, it was far from a New Left preserve in practice. This extended to its critique of 'Labourism'. This argued that it wasn't just a hostile culture that marginalized the left in national life, but that the Labour Party and trade unions in Britain, by comparison with European social democracy, were too narrowly focused on parliament and wages and lacked a broader presence in civil society or ideological strategy for cultivating this. The evidence of C42, Lee and the Festival of Labour, without suggesting British social democracy was making major inroads into civil society (or approaching the sort of penetration achieved by the Young Conservatives), indicates this was not solely for lack of interest, resources or will. It implies rather that it was popular cultural preference and the wider political culture that were constraints.[16]

Few could fail to be impressed by the scale and ambition of the Festival of Labour. Its political impact and cultural legacy was negligible, indeed its indifferent reception encouraged Labour to veer away from direct cultural provision in Lee's policy, to Wesker's detriment. But in a signal of the effort involved, 150,000 party people visited London on the weekend of 16–17 June 1962. Organized by Merlyn Rees, the Festival aimed to capture some of Wesker's cultural nous and CND's street savvy. Rees argued that it aimed to 'show that socialism is not only concerned with material welfare'. Its coincidence with C42's efforts did not prevent Wesker's involvement, but he came to wonder whether Labour was stealing his thunder. When asked if the event would have happened without Wesker's chivvying, Gaitskell replied, cryptically, 'not at all'.[17]

The Festival featured a parade of Labour, union and Co-op tableaux floats; classical and jazz concerts at the Royal Festival Hall, films at the National Film theatre. TV writer (and later Labour Lord) Ted Willis commissioned a play, besides monitoring unilateralist sentiment. There were two art exhibitions – of global and modern art (including work by Peter Blake, David Hockney, Henry Moore, Eduardo Paolozzi) at the TUC's Congress House. Battersea Park hosted sports, handicraft and Co-op fashion displays, dancing and various stalls. This saw Labour tap into a range of entertainment (Jack Hylton, BBC), arts (Michael Ayrton, Tom Driberg), sports (Denis Howell, Philip Noel-Baker) and design (Mountain and Molehill, ex-communist professional graphic designers and Misha Black) networks. As at the 1951 Festival of Britain, there was a spatial divide between the more uplifting and populist, entertaining elements. Besides the London showpiece in June 1962 there were regional festivals. The festival was as useful a marker of Labour's cultural tastes as the 1951 Festival was of its national vision.[18]

Multiple strands in Labour thinking encouraged post-materialist thinking. It was latent in British socialism's ideal of escaping the binds of class and material circumstance. Section 132 of the 1948 Local Government Act enabled local authorities to spend on leisure and arts provision. *Leisure for*

Living (1959), like the Festival of Labour, outlined its rather rarefied cultural preferences. 1950s revisionists like Crosland and Jenkins emphasized quality of life issues now basic needs had been met, shedding some of Labour's and Britain's puritanism. The agenda-setting development was Lee's White paper. This encompassed Wilson's modernizing homilies on leisure and automation, was alert to the demands of a younger generation and aligned itself with revisionism against the 'drabness, uniformity and joylessness of much of the social furniture we have inherited from the industrial revolution'. It advocated post-industrial usage of buildings and borrowed from C42 the argument that the arts, like 'all new social services have to fight long and hard before they establish themselves... yesterday it was the fight for a free health service... before it was the struggle to win education for all'.[19]

With the new minister and ACGB brought together in the Department of Education and Science, a fivefold increase in real terms spending was achieved, but as important was the political salience and conducive atmosphere Lee fashioned.[20] Lee pressed the Arts case hard, telling *Tribune* that the government's legacy here rivalled the Attlee government's NHS. Paradoxically, her spending battles were with Jenkins and Crosland, the revisionists who advocated a cultural turn in the 1950s. Her case was that it had given Labour a lead over its opponents and that relatively small investments yielded large benefits to cultural and national life, by contrast with areas of government difficulty.[21] There were, in short, economic, social, but also political benefits to the arts.

Lee argued 'the arts are not only a source of expenditure but also a source of income' and artists 'are not essentially takers... they are givers'. The government's interest in culture was rarely unaware of the economic benefits of TV, pop, tourism, hotels, heritage, the Beatles or of its taxability as SET hit theatres in 1969. The focus was less on specific, alternative agendas (as Wesker pressed and as Lee differentiated her efforts from French Culture Minister, Andre Malraux) than on generating audiences. Lee played populist to dispel the mystique and 'old-fashioned gloom and undue solemnity' surrounding the arts, arguing for better cafés and for culture's consumers besides producers. Lee wielded political weight to win funding not to direct it. This was done at 'arm's length' from direct political control by the ACGB. As Goodman put it, 'independence of arts from state dictation of content is key to central state subventions to it'.[22]

Political preferences or questions of taste were thus side-stepped. Yet a civilizing mission was very evident. The fine arts – and most ACGB funds went to museums, galleries, ballet, opera, orchestras and theatres – were conceived not just as appropriate culture, but as social and spiritual goods. As Goodman put it, 'a dose of culture could turn hooligans into citizens'. The White Paper averred that 'the exclusion of so many for so long from the best of our cultural heritage can become as damaging to the privileged minority as the under-privileged majority'. Access was the key and Lee warned: 'before we arrogantly say that any group of our citizens are not capable of appreciating the best in the arts, let us make absolutely certain that we have put the best within their reach'.[23]

Labour was a firm believer in a cultural hierarchy that it believed Britons might be enticed to ascend. As with much of the permissive legislation enacted in the 1960s, arts policy was at odds with popular opinion, but with the difference that it endeavoured not to modernize the traditional, but to promote access to it. Jazz, much in evidence at the Festival of Labour and made eligible for ACGB funds in 1967, was as modern as its tastes ran. The White Paper extolled how 'in the world of jazz the process has already happened; highbrow and lowbrow have met'. This agenda was challenged by self-made and commercial pop culture, not to mention the counter-culture in 1960s Britain. But since the ACGB's outlook was permissive, this was not the setback it was for C42's more particular agenda – indeed it could even claim some credit for this.[24]

Lee's key innovation was regional funding. The ACGB's post-war mantra of 'few but roses' became 'the best for the most' with metropolitan, profes-sional standards and elite forms distributed beyond London. As she told the Musicians' Union in 1969, 'a broadening of opportunities should not lead to a lowering of standards'. The ethos remained non-prescriptive – for Goodman they were 'only in very rare cases seeking to stimulate some local activity where at least the nucleus of existing demand is not already estab-lished'. The model here was the North East (later Northern) Arts Asso-ciation (NAA), established in 1961 with Arthur Blenkinsop (Labour MP for South Shields from 1964) as secretary. Spending tripled from 1963–67 and NAA's vision, like Lee's, saw economic and socio-cultural benefits in the arts, sounding a distinctly post-industrial language of regeneration. The majority of English regional associations, plus Scottish and Welsh Arts Councils, were set up under Lee's tenure. Regional associations were able to override the apathy that often dogged the fund-raising powers of section 132 by bringing councils together, collaborating with business and pegging this to ACGB support.[25]

Lee's approach was not short of critics. Many wanted a more assertive Minister to lead rather than follow local initiatives, fearing local politics and parsimony might curtail ambition. From Clive Barker's perspective, Lee's philosophy was prone to abdicate issues of cultural taste and stan-dards. As Barker, who organized C42's local festivals in 1962 and worked with Joan Littlewood's Theatre Workshop, saw it, these were 'two first rate projects in this country... being denied money at the precise moment when the government is going around saying "spend more money on culture"'.[26] More radical critics questioned the whole model of distributing good works from on cultural high. In this respect Lee and C42, whatever their divergent geographical emphases and cultural preferences (C42 being more prescriptive and defending folksy-proletarian besides elite forms), resembled each other. As contemporaries like John McGrath and 1980s radicals like Warpole and Mulgan saw it, for both Lee and C42 'the problem was of taking existing art to the workers, not trying to create new forms of art'. Contrasting C42 and Lee's efforts with the flourishing pop scene, Mulgan and Warpole also highlighted how in the Open University, Lee sought to enable people 'to develop new skills and abilities' where arts policy tended to stress 'people's need to learn to appreciate the skills and abilities of others'.[27] By contrast the think-tank Political and Economic Planning (PEP) wanted resources concentrated not devolved and criticized the shift away from London where standards and demand were highest. The ACGB's assistant secretary Eric White also saw this regional emphasis as evidence of political interference.[28] For Conservatives too, Lee had politicized the issue.

The language of civilizing minds and cultural improvement was more salient on the left,[29] but not hard to locate amongst Conservatives. In the context of relative affluence, these were recognizably post-materialist politics that played out in various directions. Criticisms of advertising or Whitehouse's unease at emergent popular tastes were common amongst Conservatives, as other chapters in this book show. Equally, Butler rarely tired of stressing that 'spiritual progress must keep pace with the material' and that it was Labour's redistributive appeal, driven by union wage issues, that was 'materialistic'.[30] Both parties shifted away from production-centred identities. As revisionists aimed to shed Labour's cloth cap associations, Conservatives were concerned 'not to tie the Party's public image too closely to industry', but to how affluence might be spent. Bow Group Tories declared leisure 'within the purview of the politician' as the 'post-industrial society' increased 'true leisure, as distinct from mere recuperation from work'. This invariably meant 'highbrow', with the aim that 'the leisure society' as 'successor to the industrial society' should be 'a Tory development'. And this might involve the state, since if the 'cultural pyramid was not likely to be pushed from the bottom... it must be pulled from the top'.[31]

The Arts or cognate spheres went unmentioned in previous Conservative manifestos, but Macmillan was keen to perfect the 'uses of leisure' section of 1959's manifesto. He suggested they 'pinch' from the Wolfenden report on Sport and Heathcoat-Amory agreed a lot could be done with minimal spending.[32] David Eccles at the Board of Trade went further, proposing tourism and Arts be co-ordinated in the Ministry of Works as a response to what he saw as the 'desire of a growing number of our people (especially the young) to bring something into their lives which is not money or the cruder diversions of sport and sex'. This Eccles observed in record and paperback sales, drama clubs, stately home visiting and exhibitions about 'the design of consumer goods'. The economic gains justified subsidies and co-ordinating policy and he concluded the Conservatives should 'extend the field of the arts'. After the election, as Education Minister, Eccles reiterated this in a paper on 'Leisure in our Affluent Age'. Macmillan, although acknowledging the Chancellor's concerns about cost and 'arousing expectations', was 'all for tempting the teddy boys into the geological museum'.[33] Little came of this, but Eccles, who succeeded Lee as Arts Minister in 1970, showed how these issues spanned the parties – much as Labour induced the Conservatives to conceive such matters as part of public politics – and indicated the post-materialist trend in political discussion.[34]

A leisure study group set up by Edward Heath reported in 1965. It was chaired by ex-athlete and MP Chris Chataway and included Bow Groupers, an entertainment advisor to the Rank group, Ray Kelly, and Nicolas Scott, ex-YC chairman, future MP and advertising executive. Much of the report's research detailed leisure trends – from perennial favourites like bingo and DIY to the decline in bowling alleys and the growth in overseas holidaying, yachting (whose participants had quadrupled in the previous decade) and caravanning, which saw Caravan Club membership hit 48,000 in 1960.

Commercial forces alone promised fitful development, but state intervention was not easily seen as a remedy. A Sports Council along ACGB lines was rejected. Even short of its more totalitarian aura of 'state gladiators', sport was not to be encouraged to rely on the state – although it wanted to enhance international performance and David Howell had been a 'PR success' as Wilson's Sports Minister. Elsewhere it was more paternalist. 'The first reaction of some Conservatives' it admitted was 'to preserve freedom of choice, from a belief that it is no function of government to designate one activity as more desirable than another and from a conviction that where demand exists the market will provide'. 'But even a cursory study of the problems and likely trends must surely convince the least paternalist "free marketeer" that without planning and some spending by the community as a whole the more intensive use of leisure that is a feature of this age will render this a wretched country' and 'if the beauties of the coast and countryside are to survive the millions who swarm from the great conurbations'. The report was 'struck by the political importance' of such issues and saw them as Conservative territory, where 'imaginative plans for recreation would reinforce our image as the party of prosperity'.[35]

But this didn't convince Keith Joseph, who in 1967 was moved by the state-minded thinking on display here and in arts policy, to create his own policy group on tourism, independent of the party research department. Joseph embodied Conservative uncertainties about the role of the market and state in the cultural sphere, if also a growing awareness of its importance. A 1956 sub-committee on automation with Joseph as secretary had faith that the resources of Britons' voluntary social life meant that reduced working hours would result in 'a great growth in happiness, that travel will become a widespread pleasure, and that the arts and the appreciation of them will flourish'. But as chair of a party Arts and Amenities Committee in 1959, he held, 'a comprehensive policy embracing... sport, recreation and the arts' was the 'government's clear duty', because 'leisure, wrongly used, constitutes a real threat to society'. As Housing Minister in the early 1960s, he resisted lobbying from the ACGB and the actors union Equity, to restrict developers altering the usage of theatres. He felt it did 'not matter from the point of view of its effect on the neighbourhood whether a building is used as a theatre, a cinema, a bowling alley or a bingo saloon'.[36]

An Arts policy group was also assembled in 1965. After Duncan Sandys, President of the Civic Trust, resigned early on, interest only picked up under Paul Channon, who became the first shadow Arts minister in 1968. Other members included Robert Cooke MP (who contended 'our own party has lost ground here') and Sir Paul Reilly, the Director of the Council for Industrial Design, who told Heath his participation must remain secret since the CoID was 'strictly non-political'.[37] In 1968 the group's secretary, Chris Patten, outlined how arts funding would win 'Burke's nodding approval' for 'conserving' the more noble achievements of humanity. There was no ideological harm in subsidies for architecture or the environment. Patten demurred from PEP's preference for improving existing (London) excellence or Hoggart's cultural democracy, a vision he feared would see 'Joan Littlewood and Arnold Wesker' at the helm. Rather, it had to be recognized that the 'majority are not interested in going to the opera, to art galleries or even to Centre 42'. Patten believed that as 'the state has helped to nurture an appetite for the arts', it had a 'responsibility' to satisfy this. Patten wanted to boost business support via tax concessions as in the USA, seeing diverse patronage as a safeguard against political control of the arts. In short, the state had to give Britons 'some outlet for their educated tastes without dictating what those tastes should be'.[38]

The group was addressed by NAA Director Alexander Dunbar who wondered if tax breaks were the way to induce private sector interest. 'Apathy not philistinism was the main enemy of the arts' he argued, not that it was any good reverting to 'taking the arts to the canteens'. William Emrys Williams, ACGB Secretary-General until 1963, who now headed the Institute of Directors' Arts Advisory Council, was also wary. Tax concessions implied 'tacit avowal of a government conviction that culture had a particular priority' and offered material reasons rather than persuading business of the intrinsic merits of the arts and their responsibility to become 'a voluntary third force of patronage'. Goodman attended in 1968 and argued for making the ACGB chair a full-time, remunerated post whose incumbent would deal directly with the Treasury. A Minister, excellent as Lee had been, was not needed. This appealed to most Conservatives (Edward Boyle was a notable demurer) as a 'repudiation of the Ministry of Culture approach to the arts'.[39]

Audiences

Wesker's point of departure was that despite the commercial and critical acclaim of his plays, their audience was not working class enough. Thousands went to the theatre, but more to the cinema and millions watched TV every night, which left Wesker wondering 'is anybody listening?' His address to 1960's Oxford drama festival was sent to every Trade Union leader as *The Modern Playwright or O, Mother, Is It Worth It?* It argued that the trade union satire starring Peter Sellars, *I'm Alright Jack*, was 'a sick cultural manifestation', but charged the labour movement only had itself to blame since it offered little alternative to cultural habits and focused on material improvement. The demand for higher wages can be read as evidence of a less deferential status order, if also less civic-minded, more acquisitive culture of the 1960s (and thus that inflation was a cultural besides economic issue). But for Wesker this was an impoverishing outlook, since 'if we are not to be materially exploited neither should we be culturally exploited'. Socialism, for Wesker, was a way of life not just an economic structure, though Labour and the unions perpetuated the fragmenting of work and leisure. Wesker saw exemplars of cultural well-being in 'the Chekovs, Millers, Steinbecks and Zolas, the Beethovens... Van Goghs and yes, the Louis Armstrongs'.[40]

At the 1960 TUC, a motion drafted by Wesker and Bill Holdsworth, active in the Hemel Hempstead Left Club, was passed. This surprised Wesker, but was part of a rising trade union concern with cultural matters in this period, as the previous chapter noted amongst teaching unions. The motion requested no money, but mandated the General Council 'to ensure a greater participation... in all cultural activities'. It was moved by Ralph Bond of the Association of Cinematograph, Television and Allied Technicians. Bond's case was that 'for every pound that is spent in this country on armaments, one farthing goes to the Arts Council' and that the only difference between tap water and TV was 'that tap water is purified before we get it'. 'Our spiritual heritage, its culture, its songs, its living drama, its poetry is dying away' he argued, 'distorted and vulgarized by the purveyors of mass-production entertainment'. Bond had attended an International Confederation of Trade Unions Film Festival in Stockholm, featuring Scandinavian, West German, Austrian and American films, but not a single British contribution, he was 'sad to say'. Seconding, the NUM's William Whitehead was sure Congress was not 'satisfied that culture and art mean rock 'n' roll... *yogi bear* and *Rawhide* with bluinite detergent', but rather 'William Morris, Shakespeare, Shaw... Benjamin Britten'. The General Council averred the efforts of the Workers' Educational Association (WEA) and how the provisions of European trade unionism was tribute to the sizeable dues they extracted, some four times the British level. But when a speaker attacking sex and violence in cheap literature in support of the motion, was interrupted by the Congress President – 'I hope delegates will be brief as I want to take the economic section after this' – in a manner symptomatic of the motion's critique of dominant materialist outlooks, the matter was sealed.[41]

Wesker's project was decidedly post-materialist. C42 posters proclaimed: 'All Art should be Free – it is an experience not a commodity' and reasoned 'the principle of free art, like free education and medicine, would be accepted within a couple of decades if it could be proved that a majority of the population will respond to the cultural experience'. Writer Doris Lessing told the first C42 council of management how: 'Under the glossy mask of false prosperity which is the face of Britain now, people are being starved. They are hungry for a life that has more meaning to it than money, gaining status and securing their old age... 95% of the people are educated away from art'. Wesker rarely let up on this agenda, pressing Harold Wilson in the run-up to the 1964 election that politics based solely on productivity and higher wages lacked inspiration and the arts were a way of livening up Labour's image. Wilson responded that his 'white heat' speech had really been about leisure.[42] C42 critiqued Labour's National Plan in 1966 for amounting to 'all work and no play' where it might have made commitments like C42's 'Ten Year Plan' for every community to be no further than 50 miles from an arts centre. Unlike the CA, but not unlike the NVALA, C42 was uneasy with the modern, science and electric culture. Wesker's default position was humanist socialism. He often cited DH Lawrence's *A Sane Revolution* or Lindsay Anderson's contribution to Tom Maschler's, *Declaration* that 'a socialism that cannot express itself in emotional, human, poetic terms is one that will never capture the imagination of the people – who are poets even if they don't know it'.[43]

C42's appeals to the Unions argued materialism was limiting their appeal. Its 1964 May Day ads read: 'C42 greets you on this day of celebration and reminds you how bankrupt the labour movement is of the wherewithal to celebrate'. Working-class artists like Shelagh Delaney, Brendan Behan and Albert Finney were assimilated into the commercial sector. Arts funding was 'an opportunity for the labour movement to develop its cultural wing, since, it has always been acknowledged that a fight for the "good life" really meant a struggle to be allowed to enjoy the riches of education and the arts once material standards had been improved'. Lee's initial enthusiasm for Wesker's vision endorsed the 'brave idea' that if politicians and economists had 'failed to rescue us from the torpor of a subtly totalitarian culture, the only thing left is to give the poet his chance'.[44]

That the arts were the next stage in a vision of social progress, presupposed popular interest for what C42 deemed decent culture. Whilst critical of popular tastes, Wesker had faith that they were residually decent. To believe commercial fare was 'what people want' was to imagine 'that they will never be capable of developing richer responses'. Audiences could be desensitized by violence in films like Kubrick's *Paths of Glory*. The hope for a 'generation sacrificed to the lust of movie moguls' was in films of upright values (shown at C42's festivals) like *Living Jazz* and *We are the Lambeth Boys*. The prospect, he outlined in defence of Lee's subsidies, was to 'enable the arts to survive until such time as a minority audience becomes a majority audience'.[45]

But Wesker and C42 were often seen as patronizing working-class tastes. One tactic was to query the talent of audiences to exercise appropriate cultural choice. Wesker told the Finsbury Theatre Society in 1963 'that the British public was philistine', if 'not inherently so'. His message to the 1967 American trade Unions 'Labor and the Lively Arts: A Happening' (enabled by Resolution 31 at the 1964 AFL-CIO convention, emulating C42) was 'Philistines not dying easily here'. By 1967 in an unpublished piece, Wesker argued: 'the British people seem not to be "struggling for peace" or "the happy future of mankind", but for a little private garden in a capitalist state'. In an expression of frustration with popular responses to his efforts and of the limits to a post-materialist politics, Wesker complained British worker's reflex and first response was to 'whichever master dangles the bone of material improvement, it jumps'.[46] In 1970 John Mcgrath (BBC dramatist, briefly on C42's council and founder of the radical 7:84 theatre company in 1971) charged Wesker with having been assimilated by 'the idea... that culture is a product to be sold by culturally-conscious (therefore superior) artists and intellectuals to a culturally-starved (therefore inferior) workers... a bourgeois concept of culture'.[47] This hurt because of Wesker's working-class self-identity, the pronounced affinities to this in his work, but also the less than proletarian audiences that increasingly hung out at the Roundhouse.

Such attitudes were implicit in C42's cultural repertoire and preferences. Wesker's pet hates included the furore around the Beatles and intellectuals who 'pretend to like Elvis'. In *Youth Service Magazine* he explained 'that the music of Bach is superior to the music of Elvis Presley... is an indisputable fact that Presley himself would admit'.[48] In his play *Chips with Everything* the Wing Commander is miffed when the men chose folk music in preference to Elvis. Wesker could sound conservative in his fears of commercial, American pop and counter-cultural experimentalism.

Commentators like Richard Hoggart were similarly wary of American, mass culture. But C42 exhibited what Hoggart warned of in the politics and culture of this early New Left type (and C42 festivals were 'pure new-left subculture', Sinfield estimates) in *The Uses of Literacy*: 'a nostalgia for those "best of all" kinds of art, rural folk-art or genuinely popular urban art, and a special enthusiasm for such scraps of them as he thinks he can detect today... part-pitying and part-patronizing working-class people beyond all semblance of reality'. This politically progressive but culturally traditional amalgam exalted indigenous national cultures and in highly selective ways. As historians have noted, this New Left moment (and it might be added bodies like Michael Young's Institute for Community Studies), was aiming to recover 'authentic', traditional working-class experience just as this was reckoned to have evaporated or mutated. Notably, multiculturalism only faintly registered on C42's radar. C42 was an exercise in cultural defence against new forms of popular culture as much as against elitism; anti-establishment, but defending traditional forms and struggling to rival or penetrate mainstream commercial culture. C42 was faintly suspicious of the modern. Its only non-classical musical tastes, folk and jazz, were of the 'trad' (acceptable American) type, countering electric pop – although certainly at the start of the 1960s, when there was a revival in both, not without popular as well as radical political resonance.[49]

This folksy, nostalgic cleaving to some authentic workers' (and mostly male) culture did not impress all. Playwright Shelagh Delaney, closely associated with the New Left, wondered why it was 'some people seem to think that 100 years ago, everybody was speaking poetry in pubs?' (a reference to C42 festivals performances). Working-class artists, Ron Dellar explained in *New Left Review*, felt 'resentment' when portrayed as 'romantic misfits whose works could only be... appreciated by an... upper middle class minority' as much as when they had to debase their art in 'glossy magazines'.[50]

C42 aspired to address Dellar's discontents. It argued operating in traditional cultural conditions was alienating to working-class audiences and artists alike and materially unnecessary. Influenced by Raymond Williams, C42 asked how artists might control their work and relate it 'to a community rather than a market or patron'. Its answer was 'a cultural hub in London which by its approach and work will destroy the mystique and snobbery associated with the arts'. 'If we do not succeed', it warned:

> a vast army of highly powered commercial enterprises are going to sweep into the leisure hours of future generations and create a cultural mediocrity [and]... a nation emotionally and intellectually immature, capable of enjoying nothing, creating nothing and effecting nothing. This is not an idle prophecy; it is a fact in the making. Bingo is only the beginning.[51]

The aim was then 'to gather under one roof the best professional artists' such 'that any community body can invite them to take their work out in the form of festivals. All artists are paid but the venture is non-profit making' and the aim was, in creating a new popular audience for the arts (not *vice versa*) was to see them more as participants than spectators. 'The basic principle underlying this venture', C42 believed was 'that, given the right opportunities, art will return as the natural function of any community; without it a community is soulless and in the end easily exploitable'.

'It may be an abstract cause to fight for', C42 confessed, 'but then, in its day, so was education, trade unionism, universal suffrage and the abolition of slavery'. And, as alive to what it perceived as cultural dangers the 1960s posed for ill-prepared Britons as more conservative tendencies like the NVALA, C42 averred, 'a vote in a democracy may be the individual's weapon against political abuse, but the experience of art can strengthen a man's personality against spiritual abuse'.[52] There was then meaning and theory to the nomenclature of a *Centre* 42 prior to the Roundhouse.

To the Roundhouse

For Wesker's broader project, the Roundhouse was both saviour and destroyer. It renewed its focus after 1962's provincial festivals and placed it on the national cultural agenda, but burdened it with fundraising at the expense of cultural output. It sidetracked its energies and ultimately overwhelmed rather than staged C42. As C42's funding focus shifted from trades councils to the London glitterati and Arts Council, so its audience mutated from the working class to the youthful avant-garde, a select, hippy, North London crowd. As early as 1964 as patron of Sussex University's Arts Festival, Wesker contrasted his liking for 'lively, open-minded, gay and generous' students, with more curmudgeonly crowds (and funders).[53]

The Roundhouse was a metonym for C42 until 1970, but as a creative space, the notoriety and achievements of the Roundhouse came *despite* C42 not *because* of it. C42's cultural vision was made obsolete by the sorts of popular culture the Roundhouse housed for financial expediency. 'Waiting for lefty' (as in the play by Clifford Odetts, the US playwright to whom Wesker was often compared) proved fruitless. But it was, equally, C42 that rendered the Roundhouse *space* into a cultural *place* and forged a modern role for it. The Roundhouse would not have happened so easily in a non-1960s context, much as the same context also spelt the end for C42. C42 broke up just as political theatre flourished in the form of 7:84, Red Ladder and Agitprop.[54] And just as C42 (with Unity and Littlewood's Theatre Workshop) informed these, so it influenced numerous local arts centres and 'carrot-cake' cinemas, often housed in regenerated industrial buildings.

The Roundhouse strategy itself was controversial. Barker wanted to retain a local focus. Ted Willis, touted a merger with cash-strapped Unity Theatre in 1963. Willis was a vehement critic of Wesker's focus on premises, though far from an authority since many held him responsible for London Unity's failed professional venture after the war. The *Daily Herald* proposed a merger with the Club and Institute Union, since C42 had 'more ideas than money', but the CIU had clubs and assets. But C42 was single-minded. It insisted that the 'Teesside friends of C42' (founded by Middlesbrough-born Barker, Tony Topham and Young Socialist steel worker, Mike Brown) be so-titled and not 'C42 Teesside'. They differentiated themselves from the

NAA – 'Blenkinsopians are no more interested in a worker's culture than I am in swimming the atlantic', Brown opined.[55]

The building itself already had a transient history. Built in 1847 by Robert Stephenson as a turning house, developments in rail engine and tender design rendered it obsolete (just as the pace of cultural change in the 1960s made C42's vision obsolete). From 1869 until fashion tycoon Louis Mintz acquired the 19-year leasehold and gifted it to C42 in 1964, it was a liquor warehouse.[56] Visiting the Roundhouse, 'the cathedral of the permissive society' *She* magazine dubbed it, was a trip through the sixties. It hosted two key London counter-culture moments – the Dialectics of Liberation conference in 1967 and the launch of *International Times* (*IT*) in 1966. Neither was a C42 event, but both revealed something about it. C42 rates made the Roundhouse cheap to hire as a counter-cultural space. Jim Haynes, an *IT* editor, the creator of London's ArtsLab and founder of the Edinburgh Traverse Theatre, argued Wesker's fundraising ambitions for converting the Roundhouse were too high and stalled C42 cultural output in the meantime. For ArtsLab (and as Willis would later criticize Wesker)

Figure 6.1 Wesker (right) with Billy Butlin (left), Mary Wilson and the Prime Minister at the Downing Street tea party (1967)
Source: Ransom Humanities Center, University of Texas at Austin, USA

this procedure was reversed. Dialectics of Liberation assembled such luminaries as Stokely Carmichael (monitored by the Home Office), Allan Ginsberg, Julian Beck (of Living Theatre), RD Laing, Timothy Leary and Herbert Marcuse. Whilst the dialecticians debated, Wesker was at a fundraising tea party at Downing Street with political and business leaders like Billy Butlin and Lew Grade (see Figure 6.1). This coincidence of Dialectics and the No.10 tea party encapsulated the cultural divergence of C42 and the Roundhouse. As apt a measure of how Wesker's agenda had slipped by was Haynes moving to Paris in 1968 to teach 'free love', whilst Wesker retreated to a Hay-on-Wye farmhouse, found for him by publisher Tom Maschler in the hope of re-igniting his creativity.[57]

In 1964 PM Harold Wilson had gifted the Roundhouse George Hoskins, a coffee shop entrepreneur and former civil servant, to lend gravitas to the fundraising efforts, although he was often absent as Wilson dispatched him as an aide to Uganda and Nigeria. Robert Maxwell, a Labour MP already reputed for unscrupulous business practice, joined the Roundhouse Trust (a separate body from C42, to encourage donations despite C42's debts and air of profligacy and meaning monies would not go directly to Wesker) in March 1965 at Lee's behest. He told Wesker that Lee felt his campaign 'should not be allowed to fail'.[58] This drift to put things on a more commercial footing institutionally uncoupled C42 and the Roundhouse. This saw the Roundhouse used variously for TV, adverts, ice shows, Campaign for Real Ale festivals and a British Film Institute – *Sunday Times* 'cinema city' exhibition (visited by Harold Lloyd and Gene Kelly).

Without secure funding or cultural roots, C42 and its property were overrun by popular and counter-cultural activities, far from the blend of high and authentic-folk-proletarian culture Wesker envisaged. Before 1971 performances included Andy Warhol's first play, *Pork*; bands such as The Doors; a rock version of *Othello* and Peter Brook's Experimental Theatre interpretation of *The Tempest* on trapeze (featuring Glenda Jackson). A regular 1967 event was the UFO club which pioneered (with its lead band, Pink Floyd) late night psychedelic raves illuminated by oil slide shows. Not untypical of Roundhouse fare was 1967's 'New Year Giant Freak Out All Night Rave', which saw The Who's power fail twice and a flour fight. Clement Freud reviewing the gig for the *Financial Times* thought it would have been best to arrive either drunk or lightly stoned. It was also, more soberly, a political venue favoured by the left and 1960s radicals – used by North St. Pancras Labour Party, anti-Apartheid groups, *Black Dwarf* and the Revolutionary Socialist Student Federation conference in November 1968, addressed by Daniel Cohn-Bendit. The schizophrenia of the venue was such that it also hosted traditional 'high' culture like the British School at Rome Painting Group and recordings of Beethoven by Daniel Barenboim and the New Philharmonia Orchestra.[59]

Much as it prioritized commercial over cultural value, Hoskins' regime did not mean less controversial, as Kenneth Tynan's *Oh Calcutta!* revealed when it replaced Wesker's (poorly reviewed) *The Friends* in 1970. Nor, seem-ingly caught up by C42's radicalism, did it preclude more avant-garde offer-ings. American Ed Berman's Inter-Action theatre (of which Barker was a trustee) set up in a derelict shop opposite the Roundhouse in 1969 to take advantage of its audiences and get around its economic plight ('we don't need £590,000 – yet' it proclaimed). They performed *Ham-cutlet*, a parody of *Hamlet* and traipsed the streets to escape the confines of conventional theatre. It eventually ran an ACGB-sponsored late night theatre club in the Roundhouse, creatively independent, but with C42 pocketing bar and restaurant revenues. This meant the Roundhouse, despite C42's failure to win ACGB support, was still featured in a *Daily Mail* expose of state funding that warned 'they're giving your money to spoonfeed hippy art'.[60]

C42's hand-to-mouth existence was not only a result of the physical dilapidation of the building. A do-it-yourself ethos remained from C42's regional festivals, which not even the combined (or supposed) business nous of Hoskins and Maxwell could dispel. A typical case was the anti-Vietnam war 'Angry Arts' week. Sponsored by Jonathan Miller and Vanessa Redgrave and featuring Ewen Macoll, Peggy Seeger and Harold Pinter, it was recorded as a TV documentary. Tipped off by Haynes that Roundhouse rates were reasonable – organizer Aubrey Raymond secured a deal whereby they would pay nothing if takings were under £1500. Takings totaled £1494, but the Roundhouse was still billed by the Performing Rights Society.[61]

The everyday life of the Roundhouse was a chaotic, ramshackle 'happening' – as likely to provide spiritual abuse as salvation. Until 1967 C42 maintained offices in Fitzroy Square where other tenants included Terence Conran, whose poor habits of disposing of rubbish and locking doors perturbed C42. The undoubted allure and drama of the Roundhouse could not always com-pensate for the lack of uniform wiring, adequate fire precautions and toilet facilities. In 1967 the Greater London Council (GLC) declared 'the present condition of the premises falls short of the required standard'.[62]

In 1967 the publican of the pub opposite the Roundhouse petitioned against the layabouts and noise associated with the UFO club and in 1969 the GLC Public Services Entertainment sub-committee refused an extension of an all-night music licence. UFO's reputation was hard to refute when one of its organizers, Mike Henshaw (as Green describes, a 'hip accountant' for C42 and *IT*) sponsored a legalize drugs petition. In 1967 CND shunned the Roundhouse 'whilst there is some controversy among local residents about recent functions there', a decision Wesker regretted whilst agreeing that many events were 'timid and tatty'. The police 'worried about what went on inside the Roundhouse' and raids were regular. The organizers of Dialectics were warned that police and Camden council officers were likely to raid the event.[63]

'C42 does all it can to prevent drug-taking', Hoskins argued and local police 'have told us we can do no more', but it was prey to 'irresponsible sensation-mongers'. Designer Mike Lesser's naked self-painting in jelly for *IT*'s fundraising 'Uncommon Market', initiated some torrid press coverage early in 1967. The *Daily Mail* noted this was 'not quite what Arnold Wesker had in mind'. The friendlier *Sunday Citizen* saw this as a crossroads for C42, faced with 'a largely un-sympathetic public'. Hoskins asked the 'Uncommon Market' organizers: 'could we avoid naked men in jelly – there has to be a limit on the amount of libertarianism we can afford otherwise we shall go out of existence'.[64]

Nudity, however, was good business Hoskins had decided by the run of *Oh Calcutta!* from July–September 1970, the first play with full frontal nudity on the English stage. Lucrative as it was, *Oh Calcutta!* confirmed the association, Hoskins confessed, the Roundhouse had 'in some people's minds with nude shows'. It 'packed in the pornophiles', as *Punch* put it and attracted GLC and police investigations. The play aroused the hostility of the NVALA and left the *Telegraph* wondering if 'the Lord Chamberlain's role in the world of theatre was abolished at precisely the wrong moment'. Its commercial success lost the Roundhouse a Camden Council subsidy. It also cemented the rupture between C42 and the Roundhouse. Disgruntled with *Oh Calcutta!*, with Hoskins' and other 'tycoons' scheme for a hotel and offices (hatched with Louis Seifert, the developer behind Centre Point) alongside and funding the Roundhouse and with the creative void that was C42, Wesker wound it up in October 1970. C42's death throes were characteristically acrimonious with Wesker and Hoskins trading insults over its demise. Relating the decision to architect Paul Chemetov he explained, the 'building has a certain cache in London... every slick enterprise wants to hire it', but he now had 'nightmares about it'.[65]

That the Roundhouse haunted Wesker was also made clear to French Director Jean Louis Barrault – 'I am ambivalent about everything happening in the building. It has been part of me since 1963 and is even now one of my recurring dreams'. The occasion for Wesker's missive was to explain a protest in March 1971 during a performance of *Rabelais*, which Barrault was directing at the Roundhouse. Three (naked) actors from London Living Theatre, protested what their leaflet described saw as 'the monstrous misappropriation' of the Roundhouse 'by the commercial theatre of the bourgeoisie... as if... there were not already enough places in London for this kind of bullshit'. They lamented the demise of 'Centre 42 – a theatre for the poor, the culturally underprivileged' and called on staff and actors to join their protest. 'Look at that audience' they told the press, 'they are all middle class... the Roundhouse was meant to be used by the workers'. Wesker, who was in the audience, apologized to Barrault, but also explained he was 'touched to find that others were taking up a gesture in defence of Centre 42'. The protest was 'an over-simplification, but it is near enough the truth'.[66]

Hoskins rebutted Wesker and supporters charges of naked commercialism. He argued in 1971: 'The Roundhouse has not lacked purist critics who would prefer to see it have nothing to do with "commerce" and fail nobly... They seem to think that taxation is a purifying process and that the receipt of public charity is in some way nobler than self-assistance from commercial development'. But even Hoskins believed subsidies were 'essential' (the hotel scheme aimed to exploit government tourism subsidies) and remained reliant on private largesse. Philanthropist Barnett Shine's charity enabled the purchase of the freehold and cleared C42's debts. Hoskins also had anxieties about the milieu the Roundhouse dealt with. He was proud of its diner's cosmopolitan menu and crowd, but worried that 'the Roundhouse as a social centre has been abused by those who traffic in drugs and by those who wish to while their days away lounging and sleeping in the restaurant for the price of a cup of tea'. 'We stop the pushers which causes us to be denounced as illiberal' he explained, to cater for 'the great body of people... who come here for shows and entertainment and who expect to pay their way'.[67]

C42 visions

All this could hardly have been more divergent from the offerings in C42's festivals held from September to November 1962 in Nottingham, Birmingham, Hayes and Southall, Leicester, Bristol and Wellingborough. There were local permutations (a 'prize for the best-dressed lady... not the most expensively dressed' at Wellingborough), but standard C42 fare included: pub and workplace poetry readings from Dannie Abse, Laurie Lee and Christopher Logue; folk music from Ewen Macoll, Peggy Seeger and A.L. Lloyd and art and sculpture displays (including Barbara Hepworth and L.S. Lowry) in shops and community centers. Michael Croft's National Youth Theatre performed *Hamlet* (touted as 'Shakespeare's Jimmy Porter') and a theatre folk ballad *The Maker and the Tool* was constructed by BBC radio's Charles Parker from workplace recordings. Besides Bernard Kops' play *Enter Solly Gold*, Wesker's *The Nottingham Captain* was written for the festivals with ACGB funding and dealt with the defeat of the 1817 Pentrich luddite rising (analogous with C42's fate, some felt). It was scripted to a part-jazz (by David Lee, later musical director on *TW3*) and part-classical (by Wilfred Josephs) score.[68] Jazz came from the Fortytwo Big band, lead by Tommy Watt and one of C42's more successful ventures. The 16-piece's repertoire included the 'TUC twist' and 'Wesker jumps in' and was considered 'world class' by the *Evening Standard* and well enough regarded to record with Columbia records in 1964.[69]

A sense of the cultural tastes on display here can be gleaned from Watt's philosophy. He saw jazz as a force for breaking down racial barriers and a post-industrial folk music. It was the basis of the popular music industry, but the 'emotional warmth and excitement of jazz have been debased into the outpourings of the juke box'. Jazz was an alternative to the 'regurgitated pulp being fed to the youth of this country'. It was for dancing, but also a form where the 'soloist will be allowed the full freedom of expression'. Other C42 supporters referred to the 'diabolical electric guitar' and Ray Bernard of Mountain and Molehill, who designed the Festival pamphlets, shared C42's distaste for bingo. Cultural debasement and materialism seemed to C42 to go hand-in-hand. This repertoire smacked of, as Sinfield mordantly but reasonably puts it, as 'new-left subculture exactly: relatively political and hopefully accessible instances of high culture with bits of current student subculture and uncertain gestures towards the creativity of working people'.[70] Hints of C42's grander aspirations that found full force in the Roundhouse were also apparent. Barker, who lead a films working party with Paddy Whannel and Alan Lovell, was keen to work towards a C42 chain of cinemas. Wesker unsuccessfully asked Sir Michael Balcon and Tony Richardson for a film launch to double as a C42 festival fundraiser.[71]

Wesker's vision of the Roundhouse was as nothing less than the seat of a cultural revolution. Wesker had also seen plans in 1960 on the Youth Service Development Council for the Cannon Hill Trust Midland Arts centre, which attracted ACGB and Gulbenkian funding. Once acquired in 1964, plans for the Roundhouse were outlined by Wesker in the *Allio Brief*. This provided guidelines to French theatre designer Rene Allio and architect Chemetov in re-designing the railway shed as a multipurpose, state of the arts centre. Again, C42's international aspect was apparent. Allio had worked on Roger Planchon's experimental theatre in Lyon and Malraux's Centres Dramatiques. Chemetov lead the Atelier d'urbanisme et d'architecture in Paris and had worked on the new French Communist party HQ.[72]

The *Allio Brief* 'evoke[d] the atmosphere' and aesthetics of C42's vision. The crux of this was that art should be an unextraordinary, free component of community life. Thus the Roundhouse had to avoid the impression (of which C42 was accused) of 'imposing' an 'artistic policy'. Rather, 'the public must be encouraged to adopt the new habit of calling for the artist' from the Roundhouse's 'reservoir of talent'. Architectural excellence was imperative and Wesker digressed into critiquing Coventry's new Cathedral for its 'mixed up' styles. What the Roundhouse *should* be was as assorted. C42 artists ought to be 'warlike, audacious, gay, courteous, brilliant – and no doubt drunk' and the Roundhouse 'a place of pleasure and marvelous revelation', and, 'efficient, effective, functional'.

The building should relate the artist and audience more intimately than in traditional theatres and 'result in developing a new and informed audience'. There should be meeting rooms for local Co-ops, trade unions, church and youth groups. Unlike Allio, Wesker 'like(d) the idea of skeptical youngsters lounging around in a building where there is music, theatre and debate in full swing' and felt there ought to be 'a jellied eel stall, the FortyTwo fish and chip shop, the bookstall... and the bar must be available not only for audiences... but as a pub throughout the day'. More militantly, the Roundhouse was to be a public relations war room, the place where if artists were to:

> forge a new language that will make society recognize its responsibilities to the arts – it should be here. If they are to acquire that confidence that will eliminate the artists nervous twitch of apology for his so-called 'inessential' profession – it should be here. And if all this adds up to a cultural revolution and if this revolution has a seat – it should be here.[73]

Relations with Allio and Chemetov were emblematic of C42 as a whole – charged and erratic (meetings were regularly cancelled). Wesker wryly told Allio that he had been told 'that you are a very strong Marxist and will therefore ask for a very high fee'. The fee came in at £33,334 with a projected opening in late 1966. Both were regularly revised.[74]

The Roundhouse's intoxicating Victoriana – the *Telegraph* was struck in 1964 by intense theatricality, wrought iron pillars, layers of dust – was exploited to raise funds. Vera Elyashiv's first proposal as C42's new artistic director in 1967 was a Victorian Ball, railway themed, catered by Harrods and with a guest list to include Princess Margaret and David Frost. C42 received £2000 from the National Trust's Historic Buildings Council in 1967.[75] Its immediate London competitors and colleagues, the Arts Lab and the Institute of Contemporary Arts (ICA), were also housed in a Victorian warehouse and Georgian mansion respectively. Wesker consistently asserted the case for creative use of post-industrial landscapes, supporting Misha Black and John Gielgud in 1969 in calling for the GLC to turn St. Katherine's Dock into an arts centre. Old and decaying as the Roundhouse was, it was a marker for modern, post-industrial developments. Lee's White paper name-checked the Roundhouse amongst those 'historic buildings' converted into Arts centres, a process that achieved two worthy objects, besides costing less than a new centre.[76]

Lee's focus on buildings enthused C42. Shortly before the White Paper at a conference at Coventry's Belgrade (the first full product of Section 132) on civic theatres, she emphasized a shift away from elite and West End styles towards a 'welcoming social centre open during the day' and 'multipurpose buildings'. Here she underlined 'how closely Malraux's thinking parallels much of our own', in Maisons de la Culture. This was endorsed by playwright David Turner, Hugh Jenkins MP (of artists' union, Equity and Arts Minister, 1974–76), but ex-Theatre Workshop actor John Neville wondered what would be left once the 'Metropolis' has taken its part. Neville's fears for the regions proved to be misplaced and it was C42's retreat to London that worked against it. Neville's stewardship of the Nottingham Playhouse, with its youth, educational and outreach programmes, became the model for Lee's policies. With set and stage designer Sean Kenny (who worked in the West End and with *Beyond the Fringe*) Neville hatched a design for a mobile theatre and offered it to C42, before the idea of a physical centre became all-consuming. Such 'temporary inflatable structures' were favoured by both the White Paper and business and seemed at one with the freedom and transience of the counter-culture more than C42, immured in the Roundhouse.[77]

Much as C42 sought to renovate the Roundhouse, it seemed to rub off on the movement. For architectural critic Reyner Banham, the whole project, building and cultural agenda, smacked of a 'bandaged-up load of Victoriana', a hangover from the era when socialism was passed down munificently to the workers, a sort of 'cultural soup kitchen approach' comprising 'hand outs of free art'. Banham suggested Wesker's 'chorus line of knights and dames' should instead be sent 'to Harlow New Town... to square up to the real working class'. Wesker felt it was precisely such attitudes, that saw any cultural enthusiasm as high-minded, that compelled C42 to seek elite funding and support.[78]

Financial and political reception

Funding applications, concepts and knock-backs litter C42's archives. This occupied its creative energies above all else. The 1962 Festivals left C42 £40,000 in debt and requesting small debts be written off on the basis that 'the days of the private patron have gone and the government's understanding of its duty barely extends to the arts'. The weight of this debt made Mintz's offer of the Roundhouse doubly appealing – lending the movement security after the Festivals, as well as for the conceptual reasons of a cultural hub. Thus 45 requests to run festivals in 1963 were turned down. But it locked it into ambitious plans for renovation, fundraising and a London location, just as the funding focus shifted to the regions. Lord Harewood (the Queen's cousin and director of the Edinburgh festival) launched the appeal at the Roundhouse in July 1964 with a glossy brochure in the presence of Mintz, Wilson and James Callaghan. Playwrights Pinter and Osborne and the TUC's George Woodcock and Vic Feather tuned down invitations. The appeal was for £590,000 (see Figure 6.2) over two years to come from: local and national government; the public; trade unions and Co-ops; Colleges and Universities, charities and business.[79]

Feather, the TUC's Assistant General Secretary and who attended C42's Wellingborough festival, queried whether its fundraising would prosper by looking classy or deserving. Despite arguing in 1963 that trade unionism needed to address mental as well as material poverty, Feather proved a thorn in C42's relations with the unions. According to Stanley Reed of the British Film Institute, when C42 was mentioned to him in 1962, a 'chill seemed to descend' and Feather bemoaned 'eccentrics knocking on the doors of the TUC'. Reed supposed Feather (long prone to contrast 'eccentric

Figure 6.2   The Roundhouse, replete with C42 fundraising hoarding, 1964
Source: Ransom Humanities Center, University of Texas at Austin, USA

intellectuals' to solid trade unionists) was manoeuvering the TUC away from the 1960 Congress motion. Feather had a month earlier refused to sign a letter with Wesker urging individual unions to support C42 unless asked to do so by local trades councils. Feather told Hoskins in 1963 that C42 was on too ambitious a scale. Feather was consistent, warning the NAA in 1970 off any 'worker's art'.[80]

Wesker had urged new General Secretary George Woodcock in 1960 to show 'vision'. Wesker was moved by the modernist design and sculptural accoutrements of TUC Congress House, opened in 1958, but they were less disposed to conceive trade unionism in such terms. By 1963 mutual animosities became public when Woodcock wrote in the *Observer* that the TUC has scarce experience or monies to expend on the arts and that in any case C42 'seemed a bit long-haired and starry-eyed'. By 1965 hostilities had cut off any chance of C42 receiving support, with Wesker telling the TUC General Council that they were 'old men... paralyzed by narrowness of preoccupations'.[81]

C42 called on local authorities to give what amounted to 1/80th of a penny (much less than the 1948 Act's 6d) rate. But with major re-organization in

London government between 1963–65 – the London County Council (LCC) expanding into the GLC – many local authorities deferred decisions. Even Camden, the Roundhouse's home and firmly Labour with ex-CND organizer Peggy Duff amongst the councillors, proved diffident. Keith Joseph's attempt in 1964, just before the Roundhouse appeal was launched, to prevent Deptford supporting Unity Theatre, did induce donations to C42.[82] Outer Boroughs were less willing. In 1966 Bromley Councillor Raymond Pope denounced C42 as 'proletarian piffle' and any donation as 'throwing... public money down the kitchen sink'. The GLC and LCC were preoccupied with the Roundhouse's health and safety and minded to hear how the ACGB felt about C42 before committing.[83] Likewise, Goodman was keen to see commitments from others to match any ACGB support. This was precisely Wesker's frustration with the TUC, as he explained to Woodcock, that it could be a backer of the scale that would reassure others – 'we go round and round in circles and no-one seems prepared to break it'.[84]

More joy was had with the Gulbenkian Foundation – whose extensive portfolio of arts projects included Middlesbrough's Little Theatre (post-war Britain's first new build theatre), Bristol's Arnolfini, Sussex University's Gardener Centre and NAA's youth ticket scheme. The 1959 Bridges Committee report to Gulbenkian discussed 'multi-purpose' arts centres and that whilst best suited to dispersed populations recommended it might consider 'making a grant towards the design of an Arts Centre in a big city, if such a project appears likely to materialize'. Gulbenkian funded C42 to the tune of £10,000 early in 1962, adding £3000 in 1964. Although Jim Thornton, Gulbenkian's UK and Commonwealth Director, wondered why such a 'grandiose' London base was needed.[85]

Business patronage was forthcoming from new sources, notably the ITV Companies Association Committee of Review of Grants to the Arts and Sciences, which met from 1958. As the *Manchester Guardian* saw it, they were the patrons now in era where surtax and death duties limited individual patronage. It co-funded Ballet Rambert, the Belgrade Theatre, National Trust and Civic Trust. After initial reservations, the ACGB welcomed TV as a 'third force of patronage' (as W.E. Williams put it) bolstering creativity that it might harvest. Tyne-Tees TV was NAA's largest single funder and Granada funded Joseph Trenaman as chair in TV research at Leeds University. More political recipients included Unity Theatre, PEP and the Institute of Economic Affairs. C42 and the Roundhouse Trust received small grants. After 1964 the grants were cutback as the Television Act cut into the companies profit margins and increased ACGB funding saw an 'astonishing decline in the volume of applications'.[86] As fatally, Wesker had a spat with Williams shortly before he left the ACGB for the business world. He suggested Weskerism was a 'false doctrine', premised on mass interest in the arts and later told Wesker that business would want to see that C42 was 'a sound and sane organization'.[87]

As the Roundhouse shifted from workers culture to more popular, commercial clientele, so C42 funding strategies became more business and celebrity-focused. Businesses like Shell and Esso supported the 1962 festivals, so this was not entirely a strategic departure enforced by limited public and union funds. It did attract some ostensibly unlikely bedfellows in *Deuce*, the Metropolian Police magazine, the Birmingham Small Arms Company and Muswell Hill Young Conservatives.[88] But as the *Spectator* noted in Wellingborough in 1962: 'with an eye... on Conservative local councils and the Tory working class, the festival's politics are curiously muted'. C42 believed its project transcended the usual partisan alignments. Its pitch to business was as a 'movement to revitalize the nation through the arts' in which it was hoped 'your company will play a part'.[89] Like the CA and NVALA, C42 saw itself as much a national project as a political one.

Four bids were submitted to the ACGB by 1967. After 1963's was rejected 'out of court', 1965's was duly more detailed, including sections of the *Allio Brief* to explain its 'artistic justification' and more democratic attitude, 'free of pomp'. It claimed only C42 had the experience of sourcing local festivals, noting legacies like Bristol's youth theatre and Hayes' 42 Club. The Festivals taught C42 the need for a permanent base, to proffer 'a reservoir of artistic talent', just as Oxbridge supplied the new post-Robbins universities. Professionalism was emphasized. A 'very English' paternalism and amateurism infused too many local efforts and whilst C42 believed 'art should not be reduced to a hobby'. On this, at least, C42 and the ACGB saw eye to eye. Both opposed amateurism at the 1967 Greater London Arts Association conference at the Roundhouse. From the outset Wesker insisted C42 festivals must 'not be esoteric little gatherings... or weak, amateurish efforts... they must be robust, exciting and... professional'.[90] But the 1965 bid fell on the ACGB's anxieties over the cost of securing the freehold (the leasehold expired in 1983) for the Roundhouse from British Rail. This mired C42 in what Wesker described as 'kafka-like legal traumas'. Ultimately Goodman never looked favourably on C42, as he privately confessed to the ACGB and LCC. As early as 1963 he had received a report from lawyer and civil liberties activist, Morris Ernst, that cultural initiatives by American Unions were 'not ready as yet to obtain support from the mass of workers' just as 'in England C42 has found difficulty in gaining acceptance'.[91]

Wesker's networking skills and the turnover of figures associated with C42 embraced arts, political and trade union luminaries, alternative politics, the counter-culture and satire. Few didn't pass within C42's orbit. Roger Law, best known for the 1980s TV show *Spitting Image* and whose cartoons adorned the bar wall at Peter Cook's London satire club, 'The Establishment', offered cartoons to C42. Wesker's celebrity and charisma gave the movement early impetus, enabling him to assemble union leaders Ted Hill, Frank Cousins and Bill Carron, plus Lessing, Maschler and Lee on

C42's first Council of Management. This was a movement of personality as much as ideas, long before its aspiration to a trade union audience faded.[92] Much energy was expended on schemes like the 1965 Stars Committee fronted by John Lennon, Vanessa Redgrave, Spike Milligan and Fenella Fielding. Lennon's nominal support generated media coverage. If Wesker's abrasive personality courted controversy, his core concept of a cultural hub could readily be seen as implicitly querying current government policy, cultural facilities and structures of artistic production. This explained why C42 was received coolly by many otherwise politically or creatively proximate. So Lessing told as early as 1961, the source of 'a great deal of malice being spread... about C42' was the Royal Court's Director and Wesker-sponsor George Devine, who 'seems to see this as an attack on himself'.[93]

Wesker had a talent for ingratiating himself with the famous and influential. The 'Friends of Centre 42' was bedecked with Lords, Ladys and Sirs as well as the Countess of Albemarle, John Berger, Sidney Bernstein, Gerald Gardiner, Peter Hall, Cleo Laine, J.B. Priestley, Alan Sillitoe, CP Snow, Kenneth Tynan and Raymond Williams. The (as it turned out aptly named) 'little appeal' of early 1967 aimed to work this list, but only half responded. Most audacious was an approach to Prince Philip. Wesker explained he would 'sooner have built 42 on the pennies and pounds of many hundreds and thousands', but this was not forthcoming. He visited Buckingham Palace in May 1965, where Philip blamed government funding of sports and arts for reducing the interest of private or business patrons. The request was turned down for reasons, C42 reasoned, of Wesker's left-wing associations. In another instance, Wesker simply pleaded for a millionaire to back him.[94]

C42's relationships with friends were as fraught as its internal workings. Privately, the appeals to business and celebrities were felt to be compromises, which C42 kept as quiet about as the ACGB and TUC did about their own reservations about C42. Wesker's hostility to pop and the Beatles, has been noted, but Lennon's association was keenly sought. Peter Sellars was listed amongst the Friends of C42, but *I'm Alright Jack* was regularly cited as unworthy of the labour movement. Impresario Jack Hylton was also a 'Friend', but Wesker dubbed him a 'cretinizing' cultural influence and told Goodman he would 'prefer to have Hylton's assurances in the bank'. As revealing was that on the eve of the No.10 tea party Wesker enjoined the Gulbenkian's Jim Thornton, 'let us hope that the industrial thugs who gather at Downing Street will be touched with your enlightenment'.[95]

As unforthcoming as the TUC or ACGB was ideological sustenance from the New Left. Relations had been close – Wesker wrote in the first *New Left Review*, touting his project as 'another focal point of activity' to match CND. Raymond Williams publicized C42's efforts and Tom Nairn, hoped for 'cordial relations with C42'. Like the New Left, C42 was internationally-minded. C42's experience was to bemoan the British Labour movement's focus on material issues and to be a victim of TUC indifference – a case study in what the New Left critiqued as 'labourism'. But there were limits to even the early New Left's cultural politics and thus proximity to C42. Actress and later Labour MEP Janey Buchan wrote to Wesker in 1960 explaining she had 'prodded Stuart Hall and *NLR* until I'm sick' to participate in the burgeoning fringe at the Edinburgh Festival. She despaired of the New Left's Londo-centrism and felt, '*NLR* need their heads looking at because they could have the most tremendous stage ready-made for them'.[96]

Labour's only material donations to Wesker's cause were Hoskins and Maxwell. Wesker and Lee had been close since the death of Aneurin Bevan (her husband) in 1960, often signing off 'with love'. Assurances were legion once Labour assumed office. Wilson fudged a proposed business meeting in 1965, but informed Wesker, 'I should certainly like to be associated with C42 in the future'. Two years later Lee insisted to Wesker and Hoskins that C42 had 'had more time, attention and thought... than any other part of my activity'. But privately, Lee told Wilson's secretary Marcia Williams in 1966: 'we have got to get the Roundhouse off the ground or we have got to get it off Arnold's shoulders', otherwise 'it will destroy him as a playwright'. Lee still noted common ground in that Wesker 'agreed with me that an urgent priority is to try to set up counter-attractions to the influences of commercial television, betting, drugs and all the rest of it'.[97]

But Wesker's outburst at June 1967's Labour Arts and Amenities group meeting, which Williams (who told Wilson of her 'great sympathy' for C42) had pressed for, sealed the fallout with Lee. The group chair told Lee: 'C42 is suffering from "Jenniecide"... Arnold is under the delusion that you are conspiring with Ted [Willis] to kill the C42 project'.[98] Wesker, fearing Lee might not attend the No.10 party, suggested that Willis' 'gratuitous article' in *Tribune* was his real target. To add to 1967's summer of tumult, Wesker was offered and declined a Commander of the British Empire (CBE).[99]

After this, Goodman weighed in, critiquing Wesker's project to the Prime Minister. He had 'never felt much enthusiasm for the project', since it was 'in direct contradiction to a policy that has been sedulously cultivated by Jennie and myself'. This was 'that we do not impose our views or any central views on the local regions and... that pre-packaged London culture despatched all over the place is the exact reverse of what we are trying to establish'. It would be 'unkind to all our efforts if the tea party were to suggest sponsorship of a plan at variance with our own'. It would also imperil a policy that had 'earned dividends' for the government, 'both in social results and in simple political terms'. By 1969, what vestiges of common ground Lee felt with Wesker had gone. She was annoyed Wesker gave 'no credit' to her efforts and argued that 'nowhere in the country has been created a people's arts centre such as we originally conceived'. Lee confessed she was: 'still to find any centre that wants an exclusively working class arts centre. Personally, I am opposed to this concept. As socialists, we are energetically promoting the comprehensive principle... Arnold's views seem to me out of tune'.[100]

The tea party in July 1967, came a month after Wesker's accusations against Lee. Hoskins admitted to Williams that 'we have done all humanely possible to "do it ourselves"' and 'will have to wind it up otherwise'. Sizeable donations were received from Billy Butlin, Bernard Delfont, Lew Grade and Rio Tinto Zinc, totalling almost £80,000.[101] This amounted to a survival not development package, confining C42 to being a virtual entity, existing in name and imagination alone.

Wesker's suspicions of C42 becoming tenants of the Roundhouse, rather than having a prior claim on it, that it was swallowed by the Trust, hood-winked by tycoons, railroaded by commercial imperatives and deserted by Lee and the TUC, seemed well founded. But so were those critics who argued C42 was too profligate and that cultural output should precede funding and a permanent base. Willis felt 'Wesker seems to think that he alone has the tablets of stone... on art and the rest of us are either philistines or cheats'. He insisted C42 needed to 'show us in deeds not words' as Neville had, but having created next-to-nothing was at present, 'diversionary, wrong and even harmful'.[102] There were precious few actual C42 events at the Roundhouse – mostly festival reprises like Pete Seeger's gig in January 1967. As Ruth Kustow observed the 'only time it "swings" is when it is hired out' and even then the Roundhouse had competition. For Mike Kustow, the ICA (which he directed, 1967–71) was artistically superior and ArtsLab was more 'successful as a meeting place'.[103] The legal, financial and cultural uncoupling of the Roundhouse and C42 was nowhere more apparent than when *Jackie* magazine (evidence of how the Roundhouse was a fixture in popular culture) observed in 1967, with its late night bars and psychedelic lighting, the Roundhouse was 'a really jumping scene', but during daytime reverted to 'the rather solid sign of a social and cultural arts centre'.[104]

Wesker claimed that whilst '42 has not succeeded in creating its own centre, it has created a spirit and focused attention on the arts in a way that has inspired'. Wilson took Lee from C42 and Lee took several ideas from Wesker. Itzin reckoned as fringe and youth theatres and arts centres flourished in the 1970s, that C42 had 'come true, independent of its originators'. But more often, Wesker looked ruefully back in anger. In 1967 he wrote: 'I have been too charming or innocent in my dealings with "the powers that be"... Feather... is now annoyed at my insistence that a cultural movement aimed at that wider uninitiated audience should be of such a high (and therefore expensive) artistic level. Jennie Lee, also once a friend, got annoyed with me for the same reason'.[105]

Popular reception

C42 may well have felt betrayed or neglected by its purported supporters, but the popular reception it elicited was also constraining. And for the core work this chapter demands of C42, as a site from which to read the broader political culture, this surely indicates its cultural politics had limitations. C42's local festivals met the uneven reception that the project as a whole encountered. In Bristol the Trades Council reported the poetry was 'well attended', but the 'response' to a town hall dance was 'very disappointing'. It concluded that the festival had helped shift media attention to activities other than industrial disputes. The *Bristol Evening Post*'s review asked 'can enthusiasm for such evenings extend beyond the already converted?' and suggested such 'movements need time to grow roots'.[106] In Leicester events were disturbed by anti-Semitic and anti-communist slogans, but the 'public's reception was lukewarm'. It was apparently confused by the art works, although Wesker felt the press unfairly put C42 across as 'salvation army cultural vendors'. Nottingham's Tory council refused to contribute, but poetry reading at Nottingham's Raleigh factory was, by C42's own admission, 'a fiasco' and they were 'disappointed' by the festival. At Ericsson's telephone factory in Beeston, a storeman reported: 'I like poetry', but found it 'difficult to concentrate... in such a big canteen' and a toolsetter that he would rather 'doze than listen to poetry'. There were positive legacies like the discovery of jazz singer Ann Briggs.[107] Darts matches continued in Perry Barr's 'Crown and Cushion' pub as C42's folk singers held forth, nonetheless Birmingham Trades Council felt 'a tremendous impact was made' and saw C42 as part of the move into activities 'beyond the search for bread'. C42 often did not live up to its professional mantras. 'It is by now commonplace that Centre 42 festivals are administratively chaotic', the *Spectator* concluded and Mervyn Jones found *Enter Solly Gold*, 'plainly still in a state of rehearsal'.[108]

The Festival of Labour met a similar reception, suggesting the limits not extent of its reach and networks in civil society. It was not just C42, but avowedly political left cultural agendas that struggled. Its conceptual art at Congress House attracted barely 100 festival-goers a day over its two week run and 'for many... the paintings and sculptures on view were too advanced'. Tom Driberg, the Festival's arts consultant, noted how Wesker had encountered 'philistinism' too. Several institutions spurned Labour on the basis they might suffer through association. Though a popular venue with the New Left, the Whitechapel Gallery Director Bryan Robertson told Rees it was, 'impossible for us to hold an exhibition of any kind with political sponsorship'. The British Film Institute, National School of Opera, *Daily Mirror* and Caravan Club (touted as an accommodation solution for the influx of Labour members) expressed similar anxieties. Some distinction might be drawn between association with party and politics *per se*. But that as Rees put it to Labour's Scottish Organizer, 'we have to avoid being too aggressively political', said much about the comparatively cold climate in which politics was practiced and by which it was delimited.[109]

Voicing at once the hopes and frustration of C42, Mike Brown of Teeside 'Friends of C42' told Clive Barker in 1963: 'everything would be plain sailing if people would go to the theatre'. When a month later Wesker addressed Cargofleet Workingmen's Club prior to a performance of Behan's *The Hostage*, the local paper reported the dearth of trade unionists amongst the audience as 'trade union apathy for the arts'.[110] C42's first report admitted none of the play scripts submitted to it by 1962 had proved acceptable and were more evidence of TV's corrupting impact. It also doubted 'we can initiate a public to drama by seating them on hard chairs'. This was very trying for C42's faith, as Wesker confessed to the *Observer*'s arts editor, Richard Findlater: 'this does no bode well for the sort of response we anticipate'. Most damning for C42's prospectus was the Wellingborough youth asked by the *Sunday Times* about the festival. Interviewed in a café, by a jukebox, with a Tony Curtis haircut and horse brass round his neck, this Hoggart 'juke box boy' responded: 'doesn't appeal see. Not that kind of stuff. We got all we want. Cinemas, dancing twice a week... there's six caffs, 12 pubs'.[111]

And as has been seen C42's post-festival efforts with the Roundhouse drew minimal political, financial or popular support. The North American press, intrigued by related developments in the AFL-CIO and by Wesker's Broadway success, reported his efforts as a 'missionary in the theater' were 'met with a spontaneous outpouring of indifference'. This they ascribed to the movement's 'air of knowing what was good for the people', but 'the workers having shown no great liking for Beethoven'.[112] In 1965 J.B. Priestley was supportive of Wesker's 'noble simplicity' and efforts to counter 'admass', but imagined Halifax workers faced with C42's fare remarking, 'ah couldn't make head nor tail of it'. For his part, Wesker saw in Priestley 'a popular touch which seems to have eluded me'.[113]

Conclusions

What was rejected in C42 was its cultural agenda and approach. It ended up bunkered down in the Roundhouse defying the culture surrounding it. As with consumer politics, a post-materialist context was no guarantee its post-materialist agenda would win out. But that rival tastes (popular, commercial and counter-cultural) and state alternatives marginalized it hardly suggests this was not an emergent post-materialist culture. It more firmly hints it wasn't a particularly *political* culture, or at least of the sort C42 anticipated or desired. Little wonder if C42's own strident political style and chaotic autonomy exemplified how this was envisioned. C42 was an impulse for sixties cultural politics, but these had limited traction in the broader political culture. If C42 lagged behind in cultural provision (indeed once in the Roundhouse it is hard to envision precisely *what* C42's output was to be), it is tempting to regard it as visionary in the idea of a cultural space. Its legacy was here rather than in its own cultural turns in the 1960s – in modelling rather than realizing the cultural turn. Wesker would return to Buckingham Palace to collect a knighthood in 2006. By then the Roundhouse, after a torrid interim – it remained culturally iconic and inventive but disheveled under Hoskins in the 1970s, failed in efforts to become a black arts centre with GLC support in the 1980s and preserved (but little more) by English Heritage in the 1990s – and with private financial backing, was an established arts centre. Still, echoes of C42 resounded: Pink Floyd offered financial support, there was a sponsored brick scheme, a studio 42 whose first play was *The Foolish Young Man*, politics was apparent in that it hosted Michael Moore's first UK performance. And the whole package, milking the Roundhouse's heritage not least, tied in with New Labour rhetoric of the creative industries.[114]

C42's fate can be compared with that of the New Left. Both felt culture central to politics and were influenced by the expansion in cultural workers and industries – teachers, Universities, artists. They represented an opposite fraction to Whitehouse's in terms of social mobility, generation, education and politics. But both C42 and the New Left struggled to make political headway in exploiting this or in making wider linkages to turn a fraction into a cross-section. As Rustin argues, the New Left was less the political movement it wanted to be, and more a social movement (in C42's instance, a moment). Others have reflected on how neither New Left generation were relatively slow to register issues of race, sexuality, gender, individual rights (e.g. capital punishment, abortion) that were becoming central to radical politics. Putting culture centre-stage in their politics was novel, but that culture could be quite narrow. In C42's case this was apparent in the difference between its own cultural tastes and those hosted by the Roundhouse, which did provide space for gay and black politics, if fitfully in the later 1970s and 1980s (as if C42 continued to thwart the Roundhouse's identity). That the culture wars – generational and social besides political, Curran argues – were fought out over the 1960s and its legacies in later decades notably in London politics and saw the New Left more involved in Labour politics, further suggests limits to cultural politics during the 1960s themselves.[115]

Nonetheless, C42's influence on Lee during the 1960s, even as a negative reference point, was substantial. Sinclair argues that whilst the ACGB could contain C42's prospects, its authority and remit did not extend to mass, 'pop' culture and for many Britons they made for a gayer Britain (the atmosphere Lee encouraged). As Vera Elyashiv, C42's artistic director who resigned in 1968 on the grounds that social change had undermined C42's premise that class divided cultural life, explained: 'new theatres, dance groups, bands, newspapers and fashion were created. There was nothing to stop the avalanche, helped by the Labour Government'.[116] C42 helped, inadvertently in *Redefining British Politics*, by providing a site. If this was a cultural revolution, it was not as C42 planned it, even if it nourished and hosted it and ended up being consumed by it.

7
Popular Politics? Communication and Representations of Politics

'The fundamental paradox of politics in modern Britain' Jon Lawrence argues, has been that 'as the polity became more formally democratic, so face-to-face public politics, the actual interaction between politicians and people, became less democratic'. After 1918 political parties tried to tame disorderly, heckling at public meetings that had been regarded as vibrant assertions of public opinion. The de-legitimization (not disappearance) of such robust conduct for a more rational, peaceful public came with the franchise expansion, female inclusion in this (by dint, in part, of disruptive suffrage politics), uncertainties about communicating on such a scale and fears about the lower orders being manipulated. This reinforced a trend since the 1870s secret ballot, abolition of nominations 'hustings' and other means to ostensibly democratize elections, to increase party control and curb the public character of politics.[1]

The paradox in this period was similar. Representative politics and the people seemed disengaged, despite the potential for modern means of mass communication like opinion polling and television to increase and even enhance their interaction. In supplanting the public meeting or canvassing, these methods seemed to embody how semi-detached politics was from face-to-face measures of public opinion. It was a sphere in which people were more likely to be passive spectators than active participants. Television accentuated the shift to a political citizenship practiced or consumed privately and individually. Calming and civilizing as this was, it threatened to corrode political vigour: a quiescent audience was married to a party-disciplined politics, such that a 1964 study of Parliament noted (as a mixed blessing), 'today the Commons appears to be a model of good behaviour'. It left politicians out of step with the shifting emotional contours of British culture, especially the liberation of self-expression in the 1960s, as the orderly disciplines of self-restraint in formal political discourse struggled to adapt to the 'culture of sensation' or demands of TV politics.[2] Habermas wrote in 1962 of how the commercial mass media was diminishing the public sphere as a site of open debate and participation. The press and TV were trivializing, subverting debate and making a less critical public, prone to be manipulated. Recent commentators have been as damning. TV is causally central to Putnam's influential thesis on the decline of social capital, civic engagement and public duty – tuning in was tantamount to tuning out. For Offer, TV involved a more privatized lifestyle, limited newspaper readership amongst the young and corrupted the conduct of political communication.[3] If Lawrence's recent account is more resistant of such implicit technological determinism, contending the public remains a vital and even authoritative, if remote and virtual, part of political debate, it is not hard to detect a sense of post-war decline and nostalgia for the spirit of the hustings.[4]

Party membership and electoral turnout peaked in the 1950s (dubbed the 'golden age'), but were weak indices, lending a misleading impression of politics' presence in popular culture, which was altogether slighter. As Lawrence points out, this was partly due to legal restrictions on local spending in the 1948–49 Representation of the People Acts, combined with rising costs for posters and leaflets. Then through the 1950s a chiefly organizational focus on mobilizing extant rather than persuading new voters, key marginal seats and floating voters all amounted to a 'dulling down' of electioneering.[5]

Yet the slight presence was also cultural – popular politics was a misnomer in a culture in which satire and apathy were rife. In the few films it featured in, Fielding argues, party politics was portrayed disparagingly: a sham exposed by non-party characters, in which right and left had more in common than they had with the people, politicians were self-serving; and about which many voters knew or cared little. The 1950s and 1960s seemed to have inherited features from the inter-war period, when, as McKibbin has it, England was not on the public face of it a very political culture. This was, Chapter 4 noted, a basis of YC practice in the 1950s. To judge from Almond and Verba's *The Civic Culture* which reported in 1963 that less than a third felt free to discuss politics with anyone, it remained something few talked about. As much as the comparative stability of British politics or remote power of its elites, this lack of partisanship might be read as evidence of the fragile status of party in political culture and of political language, practice and identities in the broader culture.[6]

Whilst party was not such a stable, popular presence during its alleged 'golden age', not to mention before the war or from the 1970s, there was little concerted spoiling of ballots or much demand for compulsory voting to instill participation as a civic responsibility. Party politics persisted, immunized from apathy and Crick implied (like Crosland), wary of excessive popular interest. But there was widespread anxiety at the quality of democratic politics and participation. What such despair neglected was the flourishing of extra-parliamentary groups in civil society, non-party popular politics of pressure groups, deploying newer repertoires of identity politics, even 'traditional' means of protest and street politics. This was a recognizable process in sixties Britain of the declining trust for established authority that post-materialism bred, of demands for participation from nationalists, women, consumers, students, workers, rights campaigns and of cultural politics and the notion that 'the personal is political'. These were, in part, products and evidence of this disgruntlement with party and formal politics.[7]

This chapter assesses the representations of politics in this broader context, with the form of party as salient as differences between parties. What was denuding the authority of party politics were those media that seemed to be a calming influence. The contradictory power of television as a medium was that it addressed electors relatively uninterested in politics in a private, domestic setting, yet meant that by 1959 as few as 7% of electors 'actually saw' local candidates face-to-face at meetings or canvassing. In popular perception as much as academic studies, this was assumed to be less development than decline.[8] It stresses how rather than any decline in popular politics or rise of a media-driven type, they offered a changing focus on enduring debates about the quality and conduct of politics – if TV, for instance, not only rendered politics more remote, but more intimate, enlivened it in some respects, made it more rational in others. It stresses how differences were *within* as much as *between* the parties and more saliently, between politics and the people.

Stressing how the structures and practices of formal politics could distance the electorate from it, however inadvertently, supplements rather than replaces social explanations for popular apathy or scepticism about party. The supply of, as well as demand for politics might explain popular disengagement. That the form of politics was at odds or more often somewhat marginal or even 'other' to the wider culture was a feature of British political culture. Eliasoph conceives apathy as being generated by a political culture in which public sphere discussion amongst citizens and even politicians consciously avoids the language of formal politics. This does not mean forfeiting the role of party in political history, just recognizing limits to this and that party could alienate as well as mobilize. If Lawrence's interwar stabilization produced a more torpid, quiescent, if stable, political culture after 1945, it is now commonly recognized to have become thoroughly disconnected by mutual mistrust. And its media-centredness fed this process. 2009's expenses scandal confirmed this sense of a public thoroughly distanced from and disaffected by politics. As a leading Tory candidate in 2005 contended, 'the reception... from the public while out canvassing... was the most unfriendly she had ever experienced' and related this to 'rude' questioning from broadcasters.[9]

Disenchantment with politics was legion, although political historians have tended to disregard such evidence. Many voters often considered politics with the same disregard. A National Opinion Polls survey in June

1963, for instance, found more than 70% of voters had not seen any news-paper adverts by the main parties. Of those that had, two-thirds recalled them inaccurately.[10] Studies with titles like *Anti-Politics* hinted politics was out of vogue, if also that there was simultaneously rising protest against the political establishment. Conservative journalist Henry Fairlie's doting appreciation of the political elite in 1968, admitted joking about politicians was long established (such that those who were admired were thought of as statesman not politicians), but that 'today, more than ever, the politician appears to be held in contempt'. Politicians were hardly unconscious of such sentiment. Writing *In Defence of Politics* in 1954, Hugh Gaitskell admitted 'politics is still looked upon in many quarters as a slightly odd, somewhat discreditable occupation'. This 'public view', Labour's soon-to-be-leader noted, was apparent in how bus conductors announced Parliament Square by crying, 'anyone here for the gas house?' Minister of Education Geoffrey Lloyd wrote privately in 1958 of how '"politics" has become something of a dirty word'. This was because the main parties were regarded as 'ageing and weary giants who have fought each other for so long they have forgotten what the quarrel is about'. When Margaret Thatcher asked *What's wrong with Politics?* in 1968 she acknowledged 'crit-icism of politics is no new thing' – citing Shakespeare to this end – but warned that 'we can't dismiss the present criticisms as easily as that'.[11]

In 1962 academic Bernard Crick was moved to issue a rejoinder to 'cyni-cism about the activities of politicians'. This would become a seminal state-ment *In Defence of Politics*, but was far from uncontested at the time. Political science (including Crick) was a dubious discipline in the eyes of ex-Conservative candidate, high political historian and New Right thinker Maurice Cowling. And even Crick accepted the 'anti-political' were 'very right to think politics is an achievement far more limited... than polit-ically-minded men, or men who practice this odd thing politics, normally presume'.[12]

Whether anti-politics distinguished between party, politicians and pol-itics was not always easy to discern. Characteristic in the novels and plays of the late fifties 'angry young men' (Amis, Osborne, Braine) was a repre-sentation of political parties as barely different and a 'grubby lot of rogues'. Such was their 'contempt for politics and politicians', that by conventional registers their 'anger was not political'. Similar arguments can be sustained for the satire boom in the early 1960s and the counter-culture later in the decade. For Crick, after 1962 the New Left rejected 'real political attach-ments as corruptive' and cut 'themselves off from... actual political experi-ence or influence' in favour of theoretical thinking, what he termed a 'political anti-politics'. But there was a clear distinction between the hippy-beat-libertarian ethos and the New Left, feminists and Trotskyists. As Green puts it, 'if the hippies found the left boring, then the left found them trivial'. Cultural revolt alone was 'self-indulgent anathema' to the radical left, no less than to 'career politicians' like Labour Arts Minister Jennie Lee who was close to Jim Haynes, a founder of the counter-cultural *International Times*, but thoroughly perplexed by *IT*'s declaration that 'politics is pigshit'.[13]

Such evidence has not greatly interested political historians, who have tended to take the party system as given, focusing on individual parties or competition between them. This chapter assesses the status of party itself, positioning it in longer-term debates about its relations with the people. Situating politics in a culture that was lukewarm, even hostile, it questions the proximity of party-voter relations, noting evidence of how political messages were interpreted differently from how they were intended, if they were received at all. Politics seems not to have been as privileged by contemporaries as it has been by political historians. This chapter aims to incorporate the indifferent as part of a political culture and apathy as produced by and influential in this political culture. Politics, like culture, might best be conceived as ordinary, if not so common.

In striving to be accessible and relevant, party politics was increasingly domestically-minded and conducted as marketing. As Mort has shown the subject matter and practices of politics, consumerism and opinion polling intersected ever more in this period. Mark Abrams, who transcended these spheres, is amongst this chapter's main sources. Like Christianity, politics became one culture among many, relative, not accorded the respect it had assumed in the past. Party was part of a pattern of cultural diversity and politics' diminished its exclusiveness and Unique Selling Proposition (USP) by fusing with shopping, TV and marketing. But that is not to argue that public debate was automatically devalued. Consumerism and TV were not only competition for politics, but resources of new languages, practices, and not least ways of communicating. TV appealed to many politicians as much as most viewers, if for different reasons. Indeed the case here is for a recalibration of politics and that TV made for lively, vibrant politics in many ways.[14]

Television

In 1957, for the first time, more TV than radio licences were issued. Politics could not withstand TV, but it was not simply colonized by it; it sought to control and utilize it. Politics was more altered than devalued by TV, as many contemporary and subsequent commentators have assumed. Party broadcasts often topped the ratings, with audiences of more than ten million. But this was because in a signal both of politics' assumed importance and popular distaste for it, a 1956 stipulation (in place until the 1979 election) forced both channels to show party political broadcasts (PPBs) simultaneously. It was estimated that 80% of viewers turned over or off when a party political was broadcast. TV became a major source of political information, but with the odd exception like 1958's party conferences (when Macmillan's address attracted a million more viewers than Labour's infamous defence debate), politics was a big turn off. Only a third of voters watched the 1966 election broadcasts. If TV was the pre-eminent medium, its pre-eminence was still slight and relative.[15]

In 1968's Granada Guildhall Lecture, the Leader of the House of Commons, Richard Crossman, detailed why he was 'so alarmed by... the impact so far of television on our politics'. Despite reaching into most British homes, it reinforced the tendency for politics to be a spectator rather than participatory activity, further distancing parliament and the people. Crossman further worried that:

> outside Westminster we see the decline of local democracy and the weakening of voluntary participation in most forms of community life including politics. In terms of universal suffrage we may not have had full democracy in the times of Gladstone and Disraeli. But in terms of active participation by a voluntary minority, our democracy was, I fear, more virile, more alert, more of a test for the real quality of government than it is today.[16]

Debate about television reached to the essence of politics' public standing. The logic behind the 'fourteen-day rule' barring broadcasters discussing matters before Parliament and agreed with the BBC in 1948, was 'to ensure that the BBC at no time becomes an alternative debating forum to Parliament'. So the 1955 election was largely ignored. It was reduced to seven days in June 1956, but ended by the Suez crisis. This showed that – however much Parliament wished to defend its authority – it was aware that few read its debates, that newspapers no longer reproduced them, it wasn't the only forum of public debate and that in campaigning its members had long used other means of communication.[17]

Television interviews with politicians had 'reeked of deference', with interviewers calling politicians 'Sir', but rapidly altered with broader news coverage, satire like *That Was The Week That Was* (*TW3*) and the more interrogative style of Robin Day on Independent Television News (ITN) since 1955. David Frost was 'another of those criticized for the inquisitorial tone he sometimes adopted'. Much as TV was charged with paying too little attention to politics, it was Day's 'incisive manner' that was resented by politicians and which they blamed for fuelling wider popular cynicism. By 1968 Gerald Kaufman (a *TW3* writer and later an MP) could write in *The Listener* of how TV journalists could be confrontational with politicians, whether for purposes of self-promotion or in a more fourth estate role of by claiming to hold them to account on behalf of viewers. The rumbustious audience was now a platform to be found on TV and, Kaufman added, 'any politician who falls victim to this technique is not up to the job of being a politician'.[18]

Day penned a Hansard Society pamphlet making *The Case for Televising Parliament* in 1963 in the aftermath of the Profumo scandal. That debate had exposed formal politics' 'secondhand way of using television', as MPs dashed from the chamber to offer opinions to TV reporters. The 'doubts' at the prospect of televising parliament that Rab Butler confessed in the foreword to Day's pamphlet, were whittled away. Live coverage of party conferences, first achieved in 1962 by Granada, was seen as a prelude. The state opening of parliament was televised in 1958, though for Day it was frustrating that the pageantry and symbolism should precede the 'working life' of parliament. In 1959 Aneurin Bevan had weighed in on the side of the televisers. This was surprising given his unease with modern communications, but given his status as a parliamentarian, it was significant. Bevan's case was that since at present 'the apparatus of mass suggestion are against democratic education', airing parliament would have the purpose of 're-establishing intelligent communication between the House of Commons and the electorate'. He thought it 'humiliating' for MPs to be selected and edited 'at the *ipse dixit* of... [BBC] Broadcasting House'. Bevan argued that there should be 'a special channel for the House of Commons itself... that they can turn on and listen to us at any time'.[19]

This was a proposal that made advocates of televising parliament 'blanch' – for fear of inflicting what one called 'hours of infinite boredom' on the public – and distracted from more incremental proposals. Indeed when Butler and the government Home Affairs Committee reviewed Bevan's proposals early in 1960, they used the reason that this was likely to 'arouse considerable antagonism' outside the House, to reject them. Programme-makers liked 'lively, provocative discussions' and were apt to invite 'articulate dissenters' from the party line. Familiar objections were raised by those disciplining MPs. Labour chief whip Herbert Bowden did not want to see parliament 'become an alternative to *TW3*, *Steptoe & Son* or *Coronation Street*'. But others, like Liberal Jo Grimond and Tories Iain Macleod and Bill Deedes argued for full-time broadcasting to newspapers, universities and subscribers and an edited highlights programme. For Day, broadcasting proceedings would elevate parliament's status not reduce it to the level of another TV programme. It would offset the unelected powers of newspapers, quiz panelists, other commentators and the 'alarm which the increasingly critical independence of TV journalism has aroused in both big political parties'. A *Television Hansard*, as Day titled it, would mean 'party political broadcasts could be abolished' to the benefit of the 'wretched viewer'. It would enhance parliamentary debate, modernize arcane procedures and do away with MP's 'vulgar habits' in favour of 'making public figures behave – and argue – more reasonably'. 'Television's intimacy', Day felt, 'encourages the arts of persuasion and argument' and outweighed the twin risks 'of making controversy too calm' or losing the 'exuberant crudity... that is seen at political meetings, or even sometimes in parliament'. The potential for 're-kindling interest in parliament' (he was conscious that Hansard's print sale had fallen by three quarters since 1945) as the 'nation's prime forum of debate' made it, in Day's opinion, vital that it access the 'nation's prime medium of mass communication'. He anticipated there was an audience of three million for a *Television Hansard*.[20]

A Parliamentary broadcasting experiment was initiated late in 1963. By 1966 closed circuit TV and radio coverage of the Commons was available to MPs and audio highlights were used in the BBC's *Gallery*. Costs and technology were shared between ITN, the BBC and Parliament. The final report on the experiment in 1968 emphasized the need for more microphones in the chamber and (accurately, since it was 1978 until radio was allowed and TV in 1985 in the Lords and 1989 in the Commons) predicted the BBC was unlikely to be imminently invited to make arrangements permanent.[21]

If the public were marginalized by a more media-centred delivery of politics, then it was also the case that relations between parties and broadcasters were fraught, fuelled by mutual suspicion. Notwithstanding the politics *of* TV – the issues Whitehouse raised or the scrapping of *TW3* in a charter renewal and election year – there were political debates *on* TV. Early in 1968 Labour whip John Silkin complained that jokes on *Dee Time* 'add to a general feeling of defeatism and cynicism' and BBC Controllers reflected 'such incidents could have a disastrous effect on the raising of the licence fee'.[22] And TV introduced new complications. It was not covered by the Representation of the People Acts, so precedent had to be established and after ITV's coverage of the 1958 Rochdale by-election was hotly debated. Pollsters were sensitive to pundits judging them on screen and three were disputes over issues of expenses and candidate's TV appearances conflicting with codes of proportionality in coverage were regular. Conservative candidate Peter Emery complained to the BBC about his opponent in Reading in 1959, Ian Mikardo (paradoxically, the deviser of Labour's model for election canvassing) appearing on TV's *Hustings*. The BBC dismissed the complaint, but Emery won the seat.[23]

Party misgivings about conference coverage centred on broadcast times, recording quality, lighting, editing – in sum, party control of how they were represented. Gaitskell, General Secretary Morgan Philips and MP Edith Summerskill met the BBC to discuss technical matters before allowing one single morning session of the 1955 Labour conference to be covered. The Conservatives allowed coverage from 1954, but also sought to manage what was recorded and the role of external commentators. The party made suggestions for 1955, addressing perceived BBC bias and encouraging them to avoid clips of what were described as 'senile people' amongst their delegates. TV made conferences more visual, less about policy.[24]

For the BBC's part, the head of talks Leonard Miall concluded by 1956: 'there has been a poor audience response to them and they have been very expensive' and yet 'we are in considerable bad odour with the political parties because we intend to give them much less coverage this year'.[25] Costs, besides technical issues of outside broadcasts and party demands were a factor. The BBC discouraged the Liberals from holding their conference in Holland in 1965 (to cement their European image) with the threat of no coverage. By 1965, when all three conferences were broadcast live, almost 200 BBC staff were in attendance and the BBC used this to exhibit its technical facilities for its paymaster's approval at Labour's conference. But the volumes of broadcasting staff in the conference hotels heightened politician's suspicions – in 1966 Labour's General Secretary Len Williams accused the BBC of hiding microphones in Brighton's Grand Hotel bar. And technical issues continued to dog relations. Edward Du Cann's demand for a monitor on the platform of the 1967 conference caused conflict, as did the decision to go to the scheduled broadcast of *Playschool* in the midst of Iain Macleod's 1966 address.[26]

Television had constitutional implications. Ministerial broadcasting rights agreed in 1948 were for wireless and the BBC only. A revision in 1969 was driven by both parties desire to incorporate the ITA and clip both its occasional tendency to act independently and the BBC's sense of 'supremacy'.[27] British political broadcasting, unlike advertising, was not determined by the ability to pay. But it was a partisan issue in terms of the distribution of time for broadcasts and their timing. The main parties had agreed in 1947 that only those contesting upwards of 50 seats had broadcasting rights. This meant the Co-op Party claimed broadcasting rights in 1955 and the support offered by the Beveridge (1949) and Pilkington (1962) Reports for regional broadcasting fuelled the grievance of the nationalist parties. Plaid Cymru won support from local authorities and the National Broadcasting Council for Wales, forcing Postmaster General Charles Hill to invoke his veto in July 1955. By 1964 there were Welsh language ITV and BBC broadcasts. But elite resistance remained. Party leader Gwynfor Evans pointed out the Liberals only put up 11 candidates in Wales but enjoyed broadcasting rights. Plaid and the Scottish National Party (SNP)'s failure to win seats in 1966 both hindered and fed their case.[28] In Ulster the absence of the main parties made it easier for special terms to be agreed in 1961. These stressed the different context, to enable the Unionists to broadcast without establishing a precedent for Scottish or Welsh nationalists and without Sinn Fein triggering a right to broadcasts.[29] The central, national power of broadcasting and politics (and the press) prevailed before regional, multi-party politics and multi-media outlets diversified from the 1970s.

A signal of the sensitivity of political broadcasts was found in the 'high-powered' (as Crossman, its chair 1966–68, described it) Committee on Party Political Broadcasting formed in 1947 on which the leader of the opposition, senior government ministers, chief whips, plus the BBC Director-General and ITA chair sat. The ITA's Robert Fraser expressed discontent with the compulsory broadcast of PPBs, but Wilson sought this as an assurance of central control, along with barring live audiences from election broadcasts (something the main parties by-and-large concurred on until 1974 since both suffered on ITV's *The Last Debate* during the 1959 election). By 1964 the ITA had agreed to broadcasts for parties contesting either 50 seats or 20% of those in a region and it was agreed nationalists should get five minute TV and radio slots from 1965.[30]

From 1965 Heath pressed in favour of regional broadcasts, parties using their allocated time as and when they chose and ending simultaneity. The committee thought abandoning simultaneous broadcasts might reduce viewer resentment, but feared that they were so unpopular that they might be done away with entirely if broadcasters were not bound to show them. 'You are revealing exactly why we have to have party politicals', Crossman rebuked Carleton Greene in 1967 for suggesting they at least be moved to a time of the BBC's choosing, 'because the BBC thinks it knows much better than we do how we should run our own propaganda'. Whilst resenting the compulsory element in the simultaneity rule, broadcasters were anxious at the planning and scheduling difficulties that more, shorter PPBs might bring. Heath stressed his proposals were essential to 'endear us to the public'. 'Us' implied a unanimity amongst politicians, but the Committee was uneasy that this had invigorated the claims of the SNP. Chief Whip John Silkin guessed the Conservatives would forfeit regional and simultaneity proposals to secure greater control of their own broadcasting time, but advised Wilson in the same spirit of party interest that, 'we should decide on the basis of our own interests'. And for Crossman, this meant keeping the 'captive audience' and simultaneous broadcasts as a balance to the biases the Tories enjoyed in the press.[31]

Little was done, in short, but the sensitivity of debates about compulsory broadcast in the context of PPBs unpopularity, shows historians what was at issue here was whether party could wrest or would have to cede control over broadcasting. Politics as a whole was battling to harness the potential power of television, rather than be subject to it or a subject on it. Blumer and Mcquail's research similarly worried that television was too important a medium for conveying politics to Britons to be left in the hands of politicians alone. As such 'the preferences of the consumer' should prevail against partisan propaganda and it could be a force for 'public enlightenment' and for 'counteracting skepticism and political alienation'.[32]

Crossman's 1968 lecture on 'The Politics of Television' drew on such research and was concerned that TV was blighting what he had written about a decade earlier as *The Charm of Politics*. Paralleling his 1963 introduction to Bagehot's *English Constitution*, Crossman believed television was moving Britain 'from a participatory to plebiscitary democracy', away from one where parliament is 'an active mediator between government and the people'. In 1963 he saw an 'indifferent electorate' which made for 'political stability in a free society', but was deleterious to an active democracy.

Although he identified 'signs of popular protest against the growing ineffectiveness of Parliament and the oligarchic tendencies... in our modern two-party machine politics', by 1968, he despaired that 'the active minority of citizens who participate has not grown as we expected' and more salient was a 'sense of alienation'. As other chapters have shown, from the YCs to Young and Whitehouse and varieties of consumer and cultural politics, participation was a widespread political concern. And as Fielding shows an issue on which Labour could vary from wary (Crosland) or enthusiastic (Benn) or plain dismissive.[33]

This 'growing alienation' from parliamentary and party politics came in part, Crossman claimed because 'parliament is not covered directly by television', so voters had no chance of seeing it 'seriously at work'. Crossman couched this case in familiar terms, paralleling the impact of radio and the press on politics and stressing the BBC's own shift in the mass television age away from acting as an agency of cultural improvement. For political coverage this post-Reithian ethos carried several 'dangers'. These included 'ratings', with politics 'treated as an inferior form of entertainment which has to be gimmicked up... to be made palatable to an indifferent audience'. Crossman termed this 'the trivialization effect'. Unless 'carefully controlled', television poured out programmes indiscriminately in a 'general mush'. And in a domestic sitting and, citing news coverage of the Vietnam war (and sounding not unlike like Whitehouse and the New Left), Crossman worried that 'familiarity with horror, even when treated in depth – in a serious play for instance – breeds indifference'. Political spectators were treated to extracts, focused on hecklers or 'sandwiched between a couple of "really entertaining" items'. For Crossman, the visual 'detracts from what is being said' and 'five minutes on *The World at One*' on radio, was 'far more valuable than five minutes even on a... peak evening television programme'. It wasn't only that there had been a 'steady decline in the... depth of treatment' of politics on TV or that political devotees were ill-served (though worse than sports, religious or drama fans, he alleged), but that it threatened to make 'the next general election the first in which public discussion is rendered impossible'. Not that he blamed broadcasters alone. Politicians, he admitted, found TV or an argument hard to resist 'however damaging it may be to our own cause or to the image of Parliament'.

This was not a generation of 'politicians so degenerate that they are afraid of the rough and tumble of old-fashioned politics', but Crossman preferred the electorate to weigh up arguments, calmly, without politicians being 'cross-examined like criminals'. This was, so Trenaman and Blumler's research showed, what viewers favoured. Thus, multiple PPBs in which parties would 'degrade ourselves with endless short, snappy advertising captions' were not ideal. Instead, television might cover politics in its 'natural element' – the closed party meeting, open public meeting (with 'artificial arrangements in order to prevent the heckler's desire to break up meetings') and Parliament.

It was *how* this was televised that was key. Crossman favoured the 'straight, unedited, undoctored outside broadcast' of chamber and select committee proceedings over 'snippets'.[34]

If television was an opportunity for nationalists, it was in more traditional eyes perceived as an unwelcome competitor, highlighting politics' fragile popular appeal. These were cross-party anxieties and could sound disarmingly Whitehouse-like at times. Shulman describes a 'hypersensitivity' of 'hysterical' proportions about programming during the 1966 election. An episode of the children's show *Pinky and Perky*, about how to be Prime Minister, was almost withdrawn and Labour was anxious about the scheduled broadcast of the popular spy-science fiction drama, *The Man from Uncle* on the evening of polling day, fearing its demographic would lure Labour voters away from the ballot box (as in 1959 it feared ITV's cash quiz *Dotto* and cowboy drama *Rawhide* would). Just as until 1957 there had been a 'toddler's truce' from 6–7pm, it seemed democracy needed a break from TV. *The Man from Uncle* star, Robert Vaughn, was on ITV's 1970 election panel, along with comedian-satirist Peter Cook, comedy writer Denis Norden, Methodist Lord Soper, *New Left Review*'s Robin Blackburn, novelist John Braine and host David Frost. This line-up infuriated Conservative MP John Gummer, who believed their 'main common denominator was their ignorance of politics but whose views could be invested with importance merely because they happened to be in the public eye in some other connection'. Like Herbert Bowden, Gummer was anxious politics be more than just another TV 'turn'. For Gummer the paradox was that 'on the one hand television has widened the horizons of more people than any other method of communication and on the other it imposes the attitudes and values of the metropolitan young upon a whole nation'.[35]

Bill Deedes, the Minister in charge of Government Information Services, argued similarly in a talk to the Institute of Public Relations (IPR) in 1963. Deedes considered public relations (PR) and politics close relations, but felt 'there is some irony, indeed a cause for anxiety, that today, with all the wealth of modern communications at our command, we have not got far in bridging the gulf between governors and the governed'. His nostalgic scepticism 'that a television talk to... five million people leaves me far less exhilarated than a talk to a dozen people in a village hut' and that 'the audiences feel the same' left the Minister without Portfolio, 'not sure that television is going to prove a lasting friend of democracy'.[36]

Another recurrent charge was that 'to be "good on the box"', politicians had to 'master the techniques of the medium – over-simplification, contentious generalizations', or soundbites. TV was used not to inform, but in the 1970 contest 'as a huckster's Petticoat Lane, in which the public had a choice between political detergents... "Omo" Wilson and "Daz" Heath'. If voters were consumers, so politicians were 'packages of branded goods'. The washing detergent analogy – the 1950s and 1960s' most intense advertising battle – was first aired during the 1959 election and recurrent thereafter. Never complimentary, it implied that advertising did not complement politics but sullied, corrupted and reduced its authority and – in 1997 when the *Financial Times* declared the soap powder image of politics had triumphed over informed debate – was colonizing it.[37]

A changed audience?

But was there such a degree of change to newer practices? Were they more of form than substance; were audiences so passive? In bidding for support, politics gave the impression of merging with pop, TV and shopping. As with sport, betting on elections was well established (a sort of market equivalent to polling) and liberated by 1960's relaxation of gambling laws. Some £2$\frac{1}{2}$ million was wagered on the 1966 election. Referencing The Beatles was *de rigueur* in the 1964 election. Political scientists saw Heath depicted 'as if advertising a new cigarette'. Wilson's renowned (to critics, craven) cultivation of celebrities was in this vein. During the 1966 campaign he associated with stars from *Coronation Street* and *Z-Cars*. Harry H. Corbett, star of the BBC's *Steptoe and Son* and TV émigré from Joan Littlewood's Theatre Workshop, was a recurrent Labour aide.[38]

Corbett featured in a 1969 Labour broadcast with Shirley Williams. A majority in a public survey welcomed his presence – 'he told them straight' with an 'absence of political bull'. Others felt it reinforced the notion of politics as gimmicky or craved 'an unknown Corbett'. Ludovic Kennedy's efforts for the Liberals in 1966 won a similar reception ('not the usual lot of cod's wallop'). But Kennedy's broadcast was during a documentary on Lee Harvey Oswald and this confused some viewers about death (Ludovic being a prominent euthanasia campaigner) and Kennedys. The use of celebrities could generate political interest and had the potential to break through those 'lukewarm feelings about politics' that Blumler and Ewbank reckoned helped 'insulate' the 'plain men in the street' from party propaganda. Tory broadcasts between 1964 and 1966 mixed modern 'commercial' styles with a 'contrived spontaneity' in live broadcasts to tackle voters 'scepticism barrier' – an uncertainty that was also evidence of Tories unease with the shift to TV politics.[39]

Captive audience or not, voters were not passive recipients of political messages. Jackson's study proposed TV generated not one mass response, but a range and noted the 'working class has a fairly strong degree of scepticism about politicians or pop stars'. Traditional studies revelled in questioning 'how effective' newer methods were. Jennings highlighted that there was 'no published evidence of the effectiveness of party political broadcasts', that 'it is not at all difficult for a politician to make a bad impression, especially on television' and PPBs were only viewed by 14% of voters in 1955. Though he also noted there was little new in this predicament. Ostrogorski's 1902 study had noted how few party pamphlets were read at elections.[40]

A 1969 survey of Labour slogans found only 13% remembered a recent press campaign and concluded that without 'memory aids the ability to recall accurately any... recent or current publicity was very slight'. Even 1964's successful 'Let's go with Labour' only registered 42%.[41] The recognition factor was key and business and politics shared similar risks in communicating with consumers or voters. Advertisers, like politicians, were occupied by understanding what audiences recalled from the carefully constructed messages delivered to them. Mark Abrams was attentive to this and Paul Lazarsfeld's influential (amongst pollsters and sociologists) work on voter and consumer behaviour, found both to mediate the claims of party, state and business.[42]

Debates about the psychology of TV-viewing and consumerism, elided with politics. Joseph Trenaman, the academic doyen of televised politics, shared Himmelweit's conclusions that TV's impact on unconscious values was as sizeable as any direct impact. Trenaman's research found that TV affirmed more than altered electoral behaviour, but its representation of interactions between politicians and the electorate via dress, character and language were formative of knowledge and the reputation of politics. It was in this – not just periodic elections – that Trenaman sought to 'discover the real political influence of television'. That it was enacted at home, without the sense of occasion or norms of public behaviour, made for a more relaxed attitude: enabling emotive reactions to be voiced or, alternatively, switched off. In short, as with normal TV or 'traditional' electioneering, a host of receptions were possible.[43] So whilst it was commonly understood that 'the comfortable, box-equipped living room keeps the average voter away from the hustings' and exposed to 'only mass consumer political products', TV crucially brought voters and politicians together in the living room. It did not prevent politicians being satirized (a booming TV genre) or heckled, as audiences could not be ticketed. In Sillitoe's novel *The Loneliness of the Long Distance Runner*, Colin Smith turned the volume down and became a ventriloquist for 'some Tory telling us about how good his government was going to be if we kept on voting for them... hands lifting to twitch moustaches and touching their buttonholes... so that you could see they didn't mean a word'. In Tony Richardson's 1962 film version, the politician's speech is just audible above his settee audience's derision.[44]

The energy, drama and wit of heckling was transferred into demos, agit-prop or, Thomas infers, into tabloid headlines. But as evidence from the YCs shows, heckling remained an activity practiced by the main parties as much as against them. Rather than eradicating it, TV provided opportunities for it to linger in the political culture. Television Wales and West even had a programme called *Heckler's Half Hour*. In 1966 Conservatives were planning for 'a corps of really intelligent hecklers to go with prepared questions'. This contrived spontaneity was believed better than 'irresponsible heckling' which 'could do us more harm than good'. Conservative MP Harold Gurden, writing in 1962, positively relished hecklers. He felt 'happier when the meeting is enlivened by criticism or opposition'. He advised speakers to give hecklers the chance to make fools of themselves, to remain polite and to take several interventions at a time to dull their impact. In any case, 'it isn't difficult to enlist the audience's support against hostility – mostly people like to see fair play', Gurden averred.[45]

The *News Chronicle* reported in 1950 that 'heckling is going beyond all reason', with 'continual barracking of speakers at political meetings'. According to Booker in the 1966 campaign, 'as in 1964, a major feature was the continual heckling of leading politicians by groups of teenagers'. These have to be read as much as evidence of the tenor of teenage youth culture (non-electors after all) and its eye for the media than of a persistently vibrant polity. But in 1964 concerted heckling of Douglas-Home at an un-ticketed marketplace meeting in Birmingham humiliated the PM, because it was broadcast on TV. Wilson was more adept with hecklers, repeating their charges for the benefit of the audience and to ensure his ripostes hit home. The view that heckling was 'an illegitimate and disruptive activity' was still iterated by the party authorities – to minimize humiliation by blaming opponents and appeal to the majority of voters' fears of more violent political traditions. To preserve the authority of leading figures, by 1970 the Tories held only ticketed meetings, derided as such by Labour. As with *The Last Debate* this discouraged parties and broadcasters from engaging live audiences. There seems then evidence of the persistence of the 'old ways' besides of a transition. This was less the decline of the public platform of politics than its displacement to TV.[46]

Public meetings were less apparent in local campaigning. Individual canvassing and written material had trumped them, as did TV and advertising. Some persisted more through ritual than anything else, although the 1954 guide to the *Organization of indoor and outdoor meetings* reminded local Conservative associations of their use as 'a source of encouragement to our own people'. Cars and amplifiers made public speaking easier, but thereby dulled their symbolic powers and, as with most other forms of campaigning from walkabouts to polling, were a mixed blessing; seemingly as likely to annoy as engage the public. Election studies reckoned that in 1950 many candidates addressed one a night, but by 1970 the main parties held an average of just two a week. But even in 1950, just 6% of local spending went on public meetings.[47]

Politicians relentlessly bemoaned TV's 'triviality' and the electorate's disrespect or apathy. Politicians could be as dispirited by voters as voters were by politicians. Barbara Castle lamented the evaporation of audiences at her election meetings between 1945 and 1970. Gerald Kaufman, Labour's Bromley candidate in 1955 described the election as 'boring'. Heath almost seemed to relish how in 1970: 'there are men walking the streets today – and possibly women – with eggs in their pockets just on the off chance that they will bump into the leader of the Labour Party'. For Jennings, parties attempted to control the extent of dispute in broadcast politics, but local electioneering continued to contain a deal of 'plain nonsense' and 'tub-thumping'. Lawrence rightly notes the trend towards more decorous behaviour, but politics remained a mix, as vibrant or restrained as you chose, with relations between people and party in constant renegotiation.[48]

TV politics, although foreshadowed by radio and film, undoubtedly made new demands of politicians. Oral political skills were crucial, if of a different order from public oratory. Besides 'characters', broadcasters valued succinct, reasoned delivery and the emotional charge of the Commons or of activist campaigning translated poorly into a domestic audience's environment. Broadcasting was not more authentic, just a different performance. Party efforts to practice 'sweet reasonableness' recognized this, but threatened, Jennings estimated, to make elections somnolent affairs and electors apathetic. It also chafed with Labour and Conservative MP's traditional tutelage. The shifting practice of politics, as much as educational trends, was altering the background of (still overwhelmingly male) candidates away from the trade unions and brigade of guards towards grammar school and University types.[49]

Great lengths were gone to in managing the potential and minefield of party broadcasting. Tories were advised in a party guide, *Talking on Television and Radio*, 'don't be frightened of television' and to avail themselves of the party's own broadcasting facilities. TV had made the terms of political engagement more intimate by transporting the politician into the living room and to be 'telegenic' and Tory broadcasters were urged:

> Know your audience... He does not regard himself as one among millions. Don't think in terms of a vast audience. Speak and behave as if you were also in that living room. Because that's virtually where you are... Don't approach an engagement to talk as if it were just another public meeting.

Tips included looking at the camera if addressing the viewer, but avoiding 'catching the eye' of the camera if addressing someone in the studio. For similar reasons 'looking round' (as regular committee servers were apt to do and a temptation in a busy studio) or 'looking down' (at notes) could denote 'nervousness' or 'shiftiness'. Eyes should 'express your friendliness', especially in 'the split second *after* speaking'. Posture-wise, the spine should be upright and back in the chair – slouching might have the speaker looking down their nose with an 'unfortunate impression of assumed superiority'. Speakers were encouraged to 'consciously relax', but also to avoid 'artificial control'. So whilst 'extravagant gestures' were discouraged, it was better 'to allow yourself to be free' than 'keep self-consciously still'. Voice pitch should be conversational not oratorical. Styles 'suitable in a gathering' of ten or a thousand were 'wildly out of place'. And to suit the cameras, sharp contrasts or bright colours were best avoided and make-up left to the experts.

So far as presentation went, brevity and concision were the watchwords. Recourse to 'well-worn phrases' could leave the viewer 'thinking that you are "just another politician, saying the same old thing"'. If repudiations or clarifications were essential, then performers were urged, in a classic statement of the sorts of diffusion of political tension the YCs specialized in, to 'soften the blow with a smile – just as you would in normal conversation'. Recommended practice included shortlists of the most relevant, interesting points matched to their likely audience and predicting 'sticky questions'. 'Disciplined preparation' was, paradoxically, the key to appearing 'spontaneous' on screen; so too the use of an 'informality of words', a 'conversational language – which is not often perfect prose'. Some broadcasters, the BBC's Goldie notably, felt politicians remained focused on addressing mass audiences, but the evidence here is that the 'winning qualities' were friendliness, conviction, sincerity and intelligence, but 'the tricks of the trade so useful on the platform or in committee are as inappropriate on the TV screen as they are in your best friend's living-room'.[50]

Trenaman, like Jennings, believed TV was now politics' 'principal platform', but differed from the press or public meetings. The public were more 'tolerant, impartial and inclined to want to hear all sides of any argument... they resent polemic or political abuse or the exaggerations and overstatements of the street corner orator' and did not appreciate attacks on opponents. This was engendered by its viewing in a domestic setting, which encouraged a generosity towards opponents – in 1966 broadcasts more than half of Labour voters rated a Heath broadcast as 'good-very good' – and by the popular perception that TV was, because it was more strictly regulated by the state, less partisan than newspaper coverage. It was also that TV coverage remained low key. The heterogeneous audience PPBs assembled tended to 'moderate the tone of political argument' in them. In 1959 only 6% of TV broadcast time was about the election. If 'politics was regarded as rather dull stuff by the television authorities', they were also still mindful of constraints on their action – no longer the 14-day rule so much as licence renewals and the range of political interest in broadcasting outlined in Chapter 5 from parliamentary committees, cultural studies, psychologists and the likes of the NVALA.[51]

Marketing politics

The persistence of old behaviour, if different in form, is not solely meant to imply the limits to change in political interfaces between parties, politicians and electorates. Parallels with advertising and polling seemed as novel and impressed as much as those between television and politics. And ties between consumerism and politics seemed ubiquitous in figures like Abrams, Young and Crosland, although as Moran has shown pre-dated this period.[52] The analogy was rife in political science. Samuel Beer's seminal 1965 study described parties 'bidding' to political consumers. It wasn't that politics had not been sold before, but rarely in such explicitly commercial language. 'The Product – Politics', Graham Dowson, a Rank marketing director told Conservatives, was best regarded as a consumer durable. Abrams explained in 1956 how, 'Labour faces problems similar to those of a commercial organisation', needing to know 'the reactions of consumers to our product'. But Wring has stressed how politics were about persuasion in ways that should make historians wary of assuming this was a one-way process of commercial methods either colonizing a new market in politics or politics learning from commercial expertise.[53]

Stressing that whilst the Conservatives were keener users, Beers shows how both parties wielded polling as propaganda in their claims to represent public opinion and were reluctant to allow pollsters to encroach on policy-making or their political claim to voice public opinion – the prerogative and *raison d'etre* of politicians. Paralleling debates about the impact of television, if polls promised to supplant the public meeting for gauging public opinion, this was a territory politicians were bound to defend from rival claimants. Beers and Wring position the impact of new technologies and methods as part of ongoing developments in Labour strategy, still controlled and deployed by politicians and not dominating their view of politics or society. The means of communication was a political issue in contests *within* as much as *between* the main parties. Debate in Labour was most intense after the 1959 election, turning on: the Conservatives' spending with Colman, Prentis and Varley (CPV), Labour's modern PPBs (fronted by Benn), Abrams' post-election *Must Labour lose?* poll and the conception of voters as viewers and consumers implied by these.[54]

Before the 1959 election Labour was approached by a group of advertising professionals associated with the UK wing of Erwin Wassey, a US agency later involved in running Barry Goldwater's Republican presidential campaign. The UK's fourth largest agency, they had designed the Thomas Hedley campaign in the 'soap wars' and undertaken political surveys for Hoover, the Tories and Labour during the Attlee government. Two of the group were now at McCann-Erikson in London, the world's second biggest agency. They offered 'to use, on behalf of the party, the techniques for... influencing millions of people, learned over the past twenty years'. Their 'creative power' and 'professional diagnosis... rather than lay advice' offered what would otherwise cost Labour 'thousands of pounds'. The group boasted that it had 'at its command more expertise than the agency connected with the Conservative Party' and reassured Labour that it 'had no intention' to 'influence policy'. It might 'make observations on every aspect of "the product", but it is entirely up to the client whether these observations are acted upon'. They told Gaitskell that they 'won't play at any level lower than you and Morgan' [Phillips]. Forwarded to Labour leaders through the offices of the *Daily Herald*'s A.J. Mcwhinnie (also Labour's media advisor), the 'businesslike' proposals suggested 'the Labour Party may be regarded as a manufacturer with a product (policy) to sell to the consumer (electorate)'. 'Failure to "sell"' might arise because 'it does not meet the consumer needs', 'faulty presentation', consumers being unaware of the product or confused about it by competitors. The key was to win those not presently buying it, but not 'implacably against', without 'alienating' those 'loyal to the product'. Given the client's 'restricted funds', efforts should centre on marginal areas where the minimum shift in sales could yield a maximum effect on the market share, rather than those where the vast majority already purchased it or a competing product.[55]

This approach was rejected, but it offers historians insights into how PR minds conceived politics and vice versa. From the appointment of John Harris as Labour's Director of Publicity in 1962, a more professional PR approach was evident. Although such experts as it called upon were volunteers, constituted in an *ad hoc* manner. By early 1963 a Planning group of Abrams, Harris, Percy Clark (who succeeded Harris in 1964), Peter Davis (managing director, Fleet Street Press Agency), advertising executives David Kingsley and Michael Barnes (both Labour candidates) and 'occasional' groups – advising on PR, the creative – were organized. Even holiday plans were co-ordinated to respond rapidly to the Tories' 'vast financial resources'. Besides an informality to obscure arrangements from opponents and sceptical Labour members, there was a shadowy aspect to this. A covert CPV executive was amongst Labour's 'hidden persuaders'.[56]

Using Abrams' polling to understand opinion in 'target' marginals, a 1963 Kingsley memo explained the overall aim was to effect a 'picture that the Labour Party is active, lively and go ahead (even in its advertising) in contrast with the dull, heavy-handed approach of the Conservatives'. The medium was the message. As ex-director of US agency Benton and Bowles, Kingsley touted a 'spectacular' fashioned on 'the great debate' of the 1960 Kennedy election, to encourage 'gossip about "morals"' under the Conservatives. A related emphasis, as Jonathan Boswell of the creative group discussed was 'dramatizing' economic policy to convey it in a language other than that of the technical expert or the 'fundamentalist phrases' favoured by the party faithful, but 'largely useless for the kind of people we have to win'.[57]

Reflections at the end of 1963 saw a more discriminating approach emerge. It was suggested that 'those of us who earned our living in advertising... assumed that the Labour Party was a "product" which could be "sold" in much the same way as an advertising agency sells mass-consumer items such as soap, tea, tinned salmon or biscuits' and thus 'a conventional "reminder" advertising schedule with small spaces and high frequency' was deployed. But it was recognized that as Labour was 'not... a mass-consumer product bought over the counter once or twice a week'. 'However cynical, apathetic, naïve or stupid people are', voting was not undertaken weekly and was an act 'they attach great importance to'. If 'Labour Party prop-aganda is not advertising in the <u>accepted</u> sense of the word' then this was an opportunity to 'chuck out sacred cows' of both advertising and party culture. Rather than a reminder of a brand of product to which people were 'basically indifferent', what was needed was 'a short, sharp, concentrated' campaign which 'targets stand a better-than-average chance of seeing'. And the authors, Ros Allen and Brian Murphy (of Erwin Wasey), suggested that 'if the religion of socialism is the language of priorities could we not cut down the amount of money we spend in the *Herald*', whose readers tended to be confirmed Labour voters.[58]

After the 1964 election the group was re-structured, with panels for TV (recognizing that 'this medium is pre-eminent amongst the channels of communication'), education and women. New personnel included Fred Jarvis (who headed education) and Gordon Medcalfe (of London agency Clifford Bloxham and formerly of G-Plan).[59] But by 1965 the 'Plan for an Efficient Party' campaigners were bemoaning that such help was provided 'after hours' and that Labour's keenness on controlling ad campaigns and broadcasting was not matched by funding the expertise to fashion these. As Lawrence points out, Wilson's innovation was more individual than insti-tutional within Labour, which tended to revert to media-suspicious type otherwise. Between the 1964 and 1966 elections, the Director of Publicity, press officer, the head of research and five of 11 research staff left Transport House. Parallel TUC and civil service jobs were better paid, whilst the top salary in Labour's press department was equivalent to that of a junior reporter in a London agency, despite the battles fought over the salary for Harris' post in 1962. In 1965 Labour's research secretary, Terry Pitt, earned just over £1500, whilst his Conservative counterpart Sir Michael Fraser was on £5000. Labour's abiding unease and amateurism above all continued not to prevent, but stall Labour's use of market methods.[60]

Labour interest in newer methods was stymied by a longstanding suspicion of the political biases of the press – an instinct that ran through the party, as Thomas has explicated. The power of the media impressed both advocates and opponents of its political uses. It was well illustrated in a publicity guide for agents at the 1964 election that argued, 'the press like the poor is always with us'. It was with such resignation that Labour embraced polling and advertising. Labour contained many puritan types who projected a broader set of anxieties onto advertising, from Americanization to, as Schwarzkopf argues, a Cold War battle between advocates of a free society and those that saw it as wasteful or, worse, sinister.[61]

The Advertising Inquiry Council, formed in 1958 by Labour MP Francis Noel-Baker, offered voluntary *Scrutiny* (the title of its newssheet). It assembled those concerned at advertising's economic, social and moral impacts. Mostly these were liberals and social democrats, with a substantial overlap with CA's audience: Mary Adams, Eirlys Roberts, Hoggart (future Labour MP and the Council's assistant secretary) Giles Radice and with 'observers' including the CA and London Co-op. There were conservative critics like John Betjamin and Conservative MP, moralist and Whitehouse supporter, Cyril Black, who was the Council's Honorary Treasurer. The Council urged stricter regulation and taxation of the industry. Archbishop Fisher, until recently the Archbishop of Canterbury, wrote in support of the Council in 1964 and its belief that advertising 'can exploit the gullible'.[62] Gaitskell appointed the Reith Commission in 1960 to waylay Noel-Baker's lobbying that this was 'a subject which the party should take up... along with consumer protection'. Gaitskell originally tried to get Alan Sainsbury, whom he had also tried to draft on to the Co-op Commission, to chair it. For similar reasons of commercial links of his London Press Exchange (LPE), Abrams' involvement was controversial.[63]

Left critics loaded advertising up with a range of concerns. If politicians 'have to use advertising', Hoggart told the Reith Commission in 1962, they became 'victims and perpetrators of its deceptions'. 'Properly speaking, one cannot "sell" a good cause', because 'you are not propagating the subject; you are "selling" some other hope, or aspiration, or anxiety'. The 1959 election witnessed 'the worst kind of PR stuff'. Hoggart, like CA (and like Whitehouse's view of TV), held that advertising was involved in 'manipulating the emotions' of the 'less sophisticated'. He shared the CA and satirists faith that 'irony is one of the best aids' to deflate advertising blurbs. Hoggart remained a militant critic, accusing the industry in 1965 of 'emotional blackmail exploiting human inadequacy'. The early New Left derided the American 'communicational guphology' of pollsters and psephologists and mounted an exhibition critiquing commercial advertising at Labour's conference.[64] J.B. Priestley, noted critic of 1950s' 'admass' culture, targeted *The Image Men* in a 1968 novel, mocking both the image-makers at the Institute of Social Imagistics and the politicians from both parties anxious to be shaped by them.[65]

LPE prepared a report on Labour's attitude to advertising in 1964 for the industry. It reckoned the advertising debates were an 'aunt sally' for the 'real political issue' of consumer protection. Most Labour leaders were 'fed up' with Noel-Baker's opposition and wanted a more 'mature attitude to the commercial world'. However, there were plenty in the party who wanted more informative ads, to ban cigarette advertising, regulate outdoor advertising and its influence on the press and to prosecute those that were misleading. Relations between the industry and Labour were poor. George Brown stormed out of a meeting with the Institute of Practitioners in

Advertising (IPA) after the 1959 election. That the Reith Commission saw much advertising as wasteful and Wilson saw its lucre as taxable, lead LPE to conclude warily: 'the advertising industry would do well to prepare itself for a difficult period... from 1966 onwards – if Labour wins'.[66]

Similar anxieties were aired about opinion polling. Benn's suspicion of their methods and propaganda uses by big business lobbyists outweighed any prospect of polls binding politicians and public opinion. Worse was the threat posed to democracy, that 'parliament and elections would gradually be replaced by perpetual market research surveys and perpetual mass advertising campaigns'. As evident as any specific left critique, were the fears elected politicians had that polling challenged their right to speak for voters. As Beers contends, even when established in party campaigning repertoires by the 1960s, 'politicians continued to reject the role of opinion polls in dictating party policy and to assert their role as independent interpreters of the public will'. As often, poll results were used by parties as campaign material, as open public meetings had been, to demonstrate their existing purchase on public opinion. Or polling became, as with televised politics, news stories in their own right.[67]

This explains why pollsters were perceived by many as controversial – for they contested the authority of both politicians and activists. Abrams in particular seemed an almost hidden persuader, who outlined a research, but rarely a political philosophy. Abrams noted how Graham Wallas' *Human Nature in Politics* (1908) supposed that 'advertising and party politics are becoming more and more closely assimilated in method'. From this and consumer research, Abrams deduced that in forging party identities amongst less-involved electors, repetition and familiarity were key. He also favoured detailed research on the impacts of social change to mobilize target voters in marginal seats. And the relationship between class and politics was rigidly observed, such that in 1965 he classified those who strayed from voting in accordance with their class as 'political deviants'. Abrams' Research Services Limited hosted Allan Silver's 1958 investigation of working-class conservatism, which became the classic study of deferential voting, *Angels in Marble*. This was then all quite conventional in regarding image as a mobilizing agent rather than formative of party policy or popular political identities. Polling would not, in short, contravene politician's purview. It was consistent with Trenaman's view of television, that it mobilized but rarely altered political attitudes and with a contemporary study of symbolic politics that 'linguistic cues serve chiefly to provide motive force for incipient gestures rather than to change the gestures'.[68] What was challenging then was the imported language of selling more than any underlining conception of politics.

Pollsters like Abrams seemed to have a vested interest in outlining the limits of popular political engagement. A 1969 survey of youth political attitudes reported the 'picture is predominantly one of disinterest, uninvolvement and feelings of inefficacy'. Yet they fostered the same mistrust. Like politicians, pollsters scored lowly in terms of public trust. Scenarios like the one student Max Williams recounted of polling (albeit accurately) for the 1968 Sheffield Brightside by-election without leaving the pub opposite the Labour HQ, were not uncommon. Polling's inaccuracy in the 1970 election was a shock to 'pundits, party hacks and punters alike', but had a silver lining in that the victorious Tories were pledged to abolish SET, which would enable pollsters to employ better-qualified staff rather than the 'flotsam of the labour market' as Williams put it.[69]

Politics was a minority activity amongst the Market Research Society, if one that boomed in this period with the founding of National Opinion Polls (NOP), Opinion Research Centre (later Harris), Marplan and MORI between 1958 and 1969. Its advocates claimed opinion polling to be 'more widely based than... traditional concepts' of public opinion and a means of coalescing what might otherwise remain dormant or unknown, other than through voting, public meetings or demos.[70] Polls were used to manage more than discover public opinion – politicians' power depended upon it and they mistrusted pollsters claims for this reason.

Tory spending and enthusiasm for advertising and polling was, as a rule, greater. By 1971 their spending on polls was twice that of Labour and their advertising expenditure was more than treble Labour's in the year before the 1964 election.[71] For personal and ideological reasons they meshed more readily with advertising and PR networks like the IPR and IPA. Ian Harvey MP, who wrote on advertising and was a director of CPV, chaired the IPR's advertising panel and Toby O'Brien, who ran Tory publicity from 1946, was IPR Chair 1962–63 and President 1964–65 (a post also later held by prominent YC and Conservative Minister, Peter Walker). And Tories were more regular speakers including Butler, Macleod, Maudling, Deedes and Macmillan and the IPR addressed Conservative local government conferences. Relations with Labour, as the IPR history elliptically puts it, 'never materialized'.[72]

Concerns about MP's directorships, lobbying and PR interests were not new, but more apparent at the end of the 1950s. Noel-Baker eyed the links aided by *The Business Background of MPs* first published in 1957. Finer's 1962 study described the rise of professional lobbyists and contracted MPs and how 'parliament is not above the battle between associations... it is the cockpit'.[73] Politicians with formal connections to PR/ad firms tripled between 1959 and 1965. They were more evident amongst Tories, like MPs Ian MacArthur, an Associate Director of US advertisers J Walter Thompson (JWT) and John Rodgers, deputy chairman of JWT in London. As research into the estates of those who became MPs between 1950 and 1970 has found, Conservatives were more likely to enhance their personal wealth as a consequence of being an MP. This was partly because Labour MPs were monopolized by trade unions, whereas Conservatives dealt with a range of private businesses, but also that they were judged a better source of information and influence by an industry anxious to assure its professional credentials.[74]

But neither polling expertise nor expenditure guaranteed success. James Douglas in the Conservative Research Department argued it had been a mistake not to use more polling after the Luton North by-election defeat in 1963. 'We were streets ahead of the Labour Party in 1959', but by 1963 they had 'got over their doctrinal antipathies' and closed the polling gap and it was the Conservatives who now knew 'appallingly little' of voters' 'attitudes, anxieties and aspirations'. But Douglas, who formed a psephology Group in 1960, was equally aware of the limits to such research. As Taylor has argued, dealing with pollsters proved Conservative 'scepticism of the consequences of social change to be well founded as well as exposing the limits of opinion research'. Douglas critiqued Abrams' *Must Labour Lose?* for the determinism with which it interpreted social change, however favourably for the Conservatives, and for underplaying policy.[75] Party leaders agreed. Central Office commissioned a report from NOP on the by-election defeat at Rochdale in 1958 that was 'perfectly right' on plotting voting patterns, but left the party none the wiser on why voters voted as they did. Conservatives were innately wary of the psephology emanating from David Butler and the Nuffield school, warning in 1956 of the danger 'of becoming the slaves of statistics, dominated by swings and hypnotized by public opinion polls'.[76]

Polls, like advertising and TV, promised to connect party and voters, but underlined the uncertainties of this relationship, indeed seemed to be complicating it. Defeat in 1964, as for Labour in 1959, revived Conservative interest. Douglas now headed the research department, but the party attitude remained, as one Central officer put it in 1966, 'very old-fashioned about these things. We decide what the right policy is and then we look at research... to see how best to present it'.[77] Differentiating between the parties attitudes to new techniques is then blurred. Tunstall is right that 'the major political antagonism towards advertising came from the Labour Party', whose self-conception as a movement was less wont to indulge 'image', but it was not hard to find amongst Conservatives.[78] The party's consumer pamphlet *Choice* (whose authors included Douglas and Ian MacArthur) and the Bow Group's *Advertising on trial* were wary of unalloyed free market materialism. The Whitehouse strain of moral Conservatism was evident, even amongst YCs complaining of 'mass corruption by the sheer vulgarity of commercial advertisers'. 'The old guard didn't like it', was Geoffrey Tucker's appraisal as he took over party publicity in 1968 and senior Tories like Hailsham regarded efforts in this area with scepticism and distaste. Conservative journalist Henry Fairlie reckoned that the Conservatives use of CPV in 1959 involved 'means and arguments that no British party should employ' and that increasingly real 'power lies with the advertising consultants'.[79]

And their approach was in many respects similar to that of Labour. A 1963 press advert celebrating the signing of the Nuclear test ban treaty that featured a despondent CND activist (a model, who had given his written consent to appear in a political ad) was the first time they had used a slogan without substantial text as back up. This was a response to Labour's sharper efforts and was the work of Conservative advertisers, CPV. The (Eton educated) account directors, Roger Pemberton and David Russell, whose other accounts included the army and State Express filter kings, confessed that their 1959 election adverts had been seen by some Tories as over-stressing personal affluence. They now crafted different ads for mass audiences and party workers. This eye for detail contrasted with Colonel Varley's more slapdash, yet recognizable, manner: 'we do Tory advertising the way we do gas advertising. We wouldn't tell the gas people how to make gas. Similarly we can't initiate a political policy'.[80]

Some of the elder generation – Home, Hailsham – did not use the built-in TV studio at Smith Square. The attention Conservatives lavished on preparing candidates for broadcasting then, demonstrated less enthusiasm than grudging acknowledgement of change. To judge from the account by David Walder (a new MP in 1961) of rehearsals in the Tory studio, with candidates advised to read the *Talking on Television and Radio* pamphlet, training was necessary but cursory. This squares with Kandiah's account of Central office's attitude to television. Their competitive edge was evident in their use of video by 1965, a facility Labour lacked. But this was all born less of skill than of an unease that explained their desire to exercise control over their representation on television and suspicion of the BBC. Equally, Central office recognized television's reach was greater than other media or traditional methods and 'removed many of the risks of direct politics', from heckling to local deviation from party control. They used TV to mobilize voters, but also to democratize their image (airing demotic voices to temper their plumy reputation) and respond to less deferential reporting after 1956.[81]

Evidence that the Conservatives had no innate competitive advantage over Labour, and like them saw this in local as well as centralizing terms came in 1967 from PR consultant and two-time Tory candidate Reginald Watts. Voters believed that 'politicians are the complete experts in the art of communication... hidden persuasion, subliminal conversion... brainwashing', but 'to the professional who works in the field of communications... the activities of our main political parties appear naïve and amateurish'. Party leaders should act as a 'board of directors', convince the party that its 'aim is to sell hard, its leaders, candidates and policies' and treat political meetings as a 'sales managers conference... where your salesmen – for that is what your party workers really are – are briefed on the product they have to sell'. Watts urged direct communication with 'opinion formers' (a term coined in Lazarsfeld's *Personal Influence*). True, 'in a world of OMO [a washing detergent] leaflets and hard-selling TV ads, the meagre resources of a local association may seem likely to be swamped'. But, contesting the Nuffield election studies case that local constituencies had little impact, Watt argued 'if the message being sold at the local level' tallies with a national campaign 'and/or has a specific local appeal, then the ability of a local association to isolate its target audience with greater precision does give it a great advantage'.[82]

Street politics

Modern marketed PR politics and national TV-centred campaigns were not then necessarily at odds with local campaigning as much as they seemed to causally coincide, as Lawrence surmises of this period. The latter retained more face-to-face contact in canvassing, still the major campaigning routine and key to establishing recognition since party affiliation did not appear on ballot papers until 1969. And one that was both akin to door-to-door sales and more domestic, private and peaceable than public meetings. Canvassing was as much a ritual as an efficient device for winning votes. It was a sort of inalienable right for the canvassed to meet the candidate, but prone to alienate besides mobilize voters. *Labour Woman* attested to the unpopularity yet necessity of canvassing and that 'for many the election canvass is… either a "sport" or a "punishment"'. 'For some of the electors it is a game in which their goal is to hide what they really think', whilst punishment was 'meted out to the canvasser'.[83]

Haphazard as canvassing often was, it registered recurring themes. In Lessing's account, Communists encountered neither hostility nor interest, but alienated immigrants and women, some anxious to talk irrespective of the canvasser's creed. The canvassers laughed this off to discharge fear of endangering a small Labour majority. In Walder's fictional Netherford, the Conservative candidate (Inglis) noted the contrast between the TV image – 'hair sleek, clothes brushed, sitting back urbanely behind a table' – and the canvasser 'standing in the rain, on the doorstep, hair untidy, shoes none too clean, trying to hold a pencil, a canvass card and a pamphlet all at once'. Having encountered voters who assumed he was a salesman and by-passed the unpropitious-sounding Bevins' house, he was waylaid by a voter, who regaled him about meetings and fights at the 1906 election, the spell-binding performances of Lloyd George, even Baldwin, and asked, 'why is politics so dull today, no fire in it?' Arguing the merits of calm discussion, Inglis could not persuade the voter to his evening meeting. Elsewhere 'the large white eye of television' meant door knocks went unanswered. Inglis returned to the constituency office to discover Mrs. Bevin was the ward secretary and had waited in specially.[84]

Canvassing met as uneven a reception as party TV or advertising. For Jennings, party activists rarely made good propagandists since their political interests marked them out as 'peculiar'. 'The best propaganda' was a 'private conversation in the pub or club... the canteen or the luncheon room' and was best conveyed not by the odd enthusiast, but by those who seemed least like party people. For Jennings, the YCs informal, associational practice of Conservatism was an exemplar of this. Many saw the role of local party branches as being 'to stop the voter escaping from politics by going after him at home'. Party social events tended towards the austere (even by 1951's standards) to placate loyal member's fears 'that politics may be forgotten in a round of amusement'. This in turn meant a common popular view was that there was 'a lack of liveliness about functions organized by political parties', or as recalled by Crossman in Coventry, a 'dreary kind of affair' with 'a few elderly ladies scattered around the edges of an empty dance floor' and palpably unfit to rival TV for either political or social purposes. Canvassing was tangible contact and its demise, as much as of the public meeting, could be read as distancing parties and voters, reducing social capital even. However fitful the success of the canvass with their 'numerous, young and tireless' canvassers, the Tories were advantageously equipped for this labour-intensive activity. But the consensus by 1964 was, as in this case Labour's General Secretary Len Williams put it, that 'the value of personal contact has been diminished by the dynamic intrusion into politics of the almighty telly'.[85]

Yet in CND, street politics revived as a counterpart to professional, media-centred party campaigning and domestic consumption of politics. As a pioneer and model for non-Party DIY radicalism that flourished in the 1960s, CND hinted that new political forms might revive older techniques, notably the marches and banners more often tinged with political extremism. Yet its street style was also media savvy, drawing on professional, commercial designers like Ken Garland. CND demos forged politics in a social, theatrical atmosphere and it featured noted celebrities. It was a reference point for the main parties, transgressing formal and popular politics. It polled opinion in Nottingham and Bradford in 1962 to fashion local campaigns. James Douglas' keen eye for developments in pressure groups, monitored these 'novel techniques of political propaganda'.[86]

Much as the 1962 Festival of Labour conveyed its cultural politics (see Chapter 6), so it embodied debates about Labour's presentation. Compared to the attention lavished on CND, the Festival's absence from the historiography is evidence of how formal party politics have been assumed to have taken on a more staid, discrete persona, to have lost its street cred – if also of contemporary historians' disinterest in the more carnival (literally, in this instance) aspect of politics.

Morgan Phillips proposed a 'Pageant of Labour' in 1960, telling the Party's National Executive Committee: 'our demonstrations are regarded by the general public as demonstrations against them rather than something worthwhile'. Phillips had received complaints about being held up in traffic as a Labour demonstration processed into Hyde Park. And as much as Wesker's cultural efforts, CND was the reference point for this initiative in reclaiming the streets as an effective political site. 'Why shouldn't we take a leaf from their book?', Finchley Labour Party asked the Festival organizer, future home secretary Merlyn Rees. CND's annual meeting, the same weekend as the Festival, discussed this. One activist described demos as 'old hat' and how CND were regarded as 'anti-social nuisances'. Protest styles were an issue between CND and the radical sit-down tactics of the Committee of 100.[87]

The aim was to forge a popular image for Labour that reached beyond formal politics – traditional in form, but modern in content. Besides a cultural agenda to present Labour, as the *Guardian* put it, as 'with it – or, where the cloth cap is concerned, without it' and shed what even supporters admitted was the party's rather 'musty atmosphere', this was an agenda for the culture of politics. It was designed by contrast with how, Rees argued, 'now two years before [an election] the electorate is softened up with a million pound scheme of advertising', but Labour 'cannot spend huge sums like the Tories'. Tony Benn, although a pioneer of Labour's use of TV, likewise felt the Festival was a rejection of the 'nonsense' that was 'the language (and thinking) of the ad-men' and 'clever packaging'. Rather it showed what Labour was '*really* like' and renewed a sense of a *movement* that had been questioned after the 1959 election by revisionists. Confirming this return of old-style boisterous politics were scuffles with CND hecklers of Gaitskell and festival-goers' cars (and the police) being pelted with water by local students.[88]

In other ways it was consciously modern. Floats and tableaux were traditional, but their content included science, space travel and, controversially, the merits of nuclear energy in the Sizewell and Bradwell plants. Rees stressed the use of professional experts ranging from artists, sports stars and the British Film Institute, to the architects and designers consulted for the Brighter premises competition. The ambition to enlist celebrities was a nod to the future too and the style Wilson would fashion as Labour leader. Although Jack Hylton reported '"sympathetic" stars' were 'conspicuous by their absence' in London, but several from *Coronation Street* graced the Manchester event at Belle Vue stadium with Wilson.[89] The Festival's reception was as mixed as it was in strictly cultural terms. Some found the Festival's liveliness had made it 'like Southend', others, and even supporters, experienced an 'easygoing dowdiness'.[90]

If Labour battled a dated reputation – not to mention the Co-op's image problems – politics more generally suffered because of its personal appearance. Politics' private squalor was apparent in the conditions many MPs endured in Westminster. They were 'inefficient and absurd', Hill and Whichelow attest. A 1960 *Guardian* report noted how dingy London Co-op and Labour halls were and how Conservative rooms were 'not very seductive'. The agedness, conservatism and decrepitude of many Labour constituencies had been remarked upon since at least Wilson's 1955 organizational review.[91]

Labour made this a component of the Festival, instituting a 'Brighter Premises' competition and accompanying guide to exterior and interior decorating, drawing on the 'expert knowledge' of the CoID, Civic Trust, British Lighting Council and Professor Misha Black.[92] West Lewisham's Labour HQ was used as a dummy, renovated to Black's specification at the NEC's expense, and in which the key was 'overcoming the drabness of nineteenth century architecture'. There were gardening tips, CWS paint charts and CoID approved coat hangers. The smallest detail was worth sprucing up on the grounds that 'an impression of the party is gained by new recruits from the appearance of the premises' and 'if they look uncared-for they will create an impression of inefficiency'. Tips included suggestions for colour co-ordination; to avoid typefaces that might 'be out of fashion'; to check paving to save high heels – 'the ladies will be happier'; and even 'some hints for the home too!' There was encouragement to 'enlist the help of an architect or designer' since 'the professional is usually more able and imaginative than even the most... enthusiastic amateur'. Political interiors and domesticity were considered public, professional matters.

Figure 7.1 Political domesticity: an extract from Labour's *Brighter Premises* pamphlet, 1961

Source: Labour History Archive, People's History Museum, Manchester

This was an exercise in local initiative, if at national prompting, showing that modern, image-conscious strategies were not necessarily corrosive of local politics. Len Williams held Labour 'deserves modern premises – many of which at presently undoubtedly give the wrong impression to the public', but that 'only local parties can put this right'.[93] The local was the focus for modernizing initiatives in the 1960s, like the tote-bingo schemes of Robert Maxwell's National Fund Raising Foundation. And the 'Plan for an Efficient Party', bemoaned how across 'the country cosy squalor and amateurism are our main hallmarks' and willed better salaries for Transport House pollsters and local agents.[94]

Conservatives faced similar problems. 'The typical local office' James Douglas reflected in 1959 was 'an ancient slum house', with 'a dirty plate glass window'. Given this 'scene of dinginess', Douglas found it 'difficult to persuade myself that 'tomorrow is ours' and felt that 'in terms of propaganda... a bit of money spent on paint might be a sound investment in many a constituency'. By 1965 Enoch Powell saw local party's 'dowdy rooms and an ill-paid agent' as evidence that time was up on Woolton's post-war reforms and a 'paradox' for a party of business and enterprise and inadequate to attract 'people of top ability'. Powell went so far as to argue that 'in any constituency there are no more important premises than those of the Conservative Party, since upon their working and their success the future well-being of our economy and our country depends'. This was 'the most important secular cause in the nation', but Powell wondered if:

> people find this hard to believe when they see the premises so often... antiquated, dilapidated, ill-furnished and ill-equipped? Every constituency office... ought to look the part. People today expect salesmanship... efficient presentation, and modern packaging... How can a party with its paint peeling off persuade people that it is selling them a prosperous future?[95]

Besides (and often housing) constituency offices, there were some 1500 Conservative Clubs in 1960, but many had a 'Victorian' air of decaying glories or were 'bare' with 'outdated posters'.[96] Some survived by distancing themselves from politics, not just subordinating it to social activities. In 1965 Great Yarmouth Conservative Club explained, 'there is no likelihood of membership increasing whilst we remain a political club' and renamed itself the Hall Quay Club. Labour Halls faced the same difficulties. In 1961 the Wimbledon Mothers Guild ceased to rent a room at the local Labour Hall in order to 'dispel any fear of their being connected specifically with the Labour Party' and switched to the local community centre. Topman concludes party political premises were in such cases not only overwhelmed by competitors, but 'essentially depoliticised' or else seen as 'odd' in local civil society.[97]

Satirical conclusions

If politics was not a welcome association, firmly held by a minority in a culture in which it was lightly held, it also increasingly had fun poked at it. As TV 'exposed politicians to the direct gaze of the masses', so satire stripped politics of mystique or authority. Joking was common in the wider political culture, in popular cynicism and as a means of discharging political tension in (variously) the CA's questioning of business rhetoric and the YC's light-touch politics. Formal politics even joked. Labour's 1970 campaign used waxwork dummies of opponents – a forerunner of 1980s TV satire *Spitting Image*.[98]

Mocking politics was a (dis)honourable tradition, but boomed with *TW3*, 'Beyond the Fringe', the Establishment Club and *Private Eye* starting up between 1960 and 1962. Satire focused on the belief that politics (as public service, civic duty, ideology, party) was a dubious activity. It was then best treated none-too-seriously, puncturing its claims to be a trustworthy mode of representation in addressing vital issues. Satire was both a product and critic of a more media, consumerist politics – regarding it as trivial and trivializing it. It fused a witty, lofty (most practitioners were young and Oxbridge-educated, tying them to Inglehart's sociology of post-materialism) disdain with popular antipathy and suspicions of party politicians.[99]

Politics had to compete for the attention of viewers-consumers-voters, who often thought little of it. There was nothing sacred, certainly about politics. That it 'had no moral claim to priority' and was on a par with other activities was, for Wagg, evidence of an Americanization of British political culture (and *TW3* was speedily copied by the US CBS TV network). Wagg overdraws the deference politics enjoyed before this period, but correctly identifies this populist trend. Such 'anti-politics' fostered a DIY outlook of single-issue campaigning, charity work or pointed to politics by non-party means or cultural initiatives like C42. But for the most part, satire involved 'mockery of politics *per se*', of the whole realm, politicians and pollsters alike. A *Private Eye* political 'poll' of seven housewives in 1962 found 75% responded 'get lost, mate' and that others wanted 'no more encyclopedias today'. Peter Cook satirized political PR in *The Rise and Rise of Michael Rimmer*, a 1970 film. *TW3*'s Willie Rushton contested, as an independent, the Kinross and West Perthshire by-election by which Douglas-Home arrived in the Commons in 1963. *TW3*'s irreverence amused and shocked in equal measure. Henry Brooke's defence of the death penalty, lead to the suggestion that that, 'if you're Home Secretary – you can get away with murder'. Brooke got some revenge, barring US comedian Lenny Bruce from a visit to the Establishment Club in 1963, a move that signalled comedy's political salience and politics' killjoy status.[100]

In a consumer mode, Gerald Kaufman penned a *TW3* piece road testing the 'Westminster-worthiness' of MPs. Former Labour MP for Tottenham

Alan Brown who had joined the Tories had his 'steering' identified as a weak spot; former Chancellor Selwyn Lloyd had been 'taken out of service'; and Labour (and sometime Independent) MP Michael Foot was hard to insure against veering 'over to the extreme left'. *TW3*'s most controversial sketch was 'Why?' its 'Consumer Guide to Religion', read by Frost on 12 January 1963 and that also parodied the earnest style of product assessment in *Which?* and its TV spin-off *Choice*. Judaism was expensive because of the need to hire gentiles to run businesses over the Sabbath. Catholicism had 'a superb sales organisation', but whilst the Pope was infallible he 'cannot tell you which television set is best'. Protestantism was cheaper, especially in its non-conformist version. Islam's ritual demands were 'exhausting'. Most religions offered some afterlife, but this remained untested. The 'best buy' turned out to be the Church of England – 'a jolly good little faith for a very moderate outlay'. Such sacrilege generated volleys of complaint, but as with its sceptical approach to politics, was more contributor than initiator, in this case to the crisis of faith that greeted and was manifest two months later in the publication of *Honest to God*. [101]

It also showed how subversive the relativism of appraising religion or politics like washing machines could be. *Which?*'s legacies included its widely adopted model of testing, comparison and rating was readily adopted. Like satire, it collapsed sacred, political, advertising or business authority – reduced it to a best buy, a commodity. And despite CA's earnest tone, it could be inadvertently, even deliberately, ironic. Some of this came from the US Consumers Union wry tone, born of a more populist political culture. Jim Northcott's exploration of the possibilities of a British equivalent, mined *Consumer Reports*' uproarious findings and mimicked its irreverent style, noting, for example, the product advertised as ending the need for lawn mowing that killed grass. CU and its president, Colston Warne, relished deploying humour or epigrams to expose advertising puffs or the frailty of business claims to be advancing free choice. In the late 1960s *Consumer Reports* spawned a satirical replica, *Condemner Reports*.[102]

Like CU and the satirists, CA reveled in a populist pricking of preciousness and exposing to the Reith Commission the spurious claims rather than information delivered by advertising. Irreverence was a key resource for it to combat the material advantages of business, if also one that when leveled against the claims of British business made it seem un-patriotic. It seemed quite subversive simply to quote these, exposing their rich irony: from washes 'whiter than white' to the pseudo-scientific nomenclature and unjustifiable (or untestable) claims that posed 'one of the shopper's most difficult problems'.[103]

CA founder Michael Young's *The Rise of the Meritocracy* (1958), was something of an ur-text of the new satirists, poking fun at both old elites and new meritocrats. Published by Penguin, it sold half a million, was translated into 12 languages and won the Italian Silver Casse award for best satirical essay in 1963. Raymond Williams compared it with Jonathan Swift's work and for *New Society* editor Paul Barker, the book was triumph of 'sociological analysis in the form of satire'. Even political scientists occasionally jested. Jean Blondel ventured that his early research into political life in Reading was prompted by being repeatedly asked 'what are you reading?' at Oxford and that although Professor of Government at Essex University, he had 'never advocated (openly) government by professors nor stated (in print) that Britain is the world's leading political asylum'.[104]

Satire offers signals about the broader political culture. Eliasoph argues social theorists like Adorno regard snide, ironic disengagement as corrosive of public participation, leaving commercial activity as the main civic bond. She also notes, like Goffman, that such attitudes might be seen as subversive, liberating from established norms and material for new political dialogue. But ultimately, she suggests even such 'resistance' dovetails with dominant attitudes since the 1980s that politics and public sphere debate are futile. Hay too sees popular disaffection fusing with politicians' discourse, internalizing the pejorative sense of politics as something corrupt, untrustworthy, prone to capture by powerful interests, to be kept in check or, ideally, kept out of things. Depoliticization was then, positive. Such neo-liberalism in the political sphere has been matched by public choice theory, outsourcing and displacing responsibility from representative politics for fear of 1970s-style 'overload', at once demonizing public politics, questioning its integrity and circumscribing the area of political debate. What Marquand terms 'the decline of the public' was apparent in marketized party campaigning too, conducted by analogy with commercial activity, targeting voter-consumers with branded parties. For Offer, the intimacy, directness and breadth of advertising and PPBs, by involving politics in the deceptions and low credibility of mass media campaigns, undermined the authority and trust politics sought.[105]

In this vein, the CA's individual-shopper conception of consumerism (that members if not the leadership practiced) was, critics alleged, a retreat from a more all-encompassing social-citizen mode. Similarly, Hilton argues it was now private consumerism whose values were scrutinizing and holding the public sphere to account. That strand of conservatism that saw politics as more necessity than virtue in the YCs here tallied with Bauman's account of Thatcherism as casting politics as irrelevant or a 'nuisance' to people's goals, which were better pursued individually. Such narratives of politics, whilst far from un-politically motivated, also tallied with popular sceptical apathy.[106]

Satire invariably contained an attempt to enlighten and expose, or to exploit its target's fears of ostracism.[107] It pilloried the establishment by coincidence with the Profumo-addled end of Conservative government, but equally hampered the left's claim to be a viable alternative, questioning trust in politics. The liberation of self-identity in the 1960s, querying collective institutions (state, nation, church, party), established hierarchies and identities (class, gender) and value-systems, also served to question the authority of public politics. That the 'personal was political' (a sixties feminist mantra, but evident elsewhere in consumer and cultural politics in this book) broadened the acknowledged terrain of 'the political', but vied with its public sphere orientation. Pressure groups and new social movements too strained the authority of party and government in defining 'the political'. Varied radical voices in the 1960s critiqued existing structures of politics and the state, but so did those of the New Right through the 1970s and 1980s. As Lawrence's recasting of popular involvement in public politics stresses not only a desire to control the masses, but that the 'old ways' seemed illegitimate for a rational polity to either the Left or Right – so market-driven politics was fed by critics of the political establishment as much as outright advocates.[108]

Satire then was not just a laughing matter, more indicative of the ways in which political categories and boundaries were redefined than at first glance. The representation of politics in the 1950s and 1960s is recognizable today, suggesting a process of engagement with modernity. But it was also recognizable from preceding periods, not least in anxieties about popular political audiences and the authority of formal politics. This is neither to argue for a pristine past nor that it was always thus, but that notions of contemporary disaffection are qualified by evidence of their enduring qualities and debates about them. Face-to-face politics was evermore supplanted by virtual contact between party and people, most visibly through TV, but it is difficult to conclude this necessarily degraded the quality of political debate. TV certainly altered its style and tenor, but in many ways sustained a public sphere. An irreverent public remained and even the odd politician who occasionally courted it. Politics remained lively, entertaining, contested, if less in party, then clearly in the sorts of pressure groups and extra-party networks studied here. Equally, such political forms encountered their own difficulties and similar ones to party and rarely challenged party in convening broad popular alliances. Party mutability, partly derived from their ability to exercise state power, was firmly evident. The persistence of party seems less remarkable if it is considered to have been because of its relative detachments from external social forces and the people, not despite them.

8
Conclusions

At the 1970 general election, until three days before polling, most commentators agreed that (in England at least) politics was relegated in interest and coverage to the football world cup. What does this tell historians of political culture? Since the election night results also won sizeable viewing figures, as much as anything, this bore out the cultural pre-eminence of television. It could point to the alleged comparative stability of British politics that impressed political scientists in the early 1960s or alleviate Crosland's anxieties about high levels of participation? It was not as if, as in the modern parable of Jose Saramago's novel *Seeing*, the population withdraws consent by casting blank ballots in elections, there was either mass discontent with or interest in British politics. It surely also illuminates politics' slight presence in everyday life and popular culture.[1]

Besides the work they do for historians looking to relate the political and social spheres, the core samples in *Redefining British Politics* overlap and yield other themes – adding up to more than the sum of their parts. How able these samples were to speak for broader trends is limited, but they have served to interrogate and in some cases upset handed-down narratives and to splice political culture into a broader societal context. *Redefining British Politics* marks out a more socio-cultural history of politics, something that has been rarer for the post-war period. And for no better reason than a propensity to genuflect to the terminology of contemporary debate – thus a narrow conception and perception of politics in decline, lacking ability to engage or much public authority – and what resembles a lack of imagination or confidence compared with histories of pre-1945 periods. Here narratives of the end of empire, national decline and consensus have proven imperious, if increasingly historicized as culturally influential.[2] It has not substituted newer master narratives of consumerism as Hilton proposes, whilst acknowledging their influence. It has also positioned itself differently to studies of the cultural history of elections or that focus on non-party politics, preferring to integrate these.[3]

What then does a history of 1950s and 1960s British political culture look like? A central paradox was that as politics encompassed a more plural range of issues, it also seemed incidental, even unimportant – as it took on a broader definition it appeared at the same time more culturally relative. Politics features little in Moran's take on daily life in recent British history – yet it too became more mundane, everyday in content and familiar in practice.[4] The picture then is on the one hand of disengagement between formal politics and the people. If this was not so novel, it is clear that the legitimacy of established political authority was challenged and not just by or in 'the sixties'. An irreverent public remained, sceptical of politics. It suggests that formal political identity was not that salient or weighty in British culture. On the other hand an inventive, dynamic array of debates and new initiatives, chiefly in the form of pressure groups and aspirant social movements, flourished. This is a familiar narrative of the 1960s in demands for participation and environmental, feminist, nationalist agendas, single-issues like homelessness and a host of counter-cultural agendas. This study emphasizes the pervasiveness of such developments in less ostensibly or conventionally political organizations, but that nonetheless processed the personal, culture, morality and material culture into political matters. We are left then with a less exclusive, more unstable, diffuse, transient political culture – as both a product of change in this period and the result of the more mutative, inclusive approach this demands from historians.

If *Redefining British Politics* contests dominant approaches, it also affirms some narratives. The evidence here is also of a British political culture, before British became English, Irish, Scottish and Welsh. If it is dominated by England, few signs of these devolutionary pressures were apparent. America was more of an influence and point of reference than Europe and nor do issues of race figure saliently. These and other absences doubtless reflects on the core samples used, or on their efforts to negotiate these developments, but also reinforces how politics is not best regarded as a mirror of social change and that political culture is a fluid, multiple category.

The Consumers' Association, Co-op, Young Conservatives and White-house's campaign certainly represented popular, mass, if not always majority, opinion – at least as much as those movements more commonly focused on in the literature on social movements and pressure groups. They offset some of the 1968-influenced focus on more dramatic politics. Even Wesker's spectacular visions for C42 and the Roundhouse were heavily involved in the practical rigmarole of funding an arts centre and aspired to shape mass culture and its audience. These qualities hardly make them typical, but hint that a cultural history of politics can embrace the everyday.

Nor has the focus been on successful, novel political initiatives – facets of political culture are as well illustrated by those that struggle, fail or persist. Despite its resonances with the sixties 'cultural revolution' and its staging of this in London, C42 closed itself down in 1970. C42 offers a measure of the limits of the sixties 'revolution'. Whitehouse's battle against liberal cultural trends was unsuccessful, although alerting many to the politics of TV. For both it was not simply that their reading of society and prognoses for it found scarce popular reception, but that they were contested and marginalized by other forces – the state and unions (among others) in C42's case, the media and Conservative establishment in Whitehouse's. The YCs lost members by dint of politicization as much as social factors in the 1960s and never recovered to the size and hegemony amongst middle-class young Britons they enjoyed in the 1950s. The Co-op's inherited culture struggled with the newer tastes of consumers and in competition with the CA.

The chronological reach here extends pre-1954 and notes legacies and trends for political culture after 1970. Much as elements in Co-op culture were recognizable from its Victorian inception, its enduring ethical values survived and the Co-op now trades on these. The YCs likewise exhibited features identified by historians of inter-war political culture, a low key, almost incidentally political style – one that diminished as culture became more politically conscious through the 1960s and as the YCs participated in this very process. C42 was a marker for post-industrial use of buildings and for what modern political rhetoric terms the creative industries. The Roundhouse itself was a good, if winding, marker of cultural politics from the 1960s to present day – if a path C42 or Wesker walked fitfully at best. Even Whitehouse's moral retrenchment found echoes in politics that demonized the 1960s in favour of more traditional values from Thatcher to New Labour's distancing itself from Marxist radicals. Although it was also apparent both turned 1960s liberalism to their advantage – Labour its demotic, déclassé social impetus, Thatcherism in the individual-consumer sphere.[5] The CA's focus on the consumer as a political subject has become mainstream political discourse. Most evidently, the mixing of TV and polling with modern political communication, a feature of this period, has been decisive. Party political interactions, no less than the rest of life seemed, for good or ill, more consumer-like. If this purported to recognize and address the rights of political consumers, it also constituted a more market-driven realm. This palpably strained political traditions and routines and met opposition outside the party parts of political culture in organizations that associated themselves more readily with civil society – and not least because as this study contends, politics was not best understood solely in quantitative terms. But whether it was that much of a departure (or more one in language above all else) given politics had long involved competition not only amongst protagonists, but to win the attention and support of a wider audience, seems less certain.

The Co-op, CA, C42 and NVALA have focused on politics outside party; on the development of pressure groups and social movements. They imagined themselves more as national than political movements. Whilst these bring out criticisms of party and in the cases of CA, C42 and the NVALA attempts to forge politics very much in the anti-establishment, DIY spirit of the sixties, the analytical focus has included party. For all the considerable challenges posed by pressure groups, most had at least fringe relations with the main parties. Indeed the Co-op, CA, NVALA and C42 encountered many of the problems the main parties faced in terms of participation, apathy and claiming to speak for and to those beyond their core membership and issues. Parties were not slow to assimilate ideas and practices, even personnel. There was rarely a rigid divide between party and other forms (and historians ought not to interject one), they were interrelated – and should likewise be treated as complementary, if competing, in anatomies of political culture. The discussion of the YCs, for instance, details party techniques for managing low levels of political interest amongst members as much as the scepticism about party in wider society. Internalizing these in its political practice, the YCs propagated them more widely, although they were less willing or able to do so in the second half of the 1960s. The final chapter shows the difficulties and opportunities in handling newer modes of communicating with voters, especially TV. If caused by differing instincts and values in respective party cultures, nonetheless a variety of common problems were encountered across the parties. TV posed challenges for voters, parties, other political actors and broadcasters alike.

The New Left has been an unofficial foil to several arguments in *Redefining British Politics*. This is to question some of the assumptions it imposes and the status it enjoys in discussions of cultural politics. More specifically, C42 and other cultural initiatives suggest it wasn't solely for lack of effort or interest, as the New Left charged in its characterization of 'Labourism', that the left struggled to establish a presence in cultural terrains, in civil society, in the politics of life as well as of work. Indeed C42's efforts to practically develop such an agenda received lukewarm support from the New Left itself. Not least there were the YCs, whose vibrant and mainly social lifestyle was something of an elephant in the room of the debate on party presence in civil society. Most radically, the focus on culture and media that paired the New Left with Whitehouse's ultra-conservative movement hints that cultural and post-materialist politics shared, indeed forged, key concerns and agendas in the 1960s, however divergent in their political trajectory. Post-materialist politics were not, based on the evidence of Whitehouse, necessarily progressive or modernizing, as Inglehart and much social movement literature has held. This suggests a certain autonomy of the political. Not that it was independent of social causes, but that its own culture influenced how its causes and context were interpreted. To fully apply a post-materialist agenda involves reading the dynamics of politics (its internal culture and traditions, its place and status in society) in post-materialist terms, as well as recognizing certain issues that were increasingly likely to mobilize participants.

Or put another way, the context neither determined the form that such politics might take, nor that they would win a ready popular reception. The supply of post-materialist politics in this period out-stripped or mismatched demand. Limited as popular demand was, it was emergent and more so in the ensuing decades in which cultural, consumer and moral terrains were key political disputes. These played out between and within political organizations and discourses. The left (from SDP and New Labour through Livingstone and Marxists) relations with extra-parliamentary radicalism and the unions in post-industrializing Britain since the 1970s were as generational, social and cultural as political; and Thatcher's appeal was as much around social and moral as economic orders and in style and gender disturbed party and conservative culture.[6]

It was not as if even the benighted 'seventies' saw a recession in consumer values and even wage disputes were tinged with a post-materialist air of the crumbling of established authority. The 1970s, as with periods before and after, showed post-materialism co-existent with more materialist trends. *Small is Beautiful*, a bestseller in 1973 and critique of growth economics produced by the former National Coal Board Advisor and strongly religious Ernst Schumacher, showed that the post-materialist promise of the 1960s would not be expunged by the economic difficulties of the 1970s. The 'culture wars' of the 1980s saw the meaning and legacies of 'the sixties' loom large and animus was generational, moral and cultural besides political in its alignments and positions. Culture – from heritage to comedy in the 1980s, to the creative industries that were key in national identity debates in post-industrial, late imperial 1990s Britain – was evermore a political touchstone. There seems leverage in Curran, Gaber and Petley's case that as the market won economic debates, social and cultural issues became more of a focus for political contest (if less certainty in their conclusion that the liberal left was leading these).[7] As debate on economic policy diminished after the Cold War as much as for post-materialist reasons, so socio-cultural terrains became more charged by, for example, questions of political rights and identity issues like devolution. It was not that economics had ended (there were clear economic aspects to devolution, to a medley of gender, race and consumer issues, and the market model was increasingly the norm in party political competition itself), but that it was now more about the priorities, ethics and aims of the market and less its organization – a point seemingly ratified by the relative absence of fundamental or ideological political differences (compared, say, to 1979) over the 2009 economic crisis.[8]

In a sense then, the New Left insight that culture was central to politics was right, just in a host of ways it never presumed. Politics was more parochial and less dramatic; cultural and post-materialist politics were not automatically progressive; and this was a redefinition in which, often despite themselves, political conservatives participated. Irrespective of questions raised about post-materialism, the politics of culture, consumerism, morality and personal identity were sharply contested.

Newer formations of this pressure group sort, attentive to cultural or moral agendas, had a more intimate connection and capacity to engage with, interpret and to mobilize around social and cultural shifts than political parties. By dint of being as much social as political animals, the YCs, CA and the Co-op were as sensitive to changes in youth culture and consumer behaviour as political tastes. C42 and Whitehouse struggled as much through cultural tastes as political decisions. If C42 and the Co-op were frustrated with shifting working-class tastes, those examined here also point to the middle class as a political storm centre. And why not? Historians have shown little interest in middle-class politics. This played out in some familiar ways. CA, Whitehouse and Wesker were concerned with how affluence, whether in terms of money, time or taste, was spent by those that had newly acquired it – they aspired to influence and improve (or save) working-class habits now widespread poverty seemed a thing of the past. Even the YCs offered voluntary service as a way of expending leisure alongside youthful freedoms. The YCs and Whitehouse and to a degree parts of CA's core audience showed a testiness with conventional Conservative wisdom. If middle-class politics seemed more salient, they were also less homogenous than in inter-war Britain, a fractiousness or de-alignment that would be apparent to both main parties and productive for Thatcherism.[9]

The CA's focus on consuming practices and commodities and NVALA's on the private, domestic viewing experience, aided the process of the personal becoming political. This confirms a familiar narrative of sixties history, but does so from unfamiliar origins, less dramatically or self-consciously political, but all the more potent (in the context of politics' low level presence in everyday life and popular culture) for this reason. Pressure groups challenged party, partly by affirming a pejorative sense of official politics, but this is not to argue that civil society was a more benign or less contested sphere.

Public politics by turn was more conscious of its private comportment, appearance and representation. Another recurring dichotomy was that of the professional and amateur – evident in both consumer organizations, debates about culture and the arts and no less in formal politics as it encountered modern media of TV and marketing. TV provides a vital subtext as well as context. It was the main technology and source of communicative power that the parties had to engage with in reconfiguring their activity and relationship with most voters from the mid-1950s. TV was a growing influence on how the mass of Britons viewed politics. It was, particularly after ITV started in 1955, Britons' common culture, as well as an agent of consumerism. For Wesker no less than Whitehouse, TV was the cultural counterpoint to their efforts. TV was, then, a mobilizing force and for the NVALA a political cause in itself – it did not simply transmit debate, it *was* the debate.

As economic recession bit in 2009, the idea that it is 'the economy, stupid' or that this would 'bring real politics back' were tempting. But *Redefining British Politics* has shown politics' comparative independence from socio-economic forces, if also the limits of its power to shape these, and above all, its adaptability, even creativity. This was a political culture in which politics was neither an easy nor a notably popular activity – in short, not a very political culture. Whither politics, then? This study suggests less withering from some 'golden age' and more morphing – and if not that political culture is too important to be left to political historians alone, then that they certainly ignore it at their peril.

Notes

Chapter 1

1 C. Hay, *Why We Hate Politics* (Cambridge, 2007), pp.1, 153; J.S. Nye, P. Zelikow, D. King (eds), *Why People Don't Trust Government* (Cambridge, MA, 1997).
2 J. Lawrence, *Electing Our Masters: The Hustings in British Politics from Hogarth to Blair* (Oxford, 2009); C. Brown, *The Death of Christian Britain* (London, 2009).
3 F. Jameson, *The Political Unconscious: Narrative as a Socially Symbolic Act* (Ithaca, NY, 1981).
4 K. Ross, *Fast Cars, Clean Bodies: Decolonization and the Re-ordering of French Culture* (Cambridge, MA, 1995); L. Robinson, *Gay Men and the Left in Post-war Britain: How the Personal Got Political* (Manchester, 2007).
5 As in E.H.H. Green, *Ideologies of Conservatism* (Oxford, 2002), pp.15–16; H. Pemberton, *Policy Learning and British Governance in the 1960s* (Basingstoke, 2004), p.9.
6 Hay, *Why We Hate Politics*, pp.61–65 offers 12 working definitions of 'politics'.
7 Lawrence, *Electing our Masters*, pp.8, vii; R. McKibbin, *Classes and Cultures: England 1918–51* (Oxford, 1998), p.97.
8 M. Francis, 'Tears, tantrums and bared teeth: The emotional economy of three Conservative Prime Ministers, 1951–63', *Journal of British Studies* 41 (2002).
9 B. Crick, *In Defence of Politics* (Harmondsworth, 1962, 1976 edition), pp.15, 25–26, 141.
10 N. Crowson, M. Hilton, J. McKay (eds), *NGOs in Contemporary Britain: Non-state Actors in Society and Politics since 1945* (Basingstoke, 2009).
11 S. Fielding, *Labour and Cultural Change* (Manchester, 2003), ch.1; Lawrence, *Electing our Masters*.
12 For a powerful case to this effect, A. Thorpe, *Parties at War* (Oxford, 2009).
13 Margaret Stacey, *Tradition and Change: A Study of Banbury* (Oxford, 1960), pp.54–55.
14 J. Lawrence, 'The transformation of British public politics after the first world war', *Past and Present* 190 (2006); J. Thompson, 'Pictorial lies? Posters and politics in Britain, c.1880–1914', *Past and Present* 197 (2007); L. Beers, 'Labour's Britain, fight for it now!', *Historical Journal* 52:3 (2009).
15 J. Harris, 'Civil Society in British society: paradigm or peculiarity?' in J. Harris (ed.), *Civil Society in British History: Ideas, Identities, Institutions* (Oxford, 2003), pp.5–9; R. Putnam, *Bowling Alone: The Collapse and Revival of American Community* (New York, 2000).
16 S. Fielding, 'Political History' provides a useful overview: http://www.history.ac.uk/makinghistory/resources/articles/political_history.html
17 W.L. Guttsman, *The British Political Elite* (London, 1963), p.196.
18 J. Lawrence, M. Taylor, 'Electoral sociology and the historians' in *idem.* (eds), *Party, State and Society* (Aldershot, 1997); S. Gunn, *History and Cultural Theory* (Harlow, 2006), pp.20–21, ch.3; for related pointers see, M. Jacobs, W. Novak, J. Zelizer (eds), *The Democratic Experiment: New Directions in American Political History* (Princeton, NJ, 2003).

19   G. Stedman Jones, *Languages of Class* (Cambridge, 1983); Fielding, *Labour and Cultural Change*, p.26.

20   L. Black, *The Political Culture of the Left in Affluent Britain* (Basingstoke, 2003).

21   N. Eliasoph, *Avoiding Politics: How Americans Produce Apathy in Everyday Life* (Cambridge, 1998).

22   R. Samuel, *The Lost World of British Communism* (London, 2007); S. Fielding, 'Looking for the new political history', *Journal of Contemporary History* 42:3 (2007), p.518.

23   A. Offer, *The Challenge of Affluence: Self-control and Well-being in the US and Britain Since 1956* (Oxford, 2006), p.8.

24   Fielding, *Labour and Cultural Change*, ch.1; G. Eley, *Forging Democracy: The History of the Left in Europe 1850–2000* (Oxford, 2002), pp.8–11, chs.22, 27; A. Lent, *British Social Movements Since 1945: Sex, Colour, Peace and Power* (Basingstoke, 2001).

25   An Agent, 'Propaganda and public relations', *Conservative Agents' Journal* 434 (September 1957), p.199; A. Marsh, *Protest and Political Consciousness* (London, 1977), ch.5.

26   R. Inglehart, 'The silent revolution in Europe: Intergenerational change in post-industrial societies', *American Political Science Review* 65:4 (1971).

27   R. Inglehart, *Culture Shift in Advanced Industrial Society* (Princeton, NJ, 1990), ch.10.

28   S. Majima, M. Savage, 'Have there been culture shifts in Britain? A critical encounter with Ronald Inglehart', *Cultural Sociology* 1:3 (2007), pp.293–315; J. Vernon, *Hunger: A Modern History* (Cambridge, MA, 2007); M. Glendenning, 'The conservation movement: A cult of the modern age', *Transaction of the Royal Historical Society* 6:13 (2003); J. de Groot, *Consuming History* (London, 2008)

29   D. Houtman, *Class and Politics in Contemporary Social Science* (New York, 2000), pp.xi, 136–138, 154; Majima, Savage, 'Culture shifts in Britain?', pp.294–297, 312.

30   C. McLarney, E. Chung, 'Post-materialism's "silent revolution" in consumer research', *Marketing Intelligence and Planning* 17:6 (1999); also C. Bean, E. Papadakis, 'Polarized priorities or flexible alternatives? Dimensionality in Inglehart's materialism-postmaterialism scale', *International Journal of Public Opinion Research* 6:3 (1994).

31   Inglehart, *Culture Shift*, pp.19, 334–345; Hay, *Why We Hate Politics*, pp.44–48, 79; Crick, *In Defence*, p.141.

32   I. Jennings, *Party Politics, Vol. II The Growth of Parties* (Cambridge, 1961), pp.327–335. *Vol. I Appeal to the People* (Cambridge, 1960), pp.172, 209, 228, 235.

Chapter 2

1   Leslie Adrian, 'CA for TV?', *Spectator* (1 April 1960), p.485.

2   I. Zweiniger-Bargielowska, *Austerity in Britain* (Oxford, 2000); L. Black, *The Political Culture of the Left in Affluent Britain, 1951–64* (Basingstoke, 2003).

3   P. Gurney, 'The Battle of the Consumer in Postwar Britain', *Journal of Modern History* 77:4 (2005), p.959; M. Hilton, *Consumerism in Twentieth Century Britain* (Cambridge, 2003); F. Mort, 'Competing domains: Democratic subjects and consuming subjects in Britain and the United States since 1945' in F. Trentmann (ed.), *The Making of the Consumer* (Oxford, 2006).

4 On which see A. Offer, *The Challenge of Affluence* (Oxford, 2006); M. Hilton, *Prosperity for All: Consumer Activism in an Era of Globalization* (Ithaca, NY, 2009); T. Kasser, *The High Price of Materialism* (Cambridge, MA, 2003).

5 Stephen Fay, 'The Last of the Fabians', *Sunday Times* (2 August 1964).

6 M. Hilton, 'The Fable of the Sheep, or, Private Virtues, Public Vices: The Consumer Revolution of the 20ᵗʰ Century', *Past and Present* 176 (2002); *idem.*, 'The banality of consumption' in K. Soper, F. Trentmann (eds), *Citizenship and Consumption* (Basingstoke, 2008).

7 *Which?* (Winter 1958), p.3; (Winter 1959), p.35; *Which?* went monthly in April 1959; Christina Fulop, *The Consumer Movement and the Consumer* (London, 1977), p.38.

8 CA Council minutes (20 January 1959), Consumers' Association Archive (CAA); R. Morse (ed.), *The Consumer Movement: Lectures by Colston E. Warne* (Manhattan, KS, 1993), p.200.

9 H.B. Thorelli, S.V. Thorelli, *Consumer Information Handbook: Europe and North America* (New York, 1974), p.19; CA, *Twelfth Annual Report of the Consumers' Association* (1969), pp.4, 11; Kelsey van Musschenbroek, 'Mounting action by the militant shoppers', *Financial Times* (10 March 1970); CA, *Which? and Consumers' Association* (London, 1965), p.5.

10 Eirlys Roberts, 'CA's part in the design of Products' (29 June 1966); CAA A27; *Which?* (September 1960), p.205; Manchester Consumer Group newsletter (August 1967); Mary Adams papers (MAP), S322/240.

11 *Daily Express* (12, 14 April 1962); Brook memo, CA Council minutes (14 May 1962); M. Healy, 'Reactions to the Car Supplement', CA Council minutes (12 February 1962); Goldman CA Council minutes (14 December 1964).

12 CA Council minutes (15 October 1962); *Which?* (August 1961), p.206; *Daily Mail* (23 November 1962); Michael Young, *The Chipped White Cups of Dover: A Discussion of the Possibility of a New Progressive Party* (London, 1960), pp.5, 11.

13 'CA News', *Which?* (July 1959), p.63; Press release (8 January 1965), MAP, S322/241; 'The Taste-makers', *Sunday Times* (25 May 1963).

14 *Which?* (September 1960), p.205; Manchester Consumer Group newsletter (August 1967), MAP, S322/240.

15 *Which?* (August 1959), p.99.

16 *Which?* (Autumn 1958) and 'Slimming Foods' (June 1961), pp.136–139; CA Council minutes (12 February 1962); CA, *Contraceptives* (London, 1963); Transcript, interview with Roberts, p.21; CAA A26. *Good Food Guide* (1963–4), p.vi.

17 C.A.R. Crosland, *The Future of Socialism* (London, 1956); R. Harris, A. Seldon, *Advertising and the Public* (London, 1959), p.226.

18 *Shopper's Guide* (Spring 1958).

19 CA Council minutes (28 October 1956, 17 November 1957); Transcript, interview with Goldman, p.3; CAA A26.

20 'The woman behind a hard look at cars', *Topic* (20 January 1962); Fay, 'The Last of the Fabians'; Asa Briggs, *Michael Young: Social Entrepreneur* (Basingstoke, 2001).

21 'The how and why of Which?', *Domestic Equipment Trader* (January 1964), p.31; Roberts, *Wall Street Journal* (12 July 1968); 'Results of Monthly Omnibus Questionnaires' (January 1971), p.66; CAA A11; Crosland, 'Proceedings of Consumer Assembly', London (3 November 1967), p.18, CAA A67.

22 Josephine Clifford-Smith (Membership secretary), 'Inquiries by CA members and the public' (2 January 1962), CA Council minutes (8 January 1962); Draft

for *New Society,* 'Who Reads *Which?*' (26 October 1962), p.1, CAA A27; 'Beer', *Which?* (August 1960), pp.167–169.

23 CA Council minutes (17 November 1957, 13 February 1958); On Fienburgh, James Douglas to Anthony Dumont (16 February 1959), Conservative Party Archive, CRD 2/8/19.

24 D. Tench, *The Law for Consumers* (London, 1962); H. Pemberton, *Policy Learning and British Governance in the 1960s* (Basingstoke, 2004), pp.63–66; *Times* (10 April 1980); *Which?* (October 1965), p.287. Mitchell was succeeded at the National Consumer Council by CA's Maurice Healy.

25 '*Which?* and Advertisers', *Which?* (March 1966), p.67; 'Eirlys Roberts Writes', *Which?* (June 1968), p.163; Gurney, The battle of the consumer', pp.967–968.

26 Elisabeth Houlton, *Which? Put to the Test* (Aims of Industry Study No. 15, 1967), pp.3, 12; Eirlys Roberts, *Consumers* (London, 1966), p.6; Thorelli, Thorelli, *Consumer Information,* p.18; R. Dunstan, 'Which? Hunt', *Twentieth Century,* Vol.176:4–177:1 (1968–9), p.14.

27 'Accounts for 1961/62', CA Council minutes (4 June 1962); CA, *Fifth Annual Report* (1961/2), p.3; CA, 'Notes for CA speakers' (September 1970), p.11; CAA A65. CA Council minutes (14 May, 4 June 1962).

28 Stanley Alderson, 'Buy the Improved Which?', *The Manager* (July/August 1959), pp.472–473; 'The Press Greets CR', *Which?* (Winter 1958), p.20; Healy, 'Reactions to the Car Supplement'; D. Horowitz, *Vance Packard and American Social Criticism* (Chapel Hill, NC 1994).

29 '*Which?* Layout and Design', CA Council minutes (14 May 1962).

30 Song in transcript of interview with Joan Meier, pp.172–173, CAA A13; Joan Meier to Brook (9 January 1963), discussion documents, CAA A27.

31 Sarah Franks, 'Selling Consumer Protection: Competitive Strategies of the Consumers' Association, 1957–90' (M. Phil. diss., Oxford University, 2000), pp.35–46; Gilda Lund, *You and Your Shopping* (London, 1961); Elizabeth Gundrey, *Your Money's Worth: A Handbook for Consumers* (Harmondsworth, 1962).

32 Leslie Adrian (ed. Nancy Ryan), *Consuming Interest, from The Spectator* (London, 1961), pp.ix–x, 86; *Spectator* (23 November 1962), p.844, (23 April 1965), p.544.

33 *Which?* (October 1959), p.123; Public Attitude Surveys Report 'Postal Survey conducted among subscribers to *Which?* magazine concerning attitude to RPM' (August 1961), CAA A14.

34 CA, 'Notes for CA speakers', p.7; Gallup Poll, *Enquiry into Which?* (July 1962), p.3b, CAA A31; J. Mitchell, 'Results of Questionnaire sent to members of the CA, November 1964', pp.12–15, CAA A27.

35 Paper 'C', Council minutes (13 September 1959); C. Brook, 'Where are we going?', p.14; Council minutes (2 February 1959).

36 Clifford-Smith, 'Inquiries'; Extraordinary Council minutes (23 February 1959); C.A.R. Crosland, *The Conservative Enemy* (London, 1962), p.65; Roberts, *Consumers,* p.81; Peter Goldman, 'Consumerism – Art or Science?' *Journal of the Royal Society of Arts* (August 1969), pp.4–5; Transcript, interview with Goldman, p.10; Eirlys Roberts, *Which? 25: Consumers' Association 1957–82* (London, 1982), pp.99–101.

37 *Which?* (July 1961), pp.174–175; (July 1967), pp.209–214; (March 1968), p.93, 'Au Pair girls', *Which?* (January 1969), pp.19–21; Roberts, *Which? 25,* pp.15, 45.

38 Rosemary McRobert (CA Deputy Director in the 1980s) in the Consumer Council's *Focus,* in *Which?* (September 1966), p.275; 'Results of Monthly Omnibus Questionnaire (January 1971), p.4.

39 Cooper, *Which?* (January 1969), p.3; S. Bowden, A. Offer, 'Household appliances and the use of time in the USA and Britain since the 1920s', *Economic History Review* 47:4 (1994).

40 Brook, '300,000 bewildered buyers club together', *Sunday Citizen* (23 June 1963); Goldman, 'Art or Science?', p.5; Eirlys Roberts, 'David and Goliath', *Observer* (9 June 1963).

41 Roberts, *Which? 25*, pp.8–9.

42 Hilton, 'Fable of the Sheep'; CA Council minutes (8 February 1960); Elizabeth Gundrey, *Help* (London, 1967), p.5; *Final Report of the Committee on Consumer Protection*, Cmnd. 1781 (July 1962), para.890.

43 'Consumer Bulletin' (July 1956), p.1, CAA A27.

44 Paul Fletcher, 'When we were very young', *Which?* (October 1967), pp.290–291.

45 CA Council minutes (2 February 1959, 8 February, 14 March 1960); Robert Millar, *The Affluent Sheep* (London, 1963), pp.194–196.

46 'Results of Monthly Omnibus Questionnaires' (January 1971), p.66; *Which?* (April 1968), p.128.

47 'Cumulative Index, 1957–66', *Which?* (December 1966), pp.398–400.

48 'Speaking engagements met by CA', CA Council minutes (14 May 1962).

49 'Draft programme for first half year', Association of British Consumers minutes (28 October 1956).

50 Marplan, R.5226 'Why People Join Consumers Association' (September 1966), p.9, CAA A14; *Which?* (August 1961), p.207; M. Hilton, 'The Female Consumer and the Politics of Consumption in Twentieth-Century Britain', *Historical Journal* 45:1 (2002).

51 In 'Vers de Société', Philip Larkin, *Collected Poems* (London, 1988), p.181; Andrew Robertson, 'The Campaigners', *Twentieth Century* (1968–9, double issue), pp.10–11; Adrian, *Consuming Interest*, pp.ix–x.

52 Gardiner to Young (18 November 1957), BBC Written Archives centre (BBC WAC), R34/1006/1.

53 Adams memo (7 April 1955), MAP S322/193; Elaine Burton, *Value for Money* (London, 1955); Grisewood note to Director General (24 November 1959), BBC WAC R34/1006/1; Papers from J.C. Thornton (Assistant Controller of BBC talks, (17 October, 19 December 1958, 13 January 1959), R34/1006/1.

54 Leonard Miall to Young (21 April 1958), Adams memo to Brook (14 September, 27 November 1959) and to Norman Collins (Chair ITV Companies, 5 November 1959), MAP S322/193; Adams to Director General (2 November 1959), BBC WAC R34/1006/1.

55 BBC board of management minutes (9, 30 November 1959), BBC WAC R34/1006/1; CA, *Evidence Submitted to the Departmental Committee on Consumer Protection* (March 1960), para.45, CAA A31.

56 Casper Brook memo to Adams (17 November 1960), Adams note (14 July 1961), MAP S322/193; Adrian, 'Choice Improved', *Spectator* (17 April 1964).

57 *Scrutiny* 9–10 (February–March 1962); Stanley Steward (British Electrical and Allied Manufacturers Association) to Carleton Greene (12 March 1962), Grace Goldie to Steward (3 May 1962), Claude Simmonds (Domestic Refrigeration Development Committee) to H. Grisewood (12 March, 13 July, 10 August 1962), Grisewood to Simmonds (20 July 1962), J. Dunse (Retail Distributors Association) to Carleton Greene (18 January 1962), Huw Weldon note (8 February 1966), BBC WAC T16/698.

58 C.E. Harrison (FBI President) to Sir Arthur Fforde (Chair, BBC Governors, 14 February 1962), CA Council minutes (4 June 1962).

59 'The Press Greets CR', *Which?* (Winter 1958), pp.20–21; van Musschenbroek, 'Mounting action'.

60 Houlton, *Which? Put to the Test*, p.13; 'A Magnifying Glass on Faults', *Garage and Motor Agent* (13 January 1962); Frayn in *Shopper's Guide* (July 1962), pp.16–17.

61 Richard Hoggart, *A Measured Life: Part 3 – An Imagined Life* (New Brunswick, 1994), p.63; On errors, *Which? 25*, p.38; 'Rover 110', *Which?* (June 1963), p.189.

62 *Which?* (Winter 1958), p.21; CA, 'Notes for CA speakers', p.9; Transcript, interview Alistair Macgeorge, pp.135–137, CAA A13.

63 CA solicitors' note (9 June 1961), National Archives (NA) BT 58/1174.

64 'Is your seat belt strong enough?' *Sunday Times* (15 January 1967); Jennifer Jenkins to Castle (14 December 1966), Goldman to Richard Marsh (Transport Minister, 10 May 1968), Ministry meeting (13 May 1968), Britax telegram (29 May 1968), NA MT 98/734; Transcript telephone conversation Britax-Minstry (n.d. c. May 1968), NA TS 82/111.

65 *Which?* (Winter 1958), p.3; *Which?* (June 1966), p.179; Casper Brook, 'Which? – The catalyst', *The Manager* (July 1961), pp.540–542; Sainsbury in Goldman, 'Art or Science?', p.1; K. Gales, T.M.F. Smith, 'A Pilot Study of the impact of *Which?*' (May 1961), p.11, CAA A27.

66 'The how and why of *Which?*'; Jeremy Mitchell, 'Testing for *Which?* Some Statistical Problems', *Applied Statistics* XII:2 (1963); Casper Brook, 'Research by Consumers', Economics Section, British Association for the Advancement of Science Meeting (1961), CAA A27; *Which?* (March, April 1963).

67 CA Council minutes (14 December 1964); Goldman, 'Increase in Subs' (January 1965) and note (6 January 1965, MAP S322/241.

68 S.S. Bloom, *The Launderette: A History* (London, 1988); C. Booker, *The Neophiliacs* (London, 1969), p.178; D. Sandbrook, *Never Had It So Good* (London, 2005), p.108; H. Carpenter, *That was Satire that was: The Satire Boom of the 1960s* (London, 2000) p.288; L. Adrian, 'The Persuasive Voice', *Spectator* (12 June 1964).

69 John Bloom, *It's No Sin to Make a Profit* (London, 1971), pp.30, 44, 55–81, 132–139, 160–165, 189, 224; 'Bloom at the top', *Time* (13 October 1961).

70 Bloom, *It's No Sin*, pp.182–199, 210; *Sunday Times* (22 March 1964); *Which?* (April 1964); Booker, *Neophiliacs*, p.235; Ralph Harris (IEA), *Times* (22 July 1964); Leslie Adrian, 'Choice Improved', *Spectator* (17 April 1964); 'Trouble in never-never land', *Time* (24 July 1964).

71 *Daily Express* (1 October 1964); James Thomas, *Popular Newspapers, the Labour Party and British Politics* (London, 2005), pp.51–53; Note from PM (31 August 1965), note to PM (23 April 1970), NA PREM 13/3295; B. Levin, *The Pendulum Years* (London, 1970), p.155.

72 V. de Grazia, *Irresistable Empire: America's Advance Through 20th Century Europe* (Cambridge, MA, 2005); D. Horowitz, *The Anxieties of Affluence* (Amherst, MA, 2004); Hilton, *Prosperity for All*, chs.1–2; L. Black, '"Free choice lies at the heart of our economic system": A comparative history of post-war British and American consumer organisations' in I. Theien, E. Lange (eds), *Affluence and Activism* (Oslo, 2004).

73 Transcript (broadcast 14 August 1958); Mark Abrams papers, Box 35; File 'Broadcasts, 1948–62'; Reuel Denney, *The Astonished Muse* (Chicago, 1957).

74 Eugene R. Beem, John S. Ewing, 'Business appraises consumer testing agencies', *Harvard Business Review* (March–April 1954).

75 S. McKellar, '"The Beauty of Stark Utility": Rational consumption in America – *Consumer Reports* 1936–54' in J. Attfield (ed.), *Utility Reassessed: The Role of*

Ethics in the Practice of Design (Manchester, 1999); 'Judgment at Mount Vernon', *Sales Management* (2 April 1965); 'Consumers Union: Feeding advice to hungry customers', *Business Week* (20 March 1954); L. Cohen, *A Consumers' Republic* (New York, 2002), pp.130–131; *Consumer Reports* (April 1962), p.165.

76 Ruby Turner Morris, *CU: Methods, Implications, Weaknesses and Strengths* (New London, CT., 1971), pp.54–56; 'Judgment at Mount Vernon'; Beem, Ewing, 'Business appraises consumer testing'.

77 R. Nader, *Unsafe At Any Speed* (New York, 1965); C. Warne, 'Carrying the economics of dissent into effective action' (1969), Thomas M. Brooks Papers Box 2 File 3 (Brooks 2/3), Consumer Movement Archive; *Focus* (September 1966), p.18.

78 D. Case, 'The Consumer Movement in the 1960s', Amherst College, BA, 1972, p.108, Brooks 2/24; R.D. Putnam, *Bowling Alone: The Collapse and Revival of American Community* (New York, 2000).

79 C. Warne, 'Economic and Social Aspects of Advertising', Advertising Federation of America, 29 May 1961, Brooks, 1/47; 'Judgment at Mount Vernon'; Morris Kaplan, 'Caveat Emptor' (April 1965), p.8, Brooks 2/19.

80 Judgment at Mount Vernon'; *Consumer Reports* (May 1966), p.258; C. Warne, 'Independent Consumer Testing Agency: An International Answer to Brand Name Advertising', Zurich, 27 July 1961, Brooks 1/47.

81 'Memo for the establishment of the Consumers' Foundation' (c.1928), J.C. Dismore to F.J. Schlink (11 July 1927), Michael Young papers (Yung) 6/12/2; E. Roberts, *IOCU, 1960–80* (London, 1981), pp.3, 10.

82 M. Hilton, 'Americanisation, British Consumerism and the International Organisation of Consumers Unions' in M. Kipping, N. Tiratsoo (eds), *Americanisation in 20th Century Europe* (Lille, 2001); C. Beauchamp, 'Getting *Your Money's Worth*: American models for the re-making of the Consumer interest in Britain, 1930s–1960s' in M. Bevir, F. Trentmann (eds), *Critiques of Capital in Modern Britain and America* (Basingstoke, 2002).

83 Notes of Informal Meeting, Mary Adams' House, 20 January 1959, CA Council minutes; Casper Brook, 'The Discriminating Consumer', British Institute of Management Conference (1959), p.15, CAA A27.

84 In CU, *This is Consumers' Union* (New York, 1961), Brooks 2/16.

85 Jim Northcott, *Value for Money? The Case for a Consumers' Advice Service* (London, 1953), pp.3–12.

86 R. Mayer, 'The Entrepreneurial Elite and the Spirit of Consumerism: Finances and Strategy in the US consumer movement' in A. Chatriot, M. Chessel, M. Hilton (eds), *The Expert Consumer* (Aldershot, 2006); Cohen, *Consumers' Republic* p.364; D. Bell, 'Introduction' in Michael Young, *Social Scientist as Innovator* (Cambridge MA, 1983), p.ix; S. Wagg, 'Comedians and Politics in the United States and Great Britain' in S. Wagg (ed.), *Because I tell a Joke or Two: Comedy, Politics and Social Difference* (London, 1998).

87 *Final Report of the Committee on Consumer Protection*, para.388; Thorelli, Thorelli, *Consumer Information*, pp.14–15; on fluoridation, *Consumer News* 7 (December 1963).

88 'Who Reads Which?', p.7; Paper 'C', CA Council minutes (13 September 1959).

89 Houlton, *Which? Put to the Test*, p.13; interview, Northcott, 14 February 2001; Mitchell, 'Results of Questionnaire' (1964), p.12; Gallup Poll, *Which?: Final Report* (May–September 1962), p.2, CAA A14.

90 Crosland, 'The Constitution of CA' (2 January 1964), Anthony Crosland papers, 4/1; Douglas to Young (5 December 1962), CRD 2/8/28; *New Society* (8 August 1968), pp.188–190.

91 CA Council minutes (9 January 1958); Thorelli, Thorelli, *Consumer Information*, p.14; British Association of Consumers (November 1956), CAA A27.
92 Informal Council meeting, Weybridge (14–15 October 1961), p.13; 'Weybridge File', council papers; Rodnight, 'A Small-scale Psychological Survey', p.22; Transcript, interview with MacGeorge, p.133.
93 M. Hilton, 'The polyester-flannelled philanthropists: The Birmingham Consumers group' in L. Black, H. Pemberton (eds), *An Affluent Society?* (Aldershot, 2004); *National Consumer* (Autumn 1964), p.22; *Labour Women's Conference* (1965), p.28.
94 B. Jackson, *Equality and the British Left: A Study in Progressive Thought, 1900–64* (Manchester, 2007), p.172; 'Weybridge File' notes, p.12. Young to Goldman (23 September 1966), Yung 6/12/1.
95 *Good Food Guide* (1965–6), p.6; *Which?* (Aug. 1966), p.259; CA Council minutes (14 December 1964).
96 Report of Rodgers-Brook meeting (16 December 1958), CA Council minutes (5 January 1959).
97 Director's letter 11, CA minutes (9 March 1960); 'Nominations for Ordinary membership', CA Council minutes (12 February 1962).
98 CA Council minutes (7 July, 5 August, 3 November 1958).
99 Correspondence, James Douglas (8 January 2003); John Ramsden, *The Making of Conservative Party Policy: The Conservative Research Department since 1929* (London, 1980), ch.10; Fletcher to Carberry (5 December 1955), CCO 3/4/21; CPC, *Automation and the Consumer* (1956), pp.35–36.
100 Douglas to R. Miller (27 April 1959), CRD 2/8/20; Phillip Goodhart, James Douglas, Patricia Mclaughlin, John Wood, Max Bemrose, Ian MacArthur, *Choice: A Report on Consumer Protection* (CPC, London, 1961).
101 Douglas to Sturges-Jones (24 October 1962), CRD 2/8/28; Douglas to McLaughlin (10 December 1958, 16 February 1959), CRD 2/8/19.
102 Douglas memo (25 November 1963), CRD 2/8/30; Young to Douglas (16 November 1962), CRD 2/8/28.
103 Douglas memo to Mrs. Henry Brooke (January 1959), CRD 2/8/19.
104 Ken Young, 'Orpington and the "Liberal Revival"' in Chris Cook, John Ramsden (eds), *By-Elections in British Politics* (London, 1997), p.171.
105 B. Lancaster, A. Mason (eds), *Life and Labour in a 20th Century City: The Experience of Coventry* (Coventry, 1986), p.358; Peter Goldman, *Some Principles of Conservatism* (CPC, London, 1961), p.2; M. Jarvis, *Conservative Government, Morality and Social Change in Affluent Britain, 1957–64* (Manchester, 2005).
106 L. Adrian, 'RPM is the Shopper's Enemy', *New Outlook: A Liberal Magazine* 21 (July 1963).
107 Helen Mercer, *Constructing a Competitive Order* (Cambridge, 1995), ch.8, pp.164–169; Richard Findley, 'The Conservative Party and Defeat: The Significance of Resale Price Maintenance for the General Election of 1964', *Twentieth Century British History*, 12:3 (2001); *Daily Telegraph* (16 March 1964).
108 Rodgers-Brook meeting (16 December 1958); Young in CA Council minutes (30 July 1962); M. Hilton, 'Consumer Politics in Post-War Britain' in M. Daunton, M. Hilton (eds), *The Politics of Consumption* (Oxford, 2001).
109 Transcript of interviews with Elizabeth Ackroyd, Maurice Healy. CAA, A13, pp.65, 113; 'Weybridge File' notes, pp.1–2; CA, *Evidence Submitted*, pp.15–16; *Final Report of the Committee on Consumer Protection*, para.851; *Which?* (June 1965); CA Council minutes (14 December 1964).

110 *Focus* (January 1971), pp.1, 23–24; (September 1970), p.14; C.A.R. Crosland, *Socialism Now* (London, 1974), p.87; Young to Wilson (3 July 1970), Yung 6/12/1; Thorelli, Thorelli, *Consumer Information*, p.167.

111 Labour Party, *Fair Deal for the Shopper* (London, 1961), p.6.

112 *Labour Woman* (August 1955), pp.128–129; (September 1955), pp.144–145; (November 1955), p.175; (May 1958), p.67; (February 1952), p.264; (May 1955), pp.87–88; Burton (November 1958), pp.60–61.

113 *Labour Women's Conference* (1958), pp.15–17; (1959), p.45; (1963), pp.29–30.

114 Burton to Gaitskell (24 February 1956); Northcott to Gaitskell (15 March 1952), Hugh Gaitskell papers, C10, F8; CA Council minutes (5 January 1959).

115 *Labour Women's Conference* (1970), p.27; Brook in RICA, *British Co-operatives: A Consumers' Movement* (London, 1964), pp.3, 31–32.

116 'When will the consumer wake up?', *Planning* 89 (29 December 1936), p.2; 'The Outlook for Consumers', *Planning* 63 (3 December 1935), p.3; 'Consumer Protection and Enlightenment', *Planning* 441 (25 April 1960).

117 Labour Party, *Let Us Win Through Together* (1950); *A New Hope for Britain* (1983); L. Freedman, G. Hemingway, *Nationalisation and the Consumer* (London, 1950), p.3; Labour Party Research Department, R.176, 'Consumer Advisory Service' (Nov. 1952).

118 Michael Young, *Small Man, Big World: A Discussion of Socialist Democracy* (London, 1949), p.9; Jeremy Mitchell, 'A Triptych of Organisations: CA, SSRC, NCC' in Geoff Dench, Tony Flower, Kate Gavron (eds), *Young at Eighty: The Prolific Public Life of Michael Young* (Manchester, 1995), p.10; Edward Shils, 'On the Eve', *Twentieth Century* (May 1960), p.452; CA salary documents, MAP, S322/241.

119 Young to Goldman (10 June 1970), Yung 6/12/1; Young, *Chipped White Cups*, pp.19–20; Trevor Smith, Alison Young, 'Politics and Michael Young' in Dench *et al.*, *Young at Eighty*, p.138.

120 'Customers Write … Shop Assistants Write', *Which?* (November 1967), pp.356–357.

121 *Which?* (October 1967), pp.292–293 Liberal Party, *Shopping: Better Buys* (London, 1961), *Consumer Protection* (1962); Labour, *Fair Deal*; Phillip Goodhart *et. al.*, *Choice*; M. Haynes, *Advertising on Trial: The Case for the Consumer* (Bow Group, London, 1961).

122 'The next ten years', Yung 3/1/1; 'Proceedings of Consumer Assembly', pp.34, 38.

123 Young to Abrams (24 January 1969), Yung 5/1/1; 'The New Radicalism' (25 April 1969), pp.1–2; *Social Reform in the Centrifugal Society* (New Society pamphlet, 1969), Yung 2/1/4. Besides Young, Paul Barker, Peter Wilmott and Peter Hall were 'Open Group' members.

124 Report of IOCU 3rd Conference (Oslo, June 1964), pp.133–137, CAA A21.

125 M. Young, 'The Future of Consumer Affluence' (1970), Yung 6/12/1; 'Why acquisitiveness?' (1962), Yung 3/2/4/5; Young, Wilmott, 'Does Advertising Influence People?' (1968), Yung 2/1/4.

126 Young, 'The Future of Consumer Affluence'.

127 Young to Roberts (7 July, 20 October 1970); Roberts to Young (14 July 1970); Roberts to Norman Lee (1 October 1970), Yung 6/12/1.

128 J. Southworth, 'The Wastemakers', *Focus* (April 1970), pp.2–7; 'Rubbish', *Consumer News* 24 (May 1965).

129 See C. McLarney, E. Chung, 'Post-materialism's "silent revolution" in consumer research', *Marketing Intelligence and Planning* 17:6 (1999).

130 S. Majima, M. Savage, 'Have there been culture shifts in Britain? A critical encounter with Ronald Inglehart', *Cultural Sociology* 1:3 (2007).

Chapter 3

1 *Co-operative Consumer* (January 1956), p.12.
2 'Introduction' in L. Black, N. Robertson (eds), *Taking Stock: Consumerism and the Co-operative Movement in Modern British History* (Manchester, 2009); I. Zweiniger-Bargielowska, *Austerity in Britain* (Oxford, 2000).
3 Elizabeth Gundrey, *Your Money's Worth: A Handbook for Consumers* (Harmondsworth, 1962), p.20.
4 Co-op Union, *Consumer Protection: A Memorandum submitted by the Co-operative Union Ltd. to the Molony Committee* (Manchester, 1960), p.3; Research Institute for Consumer Affairs (RICA), *British Co-operatives: A Consumer's Movement?* (London, 1964), pp.7, 20–21.
5 RICA, *British Co-operatives*, pp.5, 14, 26; C.A.R. Crosland, *A Critical Commentary on Co-operative Progress* (Manchester, 1971), p.1; S. Pollard, *The Co-operatives at the Crossroads* (Fabian Research Series 245, London, 1965), pp.12–15, 25; D. Russell, *Looking North: Northern England and the National Imagination* (Manchester, 2004)
6 S. O'Connell, *Credit and Community: Working-class Debt in the UK Since 1880* (Oxford, 2009), ch.6.
7 P. Gurney, 'The Battle of the Consumer in Postwar Britain', *Journal of Modern History* 77:4 (2005), pp.976, 962, 982; John K. Walton, 'The post-war decline of the British retail co-operative movement' in Black, Robertson, *Taking Stock*.
8 D. Nell, A. Alexander, G. Shaw, A. Bailey, 'Investigating Shopper Narratives of the Supermarket in Post-War England, 1945–75', *Oral History* 37:1 (2009); R. Millar, *The Affluent Sheep* (London, 1963), p.107.
9 M. Hilton, *Consumerism in Twentieth Century Britain* (Cambridge, 2003), p.170; H. Mercer, *Constructing a Competitive Order* (Cambridge, 1995); Gurney, 'The Battle of the Consumer', p.984.
10 J. Bailey, *The British Co-operative Movement* (London, 1955); Sir William Richardson, *The Co-operative Wholesale Society in War and Peace 1938–76* (Manchester, 1977), p.199.
11 J.A. Hough, F. Lambert, *Self-Service Shops* (Manchester, n.d., c.1951), pp.10, 13, 15.
12 *Co-operative Consumer* (January 1956), p.12; CIC minutes (22 December 1955, 26 October 1956), Hugh Gaitskell papers (Gaitskell), C309/1; Crosland (9 February 1956), R. Southern (29 October 1956), Sainsbury (11 October 1956) to Gaitskell, C309/3.
13 Walton, 'The post-war decline of the British retail co-operative movement'; 'Co-operative First Principles' (28 February 1956), pp.3–7, Anthony Crosland papers (Crosland), 14/1.
14 'Structure of the Movement' (n.d.), Crosland 14/1; J.A. Banks, G. Ostergaard, *Co-operative Democracy* (Co-op College paper 2, 1955); RICA, *British Co-operatives*, p.18. Jeffreys (27 April 1956), Gaitskell C309/2.
15 *Co-operative Independent Commission Report* (Manchester, 1958), pp.17, 61, 67–68, 249; RICA, *British Co-operatives*, p.27.
16 *CIC Report*, pp.45–46, 238; Liverpool Society visit report, Vis/Carc/24, Crosland 14/1.
17 RICA, *British Co-operatives*, p.35; A. Bonner, *British Co-operation* (Manchester, 1970), p.260; Letter to Crosland (2 November 1956) and 'CWS Retail Society', Crosland 14/1; CIC minutes (15 March 1957), Gaitskell C309/1.
18 Vis/Carc/2–4, 9, 14, 21, 24, Crosland 14/1.

19 Vis/Carc/12, 19, Crosland 14/1.

20 *CIC Report*, pp.44–49; Anon (28 November 1955), Elizabeth Wilson (31 January 1956) to Gaitskell, Gaitskell C309/3.

21 Mass Observation, Topic Collection 21/F, G, E (1947); Gurney, 'The battle of the consumer', pp.962, 982; J.T. Murray to C.A.R. Crosland (7 March 1957), Gaitskell C309/3; 'Co-operative first principles', p.10.

22 'Co-operative First/Four Principle's', Crosland 14/1; *CIC Report*, pp.24, 49–50.

23 *CIC Report*, pp.235–253, 244, 246.

24 J. Birchall, *Co-op: The People's Business* (Manchester, 1994), p.153; Pollard, *Co-operatives at the Crossroads*, p.8; *Co-operative News* (3 November 1956, 7 April 1956); L. Cohen, 'The Future of the Co-ops', *Trading Interest* (n.d., c. June 1958) pp.17–23, Crosland 14/2; *Times* (20 September 1958).

25 A. Perkins, 'First Impressions of the Commission's Report', *The Bulletin* (Co-Op Educational Secretaries Association, July 1958), p.11; 'Bouquets for Capitalism', *Sunday Times* (13 July 1958); 'Co-Operator's Choice', *Socialist Commentary* (June 1958), pp.2–3; *Daily Worker* (21 May 1958).

26 'Can the Co-ops compete?, *Economist* (10 May 1958); R. Millar, 'Why should Co-ops ape the capitalists?' *Tribune* (May 9 1958).

27 *Co-operative News* (31 May 1958); Oram to Gaitskell (29 July, 13 September 1958), Gaitskell C309/3; R. Millar, 'A Blueprint for Co-Ops of the future?', *Tribune* (2 May 1958); Gaitskell to R. Southern (7 November 1958), Gaitskell C309/3; Crosland, 'I disagree with the Central Executive', *Scottish Co-operator* (8 November 1958).

28 *Report of Proceedings Special National Congress, Blackpool* (Manchester, 1958), pp.19–33, 43–65, 69–74, 84–96.

29 *Report of Action by the Central Executive on Resolutions of the Special National Congress* (Manchester, 1959), pp.13–17; *Co-operative News* (28 February, 6 June 1959).

30 *Report of the CRDS Negotiating Committee* (Manchester, 1960); Central Executive statement (9 May 1960), leaflet *The Co-ops must fight back*, Mark Abrams papers (Abrams), Box 82, File 'CRDS, 1959–60'; PEP, 'Consumer Protection and Enlightenment', *Planning* XXVI:441 (1960), p.122.

31 Co-op Union, *Consumer Protection*, p.14; D. Ainley, *The Co-ops: The Way Ahead* (London, 1962) p.2.

32 R. Hattersley, 'New Blood' in G. Kaufman (ed.), *The Left* (London, 1966), p.152; 'Choice Improved', *Spectator* (17 April 1964).

33 RICA, *British Co-operatives*, pp.29–30; N. Hewitt, 'Some causes of Co-op failure', *Agenda* XI:3 (1962).

34 Bonner, *British Co-operation*, p.249; 'Woo your customers', *Labour Woman* (July 1960), pp.83–84; PEP, 'Consumer Protection', p.122.

35 Bonner, *British Co-operation*, p.260; S. Schwarzkopf, 'The co-operative movement and the making of British advertising and marketing culture' in Black, Robertson, *Taking Stock*; Gurney, 'The Battle of the Consumer', pp.969–971; A. Burton, *The British Consumer Co-operative Movement and Film 1890s–1960s* (Manchester, 2005), pp.224–228.

36 L. Whitworth, 'Promoting product quality: The Co-op and the Council of Industrial Design' in Black, Robertson, *Taking Stock* (Manchester, 2009); J. Woodham, 'An episode in post-utility design management: The Council of Industrial Design and the Co-operative Wholesale Society' in J. Attfield (ed.), *Utility Reassessed* (Manchester, 1999); Forsyth in RICA, *British Co-operatives*, pp.30–36.

37 London Press Exchange, 'Self-Service in the UK' (10 September 1957), Abrams 81, 'Retail Trade I'; G. Shaw, A. Alexander, 'British Co-operative Societies as retail innovators: Interpreting the early stages of the self-service revolution', *Business History* 50:1 (2008), pp.62–78; G. Shaw, L. Curth, A. Alexander, 'Selling Self-Service and the Supermarket: The Americanisation of Food Retailing in Britain, 1945–60', *Business History* 46:4 (2004); idem., 'Streamlining Shopping', *History Today* November 2002, pp.34–35.

38 Bonner, *British Co-operation*, pp.248, 250; Leonard M. Harris, 'Mass Observation Ltd'., *Buyer's Market* (London, 1963), p.31.

39 *Self-Service and Supermarket* 8:4 (April 1959), p.46; R. Towsey, *Self-Service Retailing* (London, 1964), p.186; L.A. Cherriman, R. Wilson, *The Operation of a Self-Service Store* (Co-op College papers no.9, 1962); Hough, Lambert, *Self-Service Shops*, p.13.

40 Towsey, *Self-Service Retailing*, pp.19–22, 167; G. Shaw, A. Alexander, 'Interlocking Directorates and the Knowledge Transfer of Supermarket Retail Techniques from North America to Britain', *International Review of Retail, Distribution and Consumer Research* 16:3 (2006), pp.375–394.

41 Correspondence from Alf Morris MP to Wilson; Peddie to Wilson (3 February 1967); Richardson to Jenkins (31 December 1966); Kaufman to Wilson (16 January 1967), Harold Wilson papers (Wilson) c.889; Stuart Holland to Joseph Winter (13 November 1967), Wilson c.895.

42 R. Williams, 'Working-class culture', *Universities and Left Review* 1:1 (1957), pp.29–32.

43 A.H. Halsey, G.N. Ostergaard, *Power in Co-operatives: The Internal Politics of British Retail Societies* (Oxford, 1965), pp.70–78, 94–95, ch.3; PEP, *Consumer Protection*, p.122; *Co-operative News* (7 May 1960, 4 January 1964).

44 *Special National Congress*, p.36; Crossman in G. Hodgkinson, *Sent to Coventry* (Oxford, 1970), p.xxvii; PEP, 'Consumer Protection', p.123.

45 RICA, *British Co-operatives*, pp.15–16; W. Ryrie to Chancellor (Anthony Barber, 20 October 1970) and S. Musson (Chief Registrar of Friendly Societies) to B.E. Fensome (Treasury, 2 February 1971), National Archive, NA), T326/1303; *CIC Report*, 168–173, 248–249; *Guardian* (28 May 1971).

46 Gurney, 'The Battle of the Consumer', p.963; J. Gorman, *Knocking Down Ginger* (London, 1995), p.87; CIC meeting minutes (17 March 1957) and R. Southern to Morgan Phillips (17 July, 10 December 1957), Wilson c.1297; I. Jennings, *Party Politics vol.II* (Cambridge, 1961), p.362.

47 Royal Arsenal (Vis/Carc/2), Crosland 14/1; CWS Market Research Department, *Survey among new members of the Manchester and Salford Society* (February 1958), pp.3–7, Gaitskell C309/6.

48 Birchall, *People's Business*, pp.147, 159.

49 F.A. Wells, M.D. Skillicorn, J.R. Straker, *Recruitment, Selection and Training for Management in Retail Co-operative Societies* (Co-op College papers no.10, 1963).

50 L. Harrison, J. Roper, *Towards Regional Co-operatives* (Fabian Research Series 260, 1967).

51 Rhodes in RICA, *British Co-operatives*, pp.19–28.

52 S. Pollard, 'Tradition versus Efficiency', *Socialist Commentary* (July 1958); *Co-operatives at the Crossroads*, pp.5, 12–15, 21, 28, 34, 39; Henry and Lillian Stephenson, *Eating, Sleeping and Living: A Guide to Design in the Home* (Manchester, 1964).

53 Brook in RICA, *British Co-operatives*, pp.31–36; L. Tivey, 'The Politics of the Consumer', *Political Quarterly* 39:2 (1968), pp.181–185.

54 F.D. Boggis, 'Which? Way', *Co-op Party Monthly Newsletter* (September 1963), p.53; Co-op Union, *Consumer Protection*, pp.12–13.

55 Harris, *Buyer's Market*, p.53; Millar, *The Affluent Sheep*, pp.194–196; Crosland in Eirlys Roberts, 'CA's part in the design of Products' (29 June 1966), CAA A27; Bonner, *British Co-operation*, p.249.

56 J. Douglas to Casper Brook (16 February 1959), Conservative Party Archive, CRD 2/8/19; Transcript, interview with Goldman, p.2, CAA A26.

57 Harris, *Buyer's Market*, p.53; Crosland, 'The Constitution of CA' (21 January 1964), Crosland, 4/1; C.A.R. Crosland, *The Conservative Enemy* (London, 1962), p.65; Tivey, 'Politics of the Consumer', p.185; L. Black, *'Which?* craft in post-war Britain: The Consumers' Association and the politics of affluence', *Albion* 36:1 (2004), pp.70–71.

58 Kevin Jeffreys, *Anthony Crosland: A New Biography* (London, 1999), pp.64–65; F. Inglis, *Radical Earnestness* (Oxford, 1982), pp.140, 145–146; Co-op Union accountancy department to Gaitskell (1 December 1956), Gaitskell C309/3.

59 Crosland's 1957 diary, courtesy of Susan Crosland (4 May 2008); Susan Crosland, *Tony Crosland* (London, 1983), pp.88, 90, 46; David Reisman, *Anthony Crosland: The Mixed Economy* (Basingstoke, 1997), p.16.

60 Catherine Ellis, 'Total Abstinence and a Good Filing-System? Anthony Crosland and the Affluent Society' in L. Black, H. Pemberton (eds), *An Affluent Society?* (Aldershot, 2004); Crosland on Yamey in *Cartel* 4:2 (April 1954) and 'Curbing the trade associations', *New Statesman* (9 July 1955); on Yamey and Co-op influences on legislation limiting RPM in 1956 and 1964, Mercer, *Constructing a competitive order*, pp.153–168; Riesman, *Mixed Economy*, pp.168–169; Jeremy Nuttall, *Psychological Socialism: The Labour Party and Qualities of Mind and Character, 1931 to the Present* (Manchester, 2006).

61 Hilton, *Consumerism*, pp.270–276; Ben Jackson, *Equality and the British Left: A Study in Progressive Thought, 1900–64* (Manchester, 2007), p.194.

62 Crosland, *Conservative Enemy*, p.66; A.W. Benn, *Against the Tide: Diaries 1973–76* (London, 1989), p.576.

63 Jeffreys, *Anthony Crosland*, p.168; Reisman, *Mixed Economy*, pp.184–185; Crosland in 'Proceedings of Consumer Assembly', London (3 November 1967), p.18. CAA A67; Eirlys Roberts, *Which? 25: Consumers' Association 1957–82* (London, 1982), p.59.

64 Crosland, *Conservative Enemy*, pp.62–67, 125, 146, 158; C.A.R. Crosland, *Socialism Now* (London, 1974), pp.72, 78–79.

65 Crosland, *The Conservative Enemy*, p.66; M. Young, 'Crosland and Socialism' in D. Leonard (ed.), *Crosland and New Labour* (Basingstoke, 1999), p.50.

66 Crosland, *Socialism Now*, pp.72, 88; S. Fielding, *Labour and Cultural Change 1964–70* (Manchester, 2003), ch.8; on the latter, M. Kenny, *The Politics of Identity* (Cambridge, 2004).

67 Reisman, *The Mixed Economy*, p.16; Crosland, *The Future of Socialism*, p.494.

68 Nuttall, *Psychological Socialism*, p.52.

69 Crosland, 'Co-operative First principles', p.7; *CIC Report*, p.17.

70 Crosland, *The Future of Socialism*, pp.341–342; Jackson, *Equality and the British Left*, pp.192–193.

71 *A Social Democratic Britain* (Fabian Tract 404, 1971) in Crosland, *Socialism Now*, pp.87–91.

72 Crosland, *Critical Commentary*, pp.1–9.

73 *Times* (17 February 1971).

74 'Summary of Objections' (21 July 1969), notes of No.10 meetings (21 July 1969, 22 June 1966), NA PREM 13/2857; on SET, H. Pemberton, *Policy Learning and British Governance in the 1960s* (Basingstoke, 2004), pp.166–168.

75 *Platform* (Co-op Party paper) 11 (Aug–Sept 1966); Sittingbourne Co-op to Wilson (16 May 1966), Wilson, c.1298; T.E. Graham memo to Co-op Parliamentary Group (17 April 1969), NA PREM 13/2857.
76 Notes of No.10 meetings (21 July 1969, 22 June 1966), NA PREM 13/2857; 'The Co-operative Union' (17 July 1969), NA PREM 13/2857; *Financial Times* (12 February 1971).
77 *The Future of the Co-operative Movement* in *New Statesman* (30 October 2000), p.3.
78 Gurney, 'The Battle of the Consumer', p.959.
79 R. Turner Morris, *CU: Methods, Implications, Weaknesses, Strengths* (New London, CT., 1971), p.53.

Chapter 4

1 *Rightway* 1 (Autumn 1954), p.8, Conservative Party Archive, Pub144/4; 'Young Conservatives History' (c. 1954), CCO 506/17/2.
2 BBC TV, *Hancock* 'The Blood Donor' (23 June 1961); Milicent Stephenson, 'Now Hear this', *Impact* (Spring 1964), pp.24–25; 'YCCS – Community Service', *Impact* (Summer 1967), p.17, Pub144/4.
3 Dominic Sandbrook, *Never Had It So Good: Britain in the Fifties* (London, 2005); Peter Hennessy, *Having It So Good: Britain in the Fifties* (London, 2006); Bill Osgerby, *Youth in Britain since 1945* (Oxford, 1998).
4 Catherine Ellis, 'No hammock for the idle: the Conservative Party, "Youth" and the welfare state in the 1960s', *Twentieth Century British History* 16:4 (2005), pp.441–470.
5 I. Jennings, *Party Politics Vol. I: Appeal to the People* (Cambridge, 1960) pp.179, 212 reports the higher figure. Catherine Ellis, 'The Younger Generation: The Labour Party and the 1959 Youth Commission', *Journal of British Studies* 41:2 (2002).
6 P. Whiteley, P. Seyd, J. Richardson, *True Blues: The Politics of Conservative Party Membership* (Oxford, 1994), pp.42–43, 228; David Jarvis, '"Behind every great party": Women and Conservatism in twentieth-century Britain' in A. Vickery (ed.), *Women, Privilege and Power* (Stanford, CA 2001), p.289.
7 Richard Crossman, Labour MP in *YC and Unionist Organization* (June 1959), CCO 4/8/389; N. McCrillis, *The British Conservative Party in the Age of Universal Suffrage, 1918–29* (Columbus, Oh., 1998), ch.3; M. Pugh, 'Popular Conservatism in Britain: Continuity and Change, 1880–1987', *Journal of British Studies* 27:3 (1988), pp.259, 263.
8 John Holroyd-Doveton, *Young Conservatives: A History of the Young Conservative Movement* (Bishop Auckland, 1996); Timothy Evans, *Conservative Radicalism: A Sociology of Conservative Party Youth Structures and Libertarianism, 1970–92* (Oxford, 1996).
9 Jo-Anne Nadler, *Too Nice to be a Tory* (London, 2004), pp.46–64.
10 E.H.H. Green, *Ideologies of Conservatism* (Oxford, 2002), pp.281–283, 1–17; M. Oakeshott, 'On being Conservative' (1956) in *Rationalism in Politics and Other Essays* (London, 1967), p.168; R. McKibbin, *Classes and Cultures: England 1918–51* (Oxford, 1998), p.98; Leon D. Epstein, 'The politics of British Conservatism', *American Political Science Review* 48 (1954), pp.27–28; B. Harrison, *Seeking a Role: The United Kingdom, 1951–70* (Oxford, 2009), p.438.
11 R. Samuel, *The Lost World of British Communism* (London, 2007); L. Black, 'The Lost World of Young Conservatism', *Historical Journal* 51:4 (2008).

12 See D. Jarvis, 'The shaping of Conservative electoral hegemony, 1918–39' in J. Lawrence, M. Taylor (eds), *Party, State and Society* (Aldershot, 1997), pp.132–135; A. Light, *Forever England: Femininity, Literature and Conservatism between the Wars* (London, 1991), pp.14–16; S. Fielding, 'Looking for the new political history', *Journal of Contemporary History* 42:3 (2007).

13 M. Jarvis, *Conservative Governments, Morality and Social Change in Affluent Britain, 1957–64* (Manchester, 2005); Green, *Ideologies*; P. Williamson, *Stanley Baldwin: Conservative Leadership and National Values* (Cambridge, 1999); M. Francis, 'Tears, Tantrums and bared teeth: The emotional economy of three Conservative prime ministers, 1951–63', *Journal of British Studies* 41:3 (2002).

14 M. Francis, I. Zweiniger-Bargielowska (eds), *The Conservatives and British Society 1880–1990* (Cardiff, 1996); S. Ball, I. Holliday (eds), *Mass Conservatism* (London, 2002).

15 Philip Abrams, Alan Little, 'The Young Activist in British Politics', *British Journal of Sociology* 16 (December 1965), p.319; A. Povey, 'A Fremlin's View of the YCs', *Looking Right* (Autumn 1969), p.25, Birmingham Central Library (BCL).

16 *Looking Right* (July 1967), p.17; (March 1966), p.34; Templedown branch programme April–June 1961, CPA CCO 4/8/389; *Rightway* 11 (Summer 1958), pp.3–4.

17 *Buff Orpington* (January 1956), p.15, British Library (BL); Oakeshott, 'On being Conservative', p.169.

18 W.D. Hayne, 'The belief of a conservative', *Buff Orpington* (January 1956), pp.6–7; Nick Crowson, *The Conservative Party and European Integration Since 1945* (London, 2007), p.122; Viscount Hailsham, *The Conservative Case* (Harmondsworth, 1959), p.16; B. Crick, *In Defence of Politics* (Harmondsworth, 1962, 1976 edition), p.111.

19 D. Walder, 'Young Conservative Identikit', *Crossbow* (November–December 1967), p.26; N. Stevenson (ed.), *Trust the People: Selected Essays and Speeches of Peter Walker* (London, 1987), pp.11, 47.

20 Abrams, Little, 'The Young Activist', pp.317, 319; *Looking Right*, 1959 YC handbook, BCL; 'The Young Britons' (n.d. c. 1960), and memo (23 May 1962), CCO 506/8/2; Jennings, *Party Politics I*, p.214.

21 Swinton YC course 'Methods of Recruiting' (19–21 February 1960), CCO 4/8/389; P. Bailey, 'Cockroaches Beware!', *Rightway* 1 (Autumn 1954), pp.2, 4 (Autumn 1955), p.2.

22 R. Northam, 'Those things for which we fight', Swinton YC course (18–20 April 1958), CCO 4/8/391; Eldon Griffiths, 'The Search for Higher Standards', *Impact* (Spring 1966), pp.26–27; J.S. Gummer, 'RIP–CND', *Impact* (Spring 1964).

23 *Rightway* 10 (Autumn 1957), p.4; Nadler, *Too Nice to be a Tory*, pp.18, 25; *Looking Right* (Autumn 1969), pp.17–18; (October 1966), p.34.

24 David Walder, *The Short List* (London, 1964), p.33; Milicent Stephenson, 'Now Hear this', *Impact* (Spring 1964), pp.24–25.

25 Ellis, 'No hammock', pp.446–447, 469; South-West Area YCs, *The By-Pass People: A Report on Tourism and Communications in the South-West* (1967), CCO 20/47/2; Green, *Ideologies*, pp.286–290, ch.9.

26 Epstein, 'Politics of British Conservatism', p.41; East Midlands Area YCs Executive Committee minutes (4 November 1956, 24 January 1959), ARE5/16/1, (27 February 1963), ARE5/16/2; South East Area minutes (2 March 1955), ARE9/16/2; *Impact* (Spring 1966), pp.17–18; (Summer 1967), p.13.

27 Holroyd-Doveton, *Young Conservatives*, pp.144, 157. As put by Geoffrey Johnson-Smith, Conservative Party Vice-Chair, *Impact* (Winter–Spring, 1968–69), p.9.

28 Abrams, Little, 'The Young Activist', pp.318–319; Correspondence Josephine Smith (Birmingham, 31 August 2006); Nadler, *Too Nice to be a Tory*, pp.19, 27–28.

29 'Camulodunum MCMLXV', *Impact* (February 1965), p.11; E. Wilson, 'All the Rage', *New Socialist* (November/December 1983), p.26; National YCs Advisory Committee minutes (9 January 1960), CCO 506/19/6; GLYC's *Glance* (December 1966), CCO 20/47/2.

30 *Rightway* 6 (Spring 1956), p.3; *Rightway* 2 (New Year 1955), p.5; *Rightway* 12 (Autumn 1958), p.6.

31 Transport Bill Press release (9 February 1968), CCO 20/47/3; Peter Walker, *Transport Policy* (London, 1968); National Advisory Committee minutes (1 July 1967), CCO 506/19/6; *Impact* (Spring 1966), p.6.

32 Peter Barwell (Birmingham, correspondence, 6 September 2006); *Looking Right* 1959 YC handbook, pp.11, 14; 1960 handbook, Barwell in *Looking Right* (January 1961), p.15; (October 1963), p.19.

33 Birmingham YCs Annual report, 1963 in Central Council minutes, BCL. *Looking Right* (Winter 1968), p.25; *Looking Right* 1959 YC handbook, p.18; (January 1961), p.13.

34 *Impact* (February 1965), p.3; Zig Layton-Henry, 'The Young Conservatives, 1945–70', *Journal of Contemporary History* 8 (1970), p.148; 'Sally Joins the YCs', *Rightway* 7 (October 1956), pp.6–7; David Jarvis, '"Mrs. Maggs and Betty": The Conservative appeal to women voters in the 1920s', *Twentieth Century British History* 5 (1994).

35 Swinton YC leadership course programmes (February 1960, April 1958), CCO 4/8/389, 391.

36 Layton-Henry, 'The Young Conservatives', p.148; Young Conservative and Unionist Organisation, *The Macleod Report 1965* (London, 1965), p.5; *Looking Right* (Summer 1969), p.31.

37 Walder, 'Young Conservative Identikit', pp.24–26; *Looking Right* (Summer 1969), pp.17–18.

38 Correspondence, Richard Tomlinson (Birmingham, 29 August 2006); Epstein, 'Politics of British Conservatism', p.41; Peter Walker, *Staying Power* (London, 1991), p.55; Abrams, Little, 'The Young Activist', p.328.

39 A. Clark, *Mrs Thatcher's Minister* (New York, 1994), p.162; *Trend* (Summer 1964), pp.8–9 (BL).

40 *Looking Right* (Autumn 1969), p.18; correspondence, John Wood, Rushcliffe YCs (6 September 2006).

41 J. Lawrence, 'Class and gender in the making of urban Toryism, 1880–1914', *English Historical Review* CVIII:428 (1993); G. Eley, *Forging Democracy* (Oxford, 2002), ch.22; J. Green, *Days in the Life: Voices from the English Underground 1961–71* (London, 1988), p.418.

42 Editorial minutes (16 April 1964), CCO 506/18/2; correspondence, Juliet Gardiner (10 November 2006); Holyroyd-Doveton, *Young Conservatives*, pp.154–155; Young Conservatives, *Action '67 Rally Programme* (1967).

43 A. Driscoll, 'Birdwatching', *Roundabout Rushcliffe* 2 (1 May 1966), p.16; *Blue Horizon* (Lowestoft) (December 1969), p.25 (BL); *Rightway* 9 (Summer 1957), p.8; Jarvis, 'Behind every great party', p.304.

44 Beatrix Campbell, *The Iron Ladies* (London, 1987), pp.1, 265; G.E. Maguire, *Conservative Women* (Basingstoke, 1998), p.163; Povey, 'A Fremlin's View',

p.25; Juliet Gardiner, 'Votes for Women', *Impact* (Spring–Summer 1968), p.21.

45 *Times*, 18 September 1964; Julian Critchley, *A Bag of Boiled Sweets* (London, 1995), pp.32–33; Correspondence, Gerald Blackburn (Birmingham, 30 August 2006); *Buff Orpington* (January 1956), p.14; 'They're Better in the North', *Impact* (Winter 1967–68), p.24; *Looking Right* (October 1966), p.34.

46 *Roundabout Rushcliffe* 4 (5 September 1966), p.4; *Progress* 6:1 (Spring 1965), p.22; Peter Fryer, *Mrs Grundy: Studies in English Prudery* (London, 1965), p.283; *Crossbow* (October–December 1967).

47 'Miss YC 1964', CCO 506/17/1; *Impact* (Spring–Summer 1968), p.30; compare *Looking Right* (Spring 1968), p.34 with (September 1971), p.27; (March 1966), p.32; (July 1963), p.24.

48 Rally, CCO 4/8/389; *Rightway* 12 (with *Popular Pictorial*, Autumn 1958), pp.12; 10 (Autumn 1957); 11 (Summer 1958), p.6.

49 Circular to YC Area Organizers (3 August 1962), CCO 4/9/489; National Advisory Committee Area Reports (7 December 1963), CCO 4/9/489; National Advisory Committee minutes (10 June, 1 July 1967), CCO 506/19/6; Mary Dutton (Area YC organizer, Wales and Monmouthshire) to Tony Durant (3 February 1964); Margaret Fundell to Durant (10 February 1964), CCO 506/17/1.

50 *Rightway* 5 (New Year 1956), p.6; (Spring 1956), p.5; *Trend* (Winter 1965–66), p.13; J. Gardiner, 'The world of women's magazines', *Impact* (Winter–Spring 1968–69), pp.12–13; C. Rose, 'Clothestrophobia', *Progress* 6:2 (1965), pp.38–39.

51 *New Statesman* (28 February 1964).

52 *Looking Right* (Winter 1969), p.37; Shaw, interview, 6 February 2007; Harrison, *Seeking a Role*, p.438.

53 'Report on Immigration' in Birmingham YC Central Council minutes (7 July 1965), BCL; David Atkinson, '20000 miles through 36 countries', *Impact* (Spring–Summer 1968), p.26; Layton-Henry, 'Young Conservatives', p.151; Crowson, *Conservative Party*, p.123.

54 *Rushcliffe Roundabout* 2 (1 May 1966), pp.6–7; *Rushcliffe Roundabout* 5 (8 November 1966), pp.14–15; *Trend* (Summer 1964).

55 Oakeshott, 'On being Conservative', p.169; Correspondence, Richard Tomlinson; East Midlands Area YC minutes (22 February 1952), ARE5/16/1; Walder, *Short List*, pp.153–154; Layton-Henry, 'The Young Conservatives', p.147; E. Heath, *The Course of my Life* (London, 1999), p.126; *Looking Right* (March 1966), p.36.

56 Holroyd-Doveton, *Young Conservatives*, p.156; Iris Harvey, 'Have we Young Conservatives any opposition?' *Swinton College Journal* 3:2 (December 1954); Walder, *Short List*, pp.87, 120.

57 *Impact* (Winter–Spring 1968/69), p.9; Gabriel A. Almond, Sidney Verba, *The Civic Culture* (London, 1989 (1963)), pp.97–101; Tony Shaw, interview, 6 February 2007; Eileen Atherton, correspondence (Nottingham, 21 October 2006); *Looking Right* (July 1967), p.32.

58 Raphael Samuel, 'Lost World of British Communism', *New Left Review*, 154 (1985), p.10; *Challenge* (8 October 1955); (February 1968), p.11; M. Waite, 'Sex, drugs and rock n' roll (and Communism)' in G. Andrews, N. Fishman, K. Morgan (eds), *Opening the Books: Essays on the Social and Cultural History of the British Communist Party* (London, 1995), p.216.

59 Alan Birch, *Small Town Politics* (Oxford, 1959), pp.76–77; E.P. Thompson, 'The New Left', *New Reasoner* 9 (Summer 1959), p.2; Gaitskell in *Looking Right* (January 1963), p.22; Jennings, *Party Politics I*, pp.215–221.

60 Ray Gosling, *Lady Albemarle's Boys* (London, 1961), p.16; *Lady Albemarle's Boys* 6. A. Jackson, 'Labour as Leisure: The *Mirror* and DIY Sailors', *Journal of Design History* 19 (2006).

61 *Times*, 20 April 1959; John Vaizey, 'Idealism and the Young', *Observer*, 29 November 1959.

62 *Trend* (Winter 1965–66), p.1; *Impact* (Spring 1964), p.2; (Spring 1965), pp.26–27. National Advisory Committee Minutes (13 June 1964), CCO 506/19/6.

63 Graham Dowson, 'The Product – Politics', *Impact* (Summer 1967), pp.9–11; Birmingham YCs General Purposes committee minutes (19 May 1958), BCL.

64 Abrams, Little, 'The Young Activist', p.318; Broadcasts in CCO 4/8/390; R. Worley, 'The Unhidden Persuaders', *Progress* 6:2 (Summer 1965), pp.10–11.

65 *Rightway* 7 (October 1956), pp.7–8; *Rightway* 6 (Spring 1956), p.5; *Rightway* 8 (Winter 1957), pp.7–8; *Rightway* 10 (Autumn 1957), p.7; *Rightway* 11 (Summer 1958), p.3; *Rightway* 12 (Autumn 1958), p.12; Moss, correspondence (7 February 2006).

66 National Advisory Committee minutes (9 January 1960), CCO 506/19/6; Ted Dexter, 'Cricket in mind', *Impact* (Spring 1964).

67 Holyroyd-Doveton, *Young Conservatives*, pp.50, 152; Walder, *Short List*, p.99; South East Area YC Advisory Committee minutes (30 April 1955), ARE9/16/2.

68 South East Area YC Advisory Committee minutes (13 April 1954), ARE9/16/1; 'Buxton 1966' *Roundabout Rushcliffe* 6 (16 December 1966), pp.14–15; *The Whip* (April 1958), p.4 (BL).

69 Membership figures (27 July 1967), CCO 20/47/2; Holyroyd-Doveton, *Young Conservatives*, p.61; V. Jennings, 'Policy-makers amid the party-goers', *Looking Right* (September 1965), p.31; *Macleod Report*, pp.4–7, 13, 26; on the Young Britons, Viscountess Davidson's Letter (8 October 1965), CCO 506/8/4.

70 'Review of the YC Movement', pp.2–4, East Midlands Area EC minutes (27 March 1965), ARE5/16/2.

71 See Hera Cook, 'No turning back: family forms and sexual mores in modern Britain', http://www.historyandpolicy.org/papers/policy-paper-17.html (accessed 18 June 2008).

72 *Looking Right* (Autumn 1969), pp.17–18; Psephology group minutes (18 July 1960), CRD 2/21/6; Ellis, 'No hammock', pp.454, 466; 'Camulodunum MCMLXV', p.11; *Macleod Report 1965*, p.13.

73 'YCCS – Community Service', *Impact* (Summer 1967), p.17; *Trend* (Winter 1965–66), p.25; '65 Generation YC', *Impact* (February 1965), p.25.

74 T.R. Fairgieve (President, Scottish Conservative and Unionist Association) to Edward Du Cann, 9 November 1965, CCO 20/47/1; correspondence Peter Barwell, John Wood; *Macleod Report*, p.22; Whiteley, Seyd, Richardson, *True Blues*, p.44.

75 'They're better in the North', p.24; National Advisory Committee minutes (6 March 1965), CCO 506/19/6; Walder, 'Young Conservative Identikit', pp.24–26.

76 'Survey of Young people – Pilot Survey 1' (May 1966), CCO 180/34/1/2; Opinion Research Centre, 'The Young Conservatives' (July 1966), CCO 180/34/1/3.

77 Lear in Jennings, 'Policy-makers'; J.S. Gummer, 'The 1234567890 ages of a Young Conservative', *Impact* (Spring 1966), pp.5–7; Alan Haslehurst, 'The Diagnosis', *Impact* (February 1965), p.28.

78 *Blue Horizon* (December 1969), p.4; correspondence, Louise Longson, 9 October 2009; *Looking Right* (Autumn 1969), pp.17–18, 25; (January 1965), p.28; Birmingham YCs annual report 1967; General Purposes committee (20 November 1968), BCL. On Shaw Correspondence, R. Tomlinson, 17 December 2008.

79 I. Macleod, 'On ideals of service', *Looking Right* (April 1962), p.32.
80 'YCCS – Community Service', p.17; (Spring 1966), pp.17–18; *Looking Right* (Summer 1969), p.31; (September 1970), pp.19–21; Holyroyd-Doveton, *Young Conservatives*, pp.189–190.
81 East Midlands EC minutes (14 January 1967, 20 January 1968), ARE5/16/3; Le Bosquet, 'A New Concept' (n.d., c. 1967/8), CCO 20/47/2; *Looking Right* (Summer 1968), p.36.
82 *Impact* (Spring–Summer 1968), p.22; East Midlands EC minutes (14 June 1968, 4 October 1969), ARE5/16/3; Action Notes (n.d., c.1968/9), CCO 20/47/3; *Looking Right* (Summer 1969), p.31.
83 Hugh Holland, 'Homelessness', *Looking Right* (Winter 1969), p.25; Garry Jones, 'Revolt!', *Impact* (Spring–Summer 1968), p.12.
84 Layton-Henry, 'The Young Conservatives', p.151; Juliet Gardiner, 'I took my flower to a YC ball but nobody asked me to frug!', *Impact* (Winter 1967/8); (Spring–Summer 1968), pp.22, 28. Correspondence, Gardiner; H. Morgan, 'Pop Pirates', *Impact* (Spring 1966); (Winter 1967), p.14.
85 *Impact* (Spring–Summer 1968/69), p.26; Central Office circular (13 August 1961), CCO 4/8/390; Crowson, *Conservative Party*, p.122.
86 *Progress* 6:2 (1965), p.33; Gummer, correspondence (15 May 2006); *Trend* (Winter 1965–66), p.4.
87 *The Whip* (April 1958), p.7; South East YC Advisory committee minutes (21 March 1956), ARE9/16/2.
88 East Midland Area YC Executive Committee minutes (14 January 1967, 7 July 1968), ARE5/16/3; Le Bosquet, 'Chairman's Proposals' (14 June 1968), ARE5/16/3; G. Jones, 'Revolt!', *Impact* (Spring–Summer 1968), p.12; A. Craig, 'Conservatives and Campus protests', *Impact* (Winter–Spring 1968–69), pp.16–17.
89 Layton-Henry, 'The Young Conservatives', p.153; GLYC Executive Committee minutes (11 October 1967, 10 October 1969), CCO 20/47/2; *Democratory*, CCO 20/47/3,5; Holyroyd-Doveton, *Young Conservatives* pp.76–81.
90 Greater London Young Conservatives (GLYCs), *Set the Party Free* (London, 1969), p.20; Whiteley, Seyd, Richardson, *True Blues*, pp.31–32. Green, *Ideologies*, pp.283–284.
91 Layton-Henry, 'The Young Conservatives', p.155; Chairman to Heath, 13 July 1967, CCO 20/47/2; Chalker, *Evening News*, 5 July 1969; Haslehurst-Heath correspondence (16–20 October 1969), CCO 20/47/3; P. Seyd, 'Democracy within the Conservative party', *Government and Opposition* 10 (1975).
92 McKibbin, *Classes and Cultures*, pp.96–98, 202–205; 'Classes and Cultures: A Postscript', *Mitteilungsblatt des Instituts für die Geschichte der sozialen Bewegungen* 27 (2002), pp.154–165.
93 Light, *Forever England*, pp.14–18, 106, 211–213, 221; Crick, *In Defence of Politics*, pp.111–123.
94 V. de Grazia, *Irresistible Empire* (Cambridge, MA 2005), ch.1; Helen McCarthy, 'Parties, voluntary associations and democratic politics in interwar Britain', *Historical Journal* 50 (2007).
95 Jean Blondel, *Voters, Parties and Leaders* (Harmondsworth, 1966), pp.12, 94–100, 129; Philip Tether, 'Clubs: A neglected aspect of Conservative Organization', *Hull Papers in Politics* 42 (1988), pp.2–4, 57–66. Jennings, *Party Politics I*, p.215.
96 Ronald Frankenberg, *Communities in Britain* (Harmondsworth, 1967), p.152; G. Smith, 'The Successful Agent', *Conservative Agents' Journal* 435 (October 1957); Heath, *The Course of my Life*, p.126.

97 Frankenberg, *Communities*, ch.6; Margaret Stacey, *Tradition and Change: A Study of Banbury* (Oxford, 1960), pp.50–55; Hugh Berrington, 'Banbury', in David Butler (ed.), *The British General Election of 1955* (London, 1969), p.132; Margaret Stacey, Eric Batstone, Colin Bell, Anne Murcott, *Power, Persistence and Change: A Second Study of Banbury* (London, 1975), pp.40–69.

98 Mark Arnold-Foster, 'Tory Funds', *Guardian*, 29 January 1964; Neill Nugent, 'The Ratepayers' in R. King, N. Nugent (eds), *Respectable Rebels* (London, 1979), p.27; Samuel, 'Lost World', p.10.

99 Jennings, *Party Politics I*, pp.172–173, 215–221, 216; RHR, 'The Jews and the Tory party', *Conservative Agents' Journal* 513 (February 1965); James Douglas to Ian Fraser (22 January 1959), CRD 2/8/20.

100 Nadler, *Too Nice to be a Tory*, pp.46, 52–58; Richard Hoggart, *Townscape with Figures* (London, 1994), pp.202, 170–174, 136–139, 12–13, xvii–xviii.

101 *Looking Right* (Spring 1969), p.26; E.H.H. Green, 'The Conservative party, the state and the electorate, 1945–64' in Lawrence, Taylor, *Party, State and Society*; East Midlands Area Chairman's Report (1966), ARE5/16/2; Harrison, *Seeking a Role*, pp.204–210.

102 Jennings, *Party Politics I*, pp.210, 228.

103 Francis, 'The emotional economy'.

Chapter 5

1   'Introduction' in M. Collins (ed.), *The Permissive Society and its Enemies* (London, 2008).

2   M. Whitehouse, *Cleaning-up TV: From Protest to Participation* (London, 1967), p.23.

3   See A. Lent, *British Social Movements since 1945: Sex, Colour, Peace and Power* (Basingstoke, 2001); H. Nehring, 'The growth of social movements' in H. Jones, P. Addison (eds), *Companion to Contemporary Britain, 1939–2000* (Oxford, 2005); P. Byrne, *Social Movements in Britain* (London, 1997).

4   See T. Frank, *What's the Matter with America? The Resistible Rise of the American Right* (London, 2004).

5   B. Campbell, *The Iron Ladies* (London, 1987), p.4.

6   F. Parkin, *Middle Class Radicalism: The Social Bases of the British Campaign for Nuclear Disarmament* (Manchester, 1968); R. Inglehart, *Culture Shift in Advanced Industrial Society* (Princeton, NJ, 1990).

7   D. Dworkin, *Cultural Marxism in Postwar Britain: The New Left and the Origins of Cultural Studies* (Durham, NC, 1993); H. Nehring, 'CND, 'generation' and the politics of religion, 1957–64' in J. Garnett *et al.* (eds), *Redefining Christian Britain* (London, 2007).

8   Y. Jewkes, *Media and Crime* (London, 2004), p.69.

9   S. Fielding, *Labour and Cultural Change 1964–70* (Manchester, 2003), pp.18–20, ch.8.

10 D. Nash, *Blasphemy in the Christian World* (Oxford, 2007).

11 Minutes, meeting to discuss VAL council (25 February 1965), NVALA Archive, Box 1 (NVALA 1); *The Viewer* 3 (March 1968); Whitehouse to Lord Aylestone (15 April 1968), NVALA 47; K. Bird report (6 May 1964), BBC Written Archives Centre (BBC WAC) T16/585.

12 Clean-Up TV circulars (14 March 1965, 30 September 1964), NVALA 1; NVALA's views of the seaside disturbances, *Wolverhampton Express and Star* (25 May

1964); C.G.F. Nuttall, 'TV commercial audiences in the UK', *Advertising Research* 2:3 (September 1962), pp.19–28.

13 Whitehouse to Wilson (8 August 1967) to Roy Jenkins (18 July 1967), NVALA 16 (2000); *The Viewer and Listener* (Summer 1970), p.1.

14 Minutes, meeting (25 February 1965); Whitehouse to Short (4 July 1966), NVALA 59.

15 Dance to *Times* (11 August 1964), NVALA 80.

16 Campaign circulars (30 September 1964, 27 April 1965), NVALA 1 'Clean up TV campaign'.

17 Short to Whitehouse (3 May 1967); Whitehouse to Wilson (24 June 1967), NVALA 16 (2000 Accession). Minutes meeting (26 March 1968), NVALA 44; M. Tracey, D. Morrison, *Whitehouse* (Basingstoke, 1979), ch.8.

18 *Observer* (10 November 1968); Minutes meeting (26 March 1968), NVALA 44; Curran to Whitehouse (19 June 1966), NVALA 17 (2000).

19 Press statement (5 June 1969), NVALA Box 44; International efforts, NVALA 26 (2000); *The Viewer* (March 1968); J. Capon, *And There was Light* (London, 1972).

20 M. Tracey, D. Morrison, *Whitehouse*, pp.188–190; Charles Stuart (ed.), *The Reith Diaries* (London, 1975), 12 September 1963, p.510.

21 *The Viewer and Listener* (Summer 1970); Whitehouse to John Stonehouse (27 March 1969), NVALA 59; D. Holbrook, 'Mary Whitehouse' *Political Quarterly* 51:2 (1980), p.158; Letter (30 January 1981), NVALA 123.

22 Whitehouse, *Cleaning-up TV*, pp.148–149, 165.

23 'Censorship? Television and NVALA' (n.d., c.1967), NVALA 108.

24 Speech, 16 December 1968, NVALA 59; Circular Letter to MPs (14 February 1966), NVALA 54; Clean-up TV 'Draft Constitution', NVALA 1.

25 Whitehouse, *Cleaning-up TV*, pp.54–56.

26 K. Bird report (6 May 1964); Sims memo (16 January 1967), Whitehouse speaker File II, 1963–72'.

27 Attenborough to Richard Cawston (Head of Documentaries 16 July 1968), Newman to Adam (6 January 1965), WAC T16/699; Controllers' meeting minutes (7, 14 December 1965), BBC WAC T16/585; BBC Board of Management minutes (2 December 1968), WAC R103/285/1.

28 *Daily Mail* (13 March 1967); Grace Wyndham Goldie, *Facing the Nation: Television and Politics 1936–76* (London, 1977).

29 M. MacMurraugh-Kavanagh, 'The BBC and *The Wednesday Play*, 1962–66: Institutional Containment vs. "Agitational Contemporaneity"' in J. Thumim (ed.), *Small Screens, Big Ideas* (London, 2002), p.150; A. Marwick, *The Sixties* (Oxford, 1998), p.477; Adam's annotations on Newman's memo (6 January 1965), BBC WAC T16/699.

30 Whitehouse to Carleton Greene (5 November 1968), NVALA 42; Whitehouse to Barnett (14 November 1968), Hill (16 May 1969); Barnett-Skelhorn correspondence (18 November 1968, 6 January 1969); Hill to Quentin Hogg (16 June 1969); Skelhorn to Whitehouse (17 June 1969), NVALA 34; *BBC Audience Research Newsletter* (January 1969), p.3; Lincolnshire police reports reports (20 May 1969), NVALA 57.

31 Advice (26 April 1967); BBC management minutes (22 May, 5 June 1967), WAC R134/609/1,2.

32 *National VALA News* (November 1967); Whitehouse to Wilson (25 October 1964, 19 July 1966), National Archives (NA) HO256/719.

33 '1968/9 Licence campaign', NVALA 13 (2000); *Wolverhampton Express and Star* (22 July 1968).

34 *Birmingham Post* (13 May 1968); Whitehouse, Hill, Callaghan correspondence (13, 28 May 1968), NVALA 108; Whitehouse's 1968 convention address, NVALA 7 (2000); Whitehouse to Callaghan (23 February 1968), NVALA 58.

35 Goodwin (author of anti-*Honest to God* tract, *The Principles of Broadcasting*) to Buckland (13 April 1964), NVALA 79; Barnett to B. Charles-Dean (14 April 1965), Monsignor P. Casey to Whitehouse (4 March 1965), NVALA 80.

36 *NVALA – What is it?* (1966), NVALA 1; *The Viewer and Listener* (Summer 1970); M. Tracey, D. Morrison, 'Opposition to the Age' (Social Science Research Council report, 1978), p.29, NVALA 76; 'Guidance notes' in NVALA 19.

37 Note (17 June 1965); Whitehouse to Wilson (10 June 1965), NA HO256/719.

38 *The Viewer and Listener* (Summer 1970), p.6; Whitehouse to Wilson (2 January 1967); PM's Private Secretary to GPO (30 January 1967), HO256/719; Wilson-Whitehouse correspondence (10, 12 January 1967), NVALA 16 (2000); Mason to Whitehouse (6 May 1968), Whitehouse to Chataway (26 October 1970), NVALA 59.

39 Normanbrook to Burke Trend (7 September 1965); memos from PM's Office (8 September, 9 September 1965), NA HO256/719; Whitehouse to Wilson (6 September 1965), NVALA 59; T. Shaw, 'The BBC, the state and Cold War culture: the case of television's *The War Game* (1965)', *English Historical Review* CXXI:494 (2006).

40 *Daily Mail* (20 May 1970); K. Bird report (6 May 1964); Bernard Levin, *The Pendulum Years* (London, 1970), p.338.

41 Whitehouse to Charles Curran (18, 23 September 1969), NVALA 2000 accession Box 17; G. McCann, *Frankie Howerd* (London, 2004), pp.238–241.

42 *Sunday* Press (Eire) (17 March 1967); 'TV supplement', *New Left Review* 7 (1961), p.43.

43 (London) *Evening News* (2 March 1967); C. Booker, *The Neophiliacs* (London, 1969), p.256; *Humanist News* (April 1967), p.11.

44 Minutes (25 February 1965), NVALA 1; Dance to Whitehouse (15 June 1967), NVALA 80; R. Wallis, 'Moral indignation and the media: an analysis of the NVALA', *Sociology* 10 (1976).

45 Secretary's Report 1968 Convention, NVALA 7 (2000); D. Cliff, 'Religion, morality and the middle class' in R. King, N. Nugent (eds) *Respectable Rebels: Middle Class Campaigns in Britain in the 1970s* (London, 1979).

46 Whitehouse-Lamb correspondence (1968), NVALA 37; Normanbrook to Whitehouse (21 June, 22 September 1965), NVALA 42.

47 *Melody Maker* (17 October 1970); M. & W. Priest to Whitehouse (9 May 1965), NVALA 87; Muggeridge to Whitehouse (3rd July 1967), NVALA 2000 Box 7; R. Ingrams, *Muggeridge: The Biography* (London, 1995).

48 Meeting minutes (25 February 1965); K. Bird report (1964).

49 Whitehouse to Wilson (24 June 1967), NVALA 16 (2000); J. Lawrence, *Electing Our Masters* (Oxford, 2009), pp.122–125; R. Inglehart, 'The silent revolution in Europe: intergenerational change in post-industrial societies', *American Political Science Review* 65:4 (1971)

50 H. McLeod, *The Religious Crisis of the 1960s* (Oxford, 2007), p.229; Frank, *What's the Matter with America?* pp.93, 168, 234; R. Perlstein, *Before the Storm: Barry Goldwater and the Unmaking of the American Consensus* (New York, 2001).

51 *Viewer and Listener* (Summer 1970), p.1. 'Draft Constitution'.

52 'NVALA Misc', NVALA 1; Obituary, *Guardian* (30 June 2000).

53 Black to Pattulo (4 December 1964), NVALA 80.

54 'Letters from the public to MW', NVALA 77–9; *Baptist Times* (6 April 1967), *English Churchman* (7 April 1967); Rotary International and others (August 1968), NVALA 13 (2000).

55 *Catholic Teacher* 159 (Summer 1965), p.10; *Catholic Herald* (5 November 1965); Curran to Shiell (19, 27 July 1965), WAC R44/1, 188/1; Higgins to Adam (6 November 1965), WAC T16/699; Higgins to *Catholic Herald* (1 January, 14 March 1966), Higgins to Curran (7 January 1966), WAC R44/1, 189/1.

56 Joanne Halifax (MU Central President) to Whitehouse (12 February 1964), NVALA 80; 'Summary of Diocesan Mothers' Union Reports ... to the manifesto from 'the women of Britain' (n.d., 1964); Norfolk Group report (1964); *Church Times* (3 July 1964); Stephens memo (n.d., 1964), WAC T16/585.

57 *Viewer and Listener* (Summer 1970), p.1; *What NVALA Believes* (1966), NVALA 1; Whitehouse in *The Spectator* (16 September 1966).

58 *The Viewer and Listener* (Summer 1970); Whitehouse to Wilson (1 January 1968), NVALA 59.

59 Parkin, *Middle Class Radicalism*, pp.38, 52; Wallis, 'Moral Indignation', p.278.

60 Whitehouse, 'The Scientist, the bomb and the Housewife', *Weekly Scotsman* (27 July 1955) and 'A Mother's approach to social problems', 'Mothers and Sons', *Sunday Times* (1 November, 6 December 1953); BBC *Woman's Hour* (1 June 1953), NVALA 21 (2000) and BBC WAC 'Mary Whitehouse Speaker File I 1953–62'; GP Pratt to Whitehouse (18 September 1970), NA HO264/196; McLeod, *Religious Crisis*, p.215.

61 Circular (25 October 1964); Minutes meeting (25 February 1965), NVALA 1; J. Trenaman, 'The Responsibility of the Receiver' in SCTV, *Television: Responsibility and Response* (London, 1959), pp.22–23.

62 C. Brown, *The Death of Christian Britain* (London, 2001), pp.1, 7, 191–193; P. Fryer, *Mrs Grundy: Studies in English Prudery* (London, 1963); 'Scrapped: The BBC Good taste Guide', *Daily Mail* (15 January 1963).

63 For an overview, C. Brown, *Religion and Society in Twentieth-century Britain* (Harlow, 2006), ch.6; M. Roodhouse, 'Lady Chatterley and the monk: Anglican radicals and the Lady Chatterley trial of 1960', *Journal of Ecclesiastical History* 59:3 (2008); McLeod, *Religious Crisis*, pp.89, 238–241.

64 Muggeridge to Whitehouse (3, 23 July 1967), NVALA 7 (2000); Whitehouse, *Cleaning-up TV*, p.50. M. Tracey, D. Morrison, *Whitehouse*, pp.188–190.

65 *The Viewer and Listener* (Autumn 1970), p.1; D. Edwards, J. Robinson (ed.), *The Honest to God Debate* (London, 1963); A. Lunn, G. Lean *The Cult of* Softness (London, 1965), pp.6–8; McLeod, *Religious Crisis*, pp.99, 228–233, 264–265; Whitehouse in *Free Press* (Pontypool, 7 July 1967), *Cleaning-up TV*, p.50.

66 Angela Bartie, 'Festival City: the arts, culture and moral conflict in Edinburgh, 1947–67' (PhD. Dundee University, 2006), ch.5; Brown, *Religion and Society*, pp.198–201, 232–251, 266; Howard to Whitehouse (11 August 1964); NVALA 80.

67 T. Driberg, *The Mystery of Moral Re-armament* (London, 1964); Clean-Up TV newsletter (30 September 1964, 14 February 1965); P. Boobbyer, 'The Cold War in the plays of Peter Howard', *Contemporary British History* 19:2 (2005).

68 Buckland to Whitehouse (28 June 1966) NVALA 80; BBC Solicitor's notes (Halloran, 10 April 1967; Willis, 28 April, 23 May 1967), WAC R134/609/1; *Association of Broadcasting Staff Bulletin* (June 1967); Jack Williams, *Entertaining the Nation? Social History of British TV* (Stroud, 2004), p.138.

69 *Spectator* (10 September 1965), p.323; Hood, 'The Corporation', *Encounter* (April 1965).

70   M. Jarvis, *Conservative Governments, Morality and Social Change in Affluent Britain, 1957–64* (Manchester, 2005) pp.143–147, 163; Brown, *Religion and Society*, pp.267–270; see also S. Mitchell, *The Brief and Turbulent Life of Modernizing Conservatism* (Newcastle, 2006).

71   Gaitskell to Hoggart (24 July 1962), Richard Hoggart papers, MS.247/5/9/91; Campbell, *Iron Ladies*, p.99; Heath to Whitehouse (31 August 1967), NVALA 59; *The Viewer* (March 1968).

72   Chair Hemel Hempstead Conservative Association to Whitehouse (n.d., c.1969), NVALA 20; *Conservative Party Annual Conference Report* (1958), p.96. Jarvis, *Conservative Governments*, p.53.

73   B. Pym, *Pressure Groups and the Permissive Society* (Newton Abbot, 1974), pp.12, 148; A. Marsh, *Protest and Political Consciousness* (London, 1977); H.H. Wilson, *Pressure Group* (London, 1961).

74   Jasper More to Frank Pearson (the PM's PPS, 24 June 1964), NA PREM 11/4646; Jarvis, *Conservative Governments*, p.146; 1966 Convention speech in Whitehouse, *Cleaning-up TV*, pp.228–229.

75   Minutes (25 February 1965), NVALA 1; Executive minutes (15 February 1967), NVALA 10 (2000); Broadcasting Committee minutes (14 June 1967, 9 December 1970), Conservative Party Archive, CRD 3/20/1; J. Critchley, *Counsel for Broadcasting* (London, 1971).

76   Holbrook, 'Mary Whiethouse', pp.155, 162.

77   Benn to G. Thomas (22 December 1965), NVALA 16 (2000); Fielding, *Labour and Cultural Change*, p.196; Williams, *Entertaining the Nation*, p.138.

78   Bray in *Times* (28 July 1969); Bob Edwards letter (n.d., c.1966), NVALA 7 (2000); Nugent (23 September 1964), Prior (14 September 1964) to Whitehouse, NVALA 16 (2000); Wilson, cited in Shaw, 'The BBC, the state and Cold War Culture', p.1368.

79   B. Harrison, *Seeking a Role* (Oxford, 2009), pp.525–526.

80   C. Doughty to Whitehouse (6 February 1965), NVALA 80; Bryan to Whitehouse (5 June 1969), NVALA 45; More to Whitehouse (4 June 1964), NVALA 16 (2000); J.S. Gummer, *The Permissive Society* (London, 1971); *Viewer and Listener* (Summer 1970), p.4; *The Listener* (9 November 1972).

81   Stonehouse, speech to Manchester University symposium on broadcasting (16 December 1968), NVALA, 59; *Peace News* (4 January 1963).

82   L. Black, 'Whose finger on the button? British television and the politics of cultural control', *Historical Journal of Film, Radio and Television* 25 (2005), pp.548–553; A. Offer, *The Challenge of affluence* (Oxford, 2006), pp.127–128; C. Pattie, P. Seyd, P. Whiteley, *Citizenship in Britain* (Cambridge, 2004), p.261; P. Norris, 'Does TV erode social capital? A Reply to Putnam', *Political Science and Politics* 29 (1996).

83   A. Fox, *The Emerging Ethic* (Portlaw, 1971); *Guardian* (2 December 1965), *Spectator* (17 December 1965). Whitehouse, *Cleaning-up TV*, pp.133–146; Kenneth Adam memo (30 November 1965); BBC WAC T16/585; NVALA Circular (1 January 1966), NVALA 1.

84   SCTV, *Television: Responsibility and Response* (1959); *Tonight and Tomorrow* (1960 conference report); *Schoolmaster* (23 November 1962); SCTV, *Pilkington and After* (London, 1962).

85   Mary Adams, 'Television Consumers', *Consumer News* 8 (January 1964), reproduced in *Television Viewers Council Annual Conference* (1963), pp.31–32; *Punch* (22 July 1963).

86 Benn to Adams (25 May 1965), Mary Adams papers (MAP), BBC WAC S322/239; Whitehouse, *Cleaning-up TV*, pp.192–194; Ken Jones, 'Community Television', *Adult Education* XXXVII:6 (1965). B. Groombridge, *Television and the People: A Programme for Democratic Participation* (Harmondsworth, 1972).

87 CCCS annual reports (1965), pp.14–15; (1965–66), pp.17, 20; (1968–69), p.12 in Hoggart, MS. 247/6/4/3, 4, 9; Powell, 'Television Providers and the Public', pp.6–29, MAP S322/241.

88 *The Scotsman* (18 December 1965); Shaw to Hoggart (n.d., c.1962, 10 July 1962), Hoggart MS.247/5/9/55; for example, S. Fay, 'The Late New Left', *Spectator* (21 September 1962), pp.390–394.

89 *New Society* (16 February 1967), p.245; similarly Hoggart's obituary, *Guardian* (24 November 2001).

90 'Unbent Springs', BBC Home Service (27 April 1955), Hoggart MS.247/3/114/1; R. Hoggart, *The Uses of Literacy* (Harmondsworth, 1957), pp.137, 154, 161; see C. Ellis, 'Relativism and reaction: Richard Hoggart and conservatism' in S. Owen (ed.), *Richard Hoggart and Cultural Studies* (Basingstoke, 2008).

91 R. Hoggart, 'The Difficulties of Democratic Debate', *Teachers College Record* 64:8 (May 1963), pp.653–654; For criticisms of Pilkington's methodology, Barbara Wooton, *Times* (25 July 1962).

92 Hoggart's review, *New Society; National VALA – What Is It?* (1966), NVALA 1; Cliff, 'Religion, morality', pp.138–139; M. Donnelly, *Sixties Britain* (Harlow, 2005), pp.80–81; Marwick, *Sixties*, p.477; Sherrin in M. Whitehouse, *Who Does She Think She Is?* (London, 1972), p.63.

93 Hoggart to Whitehouse (7 February, 11 March, 1 June 1966), Hoggart MS.247/4/6/218–220; D. Holbrook 'Magazines – with special reference to the exploitation of pseudo-sexuality' in Denys Thompson (ed.), *Discrimination and Popular Culture* (Harmonsworth, 1970), which quotes extensively from Raymond Williams' *Communications* on the power of the media; Holbrook, 'Mary Whitehouse', pp.154–163.

94 Dworkin, *Cultural Marxism*, p.117; S. Hall, P. Whannel, *The Popular Arts* (London, 1964), pp.23–24.

95 S. Hall, 'The supply of demand', in E.P. Thompson (ed.), *Out of Apathy* (London, 1960), p.82.

96 *Christian Science Monitor* (30 October 1970); Birdwood (15 September 1970), NVALA 35.

97 Report from Wigmore Hall (15 July 1969), ACGB papers 59/1; *Daily Mirror* (22 July 1969); *The Viewer and Listener* (Autumn 1970), p.2.

98 H. Himmelweit, A.N. Oppenheim, P. Vince *et al*, *Television and the Child* (Oxford, 1958), p.20; Whitehouse, *Cleaning-up TV*, p.73; Himmelweit, correspondence with Kenneth Adam (1, 8 November 1960) and Cecil McGivern (producer, *Mainly for Women*) (11, 13 November 1959), WAC T16/689.

99 SCTV minutes (13 February 1963), MAP S322/125/1; Cliff, 'Religion, morality', pp.138–139; W.A. Belson, *Television and the Family* (London, 1959), pp.xvii, 127–134; Minutes Commons meeting (26 March 1968); J.P. Murray, 'The violent face of television: 50 years of research and controversy' in E. Palmer, B. Young (eds), *The Faces of Televisual Media* (Mahwa, NJ, 2003), p.149; *British Journal of Psychology* 50:2 (May 1959).

100 J.D. Halloran, R.L. Brown, D.C. Chaney, *Television and Delinquency* (3rd working paper, Leicester, 1970), pp.13–17, 178–80; Halloran, 'Introduction' and 'The Social Effects of Television' in J.D. Halloran (ed.), *The Effects of Television* (London, 1970), pp.22, 63.

101   *BBC Audience Research Newsletter* (June 1970); Jarvis, *Conservative Governments*, pp.142–144.

102   *The Viewer and Listener* (Summer 1970), p.1; Barnett in minutes (25 February 1965), NVALA 1; Open Letter to Greene *The Viewer* 3 (March 1968); 'Television and Youth', *New Society* (18 July 1963), pp.3–4.

103   NVALA 19, 15 (2000); NVALA Schools Broadcasting Monitoring Project (May 1970) Report, p.15 in BBC WAC R103/285/1; 1966 Mansfield survey results in Whitehouse, *Cleaning-up TV*, Appendix IV.

104   J.D. Halloran, P. Eliot, G. Murdock, *Demonstrations and Communication* (Harmondsworth, 1970), p.300; Harrison, *Seeking a Role*, p.469.

105   *Humanist News* (April 1967), p.11; Cliff, 'Religion, morality', p.143; J. Gusfield, *Symbolic Crusade and Status Politics: The American Temperance Movement* (Chicago, 1976, 1st edition 1963).

106   Wallis, 'Moral indignation', pp.273–274, 282–286.

107   See Maurice Cowling's *Mill and Liberalism* (Cambridge, 1963), a critique of contemporary liberalism, which resonates with Whitehouse's in attacking a rational, post-Christian liberal elite or clerisy.

108   J. Goodwin, J. Jasper (eds), *The Social Movements Reader* (Oxford, 2003), pp.ix, 3.

109   Cliff, 'Religion, morality', p.144; poll of 1500 NVALA members, *Liverpool Post* (18 October 1969).

110   Tracey, 'Opposition', p.43; *National VALA News* (November 1967), p.4; White-house to Heath (27 June 1970), NVALA 59; Essex VALA leaflet, WAC R78/2, 348/1; Parkin, *Middle Class Radicalism*, p.33.

111   Parkin, *Middle Class Radicalism*, pp.38, 49, 56.

112   Inglehart, *Culture Shift*, pp.177, 211, ch.10; *idem.*, 'The silent revolution in Europe'.

Chapter 6

1   R. Inglehart, *Culture Shift in Advanced Industrial Society* (Princeton, NJ, 1990), p.335; also M. Veldman, *Fantasy, the Bomb and Greening of Britain, 1945–80* (Cambridge, 1994).

2   F. Coppieters, 'Arnold Wesker's Centre Fortytwo: a cultural revolution betrayed', *Theatre Quarterly* 5:18 (1975), p.51; A. Marwick, *The Sixties* (Oxford, 1998), p.343.

3   L. Black, "Making Britain a gayer and more cultivated country': Wilson, Lee and the creative industries in the 1960s', *Contemporary British History* 20:3 (2006).

4   D.A.N. Jones, 'Politics in the Theatre', *Times Literary Supplement* (22 July 1967); D. Thomas, D. Carlton, A. Etienne, *Theatre Censorship: From Walpole to Wilson* (Oxford, 2007).

5   A. Davies, *Other Theatres: The Development of Alternative and Experimental Theatre in Britain* (Basingstoke, 1987); C. Itzin, *Stages in the Revolution: Political Theatre in Britain Since 1968* (London, 1979); D. Shellard, *British Theatre Since the War* (New Haven, CT, 2000), ch.4.

6   *New York Times* (26 February 1961); *Daily Mail* (5 June 1964).

7   NVALA Annual Convention (May 1968), NVALA 2000 accession, Box 7.

8   Meeting 21 January 1965, NA PREM 13/358; *Tatler* (25 August 1965); payments, Arnold Wesker papers (AW) 276/3; *The Nation* (25 March 1961); *New York Daily Post* (28 October 1963).

9   Carl Foreman (Open Road films) to Wesker (19 November 1963), AW 134/3; A. Wesker, *Fears of Fragmentation* (London, 1970), pp.103–104; Wesker to Goodman (11 October 1965), AW 144/11.

10 Founding Meeting, CO100 AW, 119/1; Wesker to John Papworth (22 February 1962), AW 119/2; A. Wesker, *As Much as I Dare* (London, 1995), pp.610, 619; *Daily Express* (16 September 1961).

11 Jeremy Hawthorne, 'Wesker: The Last Season?', *Mainstream* (October 1965); Wesker's riposte, *Daily Worker* (3 February 1966); A. Wesker, 'Aie Cuba! Aie Cuba!' in *The New Man in Cuba* (British-Cuba Association, Nov. 1969), pp.15, 21; Levin, *Daily Mail* (25 March 1970); R. Williams (ed.), *May Day Manifesto 1968* (Harmondsworth, 1968), pp.9–10.

12 *Sunday Times* (28 December 1969); M. Page, 'Whatever happened to Arnold Wesker?', *Modern Drama* 11 (1968); M. Patterson, *Strategies of Political Theatre: Post-war British Playwrights* (Cambridge, 2003), ch.2.

13 'Experts prepare for an age of culture', *Sunday Times* (25 November 1962); S. Hall, P. Whannel, *The Popular Arts* (London, 1964), p.379; *The Warning Voice*, Mark Abrams papers Box 70, File 'Leisure 1956–67 2/2'; N. Shrapnel, 'Parsimony and Puritanism', in *A New Britain* (Guardian, 1963), pp.61–66.

14 *Labour Party Annual Conference Report* (1963), p.135; DEA, NA EW23/50; Society of Industrial Artists and Designers, ACGB papers (ACGB) 62/76; *A Policy for the Arts: The First Steps* (Cmnd. 2601, 1965), paras. 66, 71; I.P. Henry, *The Politics of Leisure Policy* (Basingstoke, 2001), pp.19–22.

15 L. Chun, *The British New Left* (Edinburgh, 1993), pp.60–64; M. Rustin, 'The New Left as a social movement', in Oxford University Socialist Discussion Group (eds), *Out of Apathy* (London, 1989), pp.121–127; D. Dworkin *Cultural Marxism* (Durham, NC, 1997).

16 J. Green, *All Dressed Up* (London, 1998), pp.239–244; Williams, *May Day Manifesto*; L. Black, 'Arts and crafts: social democracy's cultural resources and repertoire in 1960s' Britain', in I. Favretto, J. Callaghan (eds), *Transitions in Social Democracy* (Manchester, 2007).

17 Interview, Lord Merlyn-Rees (29 November 2001); Minutes PR Group (29 July 1960); Rees speech (10 March 1962), File 'Miscellaneous', Festival of Labour papers Box 1 (FOL 1); Wesker to Topolski (10 August 1960), AW 136/10; Gaitskell, *Daily Mail* (14 June 1962).

18 B. Conekin, *The Autobiography of a Nation: The 1951 Festival of Britain* (Manchester, 2003).

19 Black, 'Arts and crafts'; Cmnd. 2601, para.100.

20 C. Gray, *The Politics of the Arts* (Basingstoke, 2000), pp.47–51; Martin Priestman, 'A Critical Stage: Drama in the 1960s', in Bart Moore-Gilbert, John Seed (eds), *Cultural Revolution? The Challenge of the Arts in the 1960s* (London, 1992), p.122.

21 *Tribune* (21 July 1967); Lee to Jenkins (10 February 1969), Jennie Lee papers (JL) 2/2/2/1.

22 Royal Academy address (5 May 1970) JL 2/2/2/2; BBC Home Service Transcript, 19 March 1966, JL 4/1/2/7; Goodman to Wilson (30 June 1967), Lee to M. Williams (26 November 1969), Harold Wilson papers, c.872; Cmnd. 2601. para. 5.

23 Goodman in Geoff Mulgan, 'Culture: The Problem with being Public' in D. Marquand, A. Seldon (eds), *The Ideas that Shaped Post-War Britain* (London, 1996), p.207; Cmnd. 2601. paras.49, 99; *House of Commons Debates*, 27 April 1965, cols.294–295.

24 Cmnd. 2601. para.71.

25 May Day Concert message, JL 2/2/2/1; Goodman, *Not for the Record* (London, 1972), p.144; NAA, *Annual Report* (1965–66), pp.4, 7.

26 Mervyn Jones, 'Labour and the Arts', *New Statesman* 18 February 1966; Clive Barker, 'Vintage 42', *Twentieth Century* (Winter 1966), p.49; Barker obituary *Guardian* (19 April 2005).

27 G. Mulgan, K. Worpole, *Saturday Night or Sunday Morning?* (London, 1986), pp.28–29.

28 Political and Economic Planning, 'Public Patronage of the Arts', *Planning* XXXI: 492 (November 1965); Eric White, *The Arts Council of Great Britain* (London, 1975), pp.72–74.

29 J. Nuttall, *Psychological Socialism: Labour and the Qualities of Mind and Character* (Manchester, 2006).

30 R.A.B. Butler, 'Conservatism today and tomorrow', *Swinton College Journal* 1:1 (1951); and in general, M. Jarvis, *Conservative Governments, Morality and Social Change in Affluent Britain, 1957–64* (Manchester, 2005).

31 J. Ramsden, *The Making of Conservative Party Policy* (London, 1980), pp.200–201; D. Fairbairn, 'An Approach to Leisure: Conservatism in a Post-Industrial Society', in Bow Group, *Principles in Practice* (London 1961), pp.87–88; R. Carless, P. Brewster (eds), *Patronage and the Arts* (London, 1959), pp.68–73.

32 PM notes to Chancellor (23 April, 3 June 1959), PREM 11/2666; Steering Committee minutes (29 July 1959), p.4, (27 January 1959), pp.4–5, CRD 2/53/54.

33 Eccles to PM (6 July 1959), CRD 2/53/54; 'Leisure in our affluent Age' (23 December 1959), T 218/169; Heathcoat-Amery to PM (19 February 1960), note from PM (29 December 1959), PREM 11/2950.

34 Viscount Eccles, *Politics and the Quality of Life* (CPC: London, 1970).

35 *Report of Policy Study Group on Leisure* (4 July 1965), CRD 3/31/2.

36 K. Joseph to Sir Michael Fraser (13 October 1967), CRD 3/31/2; CPC, *Automation and the Consumer* (London, 1956), pp.14, 21, CRD 2/8/9; 'The Uses of Leisure', CRD 2/52/13; Hugh Jenkins (Assistant General Secretary, Equity) to George Woodcock (TUC) (2 January 1962), Joseph to Woodcock (15 August 1962), ACGB 38/45, Boxes 1, 2.

37 Sandys to Heath (6 December 1965), James Douglas memo (21 December 1966), Robert Cooke to Whitelaw (Chief Whip) (14 January 1965), Reilly to Heath (5 May 1967), CRD 3/3/1.

38 C. Patten, 'Conservatives and the Arts' (n.d., c.1968), CRD 3/3/2.

39 Arts Policy Group minutes (7 November 1967, 23 May, 17 June 1968), W.E. Williams, 'Industry and the Arts' (May 1968) draft report, pp.34–36, 'The Arts Council and Government Responsibility for the Arts' (14 October 1968), pp.2–3, CRD 3/3/2–3.

40 A. Wesker, *The Modern Playwright or O, Mother, Is It Worth It?* and *Labour and the Arts II: What, Then, is to be Done?* (Oxford, 1960, 1961); Wesker, 'You're Only Living Half a Life', 'Plans for Centre 42', *Tribune* (12 February 1960, 28 July 1961); J. Goldthorpe 'The Current Inflation: Towards a sociological account' in J. Goldthorpe, F. Hirsch (eds), *The Political Economy of Inflation* (Cambridge, MA, 1978), ch.8.

41 TUC, *Annual Conference Report* (London, 1960), pp.435–438; Holdsworth-Wesker correspondence, AW (2)5/6 (2nd accession); A. Wesker, 'Trade Unions and the arts', *New Left Review* 5 (1960), p.67.

42 Poster, AW 133/1; D. Lessing, 'A cultural revolution: 1st stage', C42 management minutes (12 October 1961), AW 147/4–5; Wesker to Wilson (29 June 1964), Wilson to Wesker (1 July 1964), AW 154/8–9.

43 'Ten year Plan for the Arts' (1966), AW 160/3; Wesker, 'Minority View', *Times* (8 June 1970); Wesker, *As Much as I Dare*, p.563.

44 Henshaw to David Winnick (23 April 1964), AW 133/1; TU journals Press release (14 March 1963), AW 154/4; Lee, *Encounter* (August 1962), pp.95–96.

45 Wesker, 'The Dying Audience', *Film* 16 (March–April 1958), 'The Lost generation: Thoughts about Audiences', *Definition* (7 December 1959), AW 125/1; *Daily Telegraph* (16 August 1965).

46 *Guardian* (9 February 1963); Wesker's telegram (20 May 1967), AW 133/3; commissioned by the *Moscow Literary Gazette* to discuss the *May Day Manifesto*, AW 125/4.

47 McGrath, *Black Dwarf* 15 (1970); Patterson, *Strategies of Political Theatre*, ch.2.

48 Wesker, 'It's an illusion', *Ark* (Spring 1971), p.5; Wesker, *Fears of Fragmentation*, p.106; Wesker, 'The Cultural Standards of Young People', *The Youth Officer* 2:6 (May 1963); Wesker, 'Art: therapy or experience', *Youth Service Magazine* (January 1964); *Nottingham Evening Post* (20 April 1963).

49 R. Hoggart, *The Uses of Literacy* (Harmondsworth, 1957), p.5; A. Sinfield, *Literature, Politics and Culture in Postwar Britain* (London, 1997), p.265, ch.11–12; J. Vernon, *Hunger* (Cambridge, MA., 2007), p.261; see also G. Mckay, *Circular Breathing: The Cultural Politics of Jazz in Post-war Britain* (Durham, NC., 2007); A. Horn, *Juke Box Britain* (Manchester, 2009).

50 *Sunday Citizen* (23 September 1962); Ron Dellar, 'Centre 42', *New Left Review* 11 (1961), p.60.

51 *Centre Forty Two: First Stage in a Cultural Revolution* (1962), AW 141/9

52 'Draft Appeal for funds and the 1962 series of People's Festivals', AW 137/4; Audiences were discussed in Barker, 'Vintage 42', p.49; Hall, Whannel, *Popular Arts*, p.366.

53 *Southern Weekly News* (12 June 1964).

54 Itzin, *Stages*, pp.4–5; also A. Filewod, D. Watt, *Workers' Playtime* (Sydney, 2001).

55 Interview with Barker, AW (2) 25/5; *Railway Review* (10 May 1963); Davies, *Other Theatres*, pp.140–141; *Daily Herald* (29 January 1963); Wesker to Topham (26 May 1962), Brown to Barker (24 January 1963), AW 160/2.

56 Michael Foster, 'The Roundhouse', *Architectural Association Quarterly* 3:1 (Winter 1971), pp.43–55.

57 *She* (October 1971); J. Green, *Days in the Life: Voices from the English Underground 1961–71* (London, 1988), p.119; P. Stansill, 'The life and death of *IT*', *British Journalism Review* 17:4 (2006); Haynes, Interview, Edinburgh, August 2005; D. Cooper (ed.), *The Dialectics of Liberation* (Harmondsworth, 1971).

58 *Daily Mail* (6 January 1966); Wesker to Hoskins (11 April 1965), AW 132/6.

59 Roundhouse Trust, *First Report 1965–71* (1971), pp.27–31, AW 156/5; *Melody Maker* (7 January 1967); *Financial Times* (10 January 1967); on UFO, Joe Boyd, *White Bicycles* (London, 2006).

60 A. Hunt, 'Arts in Society', *New Society* (26 June 1969), p.1002; Berman to Hoskins (18 April 1969), AW 157/6; *Daily Mail* (16 March 1970).

61 *Morning Star* (3 July 1967); Hoskins to Wegg, Prosser and Co (17 July 1967) and Raymond (31 May 1967), AW 156/6.

62 Barker to Conran (5 September 1963), AW 140/8; GLC report (27 January 1967), AW 133/6.

63 Hoskins-Henshaw correspondence (16 August, 15 September 1967), AW 157/11; *Holborn Guardian* (21 March 1969); Green, *Days in the Life*, pp.55, 117; *Sunday Telegraph* (30 July 1967); John Minnion to Wesker (24 March 1967), AW 156/7; M. Perl to J. Berke (26 July 1967), AW 156/6.

64 Hoskins to Wesker (24 March 1967), AW 156/7; *Sunday Citizen* (12 February 1967), *Daily Mail* (30 January 1967); Hoskins to *IT* (3 March 1967), AW 157/1.

65 Roundhouse Trust *First Report*, p.18; *Punch* (8 July 1970); *Daily Telegraph* (12 February 1970); Roundhouse Trust Council of management (2 June 1970),

AW 149/1; correspondence, AW 148/8; C42 Council of management (31 October 1970), AW 148/6; Wesker to Chemetov (7 October 1970), AW 149/2.

66 Wesker to Barrault (n.d. March 1971), leaflet ('A People's Theatre for the People'), AW 31/6; *North London Press* (26 March 1971).

67 Wesker to Hoskins (12 June 1970), AW 149/1; Roundhouse Trust, *First Report*, pp.23–24.

68 Hayes-Southall, Wellingborough pamphlet, AW 150/1; on Logue: 'Poetry at the canteen table', *Times* (27 July 1963); on Parker, D. Watt, '*The Maker and the Tool*, documentary performance and the search for a popular culture', *New Theatre Quarterly* 19 (2003); ACGB to Wesker (29 November 1962), ACGB 34/89.

69 Personnel in AW 154/5; *Evening Standard* (2 May 1964); Benny Green, 'Big band noise for C42', *Scene* 4 (25 October 1962).

70 T. Watts, 'Jazz' (n.d.), AW 134/2; Watt, obituary *Guardian* (30 May 2006); Leslie Ash Lyons to Henshaw (9 May 1964), AW 134/7; Bernard in J. Gorman, *Knocking Down Ginger* (London, 1995), p.121; Sinfield, *Literature, Politics and Culture*, p.265.

71 C. Barker, 'Final Exploratory report of films working party' (20 August 1961); Wesker to Balcon (9 June 1962), to Richardson (26 June 1962), AW 134/3.

72 YSDC Minutes (2 November 1960), AW 255/4; Pierre Joly, 'Oscar Niemeyer joue avec la faucille et le marteau', *L'Oeil* 219 (1973).

73 *Allio Brief* (28 August 1964), AW 133/7, Reproduced in Wesker, *Fears of Fragmentation*; Allio, 'C42: Model and designs of the Roundhouse' (1965), AW 141/4.

74 Wesker to Allio (12 August 1964), to Chemetov (2 December 1966, 19 December 1967), AW 133/7.

75 *Daily Telegraph* (1 June 1964); Roundhouse Trust Committee of Management minutes (20 September 1967), AW (2)6/1–2; 'Response to Downing Street Gathering', AW 148/7.

76 *Times* (4 July 1969); Cmnd. 2601, para.53.

77 *Stage and Television Today* (4 March 1965); Shellard, *British Theatre*, pp.86–89; Coppieters, 'Arnold Wesker's', p.39; Cmnd. 2601 para.54.

78 R. Banham, 'People's Palaces', *New Statesman* (7 August 1964); Wesker note (13 August 1964), AW 154/4.

79 Accounts, AW 132/1; Henshaw to Cullen's (24 February 1963), AW 132/2; invites, AW 144/10; Harewood's address, AW 154/8.

80 Feather to Wesker (28 April 1964), AW 154/9; V. Feather, *The Essence of Trade Unionism* (London, 1963), p.124; Reed to Wesker (27 April 1962), AW 137/3; See Feather 'Out in the Cold, Cold, Snow', *Labour Organiser* (July 1954); Feather to Wesker (12 March 1962), Hoskins-Feather lunch (13 November 1963), AW 160/6; Feather, *Arts North* (December 1970).

81 'Vision! Vision! Mr Woodcock', *New Statesman* (30 July 1960); TUC, *Congress House at Fifty* (TUC: London, 2004); *Observer* (14 July 1963); Coppieters, 'Arnold Wesker's', p.47.

82 Correspondence with metropolitan and borough councils, AW 143/1–3; Wesker to Duff (28 November 1966), Hoskins to Camden Council (23 March 1967), AW 143/5; *Evening Standard* (7 July 1964).

83 *Kentish Independent* (6 May 1966); William Hart (LCC Clerk) to C42 (8 August 1963), AW 143/7.

84 Hoskins to Maxwell (5 January 1966), AW 136/4; Wesker to Woodcock (4 August 1965), AW 144/10.

85 Bridges Committee Report (1959), paras.150–157; Gulbenkian press releases (14 February 1964, 25 February 1966, 28 February 1969), ACGB 34/208; Thornton to Wesker (24 April 1963), AW 145/5.

86 *Manchester Guardian* (1 July 1958); ACGB, *A New Pattern of Patronage* (1957–58 report), pp.5, 9–10; minutes 29 October 1958, 2 May 1962, 10 February 1964; lists of grants 1964–68, ACGB 38/42, 1–3.

87 *Sunday Telegraph* (27 May 1962), *Observer* (28 October 1962); Report of meeting (2 June 1964), AW 154/9.

88 Esso and Shell letters, AW 142/7; *Deuce* to Henshaw (1 August 1964), Henshaw to Birmingham Small Arms Company (20 August 1962), AW 154/1; C42, *Annual Report, 1961–2* (1962), pp.33–34.

89 'Cultural Collage', *The Spectator* (21 September 1962); Business appeals in AW 142/8.

90 1965 bid to ACGB (16 September 1965), ACGB 34/89; Greater London Arts Association (20 May 1967), AW 156/6; Wesker, 'Trade unions and the arts', p.67.

91 Abercrombie (ACGB Secretary-General, 1963–68) to Goodman (12 October 1965) to K. Goodacre (LCC, 30 January 1967), ACGB 34/89; Wesker to Goodman (11 October 1965), Morris Ernst to Goodman (25 February 1963), AW 144/11.

92 Lavrin to Law (12 October 1962), AW 155/2; H. Carpenter, *That Was Satire That Was* (London, 2000), p.153; C42 Council of Management (20 July 1961), AW 136/8.

93 Wesker to Lennon (18, 26 May 1965), AW 144/6–7; Lennon, *Daily Mail* (21 July 1965); Lessing to Wesker (n.d., c. June 1961), AW 136/8.

94 Roundhouse Trust, *First Report*, pp.40–41; Wesker to Duke of Edinburgh (19 January 1965), to Sir John Hunt (1 June 1965), Hunt to Wesker (19 July 1965), AW 142/7; Millionaire appeal, AW 133/1 (n.d., c.1966).

95 On Sellars, Wesker *Labour and the Arts II*; Hylton, *Scene* 7 (25 October 1962), *Topic* (6 October 1962); Wesker to Goodman (25 November 1962), AW 144/11; Wesker to Thornton (19 July 1967), AW 144/8.

96 A. Wesker, 'The Kitchen', *New Left Review* 1 (1960); Wesker 'Trade Unions and the arts', p.67; *Cambridge News* (17 May 1963); Nairn to Wesker (27 July 1962), AW 134/3; Buchan to Wesker (n.d., c. August 1960), AW 136/9.

97 P. Hollis, *Jennie Lee* (Oxford, 1997), ch.9; Lee (22 December 1964), Wilson (6 January 1965) to Wesker; Lee to Hoskins (31 May 1967), AW 146/10; Lee to Williams (24 October 1966), Wilson c.872.

98 Chair Arts and Amenities committee (19 June 1967), Hoskins to Lee (16 May 1967), JL 4/1/2/8; Williams to Wilson (2 June 1967), Ben Whitaker MP to Williams (12 June 1967), Wilson, c.872; Wesker, *As Much as I Dare* (London, 1994 edition), p.42.

99 Wesker (6 July 1967) to Lee, JL 4/1/2/8; CBE: http://www.arnoldwesker.com/current/cbe.htm

100 Goodman to Wilson (30 June 1967), Lee to M. Williams (26 November 1969), Wilson c.872.

101 Hoskins to M. Williams (14 June 1967), JL 4/1/2/8; Roundhouse Trust, *First Report*, pp.41–42.

102 Wesker, memo to C42 council (24 February 1966), AW 137/4; *Tribune* (2 June 1967).

103 *Guardian* (5 December 1969); M. Kustow 'C42: What did we achieve?, *Tribune* (11 January 1963).

104 *Jackie* (22 July 1967).

105 memo, Council of management (May 1968), AW 149/1; Wesker to David Mercer (March 1967), AW 150/7; Itzin, *Stages*, pp.103–115.
106 Bristol Trades Council Annual Report (1963–4), p.12, Bristol Record Office (BRO) 32080/tc2/2/2; Annual Report (1962–3), p.2, BRO 32080/tc1/4/29; *Bristol Evening Post* (6, 9 November 1962).
107 *Leicester Daily Press* (9 October 1962), *Leicester Mercury* (8, 15 October 1962), *Nottingham Evening Post* (18 October, 20 December 1962); C42, *Annual Report, 1961–2* (1962), p.21.
108 *Birmingham Post* (23 October 1962); Birmingham Trades Council Annual Report, 1962–3, p.11, BRO 32080/tc2/2/1; J. Corbett, *The Birmingham Trades Council 1866–1966* (London, 1966), p.166; M. Rutherford, 'Cultural Collage', *Spectator* (21 September 1962); Jones, *Observer* (16 September 1962).
109 R. Dallas, 'Festival was Outstanding Success', *Labour Organiser* (July 1962); T. Driberg, 'Festival of Labour', *Tribune* (15 June 1962) p.7; Robertson to Rees (10 January 1961), File 'Art Exhibition'; Rees to Marshall (26 January 1962), File 'Art Exhibition', FOL 2; Black, 'Arts and crafts'.
110 Brown to Barker (24 January 1963), AW 160/2; *Middlesbrough Evening Gazette* (25 February 1963).
111 C42, *Annual Report, 1961–2* (1962), p.23; Davies, *Other Theatres*, p.159; Wesker to Findlater (17 July 1963), AW 154/4; *Sunday Times* (17 September 1962).
112 *St Louis Post-Dispatch* (21 June 1964); *New York Times* (magazine, 20 November 1963); *Montreal Star* clipping (n.d. but June 1964), AW 110/1.
113 J.B. Priestley, 'Gay with the Arts?', *New Statesman* (23 April 1965); Wesker, *As Much as I Dare*, p.144.
114 J. Preston, *Kings of the Roundhouse* (London, 2005), chs.1–3; *Guardian* (12 December 1995).
115 R. Samuel, 'Born-again socialism', M. Rustin, 'The New Left as a social movement', in Oxford University Socialist Discussion Group, *Out of Apathy*, pp.51–52, 123–127; L. Robinson, 'Three revolutionary years: the impact of the counter-culture on the development of the gay liberation movement in Britain', *Cultural and Social History* 3:4 (2006); J. Curran, I. Gaber, J. Petley, *Culture Wars* (Edinburgh, 2005), ch.1.
116 A. Sinclair, *Arts and Cultures* (London, 1995), pp.147, 150; Elyashiv to Hoskins (21 January 1968), AW 137/4.

Chapter 7

1 J. Lawrence, 'The transformation of British public politics after the first world war', *Past and Present* 190 (2006).
2 A. Hill, A. Whichelow, *What's Wrong with Parliament?* (Harmondsworth, 1964), p.93; M. Francis, 'Tears, tantrums and bared teeth: The emotional economy of three Conservative Prime Ministers, 1951–63', *Journal of British Studies* 41 (2002).
3 J. Habermas, *The Structural Transformation of the Public Sphere* (Cambridge, 1989 [1962]); R. Putnam, *Bowling Alone* (New York, 2000); A. Offer, *The Challenge of Affluence* (Oxford, 2006), pp.127–131.
4 J. Lawrence, *Electing Our Masters* (Oxford, 2009).
5 Lawrence, *Electing Our Masters*, pp.138–142, 170–171.
6 Steven Fielding, 'A mirror for England? Cinematic representations of party politics, c.1944–64', *Journal of British Studies* 47:1 (2008); R. McKibbin, *Classes*

and Cultures: England 1918–51 (Oxford, 1998), p.98; G. Almond, S. Verba, *The Civic Culture* (London, 1989 [1963]), p.83.

7 B. Crick, *In Defence of Politics* (Harmondsworth, 1976 [1962]), p.152; S. Fielding, *Labour and Cultural Change* (Manchester, 2003), pp.4–5, ch.8.

8 J. Trenaman, D. McQuail, *Television and the Political Image* (London, 1961), pp.14, 230.

9 Nina Eliasoph, *Avoiding Politics: How Americans Produce Apathy in Everyday Life* (Cambridge, 1998); Caroline Spelman, 4 October 2005. http://www.bbc.co.uk/1/hi/UK_politics/4307654.stm

10 'Report on Political Advertising' (NOP/481, June 1963), pp.2–4 in Mark Abrams papers Box 68 (Abrams 68), File 'Labour Party Publicity Committee, 1963–64, 2/2'; J.D.B. Miller, *Politicians* (Leicester, 1958).

11 T. Smith, *Anti-Politics* (London, 1972); H. Fairlie, *The Life of Politics* (London, 1968), pp.16–17; H. Gaitskell, *In Defence of Politics* (London, 1954), p.3; G. Lloyd to R. Butler (12 March 1958), CPA CRD 2/53/29; M. Thatcher, *What's Wrong with Politics?* (London, 1968), p.5.

12 Crick, *In Defence of Politics*, p.16; M. Cowling, *The Nature and Limits of Political Science* (Cambridge, 1963), pp.17, 209.

13 D.E. Cooper, 'Looking back on anger' in V. Bogdanor, R. Skidelsky (eds), *The Age of Affluence 1951–64* (London, 1970), pp.265, 276; Crick, *In Defence of Politics*, pp.132–134; J. Green, *All Dressed Up* (London, 1998), pp.157, 244.

14 F. Mort, 'Competing domains: democratic subjects and consuming subjects in Britain and the USA since 1945', in F. Trentmann (ed.), *The Making of the Consumer* (Oxford, 2006).

15 I. Jennings, *Party Politics I: Appeal to the People* (Cambridge, 1960), p.167; Peter Black, *Mirror in the Corner* (London, 1972), pp.47–54, 110; R. Dalton, *Citizen Politics* (Washington DC, 2001), pp.22–23; M. Abrams, 'Television Election?' *Observer* (20 March 1966); *Daily Telegraph* (24 October 1958).

16 R. Crossman, 'The Politics of Television' (21 October 1968), NVALA 59 and *Times* (22 October 1968); B. Levin, *The Pendulum Years* (London, 1970), p.339.

17 1948 agreement, *Report of the Broadcasting Committee* ('Beveridge' Cmnd. 8117, 1949), pp.9–10.

18 J. Williams, *Entertaining the Nation? Social History of British TV* (Stroud, 2004), pp.81–83; M. Shulman, *The Least Worst Television in the World* (London, 1973), p.38; B. Harrison, *Seeking a Role* (Oxford, 2009), p.469; Levin, *Pendulum Years*, pp.339, 341.

19 Robin Day, *The Case for Televising Parliament* (London, 1963), pp.6–9; Granada TV, *Prelude to Westminster* (1962), BBC WAC T16/146/3.

20 Hill, Whichelow, *What's Wrong with Parliament?*, pp.10, 89–92; Home Office Memo 'Parliament: Televising Proceedings' (23 February 1960), NA CAB 129/100; Shulman, *The Least Worst Television*, p.35; Day, *The Case for Televising Parliament*.

21 Memo (9 August 1966), BBC News and current affairs minutes (12 August 1966) BBC WAC T59/2/1; News and Current Affairs minutes (29 November 1968), T59/2/6.

22 Grace Wyndham Goldie, *Facing the Nation: Television and Politics 1936–76* (London, 1977), pp.220–239, 248–251; Controllers Meeting minutes (26 March 1968, 9 April 1968), BBC WAC T16/157.

23 G.P. Hyett (Director NOP) to Hugh Carleton Greene (7 June 1962); Peter Emery to Sir Ian Jacobs (Director General, BBC, 19, 24 September 1959), BBC WAC T16/717; Controllers meeting minutes (6 August 1968), BBC WAC T16/148/3.

24 Harman Grisewood, meeting with parties (9 March 1955); Sir Stephen Pierssene (General-Director, Conservative Party) to Grisewood (9 May 1955); note of Labour Party meeting (6 July 1955), BBC WAC T16/146/2; Leonard Miall memo (26 January 1956); Mary Adams-Mark Chapman Walker (Conservative publicity director) notes (11 May 1954), BBC WAC S322/156.

25 'Party Conferences, 1956'; Leonard Miall, memo (27 April 1956), BBC WAC T16/146/2.

26 Leonard Miall memos (13 September, 16 October 1961), News and Current Affairs minutes (13 August, 10 December 1965, 20 May 1966, 19 January 1968), Controller's Meeting minutes (4, 18 October 1966), note from John Grist (3 November 1966), BBC WAC T16/146/3.

27 Notes to Wilson (8 July 1969, 2 April 1968) and 1948, 1969 'aide memoires', NA CAB 183/39; Goldie, *Facing the Nation*, pp.302–303, 341–344.

28 'Brief summary of radio ban history, 1947–64' (c.1964); Gordon Wilson (Secretary SNP) to Home (24 August 1964), NA BD 24/204; Evans in *Western Mail* (1 September 1964).

29 Brian Faulkener to Heath (20 February 1959); Reginald Bevins (PMG) to Rab Butler (23 June 1961); Butler to Gaitskell (8 July 1961), CPA CRD 2/20/9.

30 Committee on Party Political Broadcasting (11 December 1962, 17 December 1963, 21 January, 25 February, 16 December 1964), BBC WAC T16/518; A. Howard (ed.), *The Crossman Diaries, 1964–70* (London, 1979), p.270; Lawrence, *Electing our Masters*, pp.169, 205.

31 Committee on PPB (23 January 1967, 2 April 1968), BBC WAC T16/518; Heath to Wilson (4 November 1965), Silkin to Wilson (8 May 1968), CAB 183/39; Howard, *Crossman Diaries*, pp.270–271, 347, 509.

32 J. Blumler, D. McQuail, *Television in Politics* (London, 1968), pp.284–291.

33 Crossman, 'The Politics of Television'; *idem.*, 'Introduction' in Walter Bagehot, *The English Constitution* (London, 1963 (1867)), pp.1, 56–57; *idem.*, *The Charm of Politics* (London, 1958); Fielding, *Labour and Cultural Change*, pp.194–197.

34 Crossman, 'The Politics of Television'; Howard, *Crossman Diaries*, p.347.

35 Shulman, *Least Worst Television*, p.39; J. Gummer, *The Permissive Society* (London, 1971), pp.116–118.

36 W. Deedes, *Not a One-way Exercise* (1963), History of Advertising Trust Archive (HAT), IPR 12/4/1.

37 Shulman, *Least Worst Television*, pp.156–157; Williams, *Entertaining the Nation*, p.81; Dominic Wring, *The Politics of Marketing the Labour Party* (Basingstoke, 2005), p.145.

38 Martin Rosenbaum, 'Betting and the 1997 British General Election', *Politics* 19:1 (February 1999), p.9; L. Beers, 'Punting on the Thames: electoral betting in inter-war Britain', *Journal of Contemporary History* (forthcoming, 2010); D. Butler, A. King, *The British General Election of 1964* (London, 1965), p.39; R. Rose, 'One Man's Election', *Twentieth Century* 1043 (1970), p.10; C. Booker, *The Neophiliacs* (London, 1969), pp.279–280.

39 Mark Abrams, 'Political Broadcast Survey' (October 1969), Abrams 69 'Working Papers and correspondence regarding the Labour Party'; Jay Blumler, Alison Ewbank, 'Tories on Television', *Crossbow* (October–December 1967), pp.18, 20.

40 B. Jackson, *Working Class Community* (London, 1968), p.165; Jennings, *Party Politics I*, pp.177, 223–234.

41 Research Services Ltd. J.6643, 'Survey of impact of Political Advertising' (October 1969), Abrams 22.

42 Sidney van den Bergh (Unilever vice-chairman) 'Public Relations and Politics' (c.1960), IPR 10/2/1; C.G.F. Nuttall (LPE), 'TV commercial audiences in the UK', *Journal of Advertising Research* 2:3 (1962), pp.19–28; 'Attention to TV Commercials' (7 August 1958), Abrams 88 'Working Papers regarding television, 2/3, 1954–65'; P. Lazarsfeld, E. Katz, *Personal Influence* (Glencoe, Ill., 1955).

43 J. Trenaman, 'Some implications of a recent study of the comprehension of television programmes' (n.d., c.1958), Abrams 88 'Working Papers regarding television, 2/3, 1954–65'; Trenaman, McQuail, *Television and the Political Image*, pp.14–15, 227–236.

44 M. Abrams, 'Why the Parties Advertise', *New Society* (6 June 1963); D. Tribe, 'Galloping Consumption', *Twentieth Century*, 1039–1040 (1968–9), p.7; Alan Sillitoe, *The Loneliness of the Long-distance Runner* (London, 1966), p.170.

45 J. Thomas, *Popular Newspapers, the Labour Party and British Politics* (London, 2005); Lawrence, 'British Public Politics', pp.205–206; *Heckler's Half Hour*, CPA CRD 2/20/9; Chief organization officer memo (1966), CPA CCO 500/24/214; H. Gurden, 'Political animals', *Looking Right* (July 1962), p.23.

46 Booker, *Neophiliacs*, p.278; M. Rosenbaum, *From Soapbox to Soundbite* (London, 1997), pp.128–129; Lawrence, *Electing our Masters*, pp.209–211, 168–169.

47 Conservative Party/Central Office, *Organisation of Indoor and Outdoor Meetings* (London, 1954), p.1; Rosenbaum, *From Soapbox to Soundbite*, pp.242–245; Lawrence, *Electing Our Masters*, pp.156–159.

48 Shulman, *The Least Worst Television*, p.157; B. Castle, *Fighting All the Way* (London, 1993), pp.562–563; http://news.bbc.co.uk/hi/english/static/vote2001/in_depth/election_battles/1955, 1970; Lawrence, 'British Public Politics', p.215.

49 Jennings, *Party Politics I*, pp.177–178, 227; *The Growth of Parties Vol.II* (Cambridge, 1961), pp.340–342; Harrison, *Seeking a Role*, pp.197, 418–419.

50 John Linsey, *Talking on Television and Radio* (Conservative and Unionist Central Office, 1963 – original edition, 1957), Abrams 58 'Working Papers on the Conservative 1964 Election'; Goldie, *Facing the Nation*, pp.142, 205–206.

51 J. Trenaman, 'The Politician's Platform', *Guardian* (2 November 1961); Blumler, McQuail, *Television in Politics*, p.262; Research Services Ltd. Reports J1068 (December 1958) 'Television Enquiry VI', Abrams 9; Abrams, 'Television Election?'.

52 J. Moran 'Mass-Observation, Market Research and the Birth of the Focus Group, 1937–1997', *Journal of British Studies* 47 (2008).

53 Samuel Beer, *Modern British Politics* (London, 1965), pp.348–349; Wring, *Politics of Marketing*, p.161; Graham Dowson, 'The Product – Politics', *Impact* (Summer 1967); Labour Party Research Department, Re. 47, 'Memo on Proposed Pilot Scheme for a Public Opinion Survey' (April 1956).

54 Wring, *Politics of Marketing*, pp.48–63; Laura Beers, 'Whose opinion? Changing attitudes towards opinion polling in British politics, 1937–64', *Twentieth Century British History* 17:2 (2006), pp.195–205; Black, *Political Culture*, ch.7.

55 'Labour Party – General election campaign' in A.J. Mcwhinnie (21 January 1959), Douglas Machray (6 February 1959) to Gaitskell , Wilson papers c.866b.

56 Ros Allen, Brian Murphy 'The Past, Present and Future of LP advertising', memo (9 December 1963), Abrams 67, 'Working Papers on the LP and Advertising, 1958–64'; Planning Group minutes (5 June 1963), Abrams 68, 'LP Publicity Committee, 1963–64, 2/2'; Wring, *The Politics of Marketing*, pp.65–71.

57 Reports, Abrams 67 'Study of Public Opinion 1962–65'; D. Kingsley, 'Labour Party advertising: Aug '63 onwards'; J. Boswell, 'Getting Labour's economic plan across' (10 September 1963); Boswell to Percy Clark (12 December 1963), Abrams 67 'Working Papers on the LP and Advertising, 1958–64'; Planning and

publicity group meeting (10 December 1963), Abrams 68 'LP Publicity Committee, 1963–64, 1/2'

58 Allen, Murphy, 'The Past, Present and Future of LP advertising'.

59 D. Kingsley, 'Memo on the use of voluntary help for the publicity activities of the party' (February 1965) and memo (25 March 1965), Abrams 42 'Committee Papers and Minutes for the Publicity Group, 1965–66'.

60 Plan for an Efficient Party, *Campaign Newsletter* 4 (13 May 1966), pp.2–3; 'Our Penny-Farthing Machine', *Socialist Commentary* (October 1965); F. Teer, J.D. Spence, *Political Opinion Polls* (London, 1973), pp.171–172; Lawrence, *Electing Our Masters*, p.202.

61 Thomas, *Popular Newspapers*; Guide, Abrams 76 'General Election, 1964'; S. Schwarzkopf, 'They do it with mirrors: advertising and British cold war consumer politics', *Contemporary British History* 19 (2005).

62 *Scrutiny* 1 (May 1961), 5 (October 1961); AIQ, 'A Policy for Advertising' (July 1964), Francis Noel-Baker (16 July 1964), Fisher (6 July 1964) to Douglas-Home, NA PREM 11/4852.

63 Francis Noel-Baker to Gaitskell (11 January 1960), Sainsbury to Gaitskell (23 May 1961), Wilson papers, c.866b; on Abrams, Freeman to Gaitskell (7 July 1961), c.866b.

64 Transcript, discussion with Reith committee, pp.2–3, 8, Hoggart papers, 247/5/10/4; Hoggart *Advertisers Weekly* (October 1965) cited in J.E. Clucas, 'The Black Box' (n.d., 1967) in *IPA Forum*, 247/3/177/1; E.P. Thomspon, 'A psessay in ephology', *New Reasoner* 10 (1959), p.2; S. Hall, 'The First New Left' in Oxford University Socialist Discussion Group, *Out of Apathy* (London, 1989), p.30; Moran, 'Birth of the focus group', pp.843–845.

65 J.B. Priestley, *The Image Men* (London, 1968).

66 LPE, 'Advertising and the Labour Party' (9 March 1964), pp.1–12, HAT LPE 3/3/2.

67 A.W. Benn, 'Pollsters and Politicians', *Guardian* (13 March 1964); Beers, 'Whose opinion?, p.205; Teer, Spence, *Political Opinion Polls*, p.81.

68 Mark Abrams, 'Market analysis: How consumers make their selections' (November 1959), HAT LPE 1/3/136; 'Social Class and Politics', *Twentieth Century* (Spring 1965), p.35; A. Silver, 'Political Attitudes in Britain' (5 June 1958), Abrams 75 'Working Papers on Politics and Polls, 1956–59'; Murray Edelman, *The Symbolic Uses of Politics* (Urbana, Ill., 1964), p.123.

69 Abrams, 'Political Attitudes of Young People' (16 May 1969); Abrams 69 'Working Papers and correspondence regarding the LP'; Max Williams, 'Up the polls', *New Society* (9 July 1970).

70 David Broughton, *Public Opinion and Polling and Politics in Britain* (Hemel Hempstead, 1995), pp.2, 6; Teer, Spence, *Political Opinion Polls*, pp.10–12.

71 *Sunday Times* (11 April 1971), *Sunday Telegraph* (10 November 1963); 'Appendix' in D. Butler, A. King, *The British General Election of 1964* (Macmillan: London, 1965).

72 S. Black (ed.), *The IPR 1948–73* (London, 1973), pp.14–17, 44; Jeremy Tunstall, *The Advertising Man* (London, 1964), pp.184–186, 248–256; I. Harvey, *Techniques of Persuasion* (London, 1951).

73 F. Noel-Baker, 'The grey zone: The problems of business affiliations of members of parliament', *Parliamentary Affairs* 15 (1961); A. Roth, *The Business Background of MPs* (London, 1957); S. Finer, *Anonymous Empire: A Study of the Lobby in Great Britain* (London, 1962), p.43.

74 I. Waller, 'Pressure Groups: MPs and PROs', *Encounter* (August 1962); I. MacArthur, 'The Adman's Reply', *Impact* (Autumn 1965); Schwarzkopf, 'They do it with mirrors', p.150; A. Eggers, J. Hainmueller, 'The value of political power: Estimating returns to office in post-war British politics' (forthcoming *American Political Science Review*, November 2009), see http://www.people.fas.harvard.edu/~jhainm/Paper/VPP.pdf (accessed 18 May 2009).

75 J. Douglas to I. Fraser (14 November 1963), CPA CRD 2/8/30; Andrew Taylor, 'The Conservative Party and Mass Opinion from the 1920s to 1950s' in S. Ball, I. Holliday (eds), *Mass Conservatism* (London, 2002), pp.90–95; Douglas on Abrams, *Must Labour Lose?* and Crosland, *Can Labour Win?* (9, 17 May 1960), CPA CRD 2/21/6.

76 1959 manifesto steering committee minutes (20 March 1958), p.3, CPA CRD 2/53/34; 'Onward with psephologists', *Conservative Agents Journal* 416 (January 1956), p.17.

77 Teer, Spence, *Political Opinion Polls*, pp.162, 168.

78 Tunstall, *Advertising Man*, pp.165–166, 235; Harrison, *Seeking a Role*, p.465.

79 Nancy Wilkins, 'Anything Goes', *Impact* (February 1965), p.26; Rosenbaum, *Soapbox to Soundbite*, pp.55–56; Fairlie, *Daily Mail* (9 June 1960); Viscount Hailsham, *The Door Wherein I Went* (London, 1975), p.127; M. Haynes, *Advertising on Trial* (London, 1961); J. Douglas, I. MacArthur *et al.*, *Choice* (CPC, London, 1961).

80 'The problem of soft-selling the Tories', *Sunday Times* (22 September 1963).

81 *Sunday Times* (27 October 1963); D. Walder, *The Short List* (London, 1964), pp.106–107; M. Kandiah, 'Television enters British politics: the Conservative Party's Central Office and political broadcasting, 1945–55', *Historical Journal of Film, Radio and Television*, 15:2 (1995); 'Our Penny-farthing Machine', p.xix.

82 Reginald Watts, 'Bringing the party up to date', *Crossbow* (November–December 1967), pp.30–36.

83 Lawrence, *Electing Our Masters*, p.174; M. Brewer, 'Organising the women's day-time canvass', M. Knowles, 'American view on the canvass', *Labour Woman* (February 1952), pp.265, 270–271.

84 D. Lessing, *The Golden Notebook* (London, 2002 [1962]), pp.158–161; Walder, *Short List*, pp.118–127.

85 Jennings, *Party Politics I*, pp.210–228; S. Orneau, 'Why did we vote', *Current Affairs* 123 (January 1951), pp.7–17; J. Morgan (ed.), *Crossman – Backbench Diaries* (1981), p.622; Dennis Hackett, 'Transport House: a Labour of love', *Queen* (15 January 1964), p.40.

86 M. Rustin, 'The New Left as a social movement' in Oxford University Socialist Discussion Group, *Out of Apathy*, p.120; James Douglas to Arthur Tiley MP (24 October 1962), to Fraser (25 October 1962), CPA CRD 2/8/28.

87 Labour Party Archives, NEC minutes (22 June 1960); A.W. Mason to Morgan Phillips (5 May 1958); General Secretary's papers Box 21, GS/Pers/221; A.E. Tomlinson (Pres. Finchley CLP) to Rees (2 July 1962), File 'Correspondence – CLPs', FOL 5; *Daily Sketch* (18 June 1962).

88 *Guardian* 16 June 1962; *Daily Herald* (18 June 1962); Press release, Rees to Lowestoft CLP Annual Dinner (10 March 1962), File 'Miscellaneous', FOL 1; A.W. Benn, 'Lets repeat the Festival Every Year', *Tribune* 22 June 1962, p.7; *Daily Mirror* (18 June 1962); *South London Press* (22 June 1962).

89 'Report on the Festival of Labour' (August 1962), FOL 1; Rees, interview, 29 November 2001.

90 Nell Dunn, 'Trip to Battersea', *New Statesman* 22 June 1962, p.918.

91 Hill, Whichelow, *What's Wrong with Parliament?* pp.84–85; *Guardian* (28 January 1960); Harrison, *Seeking a Role*, pp.447–448.
92 Council of Industrial Design *Newsletter* 143 (December 1961); Merlyn Rees, 'Let's get Festive', *Transport Salaried Staff Journal* LIX: 695 (February 1962), pp.70–71.
93 Labour Party, *Brighter Party Premises* (London, 1961); London Labour Party papers, London Metropolitan Archive acc.2417/g/115; Labour Party, *Festival of Labour Brochure* (1962), p.18.
94 *Labour Fund Raiser* 4 (October 1965), p.17; Jim Northcott (Plan for an efficient Party campaign organizer, 1965–67), interview 14 February 2001; *Socialist Commentary* (October 1965), p.iv.
95 James Douglas to Mr. Bagnall (23 January 1959), CPA CRD 2/8/19; Enoch Powell, 'The Party with the paint peeling off', *Conservative Agents Journal* 513 (February 1965), pp.12–13.
96 Philip Tether, 'Clubs: A neglected aspect of Conservative Organization', *Hull Papers in Politics* 42 (1988), pp.4, 53, 68–70; Walder, *Short List*, p.86.
97 Heidi Topman, 'A study of the rise and decline of selected Labour Halls in Greater London, 1918–79' (Ph.D., Kingston University, 2006), pp.195, 224–225.
98 Blumler, Ewbank, 'Tories on Television, p.20; Wring, *The Politics of Marketing*, pp.72–73.
99 Williams, *Entertaining the Nation*, p.84; Humphrey Carpenter, *That was Satire That Was: The Satire Boom of the 1960s* (London, 2000); S. Wagg, 'Comedians and Politics in the United States and Great Britain' in S. Wagg (ed.), *Because I tell a Joke or Two: Comedy, Politics and Social Difference* (London, 1998); *idem.* 'The politics of British satirical comedy from *Beyond the Fringe* to *Spitting Image*' in D. Strinati, S. Wagg (eds), *Come on Down: Popular Media Culture in Post-war Britain* (London, 1992).
100 Wagg, 'Comedians and Politics', pp.264–265; Carpenter, pp.182, 263–265; *Private Eye* (9 March 1962).
101 G. Kaufman, 'Five year tests', R. Gillespie, C. Lewsen, 'Why? A Consumer guide to religions' in D. Frost, N. Sherrin (eds), *That Was the Week That Was: A Miscellany of Material* (London, 1963), pp.52, 78–81; Carpenter, *That was Satire*, pp.244–249; Levin, *The Pendulum Years*, p.321.
102 J. Northcott, *Value for Money?* (London, 1953); L. Black, 'A comparative history of post-war British and American consumer organisations' in I. Theien, E. Lange (eds), *Affluence and Activism* (Oslo, 2004); 'Consuming Interest?', *Spectator*, (13 December 1969), p.823.
103 CA's evidence to Reith Commission (September 1962), Abrams 41, File 3/3.
104 M. Young, *The Rise of the Meritocracy: 1870–2033* (Harmondsworth, 1958, 1963 edition), p.1; Harrison, *Seeking a Role*, p.202; G. Dench, T. Flower, K. Gavron (eds), *Young at Eighty* (Manchester, 1995), pp.131, 156, 158; J. Blondel, *Voters, Leaders and Parties* (Harmondsworth, 1966), p.1.
105 Eliasoph, *Avoiding Politics*, pp.127–129; C. Hay, *Why We Hate Politics* (Cambridge, 2007), ch.3, p.151; D. Marquand, *Decline of the Public* (Cambridge, 2004); Wring, *The Politics of Marketing*, pp.178–179; Offer, *Challenge to Affluence*, pp.130–131.
106 M. Hilton, 'The fable of the Sheep, or, Private Virtues, Public Vices: The Consumer Revolution of the 20th Century', *Past and Present* 176 (2002); Zygmunt Bauman, 'Britain's exit from politics', *New Statesman and Society* (29 July 1988).
107 F. Bogel, *The Difference Satire Makes* (Ithaca, NY., 2001), pp.3, 53.
108 Lawrence, 'British Public politics', pp.213–215.

Chapter 8

1 D. Butler, M. Pinto-Duschinsky, *The British General Election of 1970* (London, 1971), pp.154, 201, 226–228, 337; J. Saramago, *Seeing* (London, 2006).
2 G. Ortolano, *The Two Cultures Controversy: Science, Literature and Cultural Politics in Postwar Britain* (Cambridge, 2009); D. Edgerton *Warfare State* (Cambridge, 2005); J. Tomlinson, 'Thrice denied: "Declinism" as a recurrent theme in British history in the long 20th Century', *Twentieth Century British History* 20:2 (2009).
3 M. Hilton, *Consumerism in Twentieth Century Britain* (Cambridge, 2003); J. Lawrence, *Electing Our Masters* (Oxford, 2009); N. Crowson, M. Hilton, J. McKay (eds), *NGOs in Contemporary Britain* (Basingstoke, 2009).
4 J. Moran, *Queuing for Beginners* (London, 2008).
5 B. Harrison, *Seeking a Role* (Oxford, 2009), pp.523–526.
6 See E.H.H. Green, *Thatcher* (London, 2006); B. Campbell, *The Iron Ladies* (London, 1987); J. Curran, I. Gaber, J. Petley, *Culture Wars* (Edinburgh, 2005); G. Eley, *Forging Democracy* (Oxford, 2002); I. Crewe, A. King, *SDP: The Birth, Life and Death of the Social Democratic Party* (Oxford, 1995); G. Andrews, *Endgames and New Times* (London, 2004).
7 E.F. Schumacher, *Small is Beautiful: A Study of Economics as if People Mattered* (London, 1973); Curran, Gaber, Petley, *Culture Wars*, ch.1; R. Lowe, 'Life begins in the seventies', *Journal of Contemporary History* 42:1 (2007); S. Wagg, *Because I Tell a Joke or Two* (London, 1998), ch.13.
8 See C. Hay, 'Chronicles of a death foretold', *Political Quarterly* 80:4 (2009).
9 R. King, N. Nugent (eds), *Respectable Rebels* (London, 1979); R. McKibbin, *Classes and Cultures* (Oxford, 1998), chs.III, V.

Bibliography

Archival Sources

BBC Written Archives Centre, Caversham
BBC papers (BBC WAC)
Mary Adams papers (MAP)

Birmingham Central Library
Birmingham Young Conservative papers (BCL)

Bodleian Library, Oxford
Conservative Party Archive (CPA – Conservative Central Office (CCO), Area Records
   (ARE), Conservative Research Department (CRD))
Harold Wilson papers (Wilson)

Bristol Record Office
Bristol Trades Council papers (BRO)

British Library of Political and Economic Science, London
Anthony Crosland papers (Crosland)

Churchill College, Cambridge
Mark Abrams papers (Abrams)
Michael Young papers (Yung)

Consumers' Association, London
Consumers' Association archives (CAA)

Consumer Movement Archive, Kansas State University, Manhattan, KS, USA
Thomas Brooks papers (Brooks)

Essex University Library, Colchester
National Viewers' and Listeners' Association Archive (NVALA)

Harry Ransom Humanities Research Center, Texas University, Austin, USA
Arnold Wesker papers (AW)

History of Advertising Trust Archive, Raveningham
Institute of Public Relations (IPR)
London Press Exchange (LPE)

Labour History Archive and Study Centre, Manchester

Labour Party archives (LPA)
Festival of Labour papers (FOL)

London Metropolitan Archives

London Labour Party papers

National Archives, London

BD 24	Welsh Office: Radio and Television Broadcasting
BT 58	Board of Trade: Companies Department
CAB 129	Cabinet Memoranda
CAB 183	Government Chief Whip's Office
EW 23	Department of Economic Affairs: Regional Policy Department
HO 256	Home Office: Broadcasting/Post Office
HO 264	Home Office: Committee on Privacy
MT 98	Ministry of Transport, Vehicle Safety Division
PREM 11	Prime Minister's Office: Correspondence and papers, 1951–64
PREM 13	Prime Minister's Office: Correspondence and papers, 1964–70
T 218	Treasury: Arts, Science and Lands Division
T 326	Treasury: Finance, Home and General Division, Future of the CWS
TS 82	Treasury Solicitor: Ministry of Transport

National Co-operative Archive, Manchester

Co-operative Congress records, Periodicals

Open University Library, Milton Keynes

Jennie Lee papers (JL)

Sheffield University Library

Richard Hoggart papers (MS.247)

Tom Harrison Mass Observation Archive, University of Sussex, Brighton

Topic Collection 21/F, G, E (1947)

University College, London

Hugh Gaitskell papers (Gaitskell)

Victoria and Albert Museum, London

Arts Council of Great Britain papers (ACGB)

Interviews

Arnold Wesker, August 2003, Hay-on-Wye
Jim Haynes, August 2005, Traverse Theatre, Edinburgh
Lord Merlyn Rees, November 2001, House of Lords
Jim Northcott, February 2001, London

YC correspondence/interviews: Peter Barwell, Eileen Atherton, Stirling Moss, Richard
Tomlinson, John Wood, Josephine Smith, Juliet Gardiner, Gerald Blackburn, Tony
Shaw
Correspondence: Susan Crosland (4 May 2008), James Douglas (8 January 2003) and
Michael Young (19 March 2001)

Official Publications/Government Reports

Final Report of the Committee on Consumer Protection (Molony Report), Cmnd. 1781
(July 1962)
A Policy for the Arts: The First Steps, Cmnd. 2601 (1965)

Contemporary Journals/Newspapers

Adult Education
Agenda
Ark
Arts North
Association of Broadcasting Staff Bulletin
Baptist Times
Birmingham Post
Blue Horizon
BBC Audience Research Newsletter
Black Dwarf
Bristol Evening Post
Buff Orpington
The Bulletin
Business Week
Cambridge News
Campaign Newsletter (Plan for an Efficient Party)
Catholic Herald
Catholic Teacher
Cartel
Challenge
Christian Science Monitor
Conservative Agents Journal
Consumer News
Consumer Reports
Co-operative Consumer
Co-operative News
Co-operative Party Monthly Newsletter
Council of Industrial Design Newsletter
Crossbow
Daily Express
Daily Mail
Daily Mirror
Daily Sketch
Daily Telegraph
Daily Worker
Definition
Democratory
Domestic Equipment Trader

Economist
Encounter
Evening Standard
Film
Financial Times
Focus
Garage and motor agent
Glance
Good Food Guide
Guardian
Harvard Business Review
Holborn Guardian
Humanist News
Impact
International Times
Jackie
Kentish Independent
Labour Fund-Raiser
Labour Organiser
Labour Woman
Leicester Daily Press
Leicester Mercury
Liverpool Post
(London) Evening News
Looking Right
Mainstream
Manager
Manchester Consumer Group Newsletter
Manchester Guardian
Melody Maker
Middlesbrough Evening Gazette
Montreal Star
National Consumer
New Left Review
New Outlook: A Liberal Magazine
New Reasoner
New Socialist
New Society
New Statesman
New York Daily Post
New York Times
North London Press
Nottingham Evening Post
Observer
Peace News
Planning
Platform
Private Eye
Progress
Punch
Queen

Railway Review
Rightway
Roundabout Rushcliffe
Sales management
Scene
Schoolmaster
The Scotsman
Scottish Co-operator
Scrutiny
Self-service and Supermarket
She
Shoppers' Guide
Socialist Commentary
South London Press
Southern Weekly News
Spectator
Stage and Television Today
St Louis post-dispatch
Swinton College Journal
Sunday Citizen
Sunday Press
Sunday Telegraph
Sunday Times
Time
Times
Times Literary Supplement
Topic
Trading Interest
Transport Salaried Staff Journal
Trend
Tribune
Universities and Left Review
The Viewer and Listener (also *The Viewer, National VALA News*)
Wall Street Journal
Weekly Scotsman
Western Mail
Which?
The Whip
Wolverhampton Express & Star
YC and Unionist Organization
The Youth Officer
Youth Service Magazine

Contemporary Publications (published in London unless stated otherwise)

Mark Abrams; 'Social Class and Politics', *Twentieth Century* (Spring 1965).
Philip Abrams, Alan Little, 'The Young Activist in British Politics', *British Journal of Sociology* 16 (December 1965).
Leslie Adrian (ed. Nancy Ryan), *Consuming Interest, from The Spectator* (1961).
D. Ainley, *The Co-ops: The Way Ahead* (1962).

Gabriel A. Almond, Sidney Verba, *The Civic Culture* (1963, 1989 re-edition).
J. Bailey, *The British Co-operative Movement* (1955).
J.A. Banks, G. Ostergaard, *Co-operative Democracy* (Co-op College paper 2, 1955).
Clive Barker, 'Vintage 42', *Twentieth Century* (Winter 1966).
Samuel Beer, *Modern British Politics* (1965).
W.A. Belson, *Television and the Family* (1959).
A.W. Benn, *Against the Tide: Diaries 1973–76* (1989).
Hugh Berrington, 'Banbury', in David Butler (ed.), *The British General Election of 1955* (1969).
Alan Birch, *Small Town Politics* (Oxford, 1959).
Peter Black, *Mirror in the Corner* (1972).
John Bloom, *It's No Sin to Make a Profit* (1971).
Jean Blondel, *Voters, Parties and Leaders* (Harmondsworth, 1966).
J. Blumler, D. McQuail, *Television in Politics* (1968).
A. Bonner, *British Co-operation* (Manchester, 1970).
C. Booker, *The Neophiliacs* (1969).
Elaine Burton, *Value for Money* (1955).
D. Butler, A. King, *The British General Election of 1964* (1965).
D. Butler, M. Pinto-Duschinsky, *The British General Election of 1970* (1971).
R. Carless, P. Brewster (eds), *Patronage and the Arts* (1959).
L.A. Cherriman, R. Wilson, *The Operation of a Self-Service Store* (Co-op College papers 9, 1962).
Conservative Party Annual Conference Report (1958).
Conservative Political Centre (CPC) *Automation and the Consumer* (1956).
Conservative Party/Central office, *Organisation of Indoor and Outdoor Meetings* (1954).
—— John Linsey, *Talking on Television and Radio* (Conservative and Unionist Central Office, 1963 – original edition, 1957).
Consumers' Association, *Evidence Submitted to the Departmental Committee on Consumer Protection* (March 1960).
—— *Fifth* (1961/2), *Twelfth Annual Report of the Consumers' Association* (1969).
—— *Which? and Consumers' Association* (1965).
Consumers Union (USA), *This is Consumers' Union* (New York, 1961).
D. Cooper (ed.), *The Dialectics of Liberation* (Harmondsworth, 1971).
—— 'Looking Back on Anger', in V. Bogdanor, R. Skidelsky (eds), *The Age of Affluence 1951–64* (1970).
Co-operative Independent Commission Report (Manchester, 1958).
Co-operative Union, *Report of Proceedings Special National Congress, Blackpool* (Manchester, 1958).
—— *Report of Action by the Central Executive on Resolutions of the Special National Congress* (Manchester, 1959).
—— *Report of the CRDS Negotiating Committee* (Manchester, 1960).
—— *Consumer Protection: A Memorandum Submitted by the Co-operative Union Ltd. to the Molony Committee* (Manchester, 1960).
J. Corbett, *The Birmingham Trades Council 1866–1966* (1966).
Maurice Cowling, *Mill and Liberalism* (Cambridge, 1963).
—— *The Nature and Limits of Political Science* (Cambridge, 1963).
B. Crick, *In Defence of Politics* (Harmondsworth, 1962, 1976 edition).
J. Critchley, *Counsel for Broadcasting* (1971).
C.A.R. Crosland, *The Future of Socialism* (1956).
—— *The Conservative Enemy* (1962).
—— *A Critical Commentary on Co-operative Progress* (Manchester, 1971).

—— *A Social Democratic Britain* (Fabian Tract 404, 1971).
—— *Socialism Now* (1974).
R.H.S. Crossman, *The Charm of Politics* (1958).
—— 'Introduction', in Walter Bagehot, *The English Constitution* (Harmondsworth, 1963 (1867)).
—— A. Howard (ed.), *The Crossman Diaries, 1964-70* (1979).
—— J. Morgan (ed.), *Crossman – Backbench Diaries* (1981).
Robin Day, *The Case for Televising Parliament* (1963).
Reuel Denney, *The Astonished Muse* (Chicago, 1957).
T. Driberg, *The Mystery of Moral Re-armament* (1964).
R. Dunstan, 'Which?Hunt', *Twentieth Century* Vol.176:4–177:1 (1968–9).
Viscount Eccles, *Politics and the Quality of Life* (CPC, 1970).
D. Edwards, J. Robinson (ed.), *The Honest to God Debate* (1963).
Murray Edelman, *The Symbolic Uses of Politics* (Urbana, Ill., 1964).
Leon D. Epstein, 'The Politics of British Conservatism', *American Political Science Review* 48 (1954).
D. Fairbairn, 'An Approach to Leisure: Conservatism in a Post-Industrial Society', in Bow Group, *Principles in Practice* (1961).
H. Fairlie, *The Life of Politics* (1968).
V. Feather, *The Essence of Trade Unionism* (1963).
S. Finer, *Anonymous Empire: A Study of the Lobby in Great Britain* (1962).
Michael Foster, 'The Roundhouse', *Architectural Association Quarterly* 3:1 (Winter 1971).
A. Fox, *The Emerging Ethic* (Portlaw, 1971).
Ronald Frankenberg, *Communities in Britain* (Harmondsworth, 1967).
L. Freedman, G. Hemingway, *Nationalisation and the Consumer* (1950).
D. Frost, N. Sherrin (eds), *That Was The Week That Was: A Miscellany of Material* (1963).
Peter Fryer, *Mrs Grundy: Studies in English Prudery* (1965).
H. Gaitskell, *In Defence of Politics* (1954).
Peter Goldman, *Some Principles of Conservatism* (1961).
—— 'Consumerism – Art or Science?' *Journal of the Royal Society of Arts* (August 1969).
Phillip Goodhart, James Douglas, Patricia Mclaughlin, John Wood, Max Bemrose, Ian MacArthur, *Choice: A Report on Consumer Protection* (1961).
Lord Goodman, *Not for the Record* (1972).
Ray Gosling, *Lady Albemarle's Boys* (1961).
Granada TV, *Prelude to Westminster* (1962).
GLYCs, *Set the Party Free* (1969).
B. Groombridge, *Television and the People: A Programme for Democratic Participation* (Harmondsworth, 1972).
J.S. Gummer, *The Permissive Society* (1971).
W.L. Guttsman, *The British Political Elite* (1963).
Elizabeth Gundrey, *Your Money's Worth: A Handbook for Consumers* (Harmondsworth, 1962).
J. Gusfield, *Symbolic Crusade and Status Politics: The American Temperance Movement* (Chicago, 1976, 1st edition 1963).
J. Habermas, *The Structural Transformation of the Public Sphere* (Cambridge, 1989, original 1962).
Viscount Hailsham, *The Conservative Case* (Harmondsworth, 1959).
—— Hailsham, *The Door Wherein I Went* (1975), p.127.
S. Hall, 'The supply of demand', in E.P. Thompson (ed.), *Out of Apathy* (1960).

—— (with P. Whannel), *The Popular Arts* (1964).

J.D. Halloran (with R.L. Brown, D.C. Chaney), *Television and Delinquency* (Leicester, 1970).

—— (ed.), *The Effects of Television* (1970).

—— (with P. Eliot, G. Murdock, *Demonstrations and Communication* (Harmondsworth, 1970).

A.H. Halsey, G.N. Ostergaard, *Power in Co-operatives: The Internal Politics of British Retail Societies* (Oxford, 1965).

Leonard M. Harris, Mass Observation Ltd., *Buyer's Market* (1963).

R. Harris, A. Seldon, *Advertising and the Public* (1959).

L. Harrison, J. Roper, *Towards Regional Co-operatives* (Fabian Research Series 260, 1967).

I. Harvey, *Techniques of Persuasion* (1951).

R. Hattersley, 'New Blood', in G. Kaufman (ed.), *The Left* (1966).

M. Haynes, *Advertising on Trial: The Case for the Consumer* (Bow Group, 1961).

A. Hill, A. Whichelow, *What's Wrong with Parliament?* (Harmondsworth, 1964).

H. Himmelweit, A.N. Oppenheim, P. Vince, *Television and the Child* (Oxford, 1958).

G. Hodgkinson, *Sent to Coventry* (Oxford, 1970).

R. Hoggart, *The Uses of Literacy* (Harmondsworth, 1957).

—— 'The Difficulties of Democratic Debate', *Teachers College Record* 64:8 (May 1963).

D. Holbrook 'Magazines – With Special Reference to the Exploitation of Pseudo-sexuality', in Denys Thompson (ed.), *Discrimination and Popular Culture* (Harmonsworth, 1970).

—— D. Holbrook, 'Mary Whitehouse', *Political Quarterly* 51:2 (1980).

J.A. Hough, F. Lambert, *Self-Service Shops* (Manchester, n.d., c.1951).

Elisabeth Houlton, *Which? Put to the Test* (Aims of Industry Study No. 15, 1967).

IOCU, *3rd Conference Report* (Oslo, 1964).

Brian Jackson, *Working Class Community* (1968).

I. Jennings, *Party Politics vol. I* (*Appeal to the People*), II (*The Growth of Parties*), III (*The Stuff of Politics*) (Cambridge, 1960–2).

Pierre Joly, 'Oscar Niemeyer joue avec la faucille et le marteau', *L'Oeil* 219 (1973).

Labour Party, Labour Party, *Let Us Win Through Together* (1950).

—— *Fair Deal for the Shopper* (1961).

—— *Labour Women's Conference Reports* 1958, 1959, 1963, 1970.

—— *Brighter Party Premises* (1961).

—— *Festival of Labour brochure* (1962).

—— *A New Hope for Britain* (1983).

P. Lazarsfeld, E. Katz, *Personal Influence* (Glencoe, Ill., 1955).

D. Lessing, *The Golden Notebook* (2002 [1962]).

Bernard Levin, *The Pendulum Years* (1970).

Liberal Party, *Shopping: Better Buys* (1961).

—— *Consumer Protection* (1962).

Gilda Lund, *You and Your Shopping* (1961).

A. Lunn, G. Lean *The Cult of Softness* (1965).

J.D.B. Miller, *Politicians* (Leicester, 1958).

Robert Millar, *The Affluent Sheep* (1963).

Jeremy Mitchell, 'Testing for *Which?* Some Statistical Problems', *Applied Statistics* XII:2 (1963).

Ruby Turner Morris, *CU: Methods, Implications, Weaknesses and Strengths* (New London, CT., 1971).

Richard Morse (ed.), *The Consumer Movement: Lectures by Colston E. Warne* (Manhattan, KS, 1993).

R. Nader, *Unsafe At Any Speed* (New York, 1965).

New Society, *Social Reform in the Centrifugal Society* (1969).

F. Noel-Baker, 'The Grey Zone: The Problems of Business Affiliations of Members of Parliament', *Parliamentary Affairs* 15 (1961).

Jim Northcott, *Value for Money? The Case for a Consumers' Advice Service* (1953).

C.G.F. Nuttall, 'TV Commercial Audiences in the UK', *Journal of Advertising Research* 2:3 (1962).

Michael Oakeshott, *Rationalism in Politics and Other Essays* (1967).

M. Page, 'Whatever Happened to Arnold Wesker?', *Modern Drama* 11 (1968).

F. Parkin, *Middle Class Radicalism: The Social Bases of the British Campaign for Nuclear Disarmament* (Manchester, 1968).

PEP, 'Consumer Protection and Enlightenment', *Planning* XXVI:441 (25 April 1960).

—— 'Public Patronage of the Arts', *Planning* XXXI:492 (November 1965).

S. Pollard, *The Co-operatives at the Crossroads* (Fabian Research Series 245, 1965).

J.B. Priestley, *The Image Men* (1968).

Research Institute for Consumer Affairs (RICA), *British Co-operatives: A Consumers' Movement?* (1964).

Eirlys Roberts, *Consumers* (1966).

Andrew Robertson, 'The Campaigners', *Twentieth Century* Vol.176:4–177:1 (1968–9).

R. Rose, 'One Man's Election', *Twentieth Century* 1043 (1970).

A. Roth, *The Business Background of MPs* (1957).

E.F. Schumacher, *Small is Beautiful: A Study of Economics as if People Mattered* (1973).

Edward Shils, 'On the Eve', *Twentieth Century* (May 1960).

Milton Shulman, *The Least Worst Television in The World* (1973).

Alan Sillitoe, *The Loneliness of the Long-Distance Runner* (1966).

T. Smith, *Anti-Politics* (1972).

Margaret Stacey, *Tradition and Change: A Study of Banbury* (Oxford, 1960).

Standing Conference on SCTV annual conference reports, *Television: Responsibility and Response* (1959); *Tonight and Tomorrow* (1960); *Pilkington and After* (1962).

Henry and Lillian Stephenson, *Eating, Sleeping and Living: A Guide to Design in the Home* (Manchester, 1964).

Charles Stuart (ed.), *The Reith Diaries* (1975).

F. Teer, J.D. Spence, *Political Opinion Polls* (1973).

D. Tench, *The Law for Consumers* (1962).

M. Thatcher, *What's Wrong with Politics?* (1968).

L. Tivey, 'The Politics of the Consumer', *Political Quarterly* 39:2 (1968).

Ralph Towsey, *Self-Service Retailing* (1964).

J. Trenaman, 'The Responsibility of the Receiver', in SCTV, *Television: Responsibility and Response* (1959).

J. Trenaman, D. McQuail, *Television and the Political Image* (1961).

TUC, *Annual Conference Report* (1960).

Jeremy Tunstall, *The Advertising Man* (1964).

David Walder, *The Short List* (1964).

Peter Walker, *Transport Policy* (1968).

F.A. Wells, M.D. Skillicorn, J.R. Straker, *Recruitment, Selection and Training for Management in Retail Co-operative Societies* (Co-op College papers no.10, 1963).

A. Wesker, *The Modern Playwright or O, Mother, Is It Worth It?* (Oxford, 1960).

—— 'The Kitchen', *New Left Review* 1 (1960).

—— 'Trade Unions and the Arts', *New Left Review* 5 (1960).

—— *Labour and the Arts II: What, Then, Is To Be Done?* (Oxford, 1961).

—— 'Aie Cuba! Aie Cuba!', in *The New Man in Cuba* (British-Cuba Association, Nov. 1969).

—— *Fears of Fragmentation* (1970).

Eric White, *The Arts Council of Great Britain* (1975).

M. Whitehouse, *Cleaning-up TV: From Protest to Participation* (1967).

—— *Who Does She Think She Is?* (1972).

R. Williams (ed.), *May Day Manifesto 1968* (Harmondsworth, 1968).

H.H. Wilson, *Pressure Group* (1961).

Michael Young, *Small Man, Big World: A Discussion of Socialist Democracy* (1949).

—— *The Rise of the Meritocracy: 1870–2033* (Harmondsworth, 1963 [1958]).

—— *The Chipped White Cups of Dover – A Discussion of the Possibility of a New Progressive Party* (1960).

Young Conservatives, *Action '67 Rally Programme* (1967).

Young Conservative and Unionist Organisation, *The Macleod Report 1965* (1965).

Secondary Sources

G. Andrews, *Endgames and New Times* (2004).

C. Bean, E. Papadakis, 'Polarized Priorities or Flexible Alternatives? Dimensionality in Inglehart's Materialism-Postmaterialism Scale', *International Journal of Public Opinion Research* 6:3 (1994).

C. Beauchamp, 'Getting *Your Money's Worth*: American Models for the Re-making of the Consumer Interest in Britain, 1930s–1960s', in M. Bevir, F. Trentmann (eds), *Critiques of Capital in Modern Britain and America* (Basingstoke, 2002).

Laura Beers, 'Whose Opinion? Changing Attitudes Towards Opinion Polling in British Politics, 1937–64', *Twentieth Century British History* 17:2 (2006).

—— 'Labour's Britain, Fight for It Now!', *Historical Journal* 52:3 (2009).

—— 'Punting on the Thames: Electoral Betting in Inter-War Britain' (forthcoming *Journal of Contemporary History*).

J. Birchall, *Co-op: The People's Business* (Manchester, 1994).

L. Black, *The Political Culture of the Left in Affluent Britain, 1951–64* (Basingstoke, 2003).

—— '"Free Choice Lies at the Heart of Our Economic System": A Comparative History of Post-War British and American Consumer Organisations', in I. Theien, E. Lange (eds), *Affluence and Activism* (Oslo, 2004).

—— '*Which?*craft in Post-War Britain: The Consumers' Association and the Politics of Affluence', *Albion* 36:1 (2004).

—— 'Whose Finger on the Button? British Television and the Politics of Cultural Control', *Historical Journal of Film, Radio and Television* 25 (2005).

—— '"Making Britain a Gayer and More Cultivated Country": Wilson, Lee and the Creative Industries in the 1960s', *Contemporary British History* 20:3 (2006).

—— 'Arts and Crafts: Social Democracy's Cultural Resources and Repertoire in 1960s' Britain', in I. Favretto, J. Callaghan (eds), *Transitions in Social Democracy* (Manchester, 2007).

—— 'The Lost World of Young Conservatism', *Historical Journal* 51:4 (2008).

L. Black, H. Pemberton (eds), *An Affluent Society?* (Aldershot, 2004).

L. Black, N. Robertson (eds), *Taking Stock: Consumerism and the Co-Operative Movement in Modern British History* (Manchester, 2009).

S. Black (ed.), *The IPR 1948–73* (1973).

S.S. Bloom, *The Launderette: A History* (London, 1988).

F. Bogel, *The Difference Satire Makes* (Ithaca, NY., 2001).

P. Boobbyer, 'The Cold War in the Plays of Peter Howard', *Contemporary British History* 19:2 (2005).

S. Bowden, A. Offer, 'Household Appliances and the Use of Time in the USA and Britain Since the 1920s', *Economic History Review* 47:4 (1994).

Joe Boyd, *White Bicycles* (2006).

Asa Briggs, *Michael Young: Social Entrepreneur* (Basingstoke, 2001).

David Broughton, *Public Opinion and Polling and Politics in Britain* (Hemel Hempstead, 1995).

C. Brown, *The Death of Christian Britain: Understanding Secularization, 1800–2000* (2001 and 2009 editions).

—— *Religion and Society in Twentieth-Century Britain* (Harlow, 2006).

A. Burton, *The British Consumer Co-operative Movement and Film 1890s–1960s* (Manchester, 2005).

P. Byrne, *Social Movements in Britain* (1997).

Beatrix Campbell, *The Iron Ladies* (1987).

J. Capon, *And There Was Light* (1972).

Humphrey Carpenter, *That Was Satire That Was: The Satire Boom of the 1960s* (2000).

B. Castle, *Fighting All The Way* (1993).

L. Chun, *The British New Left* (Edinburgh, 1993).

A. Clark, *Mrs Thatcher's Minister* (New York, 1994).

D. Cliff, 'Religion, Morality and the Middle Class', in R. King, N. Nugent (eds), *Respectable Rebels: Middle Class Campaigns in Britain in the 1970s* (1979).

L. Cohen, *A Consumers' Republic* (New York, 2002).

M. Collins (ed.), *The Permissive Society and Its Enemies* (2008).

B. Conekin, *The Autobiography of a Nation: The 1951 Festival of Britain* (Manchester, 2003).

Hera Cook, 'No Turning Back: Family Forms and Sexual Mores in Modern Britain', http://www.historyandpolicy.org/papers/policy-paper-17.html

F. Coppieters, 'Arnold Wesker's Centre Fortytwo: A Cultural Revolution Betrayed', *Theatre Quarterly* 5:18 (1975).

I. Crewe, A. King, *SDP: The Birth, Life and Death of the Social Democratic Party* (Oxford, 1995).

J. Critchley, *A Bag of Boiled Sweets* (1995).

Susan Crosland, *Tony Crosland* (1983).

Nick Crowson, *The Conservative Party and European Integration Since 1945* (2007).

N. Crowson, M. Hilton, J. McKay (eds), *NGOs in Contemporary Britain: Non-State Actors in Society and Politics Since 1945* (Basingstoke, 2009).

J. Curran, I. Gaber, J. Petley, *Culture Wars* (Edinburgh, 2005).

R. Dalton, *Citizen Politics* (Washington DC, 2001).

A. Davies, *Other Theatres: The Development of Alternative and Experimental Theatre in Britain* (Basingstoke, 1987).

J. de Groot, *Consuming History* (2008).

M. Donnelly, *Sixties Britain* (Harlow, 2005).

D. Dworkin, *Cultural Marxism in Postwar Britain: The New Left and the Origins of Cultural Studies* (Durham, NC., 1993).

D. Edgerton, *Warfare State* (Cambridge, 2005).

A. Eggers, J. Hainmueller, 'The Value of Political Power: Estimating Returns to Office in Post-War British Politics' (forthcoming *American Political Science Review*, November 2009), see http://www.people.fas.harvard.edu/~jhainm/Paper/VPP.pdf (accessed 18 May 2009).

G. Eley, *Forging Democracy: The History of the Left in Europe 1850–2000* (Oxford, 2002).

Nina Eliasoph, *Avoiding Politics: How Americans Produce Apathy in Everyday Life* (Cambridge, 1998).

Catherine Ellis, 'The Younger Generation: The Labour Party and the 1959 Youth Commission', *Journal of British Studies* 41:2 (2002).

—— 'Total Abstinence and a Good Filing-System? Anthony Crosland and the Affluent Society', in L. Black, H. Pemberton (eds), *An Affluent Society?* (Aldershot, 2004).

—— 'No Hammock for the Idle: The Conservative Party, "Youth" and the Welfare State in the 1960s', *Twentieth Century British History* 16:4 (2005).

Charlie Ellis, 'Relativism and Reaction: Richard Hoggart and Conservatism', in S. Owen (ed.), *Richard Hoggart and Cultural Studies* (Basingstoke, 2008).

Timothy Evans, *Conservative Radicalism: A Sociology of Conservative Party Youth Structures and Libertarianism, 1970–92* (Oxford, 1996).

S. Fielding, *Labour and Cultural Change 1964–70* (Manchester, 2003).

—— 'Looking for the New Political History', *Journal of Contemporary History* 42:3 (2007).

—— 'A Mirror for England? Cinematic Representations of Party Politics, c.1944–64', *Journal of British Studies* 47:1 (2008).

A. Filewod, D. Watt, *Workers' Playtime* (Sydney, 2001).

Richard Findley, 'The Conservative Party and Defeat: The Significance of Resale Price Maintenance for the General Election of 1964', *Twentieth Century British History*, 12:3 (2001).

M. Francis, 'Tears, Tantrums and Bared Teeth: The Emotional Economy of Three Conservative Prime Ministers, 1951–63', *Journal of British Studies* 41:3 (2002).

Martin Francis, Ina Zweiniger-Bargielowska (eds), *The Conservatives and British Society 1880–1990* (Cardiff, 1996).

T. Frank, *What's the Matter with America? The Resistible Rise of the American Right* (2004).

C. Fulop, *The Consumer Movement and the Consumer* (1977).

Grace Wyndham Goldie, *Facing the Nation: Television and Politics 1936–76* (1977).

M. Glendenning, 'The Conservation Movement: A Cult of the Modern Age', *Transaction of the Royal Historical Society* 6:13 (2003).

J. Goldthorpe, 'The Current Inflation: Towards a Sociological Account', in J. Goldthorpe, F. Hirsch (eds), *The Political Economy of Inflation* (Cambridge, MA, 1978).

J. Goodwin, J. Jasper (eds), *The Social Movements Reader* (Oxford, 2003).

J. Gorman, *Knocking Down Ginger* (1995).

C. Gray, *The Politics of the Arts* (Basingstoke, 2000).

V. de Grazia, *Irresistible Empire: America's Advance Through 20th Century Europe* (Cambridge, MA, 2005).

E.H.H. Green, 'The Conservative Party, the State and the Electorate, 1945–64', in J. Lawrence, M. Taylor (eds), *Party, State and Society* (Aldershot, 1997).

—— *Ideologies of Conservatism* (Oxford, 2002).

—— *Thatcher* (2006).

J. Green, *Days in the Life: Voices from the English Underground 1961–71* (1988).

—— *All Dressed Up* (1998).

S. Gunn, *History and Cultural Theory* (Harlow, 2006).

P. Gurney, 'The Battle of the Consumer in Postwar Britain', *Journal of Modern History* 77:4 (2005).

J. Harris (ed.), *Civil Society in British History: Ideas, Identities, Institutions* (Oxford, 2003).

B. Harrison, *Seeking a Role: The United Kingdom, 1951–70* (Oxford, 2009).

C. Hay, *Why We Hate Politics* (Cambridge, 2007).

—— 'Chronicles of a Death Foretold', *Political Quarterly* 80:4 (2009).

Edward Heath, *The Course of my Life* (1999).

Peter Hennessy, *Having It So Good: Britain in the Fifties* (2006).

I.P. Henry, *The Politics of Leisure Policy* (Basingstoke, 2001).

M. Hilton, *Consumerism in Twentieth Century Britain* (Cambridge, 2003).

—— *Prosperity For All: Consumer Activism in an Era of Globalization* (Ithaca, NY, 2009).

—— 'Consumer Politics in Post-War Britain', in M. Daunton, M. Hilton (eds), *The Politics of Consumption* (Oxford, 2001).

—— 'Americanisation, British Consumerism and the International Organisation of Consumers Unions', in M. Kipping, N. Tiratsoo (eds), *Americanisation in 20th Century Europe* (Lille, 2001).

—— 'The Fable of the Sheep, or, Private Virtues, Public Vices: The Consumer Revolution of the 20th Century', *Past and Present* 176 (2002).

—— The Female Consumer and the Politics of Consumption in Twentieth-Century Britain', *Historical Journal* 45:1 (2002).

—— 'The Polyester-Flannelled Philanthropists: The Birmingham Consumers Group', in L. Black, H. Pemberton (eds), *An Affluent Society?* (Aldershot, 2004).

—— 'The Banality of Consumption', in K. Soper, F. Trentmann (eds), *Citizenship and Consumption* (Basingstoke, 2008).

Richard Hoggart, *A Measured Life: Part 3 – An Imagined Life* (New Brunswick, 1994).

—— *Townscape with Figures* (1994).

P. Hollis, *Jennie Lee* (Oxford, 1997).

John Holroyd-Doveton, *Young Conservatives: A History of the Young Conservative Movement* (Bishop Auckland, 1996).

A. Horn, *Juke Box Britain* (Manchester, 2009).

D. Horowitz, *Vance Packard and American Social Criticism* (Chapel Hill, NC, 1994).

—— *The Anxieties of Affluence* (Amherst, MA, 2004).

D. Houtman, *Class and Politics in Contemporary Social Science* (New York, 2000).

R. Inglehart, *Culture Shift in Advanced Industrial Society* (Princeton, NJ, 1990).

—— 'The Silent Revolution in Europe: Intergenerational Change in Post-Industrial Societies', *American Political Science Review* 65:4 (1971).

F. Inglis, *Radical Earnestness* (Oxford, 1982).

R. Ingrams, *Muggeridge: The Biography* (1995).

C. Itzin, *Stages in the Revolution: Political Theatre in Britain Since 1968* (1979).

M. Jacobs, W. Novak, J. Zelizer (eds), *The Democratic Experiment* (Princeton, NJ, 2003).

A. Jackson, 'Labour as Leisure: The *Mirror* and DIY Sailors', *Journal of Design History* 19 (2006).

Ben Jackson, *Equality and the British Left: A Study in Progressive Thought, 1900–64* (Manchester, 2007).

F. Jameson, *The Political Unconscious: Narrative as a Socially Symbolic Act* (Ithaca, NY, 1981).

David Jarvis, '"Mrs. Maggs and Betty": The Conservative Appeal to Women Voters in the 1920s', *Twentieth Century British History* 5 (1994).

—— 'The Shaping of Conservative Electoral Hegemony, 1918–39', in Jon Lawrence, Miles Taylor (eds), *Party, State and Society* (Aldershot, 1997).

—— '"Behind Every Great Party": Women and Conservatism in Twentieth-Century Britain', in A. Vickery (ed.), *Women, Privilege and Power* (Stanford, CA, 2001).

Mark Jarvis, *Conservative Governments, Morality and Social Change in Affluent Britain, 1957–64* (Manchester, 2005).

Kevin Jeffreys, *Anthony Crosland: A New Biography* (1999).

Y. Jewkes, *Media and Crime* (2004).

G. Stedman Jones, *Languages of Class* (Cambridge, 1983).

M. Kandiah, 'Television Enters British Politics: The Conservative Party's Central Office and Political Broadcasting, 1945–55', *Historical Journal of Film, Radio and Television*, 15:2 (1995).

T. Kasser, *The High Price of Materialism* (Cambridge, MA., 2003).

M. Kenny, *The Politics of Identity* (Cambridge, 2004).

B. Lancaster, A. Mason (eds), *Life and Labour in a 20ᵗʰ Century City: The Experience of Coventry* (Coventry, 1986).

Jon Lawrence, 'The Transformation of British Public Politics After the First World War', *Past and Present* 190 (2006).

—— *Electing Our Masters: The Hustings in British Politics from Hogarth to Blair* (Oxford, 2009).

Zig Layton-Henry, 'The Young Conservatives, 1945–70', *Journal of Contemporary History* 8 (1970).

Philip Larkin, *Collected Poems* (1988).

A. Lent, *British Social Movements Since 1945: Sex, Colour, Peace and Power* (Basingstoke, 2001).

Alison Light, *Forever England: Femininity, Literature and Conservatism Between the Wars* (1991).

R. Lowe, 'Life Begins in the Seventies', *Journal of Contemporary History* 42:1 (2007).

M. MacMurraugh-Kavanagh, 'The BBC and *The Wednesday Play*, 1962–66: Institutional Containment vs. "Agitational Contemporaneity"', in J. Thumim (ed.), *Small Screens, Big Ideas* (2002).

G. E. Maguire, *Conservative Women* (Basingstoke, 1998).

S. Majima, M. Savage, 'Have There Been Culture Shifts in Britain? A Critical Encounter with Ronald Inglehart', *Cultural Sociology* 1:3 (2007).

A. Marwick, *The Sixties* (Oxford, 1998).

A. Marsh, *Protest and Political Consciousness* (1977).

Robert Mayer, 'The Entrepreneurial Elite and the Spirit of Consumerism: Finances and Strategy in the US Consumer Movement', in A. Chatriot, M. Chessel, M. Hilton (eds), *The Expert Consumer* (Aldershot, 2006).

S. McKellar, '"The Beauty of Stark Utility": Rational Consumption in America – *Consumer Reports* 1936–54', in J. Attfield (ed.), *Utility Reassessed* (Manchester, 1999).

G. McCann, *Frankie Howerd* (2004).

Helen McCarthy, 'Parties, Voluntary Associations and Democratic Politics in Interwar Britain', *Historical Journal* 50 (2007).

N. McCrillis, *The British Conservative Party in the Age of Universal Suffrage, 1918–29* (Columbus, Oh., 1998).

G. McKay, *Circular Breathing: The Cultural Politics of Jazz in Post-War Britain* (Durham, NC, 2007).

Ross McKibbin, *Classes and Cultures: England 1918–51* (Oxford, 1998).

—— 'Classes and Cultures: A Postscript', *Mitteilungsblatt des Instituts für die Geschichte der sozialen Bewegungen* 27 (2002).

C. McLarney, E. Chung, 'Post-Materialism's "Silent Revolution" in Consumer Research', *Marketing Intelligence and Planning* 17:6 (1999).

H. McLeod, *The Religious Crisis of the 1960s* (Oxford, 2007).

Helen Mercer, *Constructing a Competitive Order* (Cambridge, 1995).

Jeremy Mitchell, 'A Triptych of Organisations: CA, SSRC, NCC', in Geoff Dench, Tony Flower, Kate Gavron (eds), *Young at Eighty: The Prolific Public Life of Michael Young* (Manchester, 1995).

S. Mitchell, *The Brief and Turbulent Life of Modernizing Conservatism* (Newcastle, 2006).

J. Moran, *Queuing for Beginners* (2008).

—— 'Mass-Observation, Market Research and the Birth of the Focus Group, 1937–1997', *Journal of British Studies* 47 (2008).

F. Mort, 'Competing Domains: Democratic Subjects and Consuming Subjects in Britain and the United States since 1945', in F. Trentmann (ed.), *The Making of the Consumer* (Oxford, 2006).

Geoff Mulgan, 'Culture: The Problem With Being Public', in D. Marquand, A. Seldon (eds), *The Ideas that Shaped Post-War Britain* (1996).

G. Mulgan, K. Worpole, *Saturday Night or Sunday Morning?* (1986).

J.P. Murray, 'The Violent Face of Television: 50 Years of Research and Controversy', in E. Palmer, B. Young (eds), *The Faces of Televisual Media* (Mahwa, NJ, 2003).

Jo-Anne Nadler, *Too Nice to be a Tory* (2004).

D. Marquand, *Decline of the Public* (Cambridge, 2004).

D. Nash, *Blasphemy in the Christian World* (Oxford, 2007).

H. Nehring, 'The Growth of Social Movements', in H. Jones, P. Addison (eds), *Companion to Contemporary Britain, 1939–2000* (Oxford, 2005).

—— CND, 'Generation' and the Politics of Religion, 1957–64', in J. Garnett *et al.* (eds), *Redefining Christian Britain* (2007).

D. Nell, A. Alexander, G. Shaw, A. Bailey, 'Investigating Shopper Narratives of the Supermarket in Post-War England, 1945–75', *Oral History* 37:1 (2009).

Neill Nugent, 'The Ratepayers', in R. King, N. Nugent (eds), *Respectable Rebels* (1979).

Jeremy Nuttall, *Psychological Socialism: The Labour Party and Qualities of Mind and Character, 1931 to the Present* (Manchester, 2006).

J.S. Nye, P. Zelikow, D. King (eds), *Why People Don't Trust Government* (Cambridge, MA, 1997).

S. O'Connell, *Credit and Community: Working-Class Debt in the UK Since 1880* (Oxford, 2009).

A. Offer, *The Challenge of Affluence: Self-Control and Well-Being in the US and Britain Since 1950* (Oxford, 2006).

G. Ortolano, *The Two Cultures Controversy: Science, Literature and Cultural Politics in Postwar Britain* (Cambridge, 2009).

Bill Osgerby, *Youth in Britain Since 1945* (Oxford, 1998).

Oxford University Socialist Discussion Group, *Out of Apathy* (1989).

M. Patterson, *Strategies of Political Theatre: Post-War British Playwrights* (Cambridge, 2003).

C. Pattie, P. Seyd, P. Whiteley, *Citizenship in Britain* (Cambridge, 2004).

H. Pemberton, *Policy Learning and British Governance in the 1960s* (Basingstoke, 2004).

R. Perlstein, *Before the Storm: Barry Goldwater and the Unmaking of the American Consensus* (New York, 2001).

John Preston, *Kings of the Roundhouse* (London, 2005).

Martin Priestman, 'A Critical Stage: Drama in the 1960s', in Bart Moore-Gilbert, John Seed (eds), *Cultural Revolution? The Challenge of the Arts in the 1960s* (1992).

M. Pugh, 'Popular Conservatism in Britain: Continuity and Change, 1880–1987', *Journal of British Studies* 27:3 (1988).

R. Putnam, *Bowling Alone: The Collapse and Revival of American Community* (New York, 2000).

B. Pym, *Pressure Groups and the Permissive Society* (Newton Abbot, 1974).

John Ramsden, *The Making of Conservative Party Policy: The Conservative Research Department Since 1929* (1980).

David Reisman, *Anthony Crosland: The Mixed Economy* (Basingstoke, 1997).

Sir William Richardson, *The Co-operative Wholesale Society in War and Peace 1938–76* (Manchester, 1977).

Eirlys Roberts, *Which? 25: Consumers' Association 1957–82* (1982).

—— *IOCU, 1960–80* (1981).

L. Robinson, 'Three Revolutionary Years: The Impact of the Counter-Culture on the Development of the Gay Liberation Movement in Britain', *Cultural and Social History* 3:4 (2006).

—— *Gay Men and the Left in Post-War Britain: How the Personal Got Political* (Manchester, 2007).

Mark Roodhouse, 'Lady Chatterley and the Monk: Anglican Radicals and the Lady Chatterley Trial of 1960', *Journal of Ecclesiastical History* 59:3 (2008).

M. Rosenbaum, *From Soapbox to Soundbite* (1997).

K. Ross, *Fast Cars, Clean Bodies: Decolonization and the Re-Ordering of French Culture* (Cambridge, MA, 1995).

D. Russell, *Looking North: Northern England and the National Imagination* (Manchester, 2004).

Raphael Samuel, *The Lost World of British Communism* (2007).

D. Sandbrook, *Never Had It So Good* (2005).

J. Saramago, *Seeing* (2006).

S. Schwarzkopf, 'They Do It with Mirrors: Advertising and British Cold War Consumer Politics', *Contemporary British History* 19:2 (2005).

—— 'The Co-operative Movement and the Making of British Advertising and Marketing Culture, 1890s–1960s', in L. Black, N. Robertson (eds), *Taking Stock* (Manchester, 2009).

P. Seyd, 'Democracy within the Conservative Party', *Government and Opposition* 10 (1975).

G. Shaw, A. Alexander, 'Interlocking Directorates and the Knowledge Transfer of Supermarket Retail Techniques from North America to Britain', *International Review of Retail, Distribution and Consumer Research* 16:3 (2006).

—— 'British Co-operative Societies as Retail Innovators: Interpreting the Early Stages of the Self-Service Revolution', *Business History* 50:1 (2008).

G. Shaw, L. Curth, A. Alexander, 'Streamlining Shopping', *History Today* (November 2002).

—— 'Selling Self-Service and the Supermarket: The Americanisation of Food Retailing in Britain, 1945–60', *Business History* 46:4 (2004).

Tony Shaw, 'The BBC, the State and Cold War Culture: The Case of Television's *The War Game* (1965)', *English Historical Review* CXXI:494 (2006).

D. Shellard, *British Theatre Since the War* (New Haven, CT, 2000).

A. Sinfield, *Literature, Politics and Culture in Postwar Britain* (1997).

Margaret Stacey, Eric Batstone, Colin Bell, Anne Murcott, *Power, Persistence and Change: A Second Study of Banbury* (1975).

P. Stansill, 'The Life and Death of *IT*', *British Journalism Review* 17:4 (2006).

N. Stevenson (ed.), *Trust the People: Selected Essays and Speeches of Peter Walker* (1987).

Andrew Taylor, 'The Conservative Party and Mass Opinion from the 1920s to 1950s', in Stuart Ball, Ian Holliday (eds), *Mass Conservatism* (2002).

Philip Tether, 'Clubs: A Neglected Aspect of Conservative Organization', *Hull Papers in Politics* 42 (1988).

D. Thomas, D. Carlton, A. Etienne, *Theatre Censorship: From Walpole to Wilson* (Oxford, 2007).

James Thomas, *Popular Newspapers, the Labour Party and British Politics* (2005).

J. Thompson, 'Pictorial Lies? Posters and Politics in Britain, c.1880–1914', *Past and Present* 197 (2007).

Hans B. Thorelli, Sarah V. Thorelli, *Consumer Information Handbook: Europe and North America* (New York, 1974).

A. Thorpe, *Parties at War* (Oxford, 2009).

J. Tomlinson, 'Thrice Denied: "Declinism" as a Recurrent Theme in British History in the Long 20th Century', *Twentieth Century British History* 20:2 (2009).

M. Tracey, D. Morrison, *Whitehouse* (Basingstoke, 1979).

TUC, *Congress House at Fifty* (2004).

M. Veldman, *Fantasy, the Bomb and Greening of Britain, 1945–80* (Cambridge, 1994).

J. Vernon, *Hunger: A Modern History* (Cambridge, MA., 2007).

S. Wagg, 'The Politics of British Satirical Comedy from *Beyond the Fringe* to *Spitting Image*', in D. Strinati, S. Wagg (eds), *Come on Down: Popular Media Culture in Post-War Britain* (1992).

—— 'Comedians and Politics in the United States and Great Britain', in S. Wagg (ed.), *Because I Tell a Joke or Two: Comedy, Politics and Social Difference* (1998).

M. Waite, 'Sex, Drugs and Rock n' Roll (and Communism)', in G. Andrews, N. Fishman, K. Morgan (eds), *Opening the Books: Essays on the Social and Cultural History of the British Communist Party* (1995).

Peter Walker, *Staying Power* (1991).

R. Wallis, 'Moral Indignation and the Media: An Analysis of the NVALA', *Sociology* 10 (1976).

D. Watt, '*The Maker and the Tool*, Documentary Performance and the Search for a Popular Culture', *New Theatre Quarterly* 19:1 (2003).

A. Wesker, *As Much as I Dare* (1995).

P. Whiteley, P. Seyd, J. Richardson, *True Blues: The Politics of Conservative Party Membership* (Oxford, 1994).

L. Whitworth, 'Promoting Product Quality: The Co-op and the Council of Industrial Design', in L. Black, N. Robertson (eds) *Taking Stock: Consumerism and the Co-operative Movement in Modern British History* (Manchester, 2009).

Jack Williams, *Entertaining the Nation? Social History of British TV* (Stroud, 2004).

J. Woodham, 'An Episode in Post-Utility Design Management: The Council of Industrial Design and the Co-operative Wholesale Society', in J. Attfield (ed.), *Utility Reassessed: The Role of Ethics in the Practice of Design* (Manchester, 1999).

Dominic Wring, *The Politics of Marketing the Labour Party* (Basingstoke, 2005).

Ken Young, 'Orpington and the "Liberal Revival"', in Chris Cook, John Ramsden (eds), *By-Elections in British Politics* (1997).

Michael Young, *Social Scientist as Innovator* (Cambridge MA, 1983).

—— 'Crosland and Socialism', in D. Leonard (ed.), *Crosland and New Labour* (Basingstoke, 1999).

I. Zweiniger-Bargielowska, *Austerity in Britain: Rationing, Controls and Consumption, 1939–55* (Oxford, 2000).

Unpublished

Angela Bartie, 'Festival City: The Arts, Culture and Moral Conflict in Edinburgh, 1947–67' (Ph.D. Dundee University, 2006).

D. Case, 'The Consumer Movement in the 1960s' (Amherst College, BA, 1972).

Sarah Franks, 'Selling Consumer Protection: Competitive Strategies of the Consumers' Association, 1957–90' (M.Phil. diss., Oxford University, 2000).

Heidi Topman, 'A Study of the Rise and Decline of Selected Labour Halls in Greater 1918–79' (Ph.D., Kingston University, 2006).

M. Tracey, D. Morrison, 'Opposition to the Age' (Social Science Research Council report, 1978).

Index